690
ROSKIND

Roskind, Robert.

Building your own
house.

$14.95

Other books in this series:

BEFORE YOU BUILD
by Robert Roskind/
Owner Builder Center

A comprehensive review of what you need to know before investing time and money in building your own house. Covers choosing the site, buying the land or lot, permits, codes and inspections, estimating and financing, establishing power, phone, water, and waste systems, and much more.

$11.95 paper, 240 pages

BUILDING YOUR OWN HOUSE
VOLUME I
by Robert Roskind/
Owner Builder Center

Takes the owner-builder step by step through everything from planning to framing. Includes sections on types of foundation, floor and wall framing, roof framing and sheathing, and windows. Profusely illustrated with photographs, diagrams, and line drawings.

$19.95 paper, 448 pages

and other useful building books from Ten Speed Press:

INSPECTING A HOME OR
INCOME PROPERTY
by Jim Yuen

This practical manual allows anyone to identify potential problems before investing in a piece of property. Inspection procedures and checklists cover structural, plumbing, electrical, and mechanical systems, pest control, evaluating additions and renovations, and doing research. Illustrated.

$12.95 paper, 176 pages

REHAB RIGHT
by Helaine Kaplan Prentice,
Blair Prentice & the City of
Oakland Planning Department.

Help in restoring just about any house built since the late nineteenth century. Classifies different house designs and design elements, and shows how to realize the full value of each. Illustrated.

$11.95 paper, 144 pages

THE STRAIGHT POOP
by Peter Hemp

A guide to common plumbing problems and how to solve them, written for the baffled layman. Illustrated.

$11.95 paper, 176 pages

Available from your local bookstore, or order direct from the publisher. Please include $1.25 shipping & handling for the first book, and 50 cents for each additional book. California residents include local sales tax. Write for our free complete catalog of over 400 books and tapes.

TEN SPEED PRESS
Box 7123, Berkeley, CA 94707

Wood screws, 7
Wood-faced paneling, 65-71. *See also* Wall
   paneling
Wooden thresholds, 156
Woodwork. *See* Casing; Jambs; Trim
Worm drive saws, 3
Wrenches, 8-9
   pneumatic, 12

Y

Y fitting, 37

Tile ceilings, *continued:*
preparation, 84
squaring the ceiling, 85-86, 87
tile installation, 86, 87
wood furring strip installation, 86-87
See also Suspended ceilings
Tiles. *See* Ceramic tile; Parquet floors;
Self-adhesive vinyl tiles; Tile ceilings
Toenailing, 176
Toilets, 43
Tongue-and-groove paneling, 65-66, 71-72
See also Wall paneling
Tools, 1-14
care of, 1-2
safety rules, 1, 11-12
See also specific tools and techniques by
name
Torpedo levels, 2, 176
Track lighting, 27-28
Tracks, 75
Trap, 30
Treads, 192, 197
Trim, 89
baseboard, 71
beveled casing, 93-94
design, 90
for doors, 93-94
home security, 167-68
painting, 133-34
prepping for painting, 131
for suspended ceilings, 80
for wall paneling, 70-71
for windows, 94-95
See also Doors; Windows
Trim brushes, 129
Trimming planes, 11
Trisodiumphosphate (TSP), 129

U

UF cable, 19
UL (Underwriters Laboratory), 17
Underlayment, 99, 107, 120
for ceramic tile, 126-27
for parquet flooring, 108
for vinyl flooring, 100, 104-5
Underwriters Laboratory (UL), 17
Uniform Building Code, 9, 37
Uniform Plumbing Code (UPC), 29, 30, 33
Union, 37
UPC (*Uniform Plumbing Code*), 29, 30, 33

V

Valances, 75
Valves, 37
bathroom sinks, 41
installing, 40
showers, 42-43
supply system, 34, 35, 40
toilets, 43
Vapor barriers, 46-47, 65
installing when insulating, 53
for wall paneling, 68

Vent system (plumbing), 37
Ventilation, 45-50
continuous ridge vent, 49
flexi-vent, 46, 50
gable vents, 49
soffit plugs, 48-49
wind turbines, 49-50
window types and, 155
Vinyl floors, 99-106, 141
applying over concrete, 106
coved edges, 103
design, 100
dry tiles, 106
permits and codes, 100
self-adhesive vinyl tiles, 104-6
sheet vinyl flooring, 100-104
See also Full-spread adhesive vinyl
floors; Perimeter bond sheet vinyl
floors; Self-adhesive vinyl tiles
Vinyl spackling (mud), 55, 61-63
Vises, 9
Vitreous tile, 119. *See also* Ceramic tile
Voltage drop, 19
Volts, 17

W

Wall paneling, 65-73
applying over drywall, 67
applying over masonry walls, 68
applying tongue-and-groove boards,
71-72
design, 66
fitting around openings, 69-70, 72
furring, 65, 68
permits and codes, 66
scribing, 65, 67, 69-70
shelves, 65-66, 72-73
tongue-and-groove paneling, 65-66, 71-72
trim, 65-66, 70-71
wood-faced paneling, 65-71
Wallboard. *See* Drywall
Wallpapering, 129, 134-38
booking, 129, 135
corners and openings, 136-38
cutting wallpaper, 135, 137-38
hanging wallpaper, 135-36
permits and codes, 129
prepping the walls, 134
sizing, 129, 134
soaking wallpaper, 135
Walls
basement, 52-54
ceramic tile, 119-26
drywall, 55-63
insulating, 51-52
kitchen, 140-41
molding for suspended ceilings, 80
painting, 129-34
paneling, 65-72
shelving, 65-66, 72-73
wall cabinets, 141-43
wallpapering, 129, 134-38

See also Ceramic tile; Drywall; Painting;
Wall paneling; Wallpapering
Washing machines, 18, 44
Water heater, 160
Water softeners, 35
Water-based (latex) paint, 130
Water-hammers, 29, 37-38
Waterproofing decks, 190
Watts, 17
Weatherizing, 151-61
air-pollution and, 151
audit, 152-54
caulking, 154-55
energy conservation, 153, 159-61
permits and codes, 152
weatherstripping, 156-59
windows, 155-56
See also Insulation; Ventilation
Weatherstripping, 151, 156-59
doors, 156-58
spring metal, 158
windows, 158-59
See also Insulation; Ventilation;
Weatherizing
Wet vent, 30
Wind turbines, 49-50
Window film, 151
Window sash, 151
Windows
adjoining or in doors, 164-65
casement window weatherstripping, 159
caulking, 154-55
coverings, 155-56
double-hung window weatherstripping,
158-59
drywall around, 58-59
home security, 170-71
jalousie windows, 151, 159
painting trim, 133
paneling around, 69, 72
storm glazing, 155
suspended ceilings and basement
windows, 84
trim installation, 94-95
valances, 75
wallpapering around, 137-38
weatherizing, 155-56
weatherizing audit, 153
weatherstripping, 158-59
See also Trim
Wire
cables versus, 19
color coding, 15, 19
connecting wires, 25-27
installing, 23-25
outdoor wiring, 28
pigtailing, 25-27
sizes, 19
voltage drop in, 19
See also Cable; Electricity
Wire nuts, 20, 25
Wiring. *See* Electricity
Wood glue, 9
Wood grades, 175

Building Your Own House

Volume II: Interiors

Building Your Own House

Volume II: Interiors

by Robert Roskind

Do It Yourself, Inc.

Ten Speed Press

Berkeley, California

1⊕
TEN SPEED PRESS
P.O. Box 7123
Berkeley, California 94707

First printing, 1991

Portions of this material were previously published in *The Do It
Yourself Show Book of Home Improvements* (Addison-Wesley
Publishing Company, Inc., ©1985). Reprinted by permission.

The author and publisher have made very effort to ensure that the
information in this book fosters safety as well as efficiency.
Because the specifics of each environment, as well as the design,
materials, and uses of each building project vary greatly, the author
and the publisher cannot be held responsible for injuries that might
result from the use of this book.

Cover design by Fifth Street Design
Illustrations by Bill Schaeffer, Marilyn Hill, Rik Olson,
    and Dan Corvello
Technical editing and additional writing (Doors and Trim, Stairs)
    by Steven George
Additional writing (Plumbing) by Peter Hemp
Developmental and production editing by Jessie Wood
Copy editing by editcetera
Proofreading by Fuzzy Randall

Library of Congress Cataloging-in-Publication Data
Roskind, Robert.
    Building your own house II / Robert Roskind.
        p.   cm.
    ISBN 0-89815-358-1 :
    1. House construction—Amateurs' manuals. 2. Building—
    Details—Amateurs' manuals. 3. Dwellings—Remodeling—
    Amateurs' manuals. I. Title. II. Title: Building your own
    house two.
TH4815.R675   1990
690'.837—dc20   90-33818
                                                CIP

Printed in the United States of America

    2   3   4   5   —   95   94   93   92

To my beautiful stepdaughter,
Julie Mattera,
a joy and a laugh in my life.
And to the light that shines within us all.

Acknowledgments

A BOOK LIKE THIS, with its numerous illustrations and its need for vast technical input, represents the merging of the energies of many people—more than I could possibly thank here.

Everyone who worked on this project put his or her heart into it. To all of those people, to the many I've met personally, and to those I've not yet had an opportunity to meet, I offer my heartfelt thanks. In particular:

To Julia Holiman, for research support, pressing details, and hours of listening to me talk.

To Marnie Poirier, writer, compiler, organizer, and the person who kept expanding to hold it all.

To Steven George, who wrote the chapters on doors and windows and on stairs, and whose technical editing enhanced the whole book.

To Peter Hemp, who wrote the chapter on plumbing.

To Bill Shaeffer, whose beautiful illustrations speak for themselves.

To Marilyn Hill, illustrator, whose cooperative spirit and attention to detail make her a pleasure to work with.

To illustrator Rik Olson and consultant Dan Corvello, whose expertise added so much to the chapter on plumbing.

To Sal Glynn of Ten Speed Press for his direction and guidance.

To Jessie Wood, developmental and production editor, who continued to impose order on the chaos.

Contents

1 Tools   1

2 Electricity   15

3 Plumbing   29

4 Insulation and Ventilation   45

5 Drywall   55

6 Wall Paneling   65

7 Ceilings   75

8 Doors and Trim   89

9 Vinyl Floors   99

10 Hardwood Floors   107

11 Ceramic Tile   119

12 Painting and Wallpapering   129

13 Kitchen Cabinets and Countertops   139

14 Weatherizing   151

15 Home Security   163

16 Decks   175

17 Stairs   191

Index   201

How to Use This Book

IN WRITING THIS BOOK, I did not intend a thorough examination of each subject. Rather, my intention was to distill the information into concise, step-by-step construction processes that even the novice builder can follow.

Except for the chapters on plumbing and electricity, each chapter is detailed enough to guide you through the process described. The actual designs you use and the specific challenges you face will of course differ according to many variables, including your taste, the tools you have to work with, and the money you have to spend. What is presented here, in a manner I've not seen elsewhere, is a usable guide to the construction process. Read each chapter and decide whether the process as shown applies to your project. If it does not, you may want to consult other do-it-yourself books, local professionals, or knowledgeable salespeople at your hardware or home center store. Be sure to consult too with your local code enforcement department; you should be familiar with all applicable codes before you begin work.

At the beginning of each project I've listed relevant safety guidelines and the most common mistakes to avoid. These lists are compiled from an accumulation of mistakes made by many people over many years. You can learn from the mistakes of others, but don't be lulled into thinking that therefore your project will proceed without any mistakes or problems. It won't. Most novices—and professionals too—underestimate the time, energy, hassles, and money that building projects demand. Add 30 to 50 percent to your initial estimates in each area.

Be sure to read the entire chapter before you begin work on any project. Throughout the book I've made every effort to tell you what you will be doing, what you will need, and what problems to watch out for; but to really prepare for a project, you need to understand the construction process as a whole before proceeding step by step.

Finally, enjoy yourself. The experience of doing your own work offers not only financial benefits but also a potential for growth and enjoyment rarely found in other endeavors. It will push you to new limits and beyond; and in the end you will have a house that feels more like a home because you took an active part in creating it.

About the Author

ROBERT ROSKIND is a cofounder of the Owner Builder Center in Berkeley, California. The center is the largest school of its kind, teaching people how to build, design, and remodel their own homes. In 1983, Roskind left the center to start the DIY Video Corporation. DIY produced the record-breaking PBS series "The Do It Yourself Show," which also airs on USA Network and The Learning Channel. DIY Video is the country's largest producer of how-to videos, with over thirty-five titles distributed nationally. Roskind has written three other books, *The Do It Yourself Show Book of Home Improvements* (Addison-Wesley Publishing Company, Inc., 1985); *Before You Build* (Ten Speed Press, 1982); and *Building Your Own House: From Foundations to Framing* (Ten Speed Press, 1984), which was selected as one of the fifty best science and technical books of 1984. Roskind lives in Oriental, North Carolina, with his wife Julia and daughter Alicia.

Building Your Own House

Volume II: Interiors

1 Tools

THIS CHAPTER DISCUSSES building your tool inventory, the importance of buying high-quality tools, and the appropriate use and care of your tools and work area.

The types of tools discussed are those for measuring and leveling, those for cutting and drilling, those for attaching and assembling or dismantling, and those for finishing. A section on pneumatic tools—air compressors and accessories—is also included.

Before You Begin

Before you began the job of constructing your new home, you should have acquired a copy of the appropriate building code from the office of your city or county building inspector. Keep this code on hand so you will know what your project requires to comply with the code.

Tools can be fun, and they can open doors to new and interesting projects, but they should never be treated as toys. If you have small children, keep your tools where they won't be accessible to curious young hands.

A workshop is a very personal place, geared to your own specific needs and to the space available. A well-organized workspace makes for an organized, smooth-flowing project, because you always know where to find that special tool when you need it. If you can't designate a separate room for your tools and projects, at least have a closet or locking toolbox that will secure your tools when you're not using them.

SAFETY

Safety should be your primary concern whenever you work with tools. Always follow these general rules.

☐ Wear protective glasses or goggles whenever you are using power tools, and when chiseling, sanding, scraping, or hammering overhead, especially if you wear contact lenses.

☐ Wear ear protectors when using power tools; some operate at noise levels that can damage hearing.

☐ Wear the proper respirator or face mask when sanding or sawing or when using substances that emit toxic fumes.

☐ Be careful that loose hair and clothing don't get caught in tools.

☐ Always use the appropriate tool for the job.

☐ Keep blades sharp. A dull blade requires excessive force and can easily slip.

☐ Don't abuse your tools.

☐ Repair or discard tools with cracks in the wooden handles or chips in the metal parts. Damaged tools can cause injury.

☐ Read the owner's manual for all tools and know the proper use of each.

☐ Keep all tools out of reach of small children.

☐ Unplug all power tools when changing settings or parts.

☐ Don't drill, shape, or saw anything that isn't firmly and properly secured.

☐ Store or dispose of oily rags properly to prevent spontaneous combustion.

☐ Keep a first-aid kit on hand.

☐ Don't work with tools when you are tired. That's when most accidents occur.

PURCHASING YOUR TOOLS

Give plenty of care and thought to the purchase of your tools. Careful investment will carry you through years of enjoyable projects.

☐ Acquire tools as you need them; don't buy unnecessary tools. If you need a tool for a special purpose, you can often rent it.

☐ Always purchase the best tool you can afford. Cheap tools are never a bargain.

☐ Purchase from reputable dealers and manufacturers.

☐ Choose the tool that has the most comfortable fit and weight for your hand.

☐ Examine tools carefully for their sturdiness and smooth finish.

☐ Check all moving parts for smooth action and freedom from play.

CARING FOR YOUR TOOLS

Caring for your tools is also extremely important, if they are to do the jobs for which they are intended.

☐ Keep your tools properly cleaned and lubricated.

☐ Keep your tools out of the weather and store them out of the way when you are not using them.

- [ ] If the storage area is damp (the basement, for example) install a dehumidifier and keep tools covered with a film of rust-inhibiting oil

- [ ] Never throw tools into the toolbox. Handle them carefully to avoid dulling the edges and nicking the surfaces.

- [ ] Hang tools with cutting edges separately to keep them from getting nicked or dulled.

- [ ] Purchase carrying cases for your power tools to protect them and to store their accessories.

Tools for Measuring and Leveling

Most Common Mistake

- [ ] Not measuring accurately. A good carpenter measures twice and cuts once.

Accuracy and care in measuring are all-important. They can mean the difference between a professional project and a sloppy one.

The **carpenter's pencil** is flat, to keep it from rolling away, with a large, soft lead that draws broad, easy-to-see lines.

A **steel tape measure** (Figure 1-1), 20' to 100' in length, is an invaluable tool that belongs in every home. The blade (the tape itself) should be at least 1" wide, with a cushioned bumper to protect the hook of the tape from damage if the

tape retracts back into the case too quickly. The play in the hook allows you to make either inside or outside measurements without having to compensate for the hook. Its flexibility allows it to measure round, contoured, and other odd-shaped objects. When making inside measurements, add the length of the tape case, which is usually marked on the case.

Squares are used for laying out work, checking for squareness during assembly, and marking angles. The **carpenter's square**, also called a **framing square**, is used for marking true perpendicular lines to be cut on boards and for squaring corners, among other things. One leg is 24" long and 2" wide, the other 16" long and 1½" or 2" wide. The better types have a number of tables, conversions, and formulas stamped on the side to simplify many woodworking tasks. (Books are also available that give this information.)

The **combination square** (Figure 1-2) is a most versatile tool. It has a spirit level that locks in place on a 12" steel rule. It is used to square the end of a board, to mark a 45-degree angle for mitering, and to make quick level checks. It can also be used as a scribing tool to mark a constant distance along the length of a board.

Levels are used to make sure your work is true horizontal (level) or true vertical (plumb). To ensure accuracy, always use the longest level possible. The **torpedo level,** used for small pieces of work, is 8" or 9" in length, with vials that read level, plumb, and 45 degrees. A **2' to 4' level** is a must for any home woodworking project, from building shelves to structural carpentry.

A **plumb bob** is a heavy, balanced weight on a string. It is dropped from a specific point to locate another point exactly below it, or to determine true vertical (Figure 1-3).

A **chalkline** is a string or line coated with colored chalk, used to transfer a straight line to a working surface easily and accurately. Pull the line out and hold it tight between the two points of measurement. Then snap it to leave a mark. Some chalklines have a pointed case that doubles as a plumb bob.

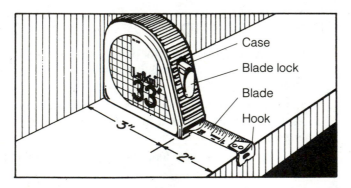

Figure 1-1. To make inside measurements easily, place the tape case against the wall and add its length (in this case, 3") to the measurement.

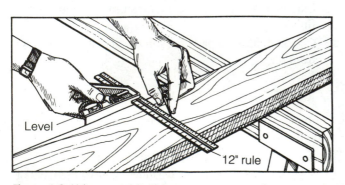

Figure 1-2. Using a combination square to prepare for a crosscut.

Figure 1-3. Using a plumb bob to determine true vertical (plumb).

Helpful Hints on Measuring

☐ When many pieces need to be cut or drilled the same, you can use one accurately cut or drilled piece as a template to mark all the others. However, for greatest accuracy, always rely on your tape measure as well.

☐ Remember the old maxim: "A good carpenter measures twice and cuts once."

Power Tools for Cutting and Drilling

Most Common Mistakes

☐ Setting a board to be cut between two supports. Instead, cantilever the board over the outside of one support to avoid binding the saw blade when the board drops. This method prevents "kick back."

☐ Choosing an inappropriate saw blade for the material being cut and for the job you are doing. Always be sure that your blade is sharp as well as appropriate for a given material.

SAWS

The **circular saw** (Figure 1-4) is one of the most popular tools in the home workshop. It consists of a replaceable blade; a blade guard, part of which is spring loaded to move out of the way as you saw; a sole plate, which may or may not be attached to a ripping fence; a cutting guide; and knobs to adjust the cutting angle and depth of the blade. Set the cutting depth to 1/8" more than the thickness of the board. Keep the sole plate flat on the surface of the wood to avoid binding. There are two basic kinds of circular saws. The **worm drive saw** is used for heavy-duty framing-type work, and many carpenters use this type of saw with a fine-tooth blade for finish work as well. The **sidewinder** is used for lighter jobs.

The **saber saw** or **jigsaw** (Figure 1-5) is used to cut curving lines and to make detailed cuts. When starting your cut from inside a piece of wood to cut an opening in paneling, drywall, or a counter top, drill a starting hole first. Most saber saws can accommodate a circle guide and angle cutting and ripping accessories.

The **reciprocating saw** is generally used to cut openings in existing walls. It is ideal for remodeling or demolition work. It can rough-cut wood, metal, leather, rubber, cloth, linoleum, and plastic.

The **chopsaw,** a motorized miter box saw, makes repeated square and angled cuts with a minimum of effort. This tool is indispensable for making high-grade finish joints, for making trim, for building decks, and for laying hardwood floors—wherever precision end cuts are needed.

The **table saw,** also called a **bench saw** (Figure 1-6), can crosscut, rip, miter, groove, and bevel. With a 7½" to 12"

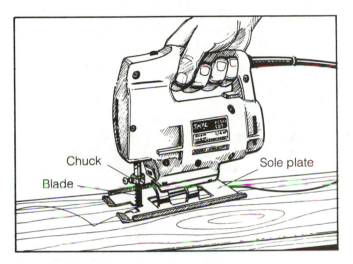

Chuck · Blade · Sole plate

Figure 1-5. A saber saw or jigsaw allows you to make fine cuts in curved and detailed patterns.

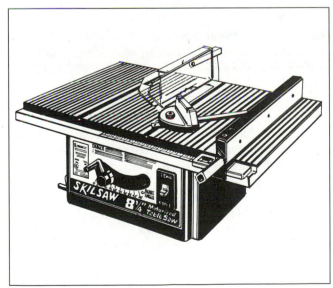

Figure 1-6. A small table saw or bench saw gives you flexibility in cutting trim, making moldings, and cabinetry work.

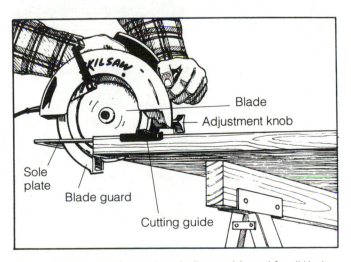

Blade · Adjustment knob · Sole plate · Blade guard · Cutting guide

Figure 1-4. The circular saw is an indispensable tool for all kinds of home building projects.

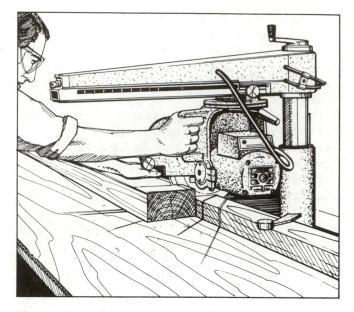

Figure 1-7. A radial arm saw is versatile like a table saw, but is used for heavier stock.

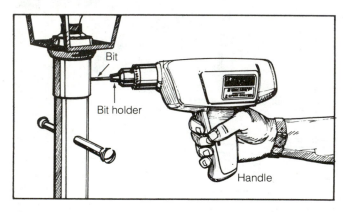

Figure 1-8. A cordless drill can be used where power is not available and where a power cord would be inconvenient.

blade, this saw can cut depths of 1½" to 3⅜". With accessories, it will cut dadoes, make moldings, and sand stock. Smaller table saws are good for general hobby and repair work.

The **radial arm saw** (Figure 1-7) holds the board stationary for crosscutting, angled cuts, notching, and lap joints, with the saw blade bearing down across the board. This saw is also useful for making wide rip cuts, up to about 24" (half the width of a sheet of plywood). The radial arm saw is usually used by professionals.

The **bandsaw** is useful for creative work where precision cutting is needed to produce complex shapes and curves.

SAWBLADES

Sawblades are available to cut tile, stucco, metal, plastic laminates, concrete, and of course wood. Blades for many of these materials are use-specific. Wood-cutting blades differ widely, depending on use. In general, the finer the teeth, the

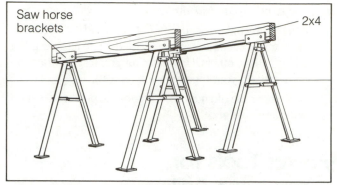

Figure 1-9. Sawhorses are easy to put together with special brackets.

finer the resulting cut. Coarse blades with large teeth tend to cut faster but rougher. If you are cutting into material that could contain hidden nails, use a special carbide-tipped sawblade, which can cut through nails easily.

DRILLS AND ROUTER

A good ⅜" **electric** or **power drill** is one of the most versatile tools in the home workshop. A variable-speed trigger and a reversing switch greatly increase the utility of the drill. A **cordless drill** (Figure 1-8) eliminates the need for cumbersome extension cords and can be used where power is not available. It can speed up many routine jobs, and is a good investment.

You'll need **drill bits** of carbon steel for soft materials like wood and plastic. High-speed steel bits work well on metals, and carbide-tipped bits are used for concrete or masonry.

Other useful **attachments** include hole saws, spade bits, buffing disks and depth stops, screwdriving bits, sanding disks, and power grinders. You can also add a paint mixer, right-angle drive, wire brushes, wood countersinks, and even rotary rasps and files.

The **router** is used to cut contours in wood for edgings and moldings and for more complex relief panels and inlay work, dovetails, and mortises, as well as trimming veneers and plastic laminates.

Helpful Hints on Cutting and Drilling

□ Always unplug your power tools when adjusting them or changing accessories.

□ Keep tool adjustment keys taped to the cord near the plug. This will remind you to unplug the tool, as well as keep you from losing the key.

□ Be sure your tools are properly grounded. Unless a tool is double-insulated, it should be plugged into a three-hole grounded outlet.

□ Watch cord placement so it does not interfere with the operation of the tool.

□ Never use a power tool in damp conditions, no matter how well grounded it is. Remember that moisture readily conducts electricity.

- For sawing and assembling, one of the most useful accessories is a pair of sawhorses (Figure 1-9). They can mean the difference between an easy, comfortable task that can be accomplished standing up, and a difficult one that requires bending repeatedly.

- When rip cutting, use a rip guide; or tack down a straight-edge to use as a cutting guide.

- Be sure that both ends of a board are well supported, and don't cut between the supports; cantilever the scrap end instead.

- When using a table saw, choose the guide that allows the longest edge of the stock to be used against the guide.

- Always secure your stock before cutting or drilling.

- Use caution when ripping small, narrow pieces. Use a push stick with a radial arm saw or table saw, and always keep your hands clear of the blade.

- When drilling into metal, squirt a lightweight oil onto the drill bit and into the hole to cool the bit.

- Predrill a pilot hole to make nailing into hardwood, as well as screwing into all types of wood, easier. A pilot hole lessens the chance of splitting the wood. The hole should be slightly smaller than the diameter of the nail or screw.

Hand Tools for Sawing and Chiseling

SAWS

The **crosscut saw** is used to cut across the grain of the wood. It has small, offset teeth. An 8-point saw is best for general use.

The **rip saw** cuts with the grain, and has much larger teeth.

Figure 1-10. Using a combination handsaw with sawhorses.

The **combination saw** (Figure 1-10) cuts both across and with the grain, but does not perform as well as saws that are designed for specific uses.

The **hacksaw** is used to cut metal, plastic, and electrical conduit.

The **backsaw** is used in conjunction with a **miter box** to cut a perfectly straight line across a piece of wood. The steel backing keeps it aligned (Figure 1-11).

The **keyhole saw** has a blade that is narrower at the tip than at the heel or handle. It is used for cutting openings in drywall or paneling and for curved cuts.

The **drywall saw** is like a keyhole saw, but it has a straight handle and a stiffer blade. Larger drywall saws, shaped more like a wood saw, are available for larger cuts, such as rough openings.

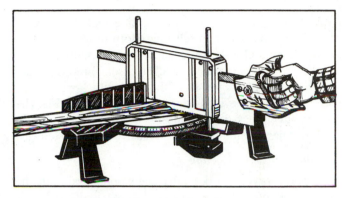

Figure 1-11. A backsaw is used with a miter box to make accurate cuts for trim and molding.

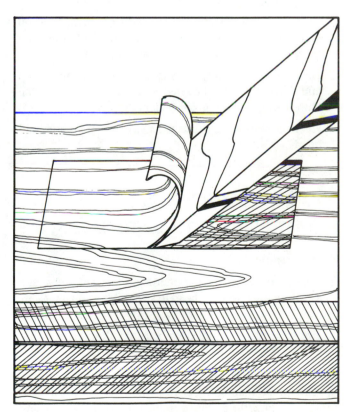

Figure 1-12. Chisels are used to chip and shave wood away.

The **coping saw** is used to follow an irregular, delicate, or intricate cut in wood. The blade is thin, fine toothed, and removable.

Helpful Hints on Sawing

☐ Don't store saws in a toolbox or where the teeth will get damaged. Hang your saws if possible; or buy a plastic tooth guard or make one out of cardboard.

☐ Keep saw blades sharp. Keep them out of contact with metal, concrete, and stone. Remove any nails from wood before sawing.

☐ Protect your saw blades by coating them with paste wax or a light grade of machine oil.

CHISELS

Chisels (Figure 1-12) are wood-cutting tools For general use, purchase a set of chisels ranging from ¼" to 1½" in width. **Socket chisels** are meant to be used with a mallet; don't use a hammer to strike a socket chisel. **Tang chisels** are for working with the weight of the hand only. For more finished work, use a beveled-edge **cabinetmaker's chisel.** The square edge of a **framing chisel** is best for forming work, while the narrow **mortise chisel** is used to break waste away.

Helpful Hints on Chiseling

☐ Approach your work so that the wood's grain lifts the edge as you strike the chisel. If the grain is allowed to direct the edge deeper into the wood, it becomes much harder to control.

☐ First mark with chisel blows the perimeter of the area you want to chisel away. Then start your blade digging into the wood slightly inside your guideline mark.

☐ Be careful not to cut too deeply. Chisels are meant to chip and shave away. The beveled edge constantly directs the chisel out of the wood for better control.

☐ Keep the cutting edge directed away from your body and hands.

Tools for Attaching, Assembling, and Dismantling

Most Common Mistakes

☐ "Choking up" on the hammer handle reduces leverage and does not allow the head to strike flat against the surface.

☐ Not predrilling a pilot hole before nailing or screwing into hardwood or near the end of a board.

☐ Using extra-leverage items to tighten clamps.

At some point in any project you will be attaching, assembling, or dismantling what you have been measuring and sawing. These operations can be done in a variety of ways.

HAMMERS AND NAILS

The **carpenter's hammer** is available in two types. The **claw hammer** is made with a curved claw, well suited to pulling nails. For ripping boards out, the **ripping hammer,** with its straight claw, fits more easily between boards. Both types are used to drive and remove nails. They come with wood (usually hickory), steel, or fiberglass handles and in a variety of face styles and weights. A 12- to 16-ounce **finishing hammer** is recommended for small workshop projects and general use; an 18- to 24-ounce **framing hammer** is used for heavier framing work. Finishing hammers have smooth faces; framing hammers have "waffled" faces.

The **tack hammer** is useful for driving tacks and brads. Some have magnetic heads.

Mallets are used primarily for striking other objects, such as chisels, or to form sheet metal. A soft-faced mallet is used with wood- and plastic-handled chisels (Figure 1-13).

The **sledge hammer** is used for heavy work on concrete, and for adjusting framing.

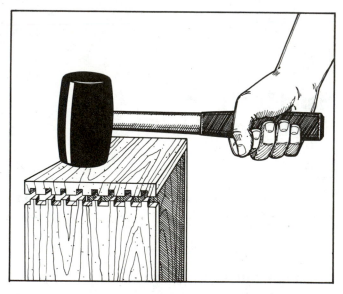

Figure 1-13. Use a mallet rather than a hammer, which may dent the wood.

Figure 1-14. Place a block of wood under the hammerhead to avoid marring the wood when pulling nails.

The **nailset** is used with a hammer to "countersink" nails by pushing them below the surface of the wood so they don't show.

Nails range from the smallest, thinnest brads to large, weighty spikes. Just be sure you are using the correct nail for the job at hand.

Helpful Hints on Hammering

☐ To withdraw a long nail without marring the wood, place a block of wood under the hammerhead for extra leverage (Figure 1-14).

☐ Use safety goggles when hammering metal. Chips often fly from steel chisels, and nailheads can break off.

☐ Whenever possible, drive the nail through the thinner piece of wood into the thicker one. Use a nail that is at least twice in length the thickness of the thinner piece of wood.

☐ Predrill a pilot hole, slightly smaller than the diameter of the nail shank, to prevent splitting the wood. Pilot holes are recommended for hardwoods, such as oak and maple, and near the ends of boards. A less effective but quicker method is to blunt the point of the nail before driving it to prevent splitting the board. To blunt the point, rest the head of the nail on a solid surface and tap the point gently with your hammer.

SCREWDRIVERS AND SCREWS

Screwdrivers should be used only to drive in and remove screws. Too often they are wrongly used—for chipping, punching holes, scraping, prying, and so forth.

The **conventional screwdriver** has a single blade and is sized to be used with screws of specific sizes.

The **phillips head screwdriver** has a cross-shaped blade that fits into the cross-shaped slot of the phillips head screw. This design reduces blade slippage and lends itself to driving with a power drill.

A **battery-powered cordless screwdriver/drill** is a very helpful tool that can be used to put a hole or a screw almost anywhere without the need to set up an extension cord. Heavy-duty types are recommended for most tasks. Holsters are available.

Screw heads are usually flat, oval, or round, and each has a specific purpose for final seating and appearance. **Flat heads** are always countersunk or rest flush with the surface. **Oval heads** permit countersinking, but the head protrudes somewhat. **Round-headed screws** rest on top of the material and are easiest to remove.

Drywall screws, also called **bugle head screws,** are countersunk phillips head screws, available in very long styles as well as in standard patterns. Originally designed to secure drywall to sheet metal framing, they are very useful for wood work. They are easy to drive compared to conventional tapered wood screws, and are even available in a finish screw pattern, called a **Robertson** screw or a **square-headed screw.**

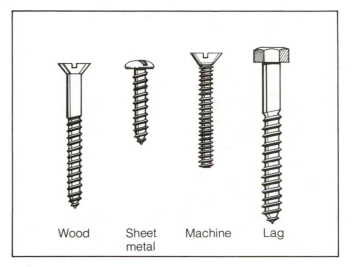

Figure 1-15. Some common screws.

Wood screws are used when stronger joining than a nail is needed, and when other materials must be fastened to wood (Figure 1-15). The conventional wood screw is tapered to help draw the wood together as the screw is inserted. Sheet metal screws can also be used to fasten metal to wood, as well as metal to metal, plastic, or other materials. **Sheet metal screws** are threaded completely from the point to the head, and the threads are sharper than those of conventional wood screws. **Machine screws** are for joining metal parts, such as hinges to metal door jambs. Machine screws are inserted into tapped (prethreaded) holes and are sometimes used with washers and nuts. **Lag screws,** or square-headed bolts with screw heads, are for heavy holding and are driven in with a wrench rather than a screwdriver.

Helpful Hints on Screwdriving

☐ When choosing screw length, remember that the screw should penetrate two-thirds of the combined thickness of the materials being joined. To avoid corrosion, consider as well moisture conditions and the makeup of the materials being fastened. If rust could be a problem, use galvanized or other rust-resistant screws.

☐ Lubricate screws with soap or wax for easier installation.

☐ Whenever possible, hold the work in a vise or clamp when inserting a screw. If this is not possible, keep your hands and other parts of the body away from the tip of the driver.

☐ To remove a screw with a damaged slot, cut another slot with a hacksaw blade if the head is exposed enough.

☐ Always make a pilot hole (usually one size smaller than the shank of the screw) before driving a screw into hardwoods and when driving a screw near the end of the board. When working with screws of larger diameter, drill a pilot hole of the same diameter as the shank of the screw into the wood to a depth of one-third the length of the screw.

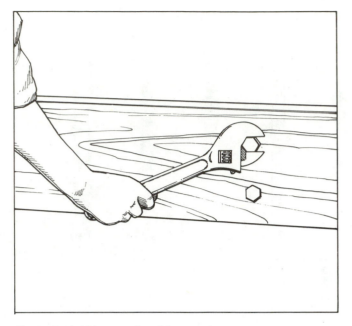

Figure 1-16. Using an adjustable wrench.

☐ To avoid damaging the screw slot and pushing the screw out of line, always keep the screwdriver shank in line with the screw shank.

WRENCHES AND PLIERS

It's not necessary to have a wide variety of wrenches and pliers, but it's handy to have some of the more common ones around the house.

An adjustable **open-end wrench** (Figure 1-16) fits any size nut that is within its opening capacity. The best choice for general use is one that opens to $15/16$".

Box or **socket wrenches** are used for removing nuts and bolts and are fitted to the size of the fastener.

The **allen wrench** is useful for recessed screws and setscrews.

Pipe wrenches are used to tighten or loosen plumbing pipes. Use two wrenches, especially when working on existing pipe—one to hold the pipe in place, the other to turn the pipe or fitting out.

The **locking wrench** works like a clamp for holding pipes and other objects in place.

The **strap wrench** is used to prevent marring chrome-plated finish and to clamp irregularly shaped items.

Slip joint pliers have jaws that lock into normal and wide opening positions.

Lineman's pliers are useful in electrical work. They have side cutters for heavy-duty wire cutting and splicing.

Channel lock pliers, with multiposition pivots, adjust for openings up to 2".

Long-nosed pliers, sometimes called **needle-nosed pliers,** can get into hard-to-reach places. They are used to shape wire and thin metal.

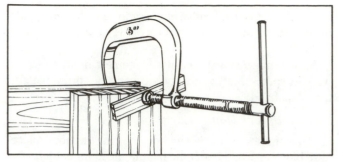

Figure 1-17. C-clamps are available with openings of different sizes.

Figure 1-18. Use wood shims for padding with bar clamps.

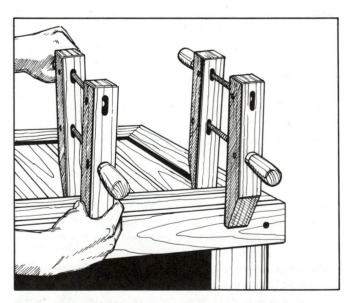

Figure 1-19. A handscrew won't mar the wood, and can be adjusted to different angles.

End-cutting nippers are used to snip wire, small nails, and brads.

Helpful Hint on Wrenching and Plying

☐ To avoid slippage and scraped knuckles, make sure the jaws of the wrench or pliers are snug in position before you manipulate the handle.

CLAMPS

Clamps are used to hold objects together while they are being worked on, or while an adhesive is drying.

The **C-clamp** (Figure 1-17) is the most common type of clamp. So named because of its shape, it has a swivel head that makes the clamp self-aligning for odd-shaped pieces.

The **bar clamp** (Figure 1-18) is useful for clamping extra-wide work.

The **vise** is a workbench tool and should be firmly secured before use. It is used for holding work to be sawed, bored, glued, or formed in some way.

The **handscrew** (Figure 1-19) has hardwood jaws that move in opposite directions because of the threading of the screws. The smooth wood and broad jaws protect the surface of the work being clamped. The handscrew is used for cabinet and furniture work.

Spring clamps are for smaller bonding uses and for securing a temporary cutting guide.

Helpful Hints on Clamping

☐ To prevent pressure damage to the surface, use padding or scraps of wood between clamps and your work.

☐ Never pound on the handle or tighten a clamp or vise with a wrench or pipe to obtain extra leverage.

ADHESIVES

The best joining is accomplished with **adhesives,** in conjunction with screws, nails, or other fasteners.

Polyvinyl (carpenter's wood glue) is a white, creamy glue that is available in plastic bottles. Mainly used for furniture, craft, and woodworking projects, polyvinyl sets in an hour, dries clear, and won't stain. However, it is vulnerable to moisture.

Resorcinol and formaldehyde are mixed just before using, and must be used at temperatures over 70 degrees. Both the resin (powdered resorcinol) and the powdered formaldehyde that you mix with water are brown and will stain light wood. Follow the manufacturer's instructions carefully.

Contact cements are used to bond veneers or to bond plastic laminates to wood for table tops and counters. Coat both surfaces thinly and allow to dry until dull before bonding. Align the surfaces perfectly before pressing them together, because once they are joined they cannot be pulled apart. Use in a well-ventilated area.

Epoxy is the only adhesive with a strength greater than most of the materials it bonds. It resists almost everything, from water to solvents. Epoxy can be used to fill cavities that would otherwise be difficult to bond. Read the manufacturer's instructions carefully; drying times vary and the resin and hardener must be mixed with precision.

The resorcinol, contact, and epoxy adhesives should be considered toxic until they cure. Take care not to get them on your skin.

Helpful Hints on Bonding

☐ Except for epoxy, too much adhesive will weaken the hold of the materials you are bonding.

☐ Rough up smooth surfaces slightly before applying adhesives so they will grip more securely.

☐ Apply a thin coat of glue, clamp securely, and allow to dry for the recommended amount of time.

☐ Wipe away excess glue immediately after clamping, except for the resorcinol and contact types. Let them dry before tooling or wiping off the excess.

FASTENERS AND CONNECTORS

You can buy ready-made fasteners and connectors for just about any job you need to do. They can be used to join wood to wood, concrete, or brick, and most meet *Uniform Building Code* requirements.

Safety plates, or **nail guards,** prevent accidental nailing into electrical wires or water and gas pipes that pass through framing.

Nail plates and **plate strips** work well as mending plates and for light-duty wood-to-wood splices.

Fence brackets simplify fence construction and allow easy disassembly when necessary.

Sawhorse brackets turn a 2x4 or 2x6 into an important support tool in just one step.

Stud shoes reinforce joists, studs, or rafters that have been drilled or notched during construction.

Foundation and masonry connectors include foundation anchors, brick wall ties, and floor jacks, among others.

Post anchors are designed to support a post from the ground up. They eliminate the need for deep post holes and prevent wood rot and termite damage.

Post caps and plates are used for a strong support where one or more beams must be connected.

Joist hangers aid in accurate, uniform connections and allow a structure to hold greater loads than do other types of fasteners.

DISMANTLING TOOLS

Everybody makes mistakes, and it helps to know how to fix things the easy way. Some dismantling tools can be a great help in "adjusting" previous work.

Pry bars, which come in various sizes, are useful demolition tools for pulling nails, ripping wood, and prying molding from walls. A pry bar offers more leverage than does a hammer.

A **catspaw** is a small pry bar with a grooved round head that is driven into a board to grab a nailhead that has been driven below the surface.

A **flat bar** is used to remove duplex nails or any nail with the head still accessible. These bars are also used to jack up drywall or door jambs, and to make minor adjustments almost anywhere.

A **reciprocating saw** with a long metal-cutting blade can also be used to cut through nails if necessary.

Finishing Tools

Most Common Mistakes

☐ Allowing a power sander to dig into the wood being finished. To avoid this, always keep the sanding machine moving over the wood.

☐ Putting the belt on a belt sander backward. This tears the seams.

☐ Using an inappropriate grit of sandpaper for the desired effect.

SANDING TOOLS

The **sanding block** or **block sander** (Figure 1-20) is wrapped with the appropriate sandpaper and rubbed across the surface by hand.

A **sanding cloth** is essential for sanding curved or round objects. It's much easier to use than a sanding block, and gives a more even finish.

The **power orbital sander,** or **pad sander** (Figure 1-21), is the ideal all-around sanding tool for finish work on walls, ceilings, floor, furniture, and other woodwork.

The **belt sander** (Figure 1-22) is designed for quick, rough sanding of large areas, or wherever heavy-duty sanding is needed.

The **disk sander** is used for fast removal of wood on uneven surfaces. Disk sanding attachments can be purchased as drill accessories.

The **drum sander** is a powerful machine used to sand floors only.

The **edge sander** is used to sand floors in areas the drum sander can't reach, such as where the floor meets the wall.

Sandpaper runs from very coarse (20 to 40 grits per inch) up to the very fine (600 grits per inch). Materials range from flint and garnet emery to aluminum oxide and silicon carbide. **Flint** is best for hand-sanding painted or pitchy surfaces, which can clog the paper. **Garnet emery** is for hand-sanding clean wood. **Aluminum oxide** is fast and long-lasting for power-sanding wood. It can also be used on plastics and fiberglass and for polishing stainless steel, high carbon steel, or bronze. **Silicon carbide** is harder than aluminum oxide and is best used for hard plastics, glass, and ceramics, or for grinding and finishing brass, copper, and aluminum.

Emery cloth is another option for metal polishing.

Steel wool is available in #3 coarse to #0000, which is very fine.

Figure 1-21. Using an orbital sander to sand a small patch.

Sanding belt

Roller

Tracking control knob

Figure 1-22. Using a belt sander.

Figure 1-20. Using a hand-held sanding block.

Use **pumice** or **rottenstone** (decomposed limestone) for a glassy finish.

Helpful Hints on Sanding

☐ Generally, you should start with a coarse paper and work to a fine paper for the smoothest finish. Whenever possible, sand with the grain of the wood.

☐ When using a power sander, do not press down on the machine. Let its own weight do the sanding. Pressing down inhibits the action of the machine.

☐ When operating any power sander, engage and disengage the machine from the material being sanded while the belt or disk is still in motion to avoid gouging the wood.

☐ To sand inward curves, wrap padding material around a stick or dowel, then wrap sandpaper over it.

☐ When sanding wood, seal heating and air-conditioning ducts and electrical outlets with plastic sheets and/or duct tape. Wood dust is highly flammable.

PLANES

Planes are used for removing very thin layers of wood, for trimming and smoothing, for straightening or beveling edges, and for adding a groove.

The **block plane** is abut 6" long and is used for small smoothing and fitting jobs.

The **trimming plane** is used for more delicate work. This tool is only 3½" in length, with a 1" blade.

The **jack plane** is 12" to 15" in length, with a 2" blade. It is used to smooth rough surfaces.

Fore and **joiner planes,** at 18" to 24" in length, are the best bet for straightening edges.

The **rabbit plane** cuts recessed grooves along an edge.

The **grooving plane** cuts a long slot.

Helpful Hints on Planing

☐ Whenever possible, plane with the grain of the wood to avoid catching and lifting chips of wood.

☐ Prevent splitting the corners of the material you are planing across the grain by approaching each corner from the outside.

☐ Always keep your blades razor sharp; dull blades require excessive force and reduce control.

☐ When it's not in use, rest your plane on its side to avoid dulling the blade.

☐ When starting cuts, apply more pressure to the front of the tool; when completing them, apply more pressure to the rear.

FILES AND RASPS

Files are used for shaping. You will find files that are round, half-round, flat, square, and even triangular. Single-cut file teeth run in one direction. Double-cut teeth, which run in opposing directions, cut more coarsely, but quicker.

Rasps differ from files in that the teeth are formed individually, not connected to one another. In general, a longer file or rasp has somewhat coarser teeth than a shorter one. Files cut smoother than rasps, but when used on wood are much slower and are susceptible to clogging.

Helpful Hints on Filing

☐ Files with an attachable handle are easier to use.

☐ Secure your work with a vise or clamps at elbow height for general filing; lower for heavier filing; and nearer to eye level for delicate work.

☐ File in the cutting direction only; lift the file on the return stroke.

☐ Keep files clean with a file brush (called a **card**) or with a small wire brush.

☐ Store files in a rack or protective sleeves to keep from dulling the teeth.

Pneumatic Tools

Pneumatic tools are fast becoming indispensable to the home builder. Pneumatic tools include an air compressor (pneumatic means "containing air") and a variety of attachments. Although pneumatic tools take some special handling, they actually save a great deal of working time and effort and are relatively easy to use. They also give professional results.

The instruction manual that comes with the compressor should list a toll-free number to call if you have any questions or problems.

Most Common Mistakes

☐ Not reading the instruction manual and safety labels.

☐ Using an improper length or gauge of extension cord. A long extension cord reduces the power and efficiency of the motor. Use extension air hose rather than cord for distance work.

☐ Using an incorrect pressure for the tool and the task.

☐ Not changing the oil every 250 hours of use or every 6 months.

☐ Failing to locate the working air compressor on a clean, dry, level site.

☐ Failing to keep the compressor properly lubricated.

SAFETY

☐ Many tasks for which an air compressor is used require safety glasses or goggles, protective clothing, and a dust- or paint-filtering mask.

☐ Make sure the pressure of the compressor has been completely relieved through the line to the tool before changing to another tool, unless a quick connection is being used.

☐ Make sure the tool has completely stopped before changing or disconnecting it.

☐ Never point the blow gun toward your eyes or any other part of your body.

☐ Never exceed recommended pressure for the tool being used or the job being done.

☐ Never override the pressure switch on a pneumatic nailgun.

☐ Never alter the three-pronged plug to fit an outlet other than the type for which it was designed.

☐ Always unplug the cord from the outlet before disengaging it from the compressor.

☐ Test safety relief valves periodically.

☐ Open the tank valve after every use.

☐ Never allow children around the compressor, whether it is in operation or stored.

☐ Never operate the compressor without the belt guard in place.

☐ Read the owner's manual completely and read all safety-oriented labels on the unit before using it.

AIR COMPRESSOR

The **air compressor** is the central power source of the pneumatic tool, and your major investment. Air compressors are available in horsepowers of ¾ to 5, or even larger, with a variety of tank sizes up to 80 gallons. The frequency and duration of use will determine the horsepower and tank size you'll need for your own projects. A 2 HP compressor is adequate for most tasks around the house. Typically, units of this size have tanks from 7½ to 20 gallons. Choose an air compressor for quality and protective features, as well as for capacity.

ATTACHMENTS

If kept properly cleaned and lubricated, air tools are virtually indestructible. They have few moving parts, so maintenance is minimal, and they run cool, because their power source is the compressor.

Most air tools are available at hardware stores and home centers. Specialty air tools can be rented. Instructions for each tool attachment are included with the purchase or rental. Read these instructions carefully before using the tool.

Two of the most obvious and useful tools are an **inflation kit** and **quick-connect couplers.** The inflation kit attachment allows you to inflate everything from beach balls to automobile tires. The quick connect couplers make it fast and easy to change tools.

The **blow gun** attachment is great for blasting away dirt, grease, and dust from hard-to-reach areas. Never point the gun at the eyes or other parts of the body.

Always be sure the **nail gun** is flat against the surface being nailed and know what is on the other side, so you won't cause damage or injury with the high pressure of the gun.

Figure 1-23. Using an air compressor with a spray gun attachment to paint.

Similarly, be sure the **stapler** is flat against the surface being stapled. Large staplers are available for heavy work like attaching roofing shingles.

The dual-action **air sander** should always be touching the surface when it is turned on. This type of sander is frequently used in automotive work and has many other uses around the house, such as rust removal and paint preparation.

The **spray gun** (Figure 1-23) speeds up paint application by 50% or more and gives a smooth finish. There are a variety of spray gun designs on the market for various types of painting.

The **sandblaster** works well for removing rust and old paint and for preparing surfaces for painting. It can also be adapted for use with soap and water for pressure cleaning, such as degreasing auto engines and garden equipment.

The **caulking gun** takes the toil out of caulking by giving a fast, strong, uniform bead. This tool can be used for any tube material, such as adhesive or grease.

The **air ratchet wrench** is great for tightening bolts, whether you are building a deck or working on an automobile engine.

The **air hammer/chisel** is used for jobs like breaking up masonry. It must be up against the surface when started.

The **air drill** makes drilling into any surface an effortless task.

The **impact wrench** is used mostly in automotive and assembly work.

Checklist of Tools for Home Projects

Tools for Measuring and Leveling

Carpenter's pencil

Steel tape measure

Carpenter's square (framing square)

Combination square

Torpedo level

2′ to 4′ level

Plumb bob

Chalkline

Power Tools for Cutting and Drilling

Saws

Circular saw

Saber saw (jigsaw)

Reciprocating saw

Table saw (bench saw)

Radial-arm saw

Chopsaw

Bandsaw

Drills and Router

3/8" variable-speed drill

Cordless drill

Router

Hand Tools for Sawing and Chiseling

Saws

Crosscut saw

Rip saw

Combination saw

Hacksaw

Backsaw and miter box

Keyhole saw

Coping saw

Chisels

Chisel set 1/4" to 1 1/2" in width

Sock

Tang chisel

Cabinetmaker's chisel

Framing chisel

Mortise chisel

Tools for Attaching, Assembling, and Dismantling

Hammers and Nails

Claw hammer

Ripping hammer

Tack hammer

Mallet

Sledge hammer

Nailset

Brads, nails, and spikes

Screwdrivers and Screws

Conventional screwdrivers

Phillips head screwdrivers

Cordless screwdriver

Screws of various kinds

Wrenches and Pliers

Open-end wrench

Box wrench (socket wrench)

Allen wrench

Pipe wrenches (2)

Locking wrench

Strap wrench

Slip joint pliers

Channel lock pliers

Long-nosed pliers

End-cutting nippers

Clamps

C-Clamp

Bar clamp

Vise

Handscrew

Spring clamps

Adhesives

Polyvinyl (carpenter's wood glue)

Resorcinol and formaldehyde

Contact cement

Epoxy

Fasteners and Connectors

Safety plates (nail guards)

Nail plates

Plate strips

Fence brackets

Sawhorse brackets

Stud shoes

Foundation and masonry connectors

Post anchors

Post caps and plates

Joist hangers

Dismantling Tools

Pry bar

Catspaw

Flat bar

Finishing Tools

Sanding Tools

Sanding block (block sander)

Sanding cloth

Orbital sander (pad sander)

Belt sander

Disk sander

Drum sander

Edge sander

Sandpapers

Steel wool

Pumice and rottenstone

Planes

Block plane

Trimming plane

Jack plane

Scrub plane

Fore and joiner planes

Rabbit plane

Grooving plane

Files and Rasps

Single cut file

Double cut file

Rasp

Pneumatic Tools

Air compressor

Blow gun

Nail gun

Air stapler

Air sander

Spray gun

Sandblaster

Caulking gun

Air ratchet wrench

Air hammer/chisel

Air drill

Impact wrench

Miscellaneous Tools

Sawhorses

Vacuum cleaner

2 Electricity

ALONG WITH THE plumbing system, installing the electrical system is among the most demanding tasks for the owner builder. It is not so much that a high degree of skill is involved in running wires, but rather that a great amount of knowledge is required. The electrical code is extensive and varies from area to area. Every electrical system is unique, and every home has its own problems that require special knowledge and experience. In addition, installing the electrical system is physically difficult and can be extremely frustrating.

In the entire process of finishing a house, electrical wiring and plumbing installation are the areas in which you should consider hiring a professional. If you decide to wire the house yourself, you should at least hire a professional consultant to oversee your work. It's also a good idea to read at least a couple of how-to books about electricity, just to determine how much of this work you want to do yourself.

The National Electric Code (NEC), written by the National Fire Protection Association, is designed to provide a basic level of safety in every electrical system in the United States. Within certain limits, each community is free to add or delete provisions in order to address specific local problems or reflect local custom.

Unlike the rest of this book, it is not the intention of this chapter to provide you with all of the information you will need to install the entire electrical system; that would require a book in itself. This chapter does not attempt to walk you through the entire process in a series of detailed steps. Rather, it offers an overview of the electrical system and its components, some of the main code restrictions, and details on installing and connecting cable, boxes, and receptacles. With the information presented here, you should be able to speak knowledgeably with your electrician about your specific needs.

A faulty or improperly installed electrical system can be the source of three major problems. First, inspectors are very demanding that the system be properly installed, and are especially wary of work done by nonprofessionals. Second, wiring mistakes are often discovered after the walls are finished. If the problem is behind the drywall, it will be difficult to repair. Most importantly, a faulty electrical system is a major fire hazard. For all of these reasons, it is a good idea to consult with a professional about all electrical work you plan to do.

Many owner-builders choose to install the branch circuits and subpanels and then have an electrical contractor install the mast and main panel and tie the circuits to the main panel.

Basic Theory

Electricity can be compared to water flowing through pipes, with a small turbine drawing power at each tap, or outlet. **Alternating current** is delivered in pulses to your appliances and lights through a black or red **hot wire.** A white **neutral wire** returns the current to the earth. A bare or green **grounding wire** serves as a safety backup for the neutral wire. The neutral wires and grounding wires are never interrupted by a breaker, as this would compromise the system's safety.

Each circuit in your electrical system is a loop. The power coming in must have a way out to perform its work. For instance, a light fixture is always connected to the neutral wire, and the switch is placed on the hot wire. The current travels through the switch and the bulb and back to the earth. With outlets, the current completes the loop through whatever appliance is plugged in and turned on.

It is vital, and required by the NEC, that you maintain standard color coding throughout your system. The color coding ensures that any electrician or inspector can open any panel, switch, or outlet box in the system and know which wires are doing what. If the neutral wire is used incorrectly to supply power to a polarized appliance or motor, damage to the appliance may occur and the potential for shocks is increased. (**Polarity** refers to the direction the power is traveling, and it must be correct to avoid damage to many electrical devices, computers in particular. If the black wire is always attached to the brass screw, the white wire is always attached to the silver screw, and the bare or green wire is always attached to the green screw, polarity will be correctly maintained throughout your system.)

Before You Begin

SAFETY

Safety is of the utmost importance with working with electricity. Develop safe work habits and stick to them. Electricity may be invisible, but it can be dangerous if it is not understood and respected.

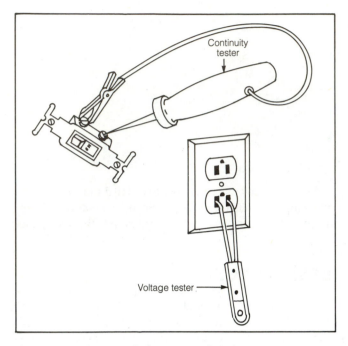

Figure 2-1. Using a continuity tester and a voltage tester.

☐ The first rule of working with electricity is, Never work on any live circuit, fixture, receptacle, or switch.

☐ Make sure the power is off at the breaker box before doing any electrical work.

☐ Avoid electrical shock by mapping and marking your switch and outlet boxes. Put the map on the door of the main power service panel.

☐ Post a warning message at the service panel that you are working on the circuit, and tape the circuit breaker in the off position.

☐ Before working with wires or electrical connections, check them with a voltage tester to be sure they are dead. One prong of the voltage tester is inserted into the hot side of the outlet and one into the neutral or ground side (Figure 2-1). If the circuit is live, the bulb will light up.

☐ Plumbing and gas pipes are often connected to electrical systems. Never touch them while working with or around electricity.

☐ Always work in a clean, dry area that is free from anything wet.

☐ Don't use metal ladders around overhead electricity.

☐ Never attempt to strip wires with a knife. Aside from endangering your fingers, you will nick the wire metal, creating an electrical hazard.

☐ Never change the size of a fuse or breaker in a circuit.

☐ Always correct the problem that caused a fuse or circuit breaker to blow before replacing the fuse or resetting the circuit breaker.

☐ Wires should be connected only at accessible boxes. Never splice wires outside a box.

☐ Ground fault circuit interrupter outlets should be used in damp areas, such as basements, bathrooms, and outdoors. Their use is required by the National Electric Code.

☐ Wear rubber-soled boots when working with electricity.

☐ Wear glasses or goggles whenever you are using power tools, especially if you wear contact lenses.

☐ Always brace the powerful right-angle drill so that it can't spin around and break your knuckles if it gets stuck while you are drilling.

☐ Use the proper protection, take precautions, and plan ahead. Never bypass safety to save money or to rush a project.

USEFUL TERMS

An **ampere** is a measure of the number of electrically charged particles that flow past a given point on a circuit per second.

A **breaker box** or **breaker panel** houses the circuit breakers or fuses and distributes power to various parts of the house.

A **circuit** is all the wiring controlled by one circuit breaker. The NEC requires that lighting circuits be supplied with 15 amps of potential, distributed in size 14 wire (minimum). (See Basic Wiring Information, later in this chapter.) Outlet circuits are always 20 amps unless they supply a large appliance. Size 12 wire is the minimum allowed for 20 amp circuits. Most larger appliances are rated at 220 to 230 volts. These circuits have special outlets and double breakers, and the outlets eliminate the chance of plugging a 110 volt appliance into a 220 volt outlet. The number of light fixtures or outlets per circuit is governed by the NEC and local additions to it. In most cases your designer or electrical contractor will be familiar with these requirements, and your plans will be accepted the first time.

A **circuit breaker** is a protective device for each circuit, which automatically cuts off power from the main breaker in the event of an overload or short. Only a regulated amount of current can pass through the breaker before it will trip.

A **continuity tester** (see Figure 2-1) has its own power supply batteries, and is used to determine if a wire has any hidden breaks, or to locate the other end of a single wire or single circuit.

A **feeder** is a single long run of heavy cable that supplies a distant subpanel or large appliance with power.

Fish tape is a long, flexible metal strip with a hook to which you fasten the cable or wire to pull it through a raceway or conduit.

The **main breaker** turns the power entering your home through the breaker box on or off. It is sometimes found in the breaker box, or it may be in a separate box at a different location.

The above-ground electrical supply from the utility company must terminate at a **mast,** an appropriately sized metal conduit with a meter socket for your utility. The size of the mast is determined by the size of your main breaker and feed wires.

The **neutral bus bar** is the bar to which the neutral wire is connected in the breaker box.

Roughing in is the placement of wires and boxes before the interior walls and insulation are installed, and before the electricity is hooked up.

The power supply from the utility poles or underground cables to the mast is called a **service drop.**

A **subpanel** is a circuit breaker box that draws its power from a main breaker box. It is used to avoid having many long circuit runs.

UL stands for **Underwriters Laboratory.** For safety reasons, each component in your system should bear the UL listed stamp. Underwriters Laboratory is an independent testing facility that tests and then monitors those components to be sure quality is maintained. Each cable, switch, outlet, and panel should bear the initials "UL" or the phrase "UL Listed."

A **volt** is a measure of the current pressure at receptacles and lights. Average household voltage is 120. There are three types of branch circuits—120 volt, 120/240 volt, and 240 volt. Most circuits in the home that are not used for large appliances are **120 volt. 120/240 volt circuits** are used for appliances that may require a lot of electricity for one operation (for example, an electric range) and a smaller amount for another operation (the clock on the range). **240 volt circuits** are used for appliances that require a lot of electricity for all their operations, such as a water heater.

A **watt** is a measure of the rate at which an electrical device, such as a light bulb or appliance, consumes energy. Watts = volts X amperes.

WHAT YOU WILL NEED

Time. The time needed will depend on the scope of the project and on your level of experience. Two inexperienced workers would need at least 5 to 8 days to rough wire a 1500-square-foot house. This isn't difficult work but if you don't follow standard procedure and know how to troubleshoot for electrical problems, it can take much longer.

Tools. Some special (although inexpensive) tools are required for working with electricity.

Long-nose (needlenose) pliers

Wire cutters

Electric drill

Tape measure

Screwdriver

Chalkline

Hammer

Circular saw

Chisel

Hacksaw

Combination square

Utility light

Fish tape

Cable stripper

Wire stripper

Colored tape

Voltage tester

Continuity tester

Safety glasses or goggles

Keyhole saw

Utility knife

Right-angle drill

Pry bar and wood wedge

Materials. After figuring the lengths of cable you will need, it's a good idea to order 10 percent extra for wastage. Depending on the extent of the wiring you are undertaking, your list may include the following materials.

Grounded receptacles

Switches

Junction boxes

Nail guards

Wire nuts

Horseshoe nails (electrical staples)

Push terminals

Screw terminals

Breakers

Track lights and fittings

Dimmer switch

Waterproof junction boxes

Ground fault interrupters

Conduit

Cable

Silicone caulking

PERMITS AND CODES

Most states and municipalities use, and have additions to, the National Electric Code (NEC). Always consult the office of your local building inspector to determine what permits or special provisions must be met. All electrical work, no matter how small the job, must pass local codes. Be sure to get the proper permits, and be certain that you are clear on how to do your work so that it will pass code. Local codes differ, so don't rely on the information given in this book—it may not pass inspection in your area. Obtain a copy of the local building code by contacting the Building Inspectors' Association in your state capital; or check with the building inspector at your county court house or your city building department.

Some minimum design requirements common to most communities are:

1. Illumination: One circuit for each 500 square feet of floor space, and at least one fixture per room. It's a good idea not to have only one lighting circuit per floor in a multilevel building. If that one circuit fails, the whole floor will be in darkness.

2. Kitchens: At least two 20 amp branch circuits for countertop outlets, and one circuit each for a garbage disposal, a dishwasher, and the refrigerator. An electric range will require a separate 220 volt outlet.

3. Laundries: One 20 amp circuit for the washer and a 30 amp 220 volt circuit for an electric drier.

4. Outlets: Two circuits each for the family room, dining room, and breakfast room, and at least one each for the living room and the garage. The NEC requires outlets to be placed no more than 6′ apart. Any wall over 2′ wide requires an outlet, as does any countertop over 12″ wide.

To some extent, meeting these requirements "designs" your installation for you. But don't forget that these are minimum requirements and may not fully address your particular needs.

Besides all these circuits, many people eventually have to add more later, for spas, pools, mood lighting, and so on. Be sure the main panel and subpanels are large enough to add future circuitry without replacing the panels themselves.

Codes specify the size and type of wire that can be used; the type and materials of the boxes; the distance between the supports for the wire; how far from the box the wire must be supported; and the size of the main breaker box, as well as many other details. The code also specifies that you must install lighting and receptacles in basements and unfinished spaces if they appear inhabitable to your inspector or planning department.

Some communities require this work to be done by a licensed electrical contractor. Never are inspectors more fearful of homeowners doing their own work than with electrical systems. The danger of electrocution, or of a house fire resulting from faulty wiring, is significant. Inspectors check electrical work very carefully. And they should. So be sure that all work is done neatly, to code, and in the manner inspectors are used to seeing it done.

DESIGN

A successful wiring project requires a plan so that you know exactly where you want your receptacles (outlets), switches, and fixtures to be placed, and the most efficient way to supply power to them. Since all of this work requires making holes in exposed framing, now is the time to add telephone cable, television cable, alarm wiring, and intercoms or other features. Just be sure to make a detailed plan, to improve your installation efficiency and so you will have a record of where you put these components.

The circuits for lighting, outlets, and heavy appliances are all isolated after the main panel. How many circuits you will need depends on the expected loads designed into the system. It's better to install the largest system you might need, and not the smallest you can get away with.

The **lighting circuits** usually terminate in ceiling fixture boxes. One 15 amp circuit provides current to as many ceiling fixtures as the 15 amp supply will carry, depending on their rated size (wattage). If there are two entrances to a room, plan for a light switch at both doors. Place switches on the unhinged side of the door. Determine the most direct route for cables, and route them accordingly.

The **outlet circuits** are either a long single run to one box, called a **dedicated circuit,** or a series of smaller pieces of cable "leapfrogging" from box to box; these are called **branch circuits.**

A **general purpose circuit** supplies power to both outlet receptacles and lighting fixtures. The code allows the use of a general purpose circuit anywhere but the kitchen or laundry. However, it is common to isolate lighting and outlet circuits in all areas of the home. That way, if you overload an outlet circuit and trip a breaker, you're not left in the dark.

Don't skimp on the receptacles. Aside from the danger of overloading outlets with extension cords and adapters, it can be just plain frustrating to have dark corners where you most need the light. Code usually requires 12′ or less between outlets on the same wall. With this maximum distance, a 6′ cord on an appliance or lamp can always reach an outlet without an extension cord. It will look better if you plan all of your outlets to be at the same height. This may be determined by local code.

The heavy feeder cable that supplies **subpanels and large appliances** is very expensive. Use the rules for notching and making holes, outlined later in this chapter, to determine the shortest possible route for these large cables.

Draw a rough plan, as in Figure 2-2, to show the general pattern of receptacles, switches, and fixtures and their circuitry. Your plan will assist you in making up your materials list and in calculating the amount of cable you will need.

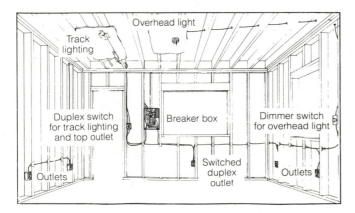

Figure 2-2. General purpose circuits.

BASIC WIRING INFORMATION

Before launching into step-by-step wiring instructions, this section reviews the basic information you need to know about wiring, boxes, receptacles, switches, circuit breakers, and fuses.

Wiring

A **cable** consists of several insulated **wires** wrapped in an outer sheath of insulation. However, the words *cable* and *wire* are often used interchangeably.

The American Wire Gauge (AWG) designation is a system for categorizing sizes and types of wire and cable (Figure 2-3). Wire sizes normally used in homes range from AWG number 10 to 14. The larger the wire, the smaller the gauge number. Wiring that runs inside the walls of a house is called cable. A run is a length of cable between two boxes. The type of cable depends on how the cable is to be used; the size of the cable depends on the amount of current (amperes) to be carried.

The larger the diameter of a wire, the greater the amount of current it can carry without overheating. Therefore, larger wires are used when larger current capacity is required. Every appliance or circuit is designated to carry a certain number of amps, and every size wire is rated as to how many amps it can carry. For instance, a 20 amp circuit requires number 12 cable, while a 50 amp stove requires a much larger cable. Check your local code for required wire sizes. Some current is lost within the wire, as heat generation. This is called **voltage drop,** and it can be significant in long cable runs. You may need to use the next larger size cable.

The insulated wires within the cable are made of either copper or aluminum, although copper is the more common. Aluminum circuit wire is not recommended because of the danger of fire, although it is often used to supply subpanels.

As explained earlier, wires are color coded so that you can tell at a glance which one is which. A black or red hot wire carries power to outlets, fixtures, and appliances. The white neutral wire carries the power back to zero potential by dumping it into the earth. A bare or green grounding wire provides backup in case of appliance failure or lighting surges to your supply lines.

Cable is referred to by the size of the wire and the number of conductors in the cable plus the ground. For example, if you are using a number 14 wire with two conductors plus ground, it is termed *14-2/w ground.* A number 12 wire with three conductors plus ground is termed *12-3/w ground.*

Type NM/NMB cable is often called by a manufacturer's name, Romex. It is sheathed in heavy protective plastic and paper with a thermoplastic covering on each wire. (Thermoplastic is plastic that won't melt from the heat of the electricity.) Type NM (nonmetallic sheathed) cable is used for most indoor wiring projects.

Type UF cable is covered with a plastic jacket that protects the insulated wires from sunlight and moisture. It can be bur-

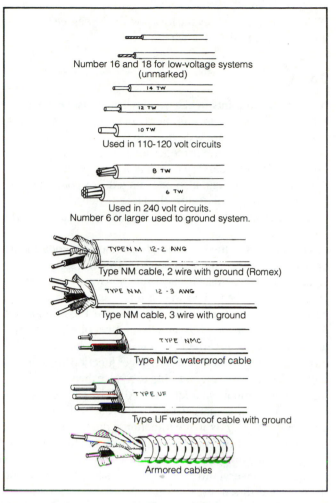

Figure 2-3. Various sizes and types of wires.

ied without any extra protection, and is used indoors and in damp areas. Terminations, spacing, and burial depth of this type is often specified by local code.

Armored cable type BX is a flexible spiral-wound steel casing enclosing two or three insulated wires and a bare, thin tapelike bond, or ground, wire. The steel casing protects against injury by nails or screws. BX cable requires special connectors and small plastic bushings, inserted into the end of the metal jacket to protect the wires' insulation at this sharp edge.

The metal jacket is cut off diagonally about 8" from the end of the cable with a hacksaw or a special BX cable-cutting tool. If you use a hacksaw you must take care not to damage the wires during cutting. This type of cable is subject to corrosion, and should be used only in dry indoor areas.

Metal conduit is rigid or flexible metal pipe or tubing that contains individual wires. It is sometimes required by code. Conduit is installed empty, and two or more wires are pulled into position with a fish tape.

Plastic PVC conduit for electrical systems is similar to the Schedule 40 PVC that is used in plumbing systems, but it is gray and uses different types of fittings. When wiring with

PVC, be sure to use only the long-sweep 90-degree bend fittings to make pulling the wire easier.

Boxes

All splices and joints in electrical wiring must be made inside of boxes, which are commonly made of steel, plastic, or fiberglass. Certain areas do not allow any but metal boxes. Many electricians prefer metal boxes because they can be disassembled if necessary to install a large group of wires. Some metal boxes can also be "ganged," or connected together to accommodate more than two switches at one location. The ground wires can also be attached directly to the metal boxes.

The purpose of the box is to protect the wire ends and to provide an area for any heat coming from the splice to dissipate. Boxes also make it easy to get to wiring connections; every box must be placed so that it is permanently accessible. All runs must be continuous from box to box. No splices may be made outside a box, and the number of wires permitted in each box is governed by code. If a switch box or outlet box is going to be too crowded, a larger junction box is used, with a piece called a **plaster ring** to reduce the visible opening to the original, smaller size. All boxes have **knockouts**—scored areas that can be knocked out to allow cable to enter and exit the box in the direction required. The knockouts are often of two or more different sizes, to accommodate large and small cables.

There are several different types of boxes, with different depths, for different uses.

Junction boxes are octagonal or square, in 3¼" and 4" sizes, with a cover plate that can be removed for access to the wires inside them.

Outlet/switch boxes are rectangular. Steel boxes can be joined together to make larger boxes. Plastic or fiberglass boxes come in different sizes to accommodate the number of switches or outlets needed.

Ceiling boxes are round and are screwed to a joist or header or attached to a crosspiece where a ceiling fixture is to be installed. They are covered by the fixture's trim ring.

Exterior boxes come in the usual varieties, junction, outlet, and switch, and are required in exterior locations. They are much more expensive than interior styles, and must be installed using appropriate weatherproof techniques.

Receptacles

The purpose of a wall receptacle is to tap the circuit to provide electrical power at a given location. The slots in the socket are designed to match the prongs of the plug on the appliance or extension cord; they vary according to the voltage and current (amperage) rating for the receptacle.

Receptacle boxes come in both flush and surface-mounted designs. Flush mounting is more desirable for inside use, except for the large receptacles used for the kitchen range or clothes drier.

Modern installations use duplex receptacles with a grounding terminal on a two-wire cable with ground circuit. These receptacles take either regular two-prong plugs or the three-prong grounding plugs found on many portable power tools and other appliances. The smallest slot is always the hot wire and the wider slot the neutral wire. The round hole connects to the grounding circuit. Some two-prong plugs have a wide tang and a narrow one to ensure that current enters the appliance correctly.

Unless you have nonmetallic cable in plastic boxes, each time a cable enters a box it must be clamped and secured. NMC clamps are available in different sizes to fit different cables, and these clamps must be secured to both the box and the cable to pass a rough electrical inspection. BX clamps are available in different sizes as well, and special 90 percent offset types are useful where clearance is a problem. The clamps and of different sizes and fit in the knockout holes.

These different sizes are intended to fit in the knockout holes in the boxes. Always be sure you are removing the appropriate size knockout plug for your clamp. Many panels have concentrically punched knockouts to accommodate larger supply or feeder cables. To remove the knockout at the right prestamped cut, just insert a flat screwdriver blade into the desired separation and lever or twist the screwdriver to separate the plug slightly from the other knockout rings. With a pair of needlenose pliers, twist or rock the plug until it comes off.

Wire nuts are commonly used to make a connection in a receptacle, switch box, or junction box. Like kinds of wires are spliced and twisted together clockwise with the ends snipped. The twisted wires are capped with a wire nut and turned clockwise to secure the connection. Wire nuts are color coded according to size. You must have the right size wire nuts to cap the number and size of the wire you are working with.

Switches and Switch Loops

Switches take many forms to meet many needs. For most residential purposes, switches come in single-pole, single-throw, three-way, and four-way. Most common is the single-pole, single-throw switch, which usually has three terminals. One terminal connects to the power supply wire, and one carries the power to the fixture. This type of switch controls the light from one location. Three-way switches have three terminals and can control a light from two locations. Four-way switches have four terminals and are used to provide light control from any number of locations between a pair of three-way switches.

A switch can serve a light fixture in two ways. It can be placed on the hot wire as a cable passes through the switch box, or a separate cable, called a **switch loop** or **leg**, can be run to the switch box to control the hot wire to the fixture. A switch loop is used when it is easier to take the cable to the fixture itself rather than through the switch box, such as when a two-story building has its circuit runs in the second floor framing, or when the runs are placed in the attic. Because the supply cable is already where the fixture will be, the switch loops reduce the effort and material that would be required to branch one circuit through three or more switch boxes.

For a single-switch control on a single fixture, the supply cable is routed first to the fixture box itself, and then another piece is routed to the switch box. The white and bare wires are attached directly to the light fixture itself, but the black wire is joined with a wire nut to the black wire of the cable going to the switch. This way, the switch controls the current supplied to the fixture. The white wire in the cable to the switch carries current to the fixture when the switch is turned on, and in this situation standard color coding is improper. You must use black tape, paint, or a felt pen to color both ends of the white wire in the cable to the switch, to indicate that they are hot wires. This is required by the NEC. The marked black end is then attached to the brass screw on the fixture.

Be sure to include this added cable, from the fixture to the switch boxes, in your material estimate.

Two- and three-way switches are basically the same as the single-pole type, but the power supply is routed through more than one conductor. These circuits require special cable, or more than one cable, to accommodate multiple controls to one fixture circuit.

Circuit Breakers and Fuses

A **fuse** is a strip of metal encased in a housing through which current passes into a circuit. The only type used in new construction is the **cartridge fuse.** Used with electric furnaces and air conditioners, cartridge fuses are manufactured to exceed their rated capacity for a short period, to accommodate the sudden peaks those appliances draw on starting. Cartridge fuses show no sign of overload, and must be tested with a continuity tester to see if they have blown. Fuses of different types should never be interchanged.

Circuit breakers are heavy-duty switches that serve the same purpose as fuses. The current is routed through a bimetal spring inside the breaker. When this spring gets too hot, it trips the breaker. When a circuit is carrying more current than is safe, the breaker switches to reset. On most breakers, the toggle-handle switch has to be flipped off and then on after the circuit trips. Always solve the problem before replacing a blown fuse or resetting the breaker.

A special kind of circuit breaker, the **ground fault circuit interrupter** (GFCI), is required by code outdoors and in areas around water, such as the bathroom and kitchen. If there is current leakage or a ground fault, the GFCI opens the circuit almost instantly, cutting off the electricity. This safety feature helps prevent shocks.

A GFCI breaker protects the entire circuit; the GFCI outlet protects only other outlets "downstream" of its location. When a GFCI breaker trips, it is reset in the same way as a regular circuit breaker.

BASIC WIRING

Most Common Mistakes

☐ While it is easy to make mistakes when working with electricity, it is just as easy to avoid them. The single most important mistake to avoid is neglecting to turn off the power before beginning. Other common mistakes include the following.

☐ Not making a plan for the work being done.

☐ Not learning about your community's specific requirements before you start.

☐ Overloading circuits by plugging too many appliances into an outlet, or by using an inadequate extension cord. (See the section on the breaker box, later in this chapter.)

☐ Not labeling circuits at the service panel.

☐ Not using UL-approved materials.

☐ Routing the wiring in an inefficient manner.

☐ Mounting outlets and switches without ensuring that they are flush with the final wall covering.

☐ Not using the correct housing box for the wiring that you plan to install.

☐ Not using weatherproof boxes for outdoor fixtures.

☐ Neglecting to seal around holes drilled through exterior walls.

☐ Not using nail guards where needed.

☐ Not having your work inspected at critical points.

☐ Failing to follow local code.

Step One
Installing the Main Breaker Box

Most Common Mistakes

☐ Using a breaker box that is too small to hold all the necessary circuits, including ones that will be needed in the future.

☐ Locating the breaker box in an inconvenient or unapproved area. (Code often designates where the box can be located.)

Caution: This is the part that even contractors often leave to electricians. If you are going to tackle this yourself, remember that the electrical inspector will scrutinize your circuit boxes and panel closely. This inspector must approve your rough electrical work and panel before your utility company will supply it with power. Work carefully and neatly; this is the heart of your electrical system.

The **breaker box** or **panel box** (Figure 2-4) holds the breakers for all the circuits in the house. It usually contains the main breaker as well. Although it is not required by code, the most logical place for the main breaker (the breaker that controls all the power to the house) is at the main panel. Sometimes, however, the main breaker is located in a separate box, or even at a different location.

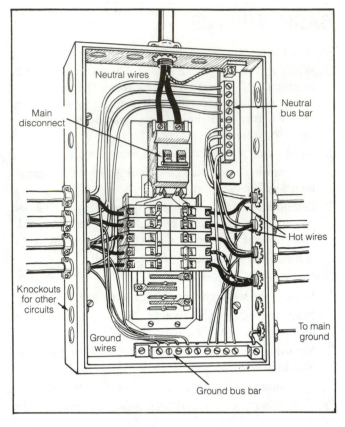

Figure 2-4. Typical breaker box.

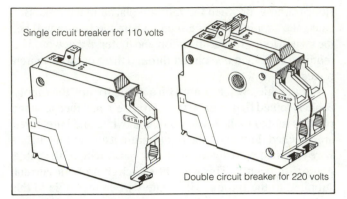

Figure 2-5. Single and double circuit breakers.

The main breaker performs two tasks. It provides a single location at which to turn off all the power, and it can limit the damage of lightning surges through the supply lines.

Circuit breakers (Figure 2-5) control the power going to a particular route of wiring. In case of an overload or a short, the breaker trips and automatically shuts off power to that circuit.

Panel boxes are available in both recessed and surface-mounted models. The recessed box is installed between two studs and securely fastened to them with screws. The box should protrude from the face of the stud by the thickness of the drywall.

After you have run the cables and installed the boxes (see next steps), attaching the wires to the breakers and buses in the panel is not difficult. Bring the neutral and grounding wires into the box and attach them to the neutral bus bar. Do this by sticking the stripped ends of the wires into any hole in the neutral bus bar; secure them by tightening down the screw heads. Some boxes have two bus bars, one for the ground wire and one for the neutral wire. Others have only one bus bar for both neutral and ground

The importance of proper grounding cannot be over-emphasized. Some communities require two grounding rods buried some distance apart. (A **grounding rod** is an 8′ copper-clad steel bar that is driven down into the soil and connected to the grounding bus.) These grounding rods are connected with one large grounding conductor to the grounding bus in the panel. This system provides an escape

route for stray current in a faulty appliance so you don't become the conductor.

Code requires joining the neutral bus with the ground bus at *one place* in the system. This is usually accomplished by the metal of the panel box itself, but some panels come with a small strap to connect these buses. In addition, the water supply, gas or oil supply, and all pool and spa electrical equipment is bonded (connected) to eliminate stray current in these components. This is typically done with a bare number 6 copper wire and pipe-to-wire clamps. Larger services, subpanels, and appliances need larger grounding and bonding wires.

Hook up the circuit breaker switch to the black hot wire by tightening the screw in the breaker over the wire, as previously described. Now it's simply a matter of snapping the breaker back into position in the box and turning the main switch back on. There are two hot buses in the main panel. The breakers are installed evenly on these buses to avoid overloading one side. This means that each succeeding 110 volt breaker is staggered from one bus to another, and a 220 volt breaker connects to both buses.

Neatness is particularly important inside your panel. There is little point in labeling your branch circuits if their wires disappear into a jumble in the box. Take your time and lay out all the wires neatly.

Tighten all screws securely; loose terminals lead to strange electrical occurrences and rapid corrosion in the panel buses. Aluminum wire ends are often treated with an antioxidant.

Step Two
Placing the Boxes

Margin of Error: ¼″

Housing boxes for outlets, switches, and lights are **roughed in** before the cables themselves are installed. In other words, all the outlets, the switch and fixture boxes, and the main panel and subpanels are installed before any wire is installed between them.

Choose the correct boxes for your needs. Check your electrical code for local recommendations. The boxes should be UL-listed and be large enough to hold the wiring, outlets, and connectors you will be using. Use a larger box with a plaster ring if necessary.

Use a ruler or other object of appropriate length, such as a screwdriver, to rest the boxes on when establishing installation points (Figure 2-6). Some boxes have nails attached to them that are hammered into the studs to secure the box to the stud. The octagonal fixture boxes used for light fixtures are attached to studs or to the ceiling joists. Ensure that your boxes will be flush with the final wall or ceiling covering by holding a small piece of the covering (drywall or paneling material) between the box and the wall stud while attaching the box. Switches are commonly located 48" above the floor. Countertop outlets are installed 42" from the floor, and regular outlets are placed so the top of the box is 14" above the floor.

Remove the knockout(s) in each box in the direction of the most efficient route for the cable to run, and install the boxes on the framing.

Step Three
Preparing the Studs for Cable

Margin of Error: 1/4". Always wire according to code. There is no room for error!

Drilling with a right-angle drill and an auger bit is the most common way to run the cable through interior, uninsulated walls. Some larger drills have right-angle attachments; or you can rent a right-angle drill.

Drill your holes in the center of the studs. Make the holes large enough to hold all the cables you will run through them. Brace yourself and the cumbersome drill so that it does not spin around if it binds.

Notching rather than drilling the studs works best when you have insulation you don't want to compress with cable. To notch a stud, follow this procedure.

1. Snap two horizontal chalklines 1" apart across the studs. These lines indicate the path the wire will follow.

2. Use a circular saw set to cut notches 1/2" deep at those lines on each stud.

3. Use a chisel to carefully remove the blocks from the notches.

4. After placing the cable, cover the notches with nail guards to prevent accidental nailing into the wire.

To avoid weakening structural members, the NEC states specific rules about the notches and holes used to route circuits. Notches in exterior (bearing) walls and plates may not exceed 25 percent of the stud width; in interior (nonbearing) walls and plates, up to 40 percent of the width is permitted.

Holes in exterior walls and plates are limited to 40 percent of the stud width, and in interior walls to 60 percent.

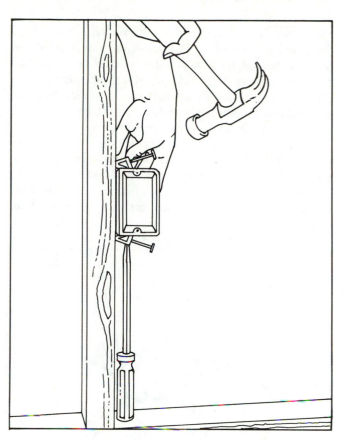

Figure 2-6. Use a ruler or screwdriver to set outlet boxes at a uniform height.

Avoid notching in all girders, headers, and beams. No top or bottom notching is allowed in the middle third of any joist. Notches within a third of each end cannot exceed one sixth the depth of the joist. No holes exceeding one third of the joist depth are ever allowed, and no holes in a joist should be any closer to the edge than 2".

Step Four
Installing the Wiring

Margin of Error: 1/4"

The NEC requires wire that is insulated and is of appropriate size for the application. The size depends on how much current the cable is expected to carry, and how far it must be carried. The most commonly used interior wiring is number 12 or 14 gauge NM sheathed cable, sometimes called Romex. Many electricians use only number 12 gauge wire even for the lighting circuits. When used behind 15 amp breakers, this provides an extra margin of safety. Of course, larger wire is required where demands will exceed 20 amps.

Within the cable are plastic-coated copper wires, colored for each function. (As explained earlier, hot wires are always black or red; neutral wires are always white; and grounding wires are bare or green.) In most cases your circuits will have to make sharp bends somewhere in their runs. Enough cable for the whole run is pulled through the straight portions of the framing and piled up just before the turn. The cable is then fed through the next straight series of holes until the cable(s) terminate. This is called **pulling cable.** Enough excess cable is provided at each end and intermediate box to be sure that components can be installed easily. Try not to let the cable twist in the corner bends or in the runs.

Beginning at the breaker box, or the hole where it will be, expose enough wire to reach the breaker switch and neutral bus bar. Use a cable stripper to prevent cutting the plastic coating on the wires (Figure 2-7). Knock out a tab in the breaker box that will provide a direct route to the switch for

the wiring, and knock out the tab in the housing box that provides the closest connection for each separate cable.

Push the wire through each hole or notch in the studs, keeping the wire smooth and free from kinks. After it is in place, secure it with horseshoe nails or staples at the notches. With holes, the staples are applied near the boxes, on the studs and joists, and at turns. The cable should never be pulled tight; some slack is necessary to allow for expansion and contraction of the building. Local code will tell you how close to the box the first horseshoe nail or staple must be (usually 8"), and how often the wire must be supported (usually every 4½').

Pull the cable to the box(es) and secure it with a staple. Put on the connector clamp and make sure that only the uncut sheathing is clamped at the box opening. Peel the jacket back far enough to allow at least 6" of wire to stick out of the face of the box.

The wire must reach from one junction box to another; do not tape two wires together to make them longer. If they must be joined, wires should be connected only at junction boxes. Code requires that a solid coverplate be placed over every junction that will not make use of a receptacle (Figure 2-8). This should not occur in a well-planned system except in basements, attics, and garages. If it does happen, consider putting outlets in those locations.

Provide at least 6" of wire to spare at each end of a run (Figure 2-9). Local code may vary on this length, so be sure to check. It's a good idea to label both ends of each wire with colored tape to make it easy to determine where it leads.

Where there is less than 1¼" between the face of the stud and the wiring, nail guards should be placed on the studs to

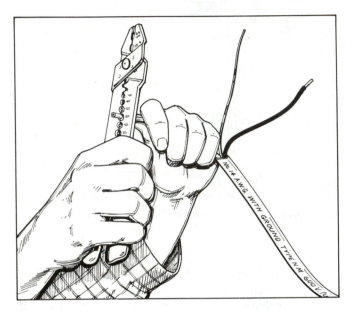

Figure 2-7. Use a cable stripper to remove insulation from wire ends.

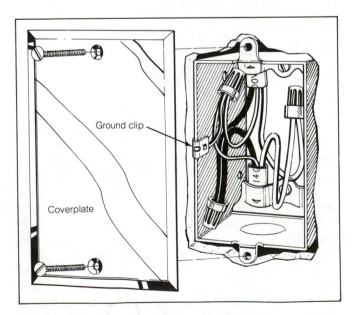

Figure 2-8. A junction box that will not make use of a receptacle must be covered with a solid coverplate.

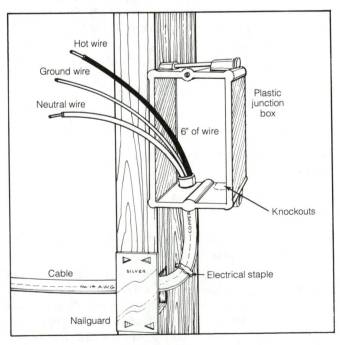

Figure 2-9. Typical box installation. Note staple, nailguard, and at least 6" of stripped wire.

protect the wire from the nails or screws that will attach the wall covering.

Now it is time to call in the inspector to check your work, before you complete the connections. This is called the **rough electrical inspection,** and it must be signed off before any of your circuitry can be covered with finish wall surfaces.

Step Five
Installing the Receptacles and Switches

Margin of Error: Exact; good tight connections, correctly done

Switches and outlets with push terminals or connections (Figure 2-10) make connecting the wiring easy, but they should be used only for copper or copper-clad wire—never for aluminum. Strip away insulation to the length indicated on the strip gauge when you push the color-coded wires into the correct push terminal. The terminal automatically clamps down when the wire goes in, so the fit is nice and tight. To release it, just insert a small screwdriver into the re-lease slot.

Some communities, however, do not allow the use of push terminals. Check with your designer, electrician, or local authorities before installing push terminal devices.

Many electricians use screw-type terminals (Figure 2-11) because they feel that the screws hold the wires more securely. If you choose to use a screw-type terminal, strip only enough insulation for the bare end to be wrapped three-quarters of the way around the screw. With long-nose pliers, make a loop on the bare end wire to hook clockwise around the terminal screw, then tighten the screw with a screwdriver.

The black wire always is attached to the brass screw or the push terminal marked +. The white wire is always attached to the silver screw or the terminal marked -. The bare copper or green wire is always attached to the green screw.

The loop of wire is installed clockwise so that turning the screw to the right to secure it also tightens the loop itself.

Step Six
Connecting the Wires

Margin of Error: Exact; good tight connections correctly done

Wire nuts are used to make connections between wires of the same color. Wire nuts come in various sizes, distinguished by color, and may differ from manufacturer to manufacturer. (Yellow, red, or gray will cover most household uses.) Always select the proper-size connector for the wires being used; wire nuts should be used only where the connection won't be pulled or strained in any way.

When using wire nuts to make connections between solid wires, strip 1½" of insulation from the wires to be joined and hold them parallel. Twist these together securely with pliers in a clockwise direction. Then cut off the ends of the wires to fit the twist-on connector. Slip the wire nut over the bare ends of the wires and twist the nut clockwise around the wires, pushing them hard into the nut. Tug gently on each wire to be sure that it is secure, then wrap electrical tape around the wire nut and the wires connected.

Pigtailing

Simple wiring connections of two cables can be handled easily. More complex types of wiring, such as lights that have switches and junctions where the wiring is continued on to

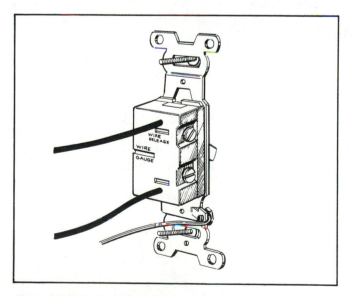

Figure 2-10. Push terminals are quicker and easier to use than screw terminals, but are not allowed in some areas.

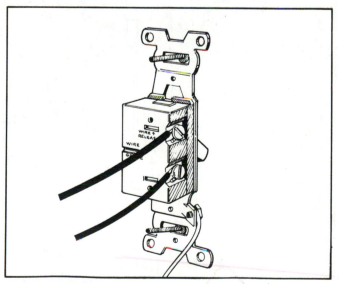

Figure 2-11. Screw terminals hold wire more securely than do push terminals.

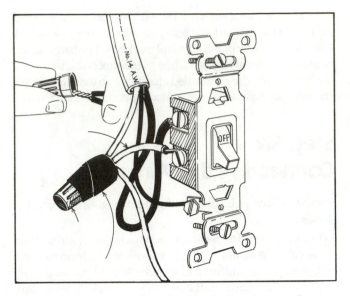

Figure 2-12. When pigtailing, always twist the wires together before attaching the wire nut.

other receptacles, involves more wires. To simplify such arrangements, wires are joined by a method called **pigtailing** (Figure 2-12).

Pigtailing connects two or more wires together with another 6" pigtail wire that has been stripped ¾" on each end. The pigtail wire is the wire you connect to the outlet or switch. This reduces the number of wires to be connected at the receptacle. When you are using pigtailing, always twist the wires together securely before twisting on the wire nut. Following are some of the common uses of pigtailing.

Connecting Wires at a Duplex Receptacle

Strip all wires ¾" and then bind all the wires of like color together with another 6" wire of the same color. Twist the ends of the wires being connected with the pigtail wire tightly together clockwise (see Figure 2-12). Then screw on a wire nut of the appropriate size. Check the security of your connection by holding the wire nut and giving a good tug to each wire. The bare grounding wires are also ganged together and joined with a wire nut, or with metal boxes, with a crimp ring. Crimp rings come in different sizes, and are required in some areas because of their superior holding power. All the ground wires are ganged and twisted, the ring is slipped over the ganged wires, and special pliers are used to lock this assembly together with the crimp.

Now it is a simple matter to connect the pigtail portion of the connection to the terminal—black to brass, white to silver, and the bare grounding wire to the grounding screw. Once pigtailed, it is easier to fold all of the wires together to fit them into the box. Then you can simply screw the duplex receptacle (outlet) onto the electrical box.

Splitting a Receptacle on a Push Terminal

Three cables (nine separate wires) come into the outlet box—one cable supplies power directly from the breaker box, another cable carries that power on to other receptacles or outlets, and the third cable comes from a wall-mounted switch so that half of that receptacle will be controlled by that switch. This type is often used in bedrooms, where you may want to control a lamp with a wall switch while still being able to plug in an alarm clock. Either the upper or the lower

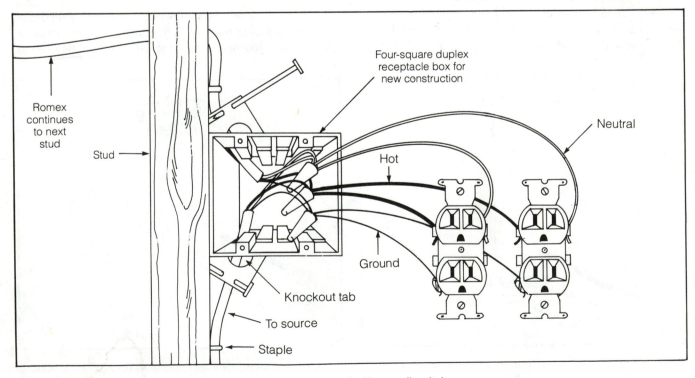

Figure 2-13. Wiring to split a receptacle so that one outlet is controlled by a wall switch.

socket always remains hot, while the other is controlled by a switch.

The white wire within the cable that goes to the switch will be hot, so it must be marked with black electrical tape at the outlet box, to distinguish it from the other neutral (white) wires. This same "hot white" wire should also be marked with black tape up at the switch; this is a switch loop, as described earlier.

Pigtail all of the same-colored wires together, as previously described, omitting the white wire that is marked with black tape.

Hook up the pigtail ground wire to the ground screw on the receptacle, and the pigtail neutral wire to a silver screw. (If it is a metal box, use two ground pigtail wires—one grounded to the receptacle and the other to connect onto the box grounding screw.) The hot pigtail wire goes into the permanently hot (lower) side. The white wire marked with black tape goes into the hot outlet side, upper or lower, depending on which socket you wish to control with the switch.

Breaking off the knockout tab on the hot side linking the two brass terminals of the outlet will allow half of the receptacle to work off of a switch, while the other half receives continuous power (Figure 2-13).

Wiring Switches

If your box and your switch are plastic, connect all grounding wires with a wire nut and push them into the box. If you are using metal boxes, pigtail all of the bare ground wires together with two separate pigtail wires. Then connect one pigtail wire to the grounding screw in the box, and the other one to the separate grounding screw on the switch. A switch is never connected to neutral wires; so join all of the white wires together with a wire nut and push them back into the box. Then pigtail the hot wires together.

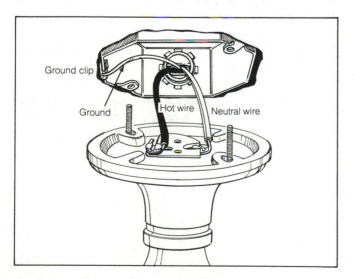

Figure 2-14. Wiring an end run ceiling fixture.

Because a switch interrupts the flow of electrical current, it should only be connected to hot (black) wires; or, in this case, a white wire marked with black electrical tape designating it to be hot. On the first switch, push the hot pigtail wire into either push terminal, and push the color-coded hot wire that goes to the overhead light into the push terminal of the same switch. On the second switch, push the black hot wire, which was pigtailed to the other black wires at the outlet, and the white wire wrapped in black tape into the back of the switch. This white wire will be made hot when the switch is turned on and will take the electrical power to the controlled outlet.

Step Seven
Hanging Light Fixtures and Receptacles

Margin of Error: Exact; well secured, properly connected, and UL approved

When you did the roughing in, the electrical boxes were attached to the studs or to the attic or second floor joist so that the plate is flush with the finished ceiling material. At this point you are ready to complete your wiring (Figure 2-14).

Pull the electrical wire through the cutout and box and strip it, just as you would for the outlets. Attach a surface-mounted hanging light with the attachment strap that is screwed to the electrical box. Follow the manufacturer's instructions. Connect the wires together, black to black, white to white, and ground to ground, using the wire nuts as previously described. Push the wires up inside the electrical box. Then it is a simple matter to attach the coverplate of the hanging light or the plate of the receptacle with the screws provided.

Track Lighting

Track lighting is connected to a ceiling box on one end.

Screw the mounting bracket into the electrical box. Push the wires of the electrical connector through the slot in the track connector, then through the slot in the box adapter. Now attach the wires to those in the box, matching colored wires and using the appropriate wire nuts. Push the wires up into the electrical box. Attach the two-piece mounting assembly to the box tabs (Figure 2-15).

Hold a ruler flat against the ceiling (or wall) so that one edge of the ruler is lined up with the center slot on the track connector. Using the ruler as your guide, draw a line along the ceiling (or wall) from this slot, as long as necessary, to where the track will end. Make marks at even intervals on the penciled line to indicate the attachment positions of the clips that will hold the track. Hold the clips in position, mark and drill pilot holes in the ceiling (or wall) at these points, and screw the clips in place. Secure the clips to the studs, rafters, or joists, or use toggle bolts if this is not possible. Partially

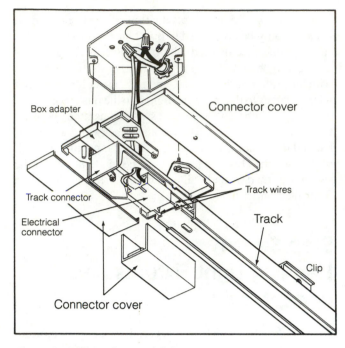

Box adapter

Connector cover

Track connector

Track wires

Electrical connector

Track

Clip

Connector cover

Figure 2-15. Wiring for a track light.

insert the side screws into the clips. Then push the track wires firmly into the electrical connector and slide the track into the track connector. Tighten the side screws of the clips to hold the track in place. The connector cover will then snap in place to cover the wires.

Recessed Light Boxes

Recessed lights are set into ceiling joists and secured so they will be flush with the finished ceiling surface. They come prewired from the socket to a small junction box built into the unit. This is due to heat buildup in these lights, and conventional cable joins high temperature rated wire in the box.

Outdoor Wiring

Outdoor wiring is essential for many uses outside the home—for security lights, porch and yard lamps, and tool operation, to name a few.

Basically, wiring for exterior use is the same as wiring indoor fixtures. However, exterior moisture-proof cables and boxes must be used. To simplify installation, choose an outdoor outlet location that is easy to get to, and close to an indoor receptacle.

Remember that the power supply can return to zero through the grounding wires, or through wet soil or concrete. You also have bonded your water pipes, gas pipe, and so on to the grounding bus in the panel. Since you can become the conductor if you are touching a faulty appliance and a water faucet, or if you are standing in a wet location, ground fault circuit interrupters (GFCIs) are required for safety.

Outdoor outlets, and those in the kitchen, bathroom, and garage, must include ground fault circuit interrupters. GFCIs measure the amount of power the hot wire brings in and the neutral wire returns. If there is a small difference, the outlet automatically shuts off, reducing your chances of receiving a fatal shock. A GFCI is a circuit breaker that is installed in the breaker box or in a special receptacle. The circuit of your exterior light is then attached into the GFCI breaker. The NEC requires GFCI protection on all outlets within 6' of all sinks or exposed plumbing, and within 12' of a pool or spa. Some local codes require GFCI protection for all pool and spa electric equipment.

Drill a hole through the exterior wall to take the power outside. Even though you want to be near the indoor receptacle, do not position the receptacles back to back. Run the cable or the conduit and install the appropriate junction box. Connect the wires as previously described, matching the color-coded wires to the correct terminal. Be sure to seal around the holes with silicone sealant, once the conduit and/or wires are in place.

Alternative Technologies

Code compliance is a matter of minimum requirements. As previously mentioned, you should install the whole system with future expansion or changes in mind. For instance, if you intend to use a personal computer in your den, consider running a dedicated circuit to that location to reduce current drops and peaks as other appliances cycle off and on.

The NEC also addresses solar-powered low-voltage systems in buildings, although the chances of fatal shocks and fires from these systems are currently quite low. As the costs of these technologies come down and efficiency rates go up, however, larger systems will become possible and concerns about safety will rise.

Nevertheless, photovoltaic and battery backup systems are easy to install and maintain. And they can be very reassuring to people who live in remote areas and to those who live where hurricanes or earthquakes occur.

3 Plumbing

EVEN MORE THAN installing an electrical system, installing the plumbing system is the most demanding task for the owner builder. A high degree of knowledge is required for this task. The *Uniform Plumbing Code* is extensive, and local codes, which vary from area to area, may take precedence. Every plumbing system is unique, and every home has its own problems that require special knowledge and experience. In addition, installing piping systems is physically demanding and can become extremely frustrating.

In the entire process of finishing a house, electrical wiring and plumbing installations are the areas in which you should consider hiring a professional. If you decide to do the plumbing yourself, you should at least have a professional consultant to oversee your work. It is also a good idea to read at least a couple of how-to books about plumbing and to keep them handy for reference.

Unlike the rest of this book, it is not the intention of this chapter to provide you with all the information you will need to install the plumbing system; that would require an entire book in itself. This chapter does not attempt to walk you through the plumbing process in a series of detailed steps. Rather, it offers an overview of the plumbing system and its components, some of the main code restrictions, and details of the actual cutting and assembling of the different types of pipe involved. With the information presented here, you should be able to speak more comfortably with your plumber about your specific needs.

Before You Begin

SAFETY

Special caution: Natural gas and propane pipe runs can look very similar to a water supply system because all three products are often piped in the same Schedule #40 galvanized steel piping. The gas piping begins at the gas meter and runs directly to the appliances and/or heating system. These lines should be clearly marked from the meter to the furnace or appliance. Some plumbing suppliers sell bright, easy to read identification tags that you can attach to the pipes. Hot water and steam heating systems require equal caution. All of these systems should be installed and repaired by an expert.

☐ *Have a fire extinguisher available at all times.*

☐ When using a torch to solder copper, wear a cotton or wool long-sleeved shirt and high-top shoes or boots.

☐ Use one of the several kinds of insulation materials available at the plumbing supply store to insulate the torch flame from the structure.

☐ Be careful about storing and discarding oily rags, which can cause fires through spontaneous combustion.

☐ When using a 1/2" drill to bore the large diameter holes needed for the piping, be sure that the drill is properly braced, according to the manufacturer's recommendations, so that if the boring bit binds up, the drill handles won't slam your hands into the wood.

☐ Wear safety glasses or goggles whenever you are using power tools or when soldering, chiseling, sanding, scraping, or hammering overhead, especially if you wear contact lenses.

☐ Be careful that loose hair and clothing do not get caught in tools.

☐ Keep blades sharp. A dull blade requires excessive force and can easily slip.

☐ Always use the right tool for the job.

☐ Don't try to drill, shape, or saw anything that isn't firmly secured.

☐ Don't work with tools when you are tired. That is when most accidents occur.

☐ Read the owner's manual for all tools and know the proper use of each.

☐ Unplug all power tools when changing settings or parts, and be sure that they are properly grounded.

☐ Keep all tools out of reach of children.

USEFUL TERMS

An **adapter fitting** is used to connect pipe of different types.

Air chambers or **air cushions** are piping configurations or devices that are used on the supply lines (usually at the fixtures) to reduce "water hammer," or water banging in the pipes.

The **building drain** is the part of the lowest piping of a drainage system that receives the discharge from soil, waste, and other drainage pipes inside the walls of the building and conveys it to the building sewer, which begins about 2' outside the wall.

A **cleanout** is a fitting that allows access into a drain, waste, soil, or sewer line so that an obstruction can be cleared.

A **closet bend** is a 90-degree fitting that carries waste from the closet flange, under the toilet, over to the closest drain.

An **escutcheon** is a doughnut-shaped ornamental plate that slides over a pipe to cover the hole in the wall where the pipe has penetrated.

A **female-threaded fitting** is any fitting in which the threads are located internally.

Finish plumbing is all the materials (and their installation) required to complete a plumbing system after the rough plumbing has been installed.

Fixtures, such as sinks, tubs, toilets, and bidets, are devices that are attached to the waste system and that require a fresh water supply in order to function.

A **male-threaded fitting** is any fitting in which threads are located externally.

A **reducer fitting** allows pipes of different diameters to fit together.

A **riser** is a water supply pipe that extends vertically one full story or more to convey water to branches or fixtures.

Rough plumbing is all parts of the plumbing system that can be completed before installation of the fixtures. This includes drainage, water supply, gas and vent piping, and the necessary fixture supports.

A **soil pipe** is any pipe that carries the discharge of water closets, urinals, or fixtures with similar functions, with or without the discharge from other fixtures, to the building drain or building sewer.

Sweating is a method of soldering copper pipe and fittings together.

A **trap** is a fitting or device designed to provide, when properly vented, a liquid seal that prevents the back passage of air without affecting the flow of sewage or waste water through the trap.

A **wet vent** is a vent that also serves as a drain.

WHAT YOU WILL NEED

Tools. Many of the tools that you will need for working with copper and plastic pipe and fittings are already in your tool chest or can be purchased or rented inexpensively.

ABS hand saw

Hacksaw

Reciprocating saw

Saber saw

Hole saw kit (sized for plumbing pipe)

Large boring bits (sized for plumbing pipe)

Adjustable wrenches

Basin wrench (telescoping)

No-hub ratchet wrench

Pipe wrenches

Chain cutter (soil pipe snap-cutter)

Hammer

Chisels

Screwdrivers

Tinsnips

Putty knife

Tape measure

Torpedo level

Chalkline

Tubing cutter

Plumber's sandcloth

Copper fitting brushes

Acid brushes

Propane torch

Striker (torch)

Goggles

Uniform Plumbing Code book

Materials. Communities differ in what piping materials you are allowed to use. A licensed plumber will know what is permitted in your area. If you are going to do the work yourself, check with the local building inspector and find out what is required. Some communities even have lists of fixture model numbers and manufacturers that you may or may not install. The inspector can also show you how to size your piping system from the tables in the *Uniform Plumbing Code (UPC)* book.

Guesstimating the amount of pipe and fittings you will need for a large job is close to a science. A good job schematic will help you estimate closer to the mark, with fewer trips to the supplier. Do some investigating to find out which suppliers in your area cater to the owner builder, and make sure that they will allow you to return any full-length pipe and extra fittings you don't use.

Some hardware stores have facilities for you to cut and thread pipe, and may even lend out tools like the soil pipe snap-cutter to customers who purchase supplies from them. These loans can be worth more than a 5 to 10 percent savings in materials from a supplier who does not offer such perks.

Of course, the materials you need will depend on the nature of the plumbing you plan to do. The following list should cover most of your needs.

ABS (or PVC) rigid plastic pipe (1½", 2", or 3")

ABS (or PVC) fittings

ABS solvent cement, cleaner, and primer

Traps

Pipe hangers

Stop valves

Closet flange and set of closet bolts

Wax ring

½" copper tubing

¾" copper tubing

Copper fittings

Faucet assemblies

Shower head

Tub spout

Plumber's putty

Roof vent

Water supply tubes

Teflon tape

Flexible tubing

Silicone caulk

Pipe joint compound

Standpipe

Filter washers

Vacuum breakers

Rags

Electrician's tape

Duct tape

Fixtures (bathtub, shower, toilet, sink)

PLANNING

Any project is only as good as the planning that goes into it. Before beginning any work, it's a good idea to map out your system in detail on graph paper, as shown in Figure 3-1. If you are not a licensed contractor, the building inspector may require a detailed plumbing schematic before issuing a permit. A detailed plan also makes it easy to compile your materials list.

Begin with the basement or crawlspace and sketch the building drain. Then sketch the branch drains, vents, and cleanouts. Trace the planned network of hot and cold water supply piping as well as the fuel gas piping, even if you are hiring a professional for this aspect. Locate your toilets, sinks, lavatories, tub, shower, hose bibbs, ice maker, wet bar, sprinkler system, and anything else you can think of that might need supply and/or waste lines.

What size water meter will you need? If your urban job is an entirely new structure, not a remodel of an existing home, then you can request a water meter of a particular size from the utility company to meet the requirements of the code. You may find that anything other than the basic $5/8$" (inside diameter) water meter will be an expensive one-time proposition. However, if you have high water requirements, or if there is a long distance from the meter to the structure, you will have to provide a larger meter.

Other issues you need to consider include the municipal water pressure in your neighborhood, and whether or not the water pressure is adequate for your demands without a booster system.

In designing your plumbing system, it's important to keep the work simple, grouping fixtures so that they are as close to the piping runs as possible. It's a good idea to have a professional plumber go over your plans to be sure that you haven't forgotten anything or created extra work for yourself, and that all obvious problems are anticipated and worked out as much as possible *before the work begins*.

All rough plumbing should be installed before the electricians begin their work, and needless to say, before insulation

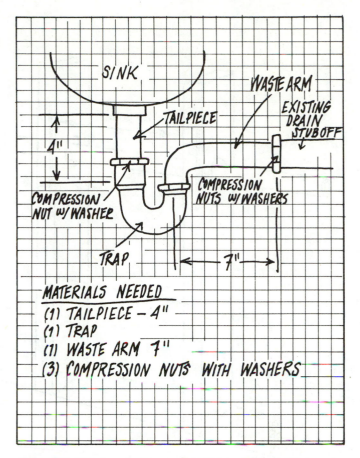

Figure 3-1. Sketch your proposed system in detail on graph paper, and use your drawings to make your materials list.

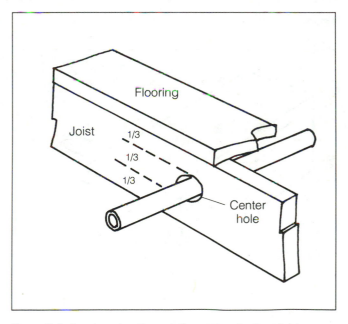

Figure 3-2. Running pipe through the center of a floor joist.

and wall coverings are in place. Your local code may require that all underfloor pipes (especially with slab construction), wires, and ducts be installed and inspected before the subfloor is put down. Some communities charge an additional

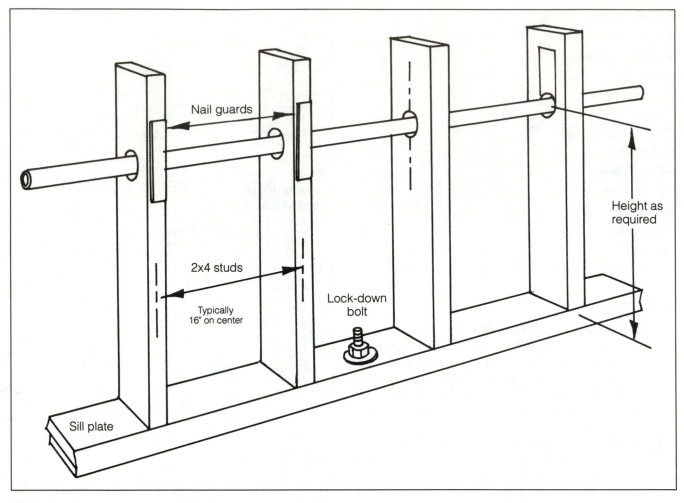

Figure 3-3. Running pipe through wall studs.

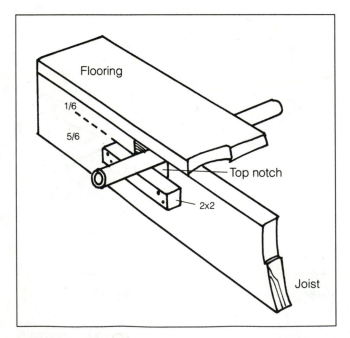

Figure 3-4. Notching a joist to run a pipe through it at the top of the joist.

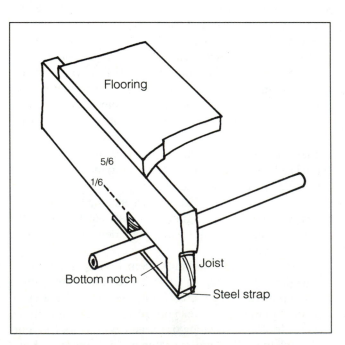

Figure 3-5. Notching a joist to run a pipe through it at the bottom.

fee for more than one rough inspection. Even if the code does not require it, it is much easier to install any underfloor piping before the subfloor is laid, especially if you have a low crawlspace.

For the structural integrity of your building, it is always best to run pipes *parallel* to framing members, especially floor joists. However, it is sometimes necessary to cut into or through the joists at some point. Always check your local building code before doing this. The code may include such regulations as the following:

☐ If a pipe must run through a floor joist near its center, you can usually drill a hole, as long as the hole is less than one-third the depth of the joist (Figure 3-2). Studwall may have holes drilled up to 40 percent of the stud depth in load-bearing walls and up to 60 percent in non-load-bearing walls (Figure 3-3).

☐ If a pipe runs through a joist near the top (Figure 3-4) or bottom (Figure 3-5), you can notch the joist. The notch should be no greater than one-sixth of the depth of the framing member. Nor should the notch be located in the middle third of the span. In studs, you may notch up to 40 percent in non-load-bearing walls.

☐ If you are notching the framing member on the top, nail a length of 2x2 under the notch on both sides of the member to give added strength.

☐ Bottom notches should be covered with a steel strap for added support.

☐ The larger DWV pipes may necessitate the removal of an entire joist or stud. Check your local building code for specifications in this situation.

CODES AND PERMITS

The plumbing industry has established standards to protect the health and safety of the community. Plumbing codes and the permit process exist to make sure that those standards are adhered to. Faulty plumbing can result in serious health and safety hazards such as fuel gas leaks, sewer gas leaks, raw sewage leaks, flooding, and electrical shorts. However, regulations governing design, methods, and materials differ from community to community. Nationwide, most communities adhere to the *UPC,* with local codes superceding it in various areas.

The main areas of code enforcement include the following issues:

☐ Type of piping materials.

☐ The proper size (diameter for length) of water supply, drain/waste/vent, and fuel gas piping.

☐ Slope of drains (inches per foot of fall).

☐ Distance from fixture traps to vent pipe.

☐ Use of certain fittings, such as sanitary T's versus Y's.

☐ Placement and number of cleanouts.

☐ Distance between pipe supports.

☐ Height of laundry standpipe traps off the floor.

☐ Height and slope of horizontal vent piping off the floor.

Contact your building inspector about any local codes that may supercede the *UPC* and about the permits that you will need. Some communities have a separate inspector for the building sewer and the outside of the structure.

In some areas plastic pipe is prohibited entirely. In other areas only ABS, not PVC, is permitted inside the structure for the drain/waste/vent system. Some codes may require you to insulate your hot water supply piping or to install vacuum breakers on your outside hose bibbs. Before beginning any work, be sure your plans conform to all local codes and ordinances. Discuss your plans with the local building inspector and find out what work you may do yourself and what, if any, must be done by a licensed plumber. Be sure to follow the code to the letter, or you run the risk of having to rip out all your hard work.

INSPECTIONS

Your plumbing work will require inspections at at least two and maybe even several stages, depending on the overall construction sequence of your particular project. Usually there are two basic plumbing inspections: rough and finish. **Rough plumbing** is all the work that goes into the project before the fixtures are installed, including the water supply systems, drain/waste/vent system, any fuel gas lines, and gas appliance flue venting. Do not cover up any of your rough plumbing work until the inspector has seen it, or you may have to uncover it for inspection.

The inspector will require a pressure test on the water supply, DWV, and fuel gas systems. For the water supply and DWV, you can usually choose either an air pressure test or a water test. Fuel gas systems can only be tested with air pressure.

After signing off on the rough plumbing, the inspector will look at the **finish plumbing.** It is at this point that the hook-up to the municipal sewer main or septic system is usually performed. Some communities require that a licensed sewer contractor make the connection to the municipal sewer main.

THE PLUMBING SYSTEM

The water-related plumbing system in your home, shown in Figure 3-6, has three main functions:

1. To carry fresh water through the supply system.

2. To use this water in the fixtures.

3. To dispose of sewage and liquid waste through the drain/waste/vent system.

To make it easier to see how each part functions, the hot and cold water supply system (Figure 3-7) and the drain/waste/vent system (Figure 3-8) are separated out from Figure 3-6.

The Supply System

The supply system carries fresh water from a well or municipal water main into your house and distributes it to your fixtures. A main shut-off valve is usually installed in the main water supply line to stop the flow of water into your home. If your water is supplied by a private well, the shut-off valve will probably be at the wellhead, or at the house where the main supply enters the building, or at both places. If your water is brought to your site by a municipal main, then you will have a water meter with a key-operated shut-off valve installed directly in front of the meter. If this is the only shut-off valve, you will need a water meter key to operate the valve. However, you will probably also have a hand-operated shut-off valve where the main supply line enters the house. Depending upon the weather conditions where you live, this hand-operated valve might be outside, at or near ground level, or inside the basement or crawlspace.

Since the 1960s, copper has become the most common material for fresh-water supply lines, due largely to ease of installation. Don't attempt to install cast iron or galvanized pipe yourself. These require the skill of a professional. As

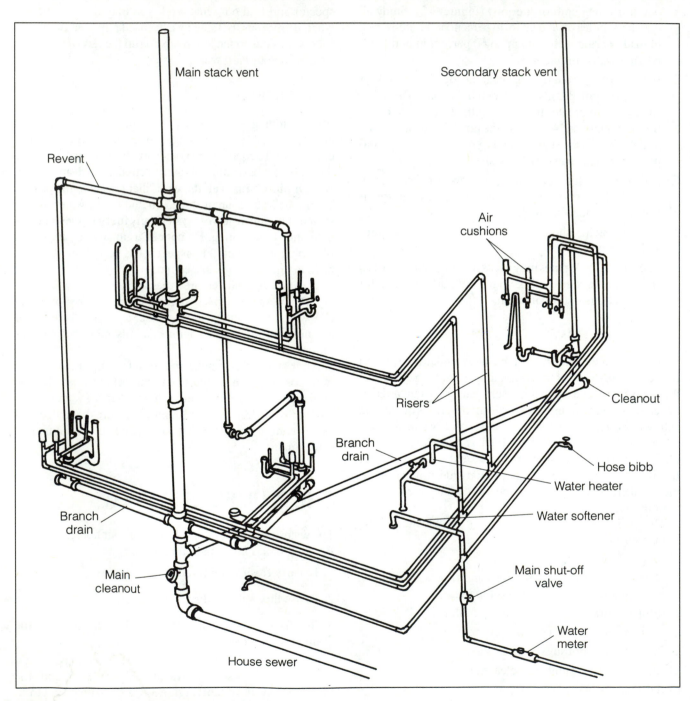

Figure 3-6. Hot and cold water supply and drain/waste vent system.

shown in Figure 3-7, the supply line enters the average-sized modern house in a ¾" pipe (inside diameter). This ¾" line continues, full size, to the cold inlet to the water heater. On the way to the water heater, branch lines lead off from the main, taking *cold water* to the various fixtures. Depending upon the distance of each fixture from the main, the branch lines may start out as ¾" and then reduce to ½", closer to each fixture. A ¾" *hot water* line leaves the water heater and threads its way through the building, with branch lines taking hot water to the fixtures. The diameter of the sections making up these branch lines depends upon the "developed length" between main and fixture.

If your home has a water softener, it is customary to soften only the hot water, and perhaps the cold water for the kitchen sink. These systems can require a fair number of gate or ball valves and check valves to isolate and direct flows. You should produce a good schematic of the finished design so that you can understand your system years from now.

Supply pipes that rise vertically from one floor to another are called **risers**. All supply lines are pressurized—although sometimes not as high as you'd like. The water supply is pressurized at its source, and this pressure drives the water throughout the system. In very cold climates, it is customary to install supply lines on a slight pitch, sloping back to a low point where valves may be installed so that the entire system can be drained down to make repairs on pipes damaged by freezing, or to drain the system for times of winter vacancy. It is very difficult to solder copper pipe that has water in it. When joining copper pipe to galvanized pipe, a **dielectric union** must be installed to prevent corrosion. Even the pipe

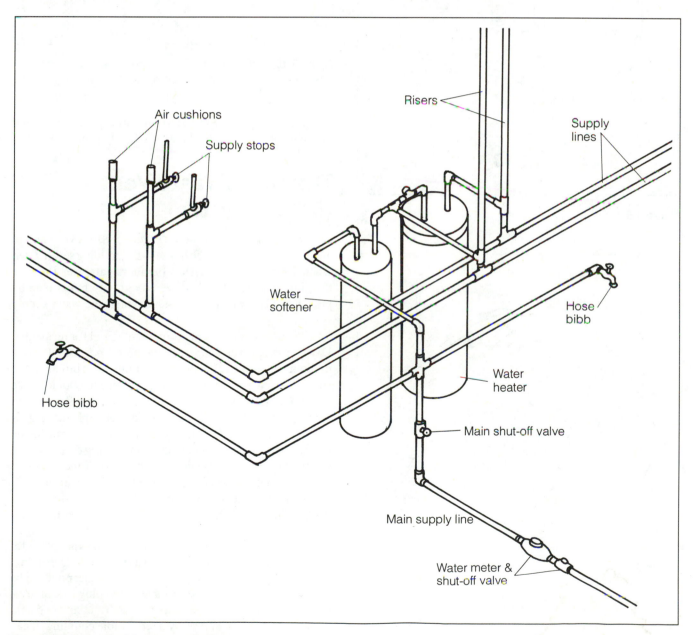

Figure 3-7. Hot and cold water supply lines.

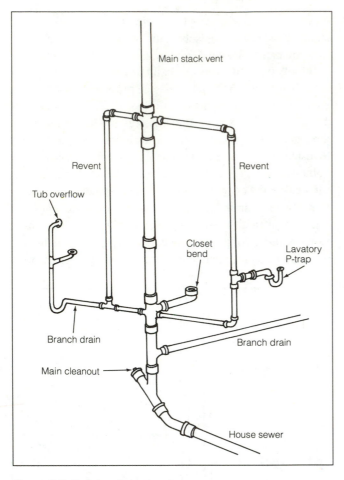

Figure 3-8. Drain/waste/vent system.

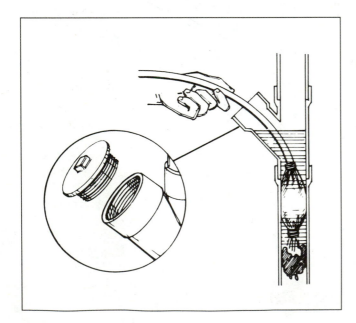

Figure 3-9. Cleanouts at key positions in drain pipes allow obstructions to be cleared away.

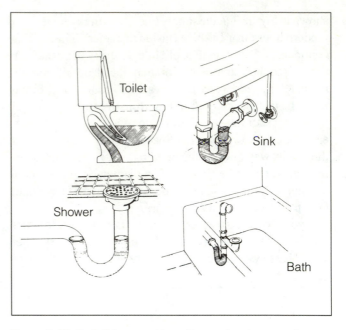

Figure 3-10. Each fixture must have its own trap to prevent noxious gases from coming up the pipes into the house.

hangers and pipe straps used to support copper pipe should be solid copper, or at least plastic coated or felt lined.

The Drain/Waste/Vent (D/W/V) System

The drain/waste/vent system (Figure 3-8) moves sewage and liquid wastes out of the house to the building sewer, from where it runs to a septic system or municipal sewer. Because the drain/waste system is driven by gravity rather than by pressure, it is harder to understand than is the water supply system.

ABS plastic is the most common material for residential DWV systems. The *Uniform Plumbing Code* establishes a minimum slope of ¼" per foot for drain/waste piping. If the slope is much greater, over a long distance the liquid waste may travel faster than the solid waste, leaving it behind to block the pipe. If the pipe does not slope enough, drainage is not sufficient and *all* wastes may back up. The drain/waste piping connects to the main drain, or **building drain**, which becomes the **building sewer**, once it is outside the structure.

Occasionally a waste line, drain line, or sewer line will clog, for any of several reasons: improper fall (slope); improper number of type of fittings; a clogged vent; objects such as toys being flushed down the toilet; or that common sewer stopper, roots. For this reason, **cleanouts** are placed at designated locations in the drain/waste system. Depending upon the type of piping and method used, a cleanout can be a hubbed female fitting with a male screw plug to seal it, attached at the end of a pipe run; or it can be a blind cap held to the end of a piece of pipe by a removable coupling. It can also be a branched fitting with a threaded branch and plug,

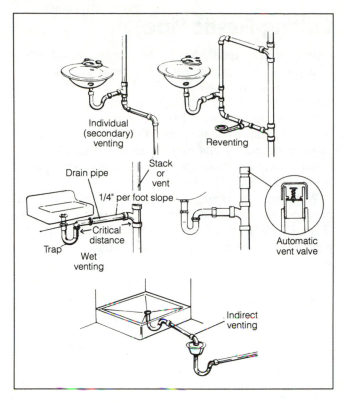

Figure 3-11. Vent types.

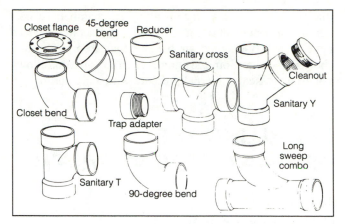

Figure 3-12. Plastic fittings.

as shown in Figure 3-9. The criteria for the placement of cleanouts is complex. Section 406 of the *UPC* explains the many variables involved.

The **vent system** is part of the drain/waste system. Vents are designed to let atmospheric pressure into the drain/waste system so that waste can flow out of the house. (This is much like opening a can of juice. You punch two holes in the can, one for the juice to flow out and the other to let atmospheric pressure in.) To ensure a safe vent system, each fixture is protected by a water seal in the trap. Without the trap and water seal, sewer gas could enter the building through the fixture (Figure 3-10). The vents terminate above the roof, sending any gases safely skyward.

All plumbing fixtures must be vented and trapped (Figure 3-11). The minimum size of the vent pipe is specified by code. Generally, a toilet vent pipe must have a minimum diameter of 2". Kitchen sinks, tubs, showers, and laundry standpipes require 1½" vents, while a single lavatory basin needs only a 1¼" vent. The section of the *Uniform Building Code* called, simply enough, "Useful Tables" will help you to determine the size vent pipe you are likely to need for your fixtures. Once again, however, your local code takes precedence over the *UPC*.

The Fixture System

The fixture system includes all fixtures in the home that use water, including sinks, toilets, showers, and bathtubs. All of these fixtures are attached to the waste system and to either the cold water supply line or to both the hot and cold lines.

Fittings and Valves

Figure 3-12 shows a sampling of various kinds of **fittings**— the connecting links that join pipes. They are used to connect lengths of pipe in a straight run, to change the direction of pipes, and to connect two intersecting pipe runs together. Common categories of fittings include the following:

A **coupling** joins two pipes in a straight run.

An **elbow** or **bend** changes the direction of a pipe run.

A **T fitting** joins two perpendicular pipes.

A **Y fitting** joins two intersecting pipes at 45 degrees.

A **union** is a straight, three-piece fitting with female threads at opposite ends and both male and female union threads in the middle, which allow the fitting to be broken in two.

A **reducing coupling** joins a larger diameter pipe to a smaller diameter one.

A **bushing adapter** allows smaller diameter pipe to be joined with larger diameter fittings.

A **cap** covers the end of the pipe.

A **plug** fits inside a threaded fitting, sealing off internal access to the pipe run.

Valves are used to control the flow of water and gas in the plumbing system. Common types of valves found in residential plumbing are the shower valve, sink faucets, angle stop (stop valve), gate valve, ball valve, and globe valve.

Air Chambers

Water supply pipes will sometimes "hammer" when a valve is shut off suddenly. This noisy, irritating condition occurs most often when water pressure is high. Because water does not compress when its flow is stopped suddenly, unsupported piping may bang against structural members; or worn valve parts may begin to "chatter." Instead of a pressure-reducing valve, you may try installing air chambers (water-hammer arresters) at fixtures. These manufactured devices have a factory-charged air bladder that absorbs the line shock in the pipe. Some designs have an air valve that allows you to increase the internal pressure with a tire pump.

INSTALLING THE DRAIN/WASTE/VENT SYSTEM

Most Common Mistakes

☐ Violating code restrictions.

☐ Not installing the DWV system with horizontal slope of at least ¼" per foot.

☐ Not properly venting or trapping all fixtures.

☐ Exceeding the fixture unit capacity of a drain or vent.

☐ Not providing enough cleanouts, or not providing cleanouts at the prescribed places.

☐ Venting the fixture too far from the fixture's trap.

☐ Reducing pipe size downstream.

☐ Not allowing for the proper insertion distance in the fittings when cutting pipe.

☐ Misunderstanding code requirements.

The type of pipe you use in the DWV system will depend on your local code. Plastic pipe is the easiest to work with, but it is not acceptable in some parts of the country.

Two types of plastic pipe are commonly used in DWV systems. PVC (polyvinyl chloride) is white to off-white in color and has the words "PVC" and "Schedule #40," along with other industry standards, printed in a continuous stripe down its entire length. ABS (acrylonitrile-butadiene-styrene) is the preferred type; it too has the material and schedule printed down its entire length.

Plastic pipe is less expensive, lighter weight, and easier to work with than cast iron or DWV-weight copper pipe and fittings. A transition cement is available to join ABS to PVC, but most codes demand that you stay with one type of plastic pipe. Most communities require Schedule #40 ABS or PVC pipe and fittings for residential DWV use. Both materials are manufactured in 20′ lengths; wholesale suppliers generally sell it at this length. Shorter, cut lengths are often available at home improvement centers and hardware stores.

One of the most difficult things about installing any residential DWV piping is boring the large 1½" to 4⅝" diameter holes that are necessary to run pipe through plates, studs, and joists. You will need special heavy duty plumber's bits and hole saws and an extremely powerful drill motor to accomplish this feat. You can rent the drill motor (Milwaukee Hole Haug), but the large-diameter bits are so expensive and easy to break that you will probably have to buy your own.

Cutting Plastic Pipe

Cutting plastic pipe by hand is best accomplished with a handsaw made expressly for this material, commonly referred to as an **ABS saw**. Modern "chopsaws" also accommodate a blade made expressly for cutting plastic. When cutting the pipe (Figure 3-13A), remember to take into account the distance that the pipe is to be inserted into the fitting on each end. Trim the rough edges with a small knife and finish with rough sandpaper to remove the burr from the freshly cut pipe (Figure 3-13B).

With a rag and cleaning solvent, clean the ends of the PVC pipe and the inside of the fittings where the pipe will join (Figure 3-13C). (You do not need to use solvent with ABS pipe; it can be wiped clean with a clean rag.)

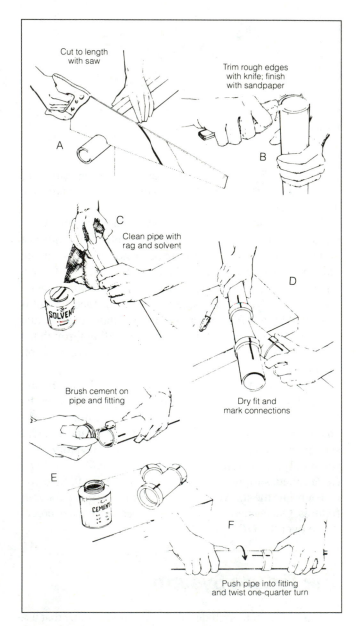

Figure 3-13. Cutting and joining plastic pipe.

When you glue the pipe and fitting together, the glue will dry almost immediately and you can never get them apart. To change the connection, you must cut off the outer fitting and start over. Therefore, you want to get it right the first time. This is easy in some cases, but often you will have a number of pipes coming into one fitting from different angles. To ensure that all of these elements meet correctly once they are permanently glued, you should "dry fit" the fittings and pipe by cutting and assembling the pieces without glue to be sure that everything fits correctly.

Make marks across fittings and pipes so that you will know exactly how to realign everything when the glue is spread and the pipes are inserted permanently into the fitting. Be sure to make the marks long enough so that they will not be covered by the glue you will spread on the pipe (Figure 3-13D).

Spread a generous amount of pipe cement around the end of the pipe and on the inside of the fitting (Figure 3-13E). Finally, insert the pipe into the fitting until it "bottoms out" and give it a little twist—about a quarter turn—to be sure that the cement is spread evenly (Figure 3-13F).

INSTALLING THE WATER SUPPLY SYSTEM

Most Common Mistakes

- ☐ Violating or ignoring code restrictions.
- ☐ Using undersized supply pipes.
- ☐ Moving or knocking copper pipe while the newly sweated fittings are still hot.
- ☐ Leaving materials smoldering after sweating fittings, thereby creating a fire hazard.
- ☐ Forgetting lines for such things as outside hose bibbs, ice makers, and wet bars.
- ☐ Placing pipe supports too far apart.
- ☐ Trying to solder a pipe joint when water has not been completely drained or contained.
- ☐ Failing to run the outside hose bibbs to bleed dirt and air from the lines after turning the water on.

The water supply lines are generally made of copper tubing and fittings. Cooper is easily joined by soldering, or sweating. It resists corrosion when not contacting or mated to ferrous metals, and its smooth surface minimizes resistance to water flow and small particles that could become lodged in the pipes. Although supply piping is not required to slope the ¼" per foot that DWV piping is, a slight slope makes it easier to drain and repair when necessary.

Hard copper supply pipe is sold in lengths of 20′. This kind of pipe is most commonly used for supply systems. Bending hard pipe results in crimping; therefore it must be cut and joined with fittings whenever a change of direction is made. It comes in three weights: K, L, and M. K is the heaviest and M is the lightest. M can be used in most areas, above the ground and within the structure.

Soft copper is sold in 60′ coils. Although it is more expensive, it can be bent around corners, which makes it easy to lay in trenches. It is used primarily for the main building water supply from the meter or wellhead to the house. It is not allowed for use within the structure in most communities. The rolled copper is available in K and L weights. Check with your building inspector to find out which type is specified in your area.

PVC and CPVC schedule #40 plastic pipe is manufactured in 20′ lengths. Most communities only allow plastic main supply lines, in the ground, up to the structure. However, a few areas do allow it for fresh water supply within the building.

Cutting and Soldering Copper Pipe

Figure 3-14 shows several kinds of copper fittings, which are joined to the pipes by soldering. The supply lines are usually installed after the DWV piping. The supply system has more flexibility, and the smaller-diameter supply lines can be run over, under, and around the larger DWV piping. It is generally easiest to begin where the water source enters the house, usually with a ¾" pipe from the source to and through the house. However, don't take any chances; design your system according to the sizing Tables 10-1 and 10-2 in the *UPC*. To install the pipe, you simply begin at one end and work your way to the other end. As the pipe is run, supports are installed according to code, at intervals of about 6′ to 10′.

Insertion distances vary for different types of joints, although ½" pipe usually inserts ½" and ¾" pipe inserts ¾". Cut your pipe with a tubing cutter. Place the pipe in the opening of the tubing cutter and twist the knob until the cutting wheel just contacts the pipe. Then rotate the cutter around the pipe, tightening the knob after each revolution until the pipe separates in two. Whether you are using hard

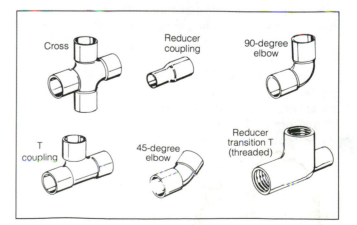

Figure 3-14. Copper fittings.

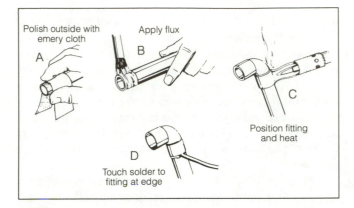

A Polish outside with emery cloth

B Apply flux

C Position fitting and heat

D Touch solder to fitting at edge

Figure 3-15. Soldering copper pipe.

or soft copper tubing, be careful not to damage it as you work.

Use the special blade on the back of the cutter to ream out the burr on the inside of the newly cut pipe. Then use plumber's sand cloth to polish the last inch of the outside of the pipe (Figure 3-15A). Use a wire fitting brush to clean the inside socket of the fitting. It is important to clean both the pipe and fitting thoroughly. The time you spend on this step now will save you a lot of time later fixing leaking joints. It's much easier to do it right the first time.

To solder your joints you will need an acetylene or propane torch, a striker, flux and acid brush, and some lead-free solid wire solder. Apply the flux with the acid brush on the inside of the fitting and around the outside of the pipe end (Figure 3-15B). Place the fitting on the pipe, twisting it back and forth a couple of times to ensure even distribution of the flux.

Heat the bottom of the pipe and fitting with the torch flame. Slowly pass the torch back and forth across the fitting to distribute the heat evenly (Figure 3-15C). Be careful not to get the fitting too hot, or the flux will burn away to nothing. To avoid overheating, touch the solder to the joint occasionally as you heat it. The moment the wire melts on contact and doesn't stick, the joint is ready.

Remove the torch and touch the soldering wire to the edge of the fitting (Figure 3-15D). Capillary action will cause the solder to pull in between the fitting and the pipe. Continue to solder until a line of molten solder shows all the way around the fitting. Be sure there are no air gaps between the solder and the fitting.

Wipe the excess solder off the surface with a clean soft rag before it solidifies, leaving a trace of solder showing in the crevice between fitting and pipe. Keep your hands well away from the heated joint, and take care not to bump or move the newly soldered joint until it has cooled.

Completing and Testing the System

Run hot and cold lines to all of the planned fixtures, and at the fixture locations screw galvanized caps onto brass nipples that are threaded into special fittings called "½" FIP by ½" copper winged 90s" that are soldered to the end of each line. Now the system can be charged with water and tested for leaks.

The tub and shower valves are usually installed in the rough phase of the plumbing. You may hook the water up to an existing main line from the meter or borrow a neighbor's water by using an adapter to hook a garden hose to your cold water supply line at the edge of the building. Be sure to leave the tub and shower valves on the "warm" setting so that cold test water can get into the hot side also and test those lines and connections. If the tub and shower valves are not installed yet, you can use a loop at the water heater's roughed-in connections to connect the hot and cold lines together here.

You'll have to drain the system of water before you can repair any leaks you may find. You can try reheating the joints, applying more flux, and then resoldering. If that fails to do the trick, you may have to cut out the offending fitting and sweat in a new fitting, using repair couplings that slide down the pipe. (It can be very difficult, or even impossible, for an inexperienced plumber to get a previously soldered fitting off the pipe by trying to reheat it and pull it free.) If you cut open the line for repairs and water continues to show up, making soldering impossible, shove a chunk of white bread into the pipe upstream of your joint. Work quickly while the bread is absorbing the water. When you turn the water on again, the bread will disintegrate and flow through the pipe and out into a bucket before you install the finish plumbing materials.

INSTALLING THE FIXTURES (FINISH PLUMBING)

This section discusses general instructions and precautions for roughing in your fixtures, as well as installation procedures for tying into the DWV and supply systems.

Bathroom Sink

The most common sink styles are cabinet-mounted, pedestal, and wall-hung. Some sinks have no holes for the valve; others have holes 4", 6", 8", or more apart for 4"-center sets, and 6" or 8" for kitchen faucets. Lavatory bowls and counter tops may have holes spaced up to 14" apart for faucets. Some sinks also have holes for spray attachments and lotion dispensers. Standard height from floor to sink rim for lavatory sinks is 31" to 32", and 36" for kitchen sinks. Common ma-

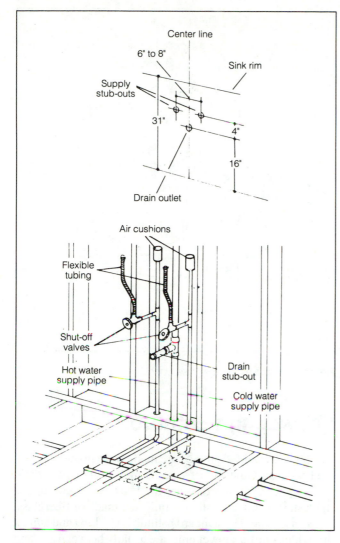

Figure 3-16. Rough plumbing for a bathroom sink.

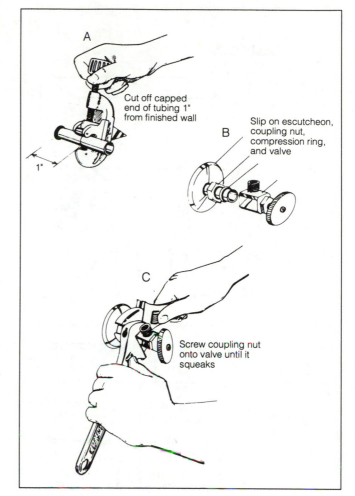

Figure 3-17. Installing a shut-off valve.

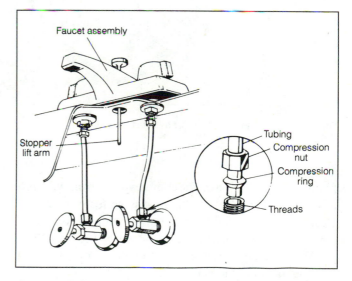

Figure 3-18. Faucet assembly.

terials include vitreous china, enameled cast iron, enameled steel, synthetic marble, and various forms of plastic.

Pipes required for roughing-in the bathroom sink include hot and cold supply stub-outs, shut-off valves, transition fittings, and possibly flexible tubing to go above the shut-off valves. Air chambers may also be required. When the roughing-in has been completed and you are ready to install your sink, your rough plumbing should resemble that shown in Figure 3-16.

Depending on the local code, you may or may not be able to wet vent the lavatory basin. Clearance from the side of a bathroom sink to a toilet tank or finished wall should be at least 4", while the distance to a tub may be as little as 2". There must also be a minimum of 21" from the front edge of the sink to a wall or fixture.

When cutting the capped lines to install your compression shut-off valves, cut the ½" copper supply pipe at least 1½" from the finished wall to allow for an escutcheon and shut-off valve compression nut and ferrule, and still have the supply pipe bottom out in the valve.

Use plumber's sand cloth to clean any drywall mud or paint off of the pipe. Cut slowly and carefully so that you don't deform the pipe (Figure 3-17A). You can also use a

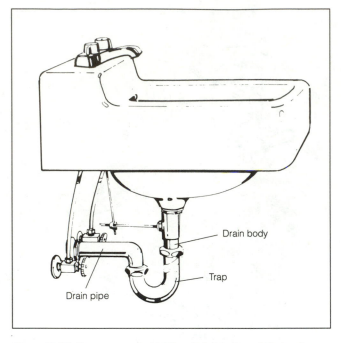

Figure 3-19. Trap connected to the drain body and drain pipe.

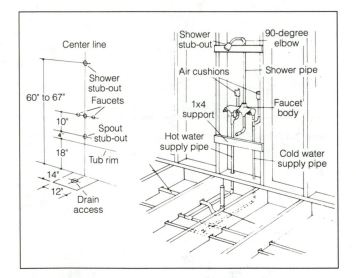

Figure 3-20. Rough plumbing for tub and shower.

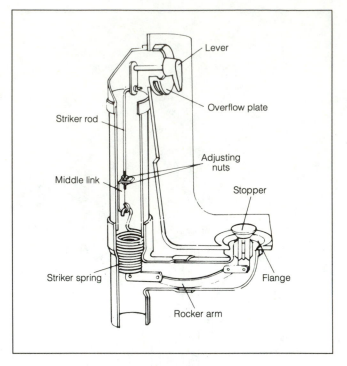

Figure 3-21. Drain overflow assembly.

Shower and Bathtub

The highest quality bathtubs are made from porcelain-covered cast iron. Other choices are enamel on steel, fiberglass, and acrylic. Cast iron tubs are the heaviest, steel tubs the lightest. Prefabricated shower units are made of fiberglass, ABS, or acrylic. The standard bathtub is 60" long and almost 30" wide . Plastic shower units are usually between 32" and 48" wide and from 78" to 84" high. The outside dimensions of a plastic tub/shower combination are usually a little wider and longer than a cast iron tub, and the actual usable space of the plastic fixture is less than that of the iron or steel tub. Installing a tub/shower or shower is one of the most difficult plumbing projects.

Pipes required to plumb a shower or bathtub include the hot and cold supply lines; pipe from valve to the tub spout, to the shower head, or to both; a trap; and drain and vent line. When roughing in has been completed and you are ready to install your tub or shower, your rough plumbing should resemble that shown in Figure 3-20.

Bathtubs and shower stalls usually require support framing. A bathtub filled with water is extremely heavy. At 80° Fahrenheit, a cubic foot of water weighs 62.19 pounds. At the same temperature, a gallon of water weighs 8.314 pounds.

Take into account the capacity of your tub, and be certain that your floor framing is up to code. The minimum floor area required for a shower stall is 1,024 square inches (32"x32"), and you should allow 24" from the stall to any other fixture or to the wall.

plumber's minihacksaw. The compression ferrule will make a water-tight seal only if the pipe is perfectly round and clean. Then slip on the escutcheon, the compression nut and compression ferrule, and finally the valve (Figure 3-17B).

Use two adjustable wrenches to tighten down the compression nut onto the valve body (Figure 3-17C). The nut will usually squeak when it is sufficiently tightened.

Assemble the faucet according to the manufacturer's instructions (Figure 3-18).

Finally, connect the trap to the waste's tailpiece and the drain pipe at the wall, as shown in Figure 3-19. Align and tighten the compression fittings carefully to prevent leaks.

Install as much of the piping as possible before installing the fixture itself. Lower the tub into place so that the continuous flange fits against the wall studs and the back edge is properly supported for its full length. If you have a plastic fixture, nail or screw the fixture in place through the flange.

Assemble the drain connections by connecting the tub overflow (Figure 3-21) with the tub drain. The trap has a slip joint that connects to the tailpiece out the bottom of the overflow T.

Hot and cold water lines are run to the tub or shower mixing valve, where they are attached by sweating them directly into the valve, in the case of valves with copper connections. A valve with threaded connections can be used with copper pipe by installing copper adapters into the threaded ports of the valve and then sweating the copper into the socket.

For the shower riser, it is best to sweat a special fitting called a "brass ½" copper by FIP winged 90" to the top of the riser to accept the threaded end of the shower arm. *Also* screw (don't nail) one or two copper pipe straps on the riser right below the "winged 90." Do the same thing for the tub spout. Use a brass nipple of the appropriate length to secure the spout snug against the waterproof finish wall of the enclosure.

The shower valve trim (handles, cover plates, tub spout, shower arm and head) are the "icing on the cake," to be installed only after the drywall has been painted and the enclosure fully cleaned. Use both teflon tape and pipe joint compound on your threaded connections, and you shouldn't have any leaks.

Toilets

Toilets come in many styles and several sizes. The degree of efficiency with which the toilet flushes depends upon many factors, price not always being one of them. *Consumer Reports* is a good place to comparison shop for performance.

Pipes required include a cold water supply stub-out with a shut-off valve, flexible tubing for above the valve, and possibly one air chamber. When the roughing-in has been com-

pleted and you are ready to install your toilet, your rough plumbing should resemble that shown in Figure 3-22.

The minimum side distance allowed from the center of the toilet bowl to a wall is 15" or 12" to a bathtub. Clearance from the front of the bowl to a wall or other fixture should be at least 21".

It is best to install the finished floor first so that this water-resistant material runs underneath the bowl. Install the angle stop (shut-off valve) now, before going any further. Closet bolts come in two lengths. *Buy the longer length.* Use only brass or stainless steel washers and nuts with the closet bolts. First bolt the closet bolts to the closet flange. Be sure to use a stainless steel washer and nut. Align the bolts so that they line up with the center of the drainpipe in the floor (Figure 3-23A).

Now place the plastic-sleeved bowl wax gasket on the closet flange, with the sleeve protruding into the drain pipe (Figure 3-23B). Using the longer closet bolts as guides, lower the bowl down onto the flange and wax. Next, drop another *two* stainless steel or brass washers down each closet bolt, and thread a brass or stainless nut as far down as you can, using your fingers. Use a ⅟₁₆" box ratchet wrench or 4" adjustable wrench to tighten each nut, going back and forth between the two nuts half a dozen revolutions each until the toilet is firmly on the floor. Go slowly after the toilet begins to compress the wax. You usually hear the wax being compressed and squishing out sideways. You may or may not

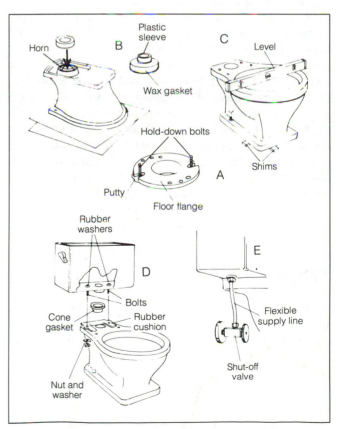

Figure 3-23. Installing a toilet.

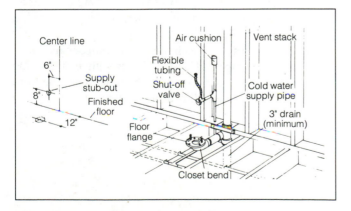

Figure 3-22. Rough plumbing for toilet.

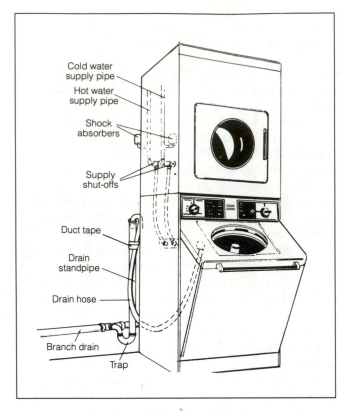

Cold water
supply pipe

Hot water
supply pipe

Shock
absorbers

Supply
shut-offs

Duct tape

Drain
standpipe

Drain hose

Branch drain

Trap

Figure 3-24. Installing a washing machine and drier.

want to level the bowl, as shown in Figure 3-23C. Shimming the bowl increases your chance of a leaking seal.

Place the rubber tank cushion (if one is needed) into position on the rear of the bowl and fit the rubber gasket onto the tank's flush valve threads on the underside of the tank (if it hasn't come from the factory already in place). Position the tank over the bowl; then install the tank bolts as shown Figure 3-23D. Now install your supply tube between the angle stop and the fill valve connection and turn the valve on, filling the tank (Figure 3-23E). Flush the toilet at least a dozen times, checking for leaks. If you have no leaks, use a minihacksaw to cut the closet bolts down to three threads above the top of the closet nuts. Then put a lump of plumber's putty inside the closet bolt covers and shove them over the tops of the bolts. The final step is to install the toilet seat.

Washing Machine

Pipes required for the clothes washer and drier installation (Figure 3-24) include hot and cold supply lines, drain line and vent line, and trap and standpipe or trap for the wash tray.

Thread brass nipples into the special fittings inside the wall. Then slip escutcheons over the nipples and thread female washing machine bibbs onto the nipples. Washing machine bibbs differ from hose bibbs in that the male hose threads for the washing machine hoses point straight down so that the machine can fit closer to the wall.

Install a 2" drain standpipe with a trap above the floor for the wasteline. Read *UPC* Section 604, "Indirect Waste Receptors," so that you understand how to rough in the standpipe and trap.

Install the hot and cold hose bibb valves and standpipe so that they can be reached when the machine is in place. The drain standpipe should always be taller than the highest water level in the machine, to protect against the possibility back-siphoning.

Hook up the washing machine supply hoses. Make sure that you have filter washers (screen cone pointing out) on the hose ends that attach to the appliance. Hand-tighten the hoses, then use pliers for a final quarter turn. Make sure to connect hot to hot and cold to cold. You may also want to use a filter washer, with a screen cone facing out, at the ends of the appliance supply hoses that connect to the washing machine bibbs.

Set the drain hose into the standpipe and secure the hose to the standpipe with duct tape. Finally, level the machine by adjusting the legs under the machine.

Clothes Drier

Allow at least 4" of clearance at the back of the drier for the venting elbow. Most driers have a vent stub-out at the bottom of the machine to attach the vent run to. Many brands also have knockouts at other locations, usually near the top and side, so that you can begin the vent run at more than one location. If you are installing a gas drier, you may want to get a professional to hook up to the gas supply.

The method that you choose to vent your drier depends on several factors. Always choose the most efficient route from the appliance to the outside. Use a hinged damper weather hood placed at least 12" off the ground to prevent backdraft. Be sure that the weather hood will not exhaust to a window well, gas vent, chimney, or any unventilated area such as an attic or crawlspace. The accumulation of lint can be a fire hazard.

Create the vent system with rigid aluminum or galvanized steel conduction pipe and wrap all joints with duct tape. Do not use sheet metal screws. Hang the rigid vent pipe from hangers on a horizontal line at the distance prescribed by your local building inspector.

4 Insulation and Ventilation

HEAT NATURALLY FLOWS from a warmer area to a cooler one. It does this in only three ways: **conduction,** the transfer of heat directly from mass to mass (Figure 4-1); **convection,** the movement of heated air from one space to another (hot air rises, heavier cool air sinks); and **radiation,** which simply means that any warm body gives off heat toward a cooler one (Figure 4-2).

The function of insulation is to minimize the transfer of heat so that the house stays warmer in cool weather and cooler in warm weather.

This chapter discusses the merits and uses of various types of insulation and explains how to evaluate R-values. "R" stands for "resistance to heat flow." The greater the R-value, the greater the insulating power. R-value requirements depend on such factors as local climate and the surface you are insulating (walls, ceiling, floor), and are regulated by local building code. Each region of the country has different requirements for adequate amounts of insulation.

This chapter also describes how to install vents in your attic. Ventilation is extremely important in an insulated attic for two reasons. First, of course, it allows hot air to escape during the summer months, so that the attic does not become superheated. And second, it prevents condensation from being trapped and causing the insulation and even the wood of the house itself to deteriorate.

In most areas, local utility companies will offer suggestions on insulating your home to reduce your energy bills. Often there is no charge for this service. You may be eligible for low-interest or interest-free loan programs. And don't forget that you may receive state or federal tax credits for energy-saving home improvements.

Before You Begin

SAFETY

- ☐ Wear a mask and goggles when working with any type of insulation or when sawing wood.

- ☐ Cover your body as fully as possible, with long sleeves, a hood, long pants, and gloves. Insulating materials can irritate your skin.

- ☐ Wear a hard hat when working in the attic, and watch your back; roofing nails may be sticking through the sheathing.

☐ To reduce fire hazards, keep the insulation at least 3" away from objects that transfer heat. Install sheet metal baffles (dams) around recessed light fixtures, chimneys, and flues.

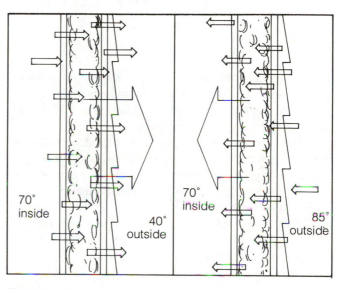

Figure 4-1. Heat is transferred from mass to mass through conduction.

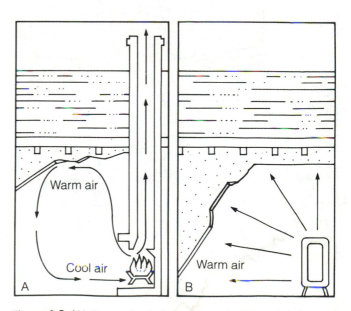

Figure 4-2. (A) Convection is the movement of heated air from one space to another (warm air rises, cool air sinks). (B) A warm body radiates heat toward a cooler one (radiant heat).

☐ When working outside on the roof, wear shoes or boots with rubber soles, stay clear of power lines, and secure extension ladders with safety hooks that clamp over the ridge.

☐ Delay your work until the roof is free of dampness from rain, frost, snow, or dew.

☐ When working high on the outside of the house, consider renting a scaffold to provide a balanced, level working surface.

☐ Do not step between attic floor joists onto the ceiling of the room below. It will give way.

☐ Some types of insulation are flammable and may give off toxic gases when they burn. Check with your local building department and fire department for special precautions or restrictions.

USEFUL TERMS

Caulking is available in several types, depending on what it is supposed to adhere to. It is a pliable material that is usually forced into a gap or crack with a caulking gun to inhibit moisture and air from entering the crack.

Cellulose is a shredded paper product, used for insulation, that has been treated with borate salts to resist burning.

Blown-in or **loose insulation** (Figure 4-3) can be cellulose, rock wool, glass fiber, vermiculite, perlite, or a combination of these materials. It is used in floors, walls, and hard-to-reach places. This type of insulation is poured between joists or blown in with special equipment. It is best suited for use in irregular-shaped areas and is the preferred option for blowing into existing finished walls.

Fiberglass blankets or **batts** (Figure 4-3) are widely used for insulating walls, floors, ceilings, roofs, and attics. They are easily fitted and stapled between studs, joists, and beams.

Flexi-vent is a strip of corrugated styrofoam designed to allow air circulation to carry away moisture that could build up under insulation.

Foam insulation (Figure 4-3) can be extruded polystyrene, isocyanurate board, or sprayed in place. The rigid panels are used on unfinished walls, on basement and masonry walls, and on exterior surfaces. The panels are glued or cut to friction fit between studs, joists, or furring strips, and must be covered with drywall or paneling for fire safety. They offer a high insulating value for a relatively thin material, but are highly flammable, and some chemically based foams may discharge poisonous fumes over a period of time. For exterior applications and in high-moisture areas, be sure to use a closed-cell, waterproof rigid panel. Sprayed in place foam insulation is usually shot directly on the roof sheathing with a foam mixer and gun. This type of insulation is most commonly used on exposed beam ceilings.

Furring is strips of wood that are used to level out a surface before finishing.

A **scab** is a piece of wood nailed into place to extend or "shim out" the surface of a rafter or stud.

Shims are thin wedges of wood used to bring furring strips level with each other when used on an uneven wall.

Silicate compound is an insulating material made of glass and sand. It does not burn or release toxic fumes. It comes in lightweight, easy-to-handle bags, and is used in the same manner as loose fill or cellulose.

Vapor barriers are used to control moisture build-up in closed areas. The most common vapor barrier is sheets of 6

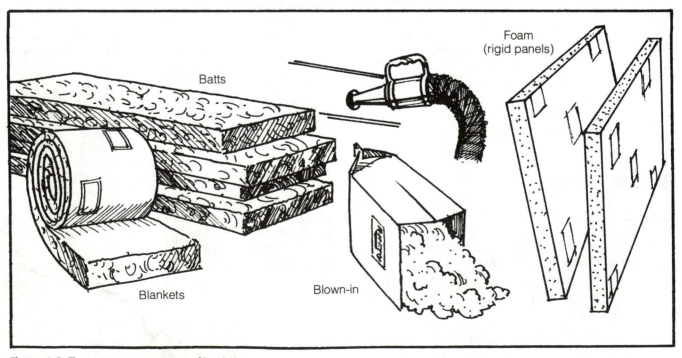

Figure 4-3. The most common types of insulation.

mil plastic attached over the insulation. In the eastern United States, vapor barriers control condensation in northern regions and humidity in the coastal and southern regions. In the West, they are usually intended to limit the accumulation of vapor to an amount that will be dispersed by normal interior heating. Elaborate vapor protection is vital in some areas and undesirable in others. Consult your local code about whether or not you should install a vapor barrier.

WHAT YOU WILL NEED

Time. The time required depends on the type of job to be done. Allow 3 to 4 person-hours per 100 square feet when installing fiberglass batts and a vapor barrier in an attic. Allow 4 to 6 person-hours per 100 square feet when installing furring, insulation, and a vapor barrier in a basement.

Tools. Most of the tools required for installation of insulation are found in the home toolbox. Others can be rented from your home building center.

Dust mask

Goggles

Gloves

Pencil and paper

Trouble light

Extension cord

String

Steel tape measure

Level

Circular saw

Hole saw

Utility knife

Spackling knife

Hammer

Drill

Shovel (for exterior application)

Staple gun and heavy-duty staples (or an air compressor with a stapling attachment)

Ramset (rental)

Caulking gun

Blowing machine (rental, if you choose to blow in your insulation)

Sump pump

Shovel (for exterior application)

Materials. As with any home project, the materials you need depend on the type of insulation used and the extent of the work to be done. Your list will include many of the following items.

For Interior Application

2x4 boards

16-penny nails

Flexi-vent material

Duct tape

2x2 furring strips

Adhesive

Shims

Spackling compound

Long straight board

Fiberglass insulation

Vapor barrier (6 mil visquine)

Cellulose

Rigid foam panels (regular or closed cell)

For Exterior Application

2" extruded foam panels

Construction adhesive

Tar paper

Sheet metal flashing

Drain pipe

Gravel

Tape

Plastic

Caulk

Waterproofing sealant

Closable vents

Drain tiles

Pipes

Soffit ventilation plugs

Sheet metal, louvred and screened vent

Continuous ridge vent

Wind turbine

PERMITS AND CODES

Codes for insulation requirements vary in different parts of the country. Check with your local building inspector. Codes also indicate regional R-factors required.

Most Common Mistakes

The most common error in insulating projects is neglecting to find out the locally required R-value and insulating accordingly. Other common mistakes include the following.

☐ Not providing for good air circulation between the roof and the insulation.

☐ Installing fiberglass batts or blankets with the paper side (vapor barrier) facing toward the outside instead of toward the heated area.

☐ Distorting, compressing, or squeezing the batt or blanket out of shape.

☐ Using paper-faced batts or blankets against a heat source like a chimney or a heating duct.

☐ Neglecting to insulate all of the small spaces and corners.

☐ Covering the vents in the eaves with insulation, thereby cutting off ventilation.

☐ Making unnecessary trips up and down the attic stairs during installation. Assemble all tools and equipment in your work area before beginning the job.

☐ Not using closed-cell (waterproof), rigid foam insulation panels on below-grade installations.

THE ATTIC

The attic is usually the single greatest heat loser in the home. The lighter heated air rises, while the heavier cool air drops (convection). That's why your feet are usually cold or why your much taller mate says it's already too hot when you want to turn the heat up.

Adequate insulation in attics is imperative to reduce heat loss. The most widely used insulation in the attic is fiberglass, which commonly comes in rolls 3½" to 6" thick. It is available in widths to fit between 16" and 24" on center framing members. It comes in two forms, batt and blanket. Batt insulation is available in 4' or 8' lengths. Blanket insulation in cut-to-fit rolls is available in lengths from 30' to 70'. Blanket insulation is generally preferable because there are fewer gaps when it is installed.

Fiberglass is available in foil-backed, paper-backed, and unfaced batts and blankets. Both the foil and the paper act as vapor barriers. Unfaced fiberglass is used in conditions of potential fire hazards and as the top layer of a two-layer application. Otherwise, paper-backed fiberglass is usually recommended.

Step One
Preparation

Margin of Error: Leave no gaps

Before you begin installing the fiberglass, you need to do some preparatory work. The first thing to do is to decide how you want to use your attic space.

Take a pencil and paper, a clipboard, and a trouble light with an extension cord with you up to the attic. Examine your attic space carefully to determine whether you will ever want to use the space for living and therefore want to heat it, or whether you prefer to insulate the main part of the house below the attic. You want to place your insulation so that it encloses the heated areas only (Figure 4-4).

If you want to finish and heat the attic space, look closely at the rafters, checking them for depth and uniformity. They must be deep enough to accommodate the depth of batting needed for your region., or you will have to use foam insulation. The rafters will also give you a point of attachment for the vapor barrier and a structure capable of supporting the finished walls of drywall or paneling.

Step Two
Ventilating the Attic

Margin of Error: Not applicable

Ventilation in the attic is extremely important. If the attic isn't properly ventilated, condensation can be trapped, causing the insulation as well as the wood structure to deteriorate. Insulation loses its R-value as it takes on moisture. Also, if heat is not vented in the summer, the attic becomes superheated. Types of ventilation include soffit plugs, gable vents, continuous ridge vents, and wind turbines (Figure 4-5). When insulating between the rafters, a 1½" space is commonly left below the roof sheathing. With soffit vents and a ridge vent, a very efficient positive airflow is obtained.

Soffit Plugs

Soffit ventilation allows air to travel from outside the house into the attic space rafters and out the gable wall vents, or out the ridge at the peak of the roof. Soffit ventilation plugs, available in various sizes, are screened and louvred so that air can pass through but insects can't. To install these vents, first drill a hole with a hole saw between each pair of rafters

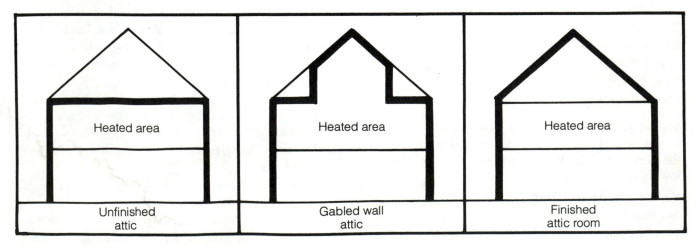

Figure 4-4. Insulation is placed to contain the heat in the heated areas only.

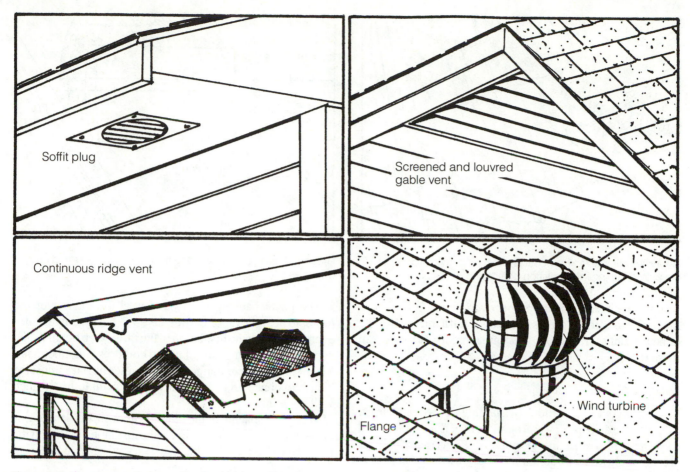

Figure 4-5. Key places where an attic should be ventilated.

all the way around the soffit (the outside roof overhang of the house). Then push in the soffit ventilation plugs.

Gable Vent

On the gable wall, near the peak, you may want to install a louvred sheet metal vent to let the air out as it moves toward the top of the attic. These gable vents are triangular, square, or round screened vents that are installed in gable walls in the same way you would install a window.

Continuous Ridge Vent

Screened continuous ridge vent is available in 10′ lengths. This kind of vent is designed to be installed along the entire ridge of the house, letting air out but keeping rain from getting in. These ridge vents are difficult to retrofit in existing homes, but they are recommended in new construction.

Wind Turbine

The wind turbine is a most effective means of ventilation. It is installed near the roof peak; wind or air rising through the turbine turns the vanes and gets the air moving near the top of the house, drawing heat and moisture out. They can be noisy, however. To install a wind turbine, follow these steps.

1. Find a good location near the peak and between rafters. Remove the roof shingles, tiles, gravel, or other roofing material down to the tar paper to expose an area slightly larger than the flange of the wind turbine. Place the flange in position and mark the flange opening on the tar paper with chalk or colored pencil.

2. Drill a starter hole, using a hole saw or a 1" or larger drill bit. Once the hole is started, use a reciprocating saw to finish cutting out the entire flange opening area. Be sure the blade is long enough and suitable for cutting tar paper and sheathing. Keep a few extra blades on hand; the long, narrow reciprocating blades tend to break easily. Wear safety glasses or goggles when sawing.

3. Use a caulking gun to apply a generous amount of roofing asphalt cement to the outer perimeter to seal the opening, then nail the flange of the base of the turbine to the roof with roofing nails. Roll some tar paper over the flange to create a double seal, and carefully replace the shingles to cover the tar-papered flange. Be sure the flange is properly interwoven with the shingles. Like the scales on a fish, each component must overlap the last piece.

4. Install the wind turbine into the base, and you're in business with a very fine ventilator. Be sure to install the turbine properly to prevent leaks. It is essential that the flange and

Figure 4-6. Staple flexi-vent material between the rafters against the roof sheathing for ventilation behind the insulation.

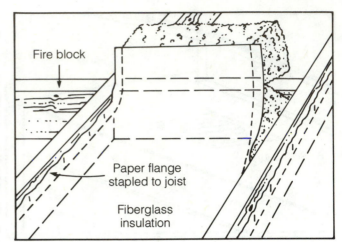

Figure 4-7. Back-cut insulation to fit around fireblocks and other obstacles.

shingles are installed in the proper overlapping fashion. You may want to call in a professional to install a turbine in a flat or nearly flat roof, because leaks are more likely to occur in these roofs.

Flexi-Vent

Complete your preparations by stapling flexi-vent material (a corrugated strip of styrofoam) between the rafters and against the roof sheathing (Figure 4-6). This material is designed to allow air circulation to carry away moisture that could build up between the roof and the new insulation. The sheets are made to fit between 16" or 24" on center rafters. Butt these strips right up next to each other and against the roof itself. Then use a staple gun or heavy duty stapler to staple them to the inside surface of the sheathing.

Step Three
Insulating the Rafters
with Fiberglass

Margin of Error: Fill entire cavity and plug holes exactly

Working on your knees in an attic for long periods of time can be very hot and tiring. You will be covered from head to toe in protective clothing and gear. Plan a few breaks into your work schedule, and try to work early in the morning before it gets too hot. Add a spray container of cold water to your toolbox to spray yourself and your fogged-up goggles.

Begin by measuring the length of each space between the rafters. Cut each piece of insulation an inch or two longer than needed, to ensure a snug fit. Use your straightedge to compress the insulation while cutting it, and use a very sharp utility knife to ensure a good straight cut across the fiberglass blanket or batt. Staple the insulation to the rafters or scabbed-on boards with a staple gun or a hammer-tacker. An air compressor with a staple gun attachment can also save you time and effort in this task.

The paper backing must be toward the interior of the room, to act as a vapor barrier. Use 3/8" heavy-duty staples every 6". Attach the insulation to the rafter scab board by the paper flange, being careful not to compress the fiberglass. Make sure the paper flange and the staples lie flat against the board, to create an even surface for attaching the finished wall material.

Where the spacing of the rafters is uneven, odd-angled, or not standard, you will need to cut the insulation to fit. Cut the fiberglass 1" wider than the necessary width, and tuck it in to create a flange for stapling.

Once the insulation is in place between all the rafters, it's time to staple up a vapor barrier of 6 mil visqine (a painter's drop cloth) over the insulation and across the face of the rafters. Although the paper or foil backing of the insulation is a vapor barrier, the visqine gives added protection against moisture forming in the cavity because it covers completely, with no breaks. As you staple the vapor barrier to the rafters, draw it as tight as possible, being careful not to puncture the plastic unnecessarily. Repair any punctures with duct tape.

When installing insulation over wires, pipes, bridging, or fireblocking, it is necessary to back-cut the fiberglass to fit over the obstacle, leaving the paper intact and the insulation uncompressed (Figure 4-7).

Step Four
Insulating the Attic Floor

Margin of Error: Fill all cavities and plugholes exactly

Fiberglass Insulation

Any floor is most easily insulated before the subfloor is applied. Just staple the flanges to the top of the joists and cover with the subfloor material. Working overhead to insulate the top ceiling is much more difficult than installing this insulation after the ceiling is in place.

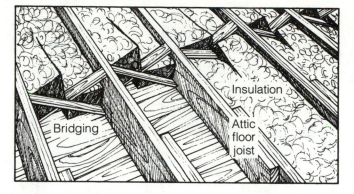

Figure 4-8. Cut insulation to fit around floor bridging.

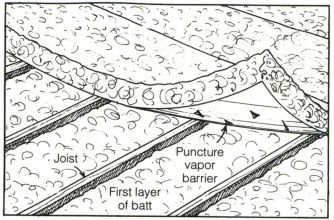

Figure 4-9. When installing two layers of batt insulation, puncture the vapor barrier of the upper layer all over so that moisture is not trapped between the layers.

Placing the fiberglass insulation between the attic floor joists effectively insulates the lower portion of your home so that you don't use expensive energy to heat unused attic space. Use this method if you don't plan to convert your attic into living space (see Figure 4-4).

Begin by unrolling the insulation between the joists, paper face down (toward the heated area of the house). Start in a corner, using a stick to tuck the insulation into the corner. Be careful not to compress the fiberglass. If there are soffit vents, leave a space at the eaves for air circulation.

Your aim in installing attic insulation is to slow the infiltration of heat from the rooms below through any cracks that may occur around the insulation. Therefore, be very careful in installing the insulation around any obstacles in the joist space, such as plumbing, heating ducts, chimney stacks, or bridging. Cut the insulation to fit snugly around the object (Figure 4-8).

The paper facing on most insulation is flammable. Therefore you must use unfaced fiberglass when working around heat sources like a chimney, flue, or heating duct. A 3" air space between the chimney and the insulation is recommended. With prefabricated flues and chimneys, check the manufacturer's recommendation.

You can insulate closely around electrical junction boxes (but not electrical fixtures boxes) because they do not give off heat. Don't cover the junction boxes, however; the code requires you to have permanent access to them. Again, be careful not to distort or compress the fiberglass. Leave about 3" around recessed lighting fixtures for air to circulate and to keep the fixture cool. Wrap pipes separately to cut off all air passage around them, and stuff scraps of fiberglass into small, hard-to-cover areas.

If one layer of fiberglass insulation between floor joists does not meet the R-value you need, a second layer can be added on top of, and at right angles to, the joists. There is less thermal loss with this method because the joists are covered, but you will no longer be able to see them. With this method, you must be careful to avoid trapping moisture between the two layers. It is best to use unfaced insulation for this layer. Or install the second layer with the paper side down and puncture the paper barrier on this second layer all over (Figure 4-9). Your main concern with this layer is that the fiber-

glass fits snug and tight, side by side and end to end. Begin this second layer in a corner, butted against the bottom of the rafters. Continue to install it end to end until you get to the center of the floor or near the stairwell. Then begin again at the opposite side and install to the center again, to avoid walking on and compressing the insulation over the joists. Finally, don't forget to insulate the hatch door to the attic.

Blown-In Insulation

Another method of insulating the attic is to pour or blow in loose insulation up to the top of the joists or beyond to provide an even surface. The loose insulation comes in large bags, and is easy to pour between the attic floor joists. Or you can rent a blower to blow the insulation between the joists. Then unfaced or punctured fiberglass insulation can be installed perpendicular to the joists. A trouble light will help you see that hard-to-reach places are adequately filled with the cellulose. To achieve a higher R-level, blow in the cellulose to fill the joist spaces past the top of the wood framing.

As you work back into the corners and around the vents in the eaves, be careful not to cover any ventilating areas. Use a long straight board to help you even out the cellulose (Figure 4-10). Drag the board along the joists to push loose piles of insulation into the spaces between the joists.

By the end of the day, your skin may itch from the small particles of glass that have found their way beneath your protective clothing. Vinegar makes an effective rinse when you bathe or shower after working with fiberglass. It almost eliminates the itching.

THE WALLS

Your choice of insulation in your walls depends on personal preference, the intended use of the space, and the R-value necessary for your area. Fiberglass (blankets or batts) is the most common material, although in some areas people install rigid foam board on the outside of the frame underneath

Figure 4-10. Use a long board to level blown-in or poured-in insulation, especially if you plan to cover it with batts or a blanket.

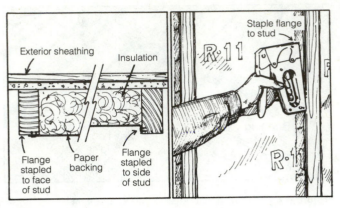

Figure 4-11. Staple the flanges of the insulation to the inside or front surface of the wall studs.

the siding, in addition to the fiberglass in the walls. The principles for installing fiberglass in the walls are the same as for installing it between the rafters. You will need a uniform surface to staple the insulation to and to hold the drywall in place (Figure 4-11).

Blown-in cellulose insulation is not recommended in new walls because it tends to settle toward the bottom of the wall, leaving uninsulated areas at the top, where insulation is most needed.

THE BASEMENT

Step One
Preparation

Margin of Error: 1/4"

Before adding insulation to the basement walls or to the crawlspace foundation, it is essential that you repair any leaks and solve any problems with dampness. Wait until the basement is thoroughly dry before you install the insulation, to be sure that all problems have been eliminated. If you are not sure whether you have a moisture problem, tape a square-foot piece of plastic to the basement wall or floor and leave it in place for a week. (Or use one of the methods described in Chapter 9, Vinyl Floors.) If condensation builds up under the plastic, you have a problem that needs to be solved.

There are several possible causes of such condensation. The most common causes are seepage, condensation, and drainage problems around the foundation, and leaks and cracks in the concrete. Taking care of these potential trouble spots will save you a great deal of time, trouble, and money later on.

Caulk any visible cracks, and control seepage by painting waterproofing sealant on the interior walls. In cold areas, it's a good idea to install closable vents in the crawlspace at the time the foundation is built. Local code will specify the location and number of these foundation vents. Open them in warm weather to air out the crawlspace and close them in winter to prevent heat loss. Some vents are automatic, and will open and close at set temperatures. You can minimize crawlspace moisture and basement seepage by diverting the most obvious sources of moisture (usually the roof downspouts) well away from the foundation.

In hilly or low-ground areas where drainage is a problem, install a "French drain" or pipes around the perimeter of the foundation to carry the water away from the foundation. You may even need a sump pump to pump out excess water. If you have a clothes drier in the basement, make sure it is properly vented to the outside; the exhaust from clothes driers is very humid.

For more information on caulking and sealing, see Chapter 14, Weatherizing. Weatherizing goes hand in hand with insulation, and many of the solutions overlap.

Insulating the basement and crawlspace sometimes calls for a different type of insulation than that used in the attic and walls. In the first place, the basement and crawlspace are more susceptible to moisture seepage, which can lead to problems like damp surfaces, stained finishes, and mildew. Water vapor moves easily through most materials used in construction, including brick and concrete blocks. A basement wall that is not adequately insulated with a moisture-resistant material will conduct warm moist air from the living space through to the cooler outer wall, where it is likely to condense. If you are not heating the basement or crawlspace, you will want to insulate beneath the first floor. This is best done before installing the subfloor; if it must be done later, it cannot be stapled correctly.

In this case, the insulation is held in place either with chicken wire or with support wires called "tiger tails," as shown in Figure 4-12. These wires are flexed, inserted between the joists over the insulation, and then released so that

Figure 4-12. You can also buy wire insulation supports, called "tiger tails," that snap between the joists to support the insulation.

Figure 4-13. Use furring strips and shims to furr out before installing rigid insulation over masonry walls.

the sharpened end digs into the joists and supports the insulation.

If you plan to heat the space below the first floor, you may want to use a closed-cell, rigid foam panel or the reflective layered type of insulation. In this case, you will insulate the basement walls, not the basement ceiling.

Rigid foam panels can be used to insulate both interior and exterior walls. The closed-cell type is not as susceptible to moisture as are other types of insulation. Use only closed-cell insulation in below-grade applications. It usually comes in 2'x8' sheets, and should be covered with a fire-resistant material, such as drywall, when exposed to the interior.

Some types of foam make an ideal habitat for certain kinds of ants. Consult your local supplier about insect problems in your area.

Step Two
Installing Rigid Foam Insulation in the Basement

Margin of Error: 1/4"

Interior Application

After correcting any moisture problems, you are ready to begin installing rigid insulation. First, you will need to install 2x2 furring strips to the wall 16" on center (Figure 4-13). Attach the furring strips with the appropriate adhesive, or with a rented ramset if you are attaching them to masonry walls. The furring gives you a firm, level surface to which you can attach drywall or paneling. Chapter 6 gives complete instructions for attaching furring strips.

To even out the slight irregularities in masonry, you will need some shim material to get the furring surfaces flush with each other. Hold a level on the face of the furring strips and shim out as needed.

Measure and cut the foam to size with a utility knife or saw. Then press the foam between the strips. It should fit snugly.

Staple a sheet of 6 mil plastic as a vapor barrier over and at the top of the insulation. Do not staple it to the furring strips or puncture it unnecessarily. Gravity and the wall covering will hold it in place.

Exterior Application

On the exterior side of the basement walls, you will need to dig a trench 2' deep all around the foundation (deeper in cold weather areas with a deeper frost line). Check with your local building inspector and follow the local code.

Use at least 2" extruded foam panels on the exterior; they are denser than regular foam and will hold up longer. Be sure they are the moisture-resistant type, made to be installed below ground, or they will become waterlogged and lose their insulating value. Place the panels right up against the concrete, butted tightly against one another. Use exterior adhesive to glue the panels to the foundation wall.

To keep water from getting in between the foam panels and the exterior foundation walls, push sheet metal flashing up under the siding and a few inches over the insulation, and hammer it in place over the foam panels with galvanized nails.

If you have a drainage problem, this is a good time to install a French drain (Figure 4-14). Install it at a slope and connect it to the municipal storm drain or other drainage outlet. Check your local building code to see how foundation drains and storm drains are installed in your area. The system, which is usually installed 1' to 3' below the ground, consists of a plastic pipe surrounded by gravel. The top half

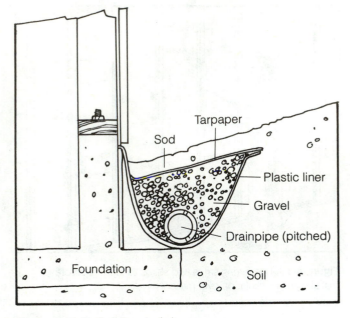

Figure 4-14. Typical French drain.

of the pipe is perforated. Water runs into the holes and down the solid lower half of the pipe, away from the foundation. A piece of tar paper on top of the gravel prevents dirt from getting in the gravel and clogging the holes in the pipe. New plastic fabric filtration materials, called **geotextiles**, can simplify these drains and reduce costs.

Backfill the excavated dirt to hold the foam panels in place around the foundation walls. Then plant grass seed or plants to prevent erosion. If you are installing a drain pipe, backfill with gravel, cover the gravel with tar paper, and cover the tar paper with the excavated dirt.

5 Drywall

BEFORE THE INVENTION of drywall, walls were usually made of hardened liquid plaster spread over wood slats (lath). Drywall is basically that same plaster, encased in large paper-covered sheets.

Drywall, often called **sheetrock, gypsum, gyp board,** or **wallboard,** is made of a crumbly fire-resistant mineral substance called gypsum, wrapped in a thick paper coating. It is durable and is easily cut, trimmed, and repaired. In this chapter you will learn how drywall can be used to cover bare stud walls.

Because of drywall's resistance to flames, most model codes require that it be used to protect wood frames. Even if the final surface will be wood paneling, drywall is often needed to protect the frame and slow the spread of fire.

Because of its unique construction, drywall can be cut, sawed, drilled, bent, nailed, glued, screwed, and painted or papered over. In addition to being easy to work with, drywall is inexpensive. Although a novice may find it difficult to finish to a smooth surface, if you practice your finishing in a closet or other area of low visibility, you can master the techniques presented here. A poorly finished job can be quite visible, especially in a well-lit room. You may find a textured finish easier to master, because it does not require the perfection of a smooth finish. Once in place, the drywall can be painted or papered (unless it is textured), which makes it ideal for designing new interiors.

Before You Begin

SAFETY

Developing and practicing safe work habits is especially important when you are working with heavy, unwieldy materials like drywall. Use the proper protection, take precautions, and plan ahead. Never bypass safety to save money or to rush a project.

- ☐ Drywall is heavy and difficult to lift and maneuver. It is best to work in pairs, especially when working on ceilings and high areas.

- ☐ Be careful not to strain your back when lifting the heavy drywall.

- ☐ Wear the proper respirator or face mask when sanding or sawing drywall.

- ☐ Use the appropriate tool for the job.

- ☐ Keep your blades sharp, and change the blade in your utility knife frequently.

- ☐ Use stepladders properly. Never climb higher than the second step from the top—use a taller ladder instead. Be certain that both pairs of legs are fully open and that the spreader bars are locked in place. When leaning the ladder against a wall, the distance between the wall and the feet of the ladder should be about one quarter the height of the ladder.

- ☐ Do not use an aluminum ladder near electrical wires.

- ☐ When setting a plank between ladders as a scaffold, be sure it extends a foot on each side and is clamped or nailed to its support.

USEFUL TERMS

A **corner bead** or **corner strip** is a protective metal cover for outside corners to prevent damage to the drywall and to allow a smoother finish.

Drywall nails have a concave head and a barbed shank or annular ring shank, or a powdered adhesive coating.

A **drywall saw** is similar to a keyhole saw. It has a stiff, pointed blade to punch through drywall and to cut curves easily.

Drywall screws are tapered number 6 screws.

Greenrock is moisture-resistant (MR) drywall that is specially treated for use in bathrooms and other damp areas. One side of these panels is usually covered with green paper.

Mud, drywall compound, or **vinyl spackling** is the substance used to cover tape and nailheads and to smooth the wall to an even, unblemished surface

A **pole sander** is a sanding block that is pivot-mounted on a long pole to let you sand the ceiling and high areas of the walls without having to stand on a ladder. It uses special precut, prepunched sandpaper.

Tape, available in **paper** or **fiberglass,** is used to cover the seams between drywall panels.

A **taping knife** is a wide, flat-bladed tool from 6" to 10" wide, used to apply drywall compound to taped seams and nail heads.

WHAT YOU WILL NEED

Time. The time you will need depends on the type and extent of job to be done.

Tools. Although you may already have a number of the tools you will need, many specialized tools, like drywall saws, pole sanders, drywall knives, and corner knives, are available to make the job easier and the finished results more professional looking.

If you plan to use adhesives to attach your drywall, a rented air compressor with a caulking attachment will make your job a great deal easier.

Ladder

Sawhorses

Steel tape measure

Level

Plane

Drywall saw

Drywall T-square

Carpenter's pencil

Drywall hammer

3/8" drill with phillips head screwdriver attachment

Chalkline and chalk

Scraper (plane)

Mud knives (4", 6", and 10" widths)

Corner mud knife

Mud trays

Drywall square

Utility knife and blades

Keyhole saw

Dust masks

Goggles

Buckets and sponges

Flashlight

Drywall sander (pole sander)

Orbital sander

Sanding block

Sandpaper in various grades

Tin snips

Materials. Standard drywall comes in several thicknesses—1/4", 3/8", 1/2", and 5/8". Thin drywall offers the advantages of being lightweight and easy to manage. Thick drywall is stiffer and tends to go up flatter. The most common thicknesses are 1/2" and 5/8". A so-called "one-hour fire-resistant wall" requires 5/8" drywall. A single layer of drywall that is thinner than 1/2" can result in a "spongy" wall. The standard panel is 4'x8', although 4'x10' and 4'x12' panels are available.

The long edges of the panels are tapered to compensate for the thickness of mud and tape used to finish the seams, where two panels butt together.

To determine the amount of drywall you will need, find the area to be covered by multiplying the length of each wall by its height. Add these numbers together and divide the result by 32, the area in square feet of a 4'x8' panel. (Of course,

if you are using 4'x10' panels, you will divide by 40.) It's a good idea to make a sketch of each wall to help you decide on the most efficient layout. The idea is to minimize the number of joints and to be sure that all panels meet over joists, and never at the corner of a window or door. Add 10 to 20 percent to cover waste.

Drywall

Joint compound

Drywall nails

Drywall screws

Drywall adhesive

Shim material

Butcher paper or cardboard for templates

Metal corner beads

Paper or fiberglass tape

PERMITS AND CODES

The thickness and type of drywall used, as well as the nailing pattern employed, are governed by local building codes in most areas. Contact the office of your local building inspector before beginning work.

DESIGN

Drywall can be installed either vertically or horizontally. You should plan your installation to create the smallest possible number of seams. Use this criterion to choose the size of drywall for your project and to plan its application. Remember that where two boards butt up against each other at their long edges, both must have a tapered factory edge where they meet. Of course, when you are using small pieces in odd-shaped areas, this will not always be possible; but do your best.

Most Common Mistake

☐ The single most common mistake in working with drywall is not practicing the finishing steps before you do the actual work. Other common mistakes are listed with each step in the process.

Step One
Prepping the Walls

Margin of Error: 1/8"

Most Common Mistakes

☐ Neglecting to install insulation, ventilation, vapor barriers, plumbing, phone lines, wiring, and ductwork before installing the drywall.

☐ Neglecting to have the rough electrical and rough plumbing inspections done before applying the drywall. These elements *must* be inspected before they are concealed.

☐ Neglecting to install nailguards (safety plates) where wires or pipes run within the studs.

☐ Joining pieces so that the seam occurs at the edge, not the center, of a window or door opening.

All electrical and plumbing work, including phone wires, cable TV lines, and alarm systems, and all insulation must be complete before the drywall is installed. You should also take care of any leaks, poor ventilation, or other repairs. It won't make your new walls look any better if a faulty pipe soaks them a few days after you put them up. The codes require you to place metal nailguards over studs to protect wires and pipes (Figure 5-1).

Once you are sure all potential problems within the walls have been addressed, you can begin your layout work for drywall application. First, observe your framework carefully to see if any studs or rafters are badly bowed and would cause the drywall to protrude or bow inward. This is especially important around doors and windows where trim will be applied later. Correct these places with shims or by chiseling, planing down, or even replacing the faulty studs if necessary before proceeding. Next, mark the centers of all wall studs on the ceiling and the floor. These marks will show you where to snap chalklines on the drywall to act as nailing guides.

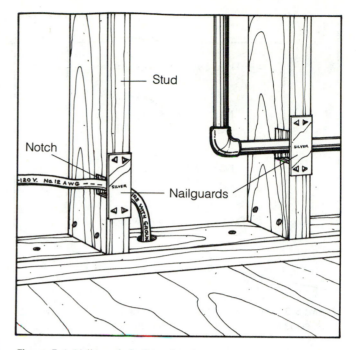

Figure 5-1. Nailguards (safety plates) protect wires and pipes from drywall nails or screws.

Step Two
Applying the Drywall

Margin of Error: ¼"

Most Common Mistakes

☐ Not getting insulation and utilities inspected before covering with drywall.

☐ Not getting nail pattern inspected if necessary (check local code) before covering nails with compound and tape.

☐ Driving nails or screws so deep that they break the paper on the panels.

☐ Not using drywall nails or screws.

☐ Not butting two panels of drywall at the beveled factory edge (although this is unavoidable at the ends).

☐ Not butting panels at the center of a stud or rafter.

☐ Applying the drywall sheets with the wrong side exposed.

☐ Creating more seams than are necessary—for example, by using small scraps.

Final taping and mudding will go much more smoothly if the joints where sheets and odd shapes of drywall meet are smooth and fit closely together. Use a scraping plane or rasp on cut edges to smooth any rough places.

When you are positioning a drywall panel, align the top of each panel with the ceiling edge or the angle break to ensure a clean edge. (Always install the ceiling panels first. The wall panels will help hold up the edges of the ceiling panels.)

All joints between boards should be positioned to meet over the center of a stud or rafter. The exception, of course,

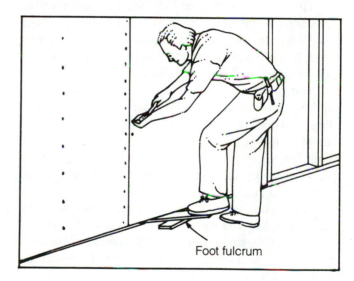

Figure 5-2. Use a foot fulcrum to support drywall while nailing. Place the nails directly across from each other in adjacent panels.

is where the long edges meet on a horizontal application. Any gaps should fall close to the floor, where a baseboard will cover them. To raise the panels, you can make a foot fulcrum with two pieces of wood (Figure 5-2).

Start a couple of drywall nails at the corners and across the top of the drywall panel before you lift it into place. Once the panel is positioned, these nails will make it easier to attach while another person holds it in place. Be sure to align each panel to meet over a stud.

There are several kinds of drywall nails. Some have cupped heads, which make them easier to cover when mudding and taping. Those with barbed shanks have greater

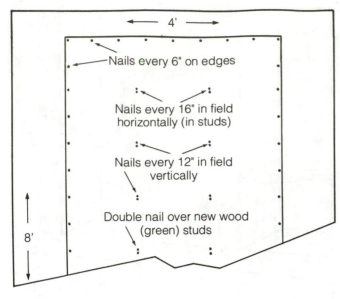

Figure 5-3. Sample nailing pattern for sheetrock. Check your local code to find nailing requirements in your area.

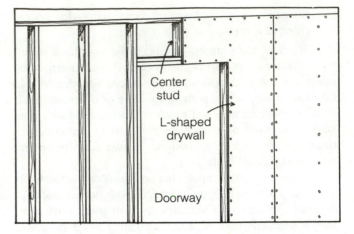

Figure 5-4. Seams should fall at the center of the window or door opening, not the edge.

holding power and reduce nail popping. Nail along the edge of the panel about every 6" or 7" on ceilings and every 8" on walls. In the middle of the panel, nail about every 12". Check your local code on this point for variance. If the studs are new wood, it is advisable to double-nail in the field, using two nails every 12" instead of one (Figure 5-3).

Hammer the nail firmly into the stud until it is forced slightly below the surface of the panel—this is called "dimpling." But don't drive it so deep that you break the paper. Be careful not to ding the edge of the panel when nailing or handling. Dings require extra mudding and finishing work. If you are using drywall screws, be sure to screw them to just below the surface of the panel.

Whether you are using drywall nails or screws, be careful not to break the paper when you are forcing the head below the surface. If the paper is broken, drive another nail or screw directly below to ensure a good hold. A special drywall hammer or a cordless electric drywall screw gun speeds the job and makes it easier.

Place nails in adjoining sheets directly across from each other where they meet at a stud. This makes mudding easier. If you miss the stud, pull out the nail or screw and dimple the hole so you can mud and tape over it properly.

In areas where the code allows it, drywall adhesive is an alternative to all these nail or screw holes. Apply the adhesive with a caulk gun onto the studs in a continuous ⅜" zigzag bead. A caulking gun attachment to an air compressor can make this method almost effortless. Follow the manufacturer's instructions when using adhesive. The adhesive minimizes the number of nail holes that need to be finished with mud and reduces nail pops. When using adhesive, however, at least one nail is needed in each corner to hold the panel in place.

When using adhesive, lay your stack of drywall panels over a stud so that the stud is in the center of the stack of panels, with the panels' back sides facing up. This creates a slight bow in the panel, which will force it into the stud and into the adhesive once the panel is applied.

As you apply the drywall, be careful not to leave a gap between boards greater than ¼", and less if possible. Larger gaps make taping more difficult. Before embedding the tape over a seam, fill this void with joint compound. Never jam the sections of drywall together; they should be lightly butted but never forced.

Step Three
Cutting Openings

Margin of Error: ¼"

Most Common Mistakes

☐ Dinging or damaging the edges of the panels.

☐ Joining pieces so that the seam occurs at the edge, not the center, of a window or door opening.

The easiest and most foolproof way to cut door and window openings in drywall is to cover a portion of the rough opening with a drywall panel, then cut along the edge of the opening with your drywall saw. By cutting out half of a doorway or window opening at a time, you will always have the framing visible as a reference.

Applying drywall around openings like doors and windows calls for a little extra care and very accurate cutting. Never try to fit around a large opening with just one panel. You'll end up with an unstable panel of thin "arms" that are likely to break off from the main piece. It's best to work with two L-shaped pieces of about the same size, with a joint that meets in the middle over the opening, as described earlier. (Figure 5-4)

Joints must always meet at a stud, and they should never occur at the edge of a door or window. The joint will even-

Figure 5-5. Snap the drywall at the cut line over the edge of your worktable.

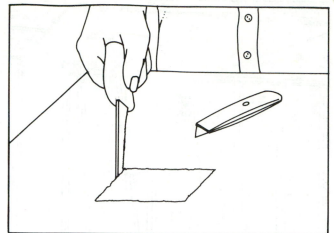

Figure 5-6. Use a drywall saw to cut out holes in your drywall.

tually crack from the stress of the movement of the door or window.

Be particularly careful not to damage the board when cutting a notch or corner. If your cuts are not clean and precise, the entire job will end up looking sloppy.

When applying drywall around right-angle openings, use a drywall T-square or a chalkline to mark the board for cutting. Cut the shorter length first with a drywall saw or keyhole saw. Then use a utility knife to score the longer cut. Use several light strokes of the knife to cut into the core. Position the cut over the edge of your worktable and snap the panel (Figure 5-5). Finish by cleanly undercutting the paper on the back side with the utility knife. Always cut with the tapered-edge side up, not the flat-edged side with the coarse paper.

Most stud walls are designed to allow for a ½" drywall ceiling, 8′ of drywall (two sheets horizontally or one sheet vertically), and a small gap above the floor. This gap keeps the drywall away from any moisture on the floor and compensates for any unevenness. The gap is hidden by the baseboard.

When cutting an opening to fit around a window, measure the opening carefully and mark it on the back of the panel, using a drywall square, a straightedge, or a chalkline. Raise the panel until it hits the ceiling, so that any gaps will fall at the floor where they will be covered by the baseboard. Cut the panel to fit the edge of the stud at the rough opening. Don't let the drywall overlap onto the jamb or into the rough opening.

For smaller openings like outlets, you can coat the rim of the opening with lipstick or colored chalk. Then fit the panel into place and apply hand pressure over the outlet area. The lipstick will transfer to the back of the panel for a cutting pattern. Cut this patch out with your drywall saw (Figure 5-6). When cutting from the back side of a panel, be careful not to tear the paper beyond the patch hole area.

Step Four
Angles and Ceilings

Margin of Error: ¼"

Most Common Mistakes

☐ Not putting up the ceiling drywall before doing the walls.

☐ Creating more seams than are necessary—for example, by using small scraps.

Cutting a complex piece of drywall is a precise job that can best be done with a paper or cardboard template. Tape the paper or cardboard over the space to be covered and mark the perimeter. Then use that template to transfer a precise pattern to the drywall. Your fit will be more exact, and your job will look more professional.

Ceilings and slanted walls, such as attic ceiling-walls, pose a serious problem in the form of gravity. More than one person is needed to support each drywall panel as it is secured in place. If an assistant is not available, you could use a 2x4 T instead. Actually, it is best to use both a brace and an assistant; as you know by now, drywall is heavy, cumbersome, and not easily aligned overhead by one person, even with the use of supports. Make a couple of supporting T's by cutting 2x4s to the height of your ceiling, less 2" to accommodate the crosspiece and the drywall thickness. Nail a 3′ section of 1x4 to the 2x4 as a brace (Figure 5-7). You can also rent a drywall jack to help you lift and hold the panels.

Drywall screws used with a screw gun (Figure 5-8) are generally more efficient and convenient than are nails for

Figure 5-7. You can make T's out of 2 x 4s to support ceiling drywall until it is nailed in place, although it is better to have an assistant as well.

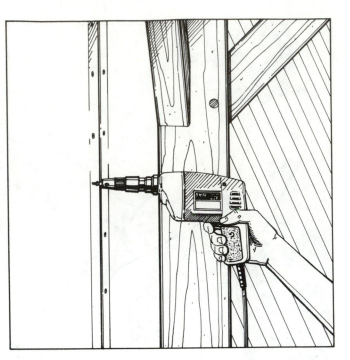

Figure 5-8. An electric screwdriver or drywall screw gun is quicker and easier than nailing.

attaching drywall, especially overhead. The pattern for fastening with screws is a maximum of 12" on center (o.c.) for ceilings and a maximum of 16" o.c. in walls with studs placed 16" o.c. When framing members are spaced 24" o.c., the pattern for using screws is a maximum of 12" o.c. for both ceilings and walls. Local codes may vary on this point, however, so be sure to determine what is acceptable before you begin.

Again, remember that ceiling pieces should always be installed before the wall boards, and the wall boards held tight against them to serve as added support for the ceiling drywall. Angled ceilings, however, may be installed after the walls.

Step Five
Curves and Odd Spaces

Margin of Error: 1/8" to exact

Most Common Mistakes

☐ Contaminating the compound with debris or dried chips of compound.

☐ Not completely covering the tape with compound.

☐ Creating more seams than are necessary—for example, by using small scraps.

As with angles, the easiest way to transfer the exact measurement from an odd-shaped space to the drywall is with a paper or cardboard template.

Tape or staple the paper to the studs and use a chalkline or pencil to mark the proper perimeter on the paper. Tape the

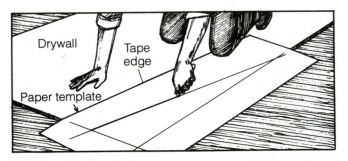

Figure 5-9. Use paper templates to cut odd-shaped pieces of drywall.

template to the drywall. Then cut right through both the pattern and the drywall (Figure 5-9).

Cut the template pieces slightly smaller than the actual space defined by the studs by cutting to the inside of the chalkline. As with other cuts of this type, use your utility knife to make the edge cuts, and a drywall or keyhole saw for the penetrations.

Fasten the drywall to the studs by the means you have chosen—nails, screws, or adhesive. With these pieces, tapered factory edges are not needed between adjoining pieces. Do smooth the cut edges for a more uniform joint, however.

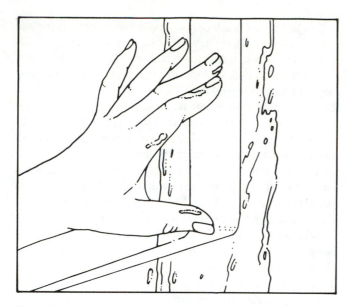

Figure 5-10. Paper tape is embedded into a layer of mud.

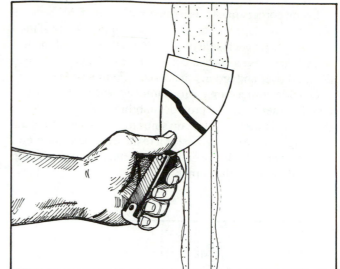

Figure 5-11. Use a 4" knife to apply a second layer of mud over the wet tape.

Step Six
Tape and Mud

Margin of Error: Exact

Most Common Mistakes

☐ Not sanding after applying each layer of drywall compound.

☐ Not sanding the final coat of drywall compound to a smooth finish.

Now is the time to muster all of your patience and diligence, because faulty workmanship will show in the taping and mudding.

Many home owners will choose to carry the project to this point, then call in a professional to finish with finesse. If you are one of the more confident, have faith that a little practice in a less noticeable area, such as inside a closet, can go a long way. If you're still not confident, select a textured application that will hide any flaws.

Materials

To achieve a smooth finish, all screw and nail heads must be covered with joint compound (mud) and the seams taped over. Joint compound has a drying time of 8 to 24 hours, depending on the thickness of application, temperature, and humidity. Allow longer for deeper cracks and crevices.

Cleanliness is very important to a smooth finish. Working from a mud tray keeps dried pieces and bits of debris out of the can. Keep the lid on the can airtight when you're not using it to keep it from drying out. Smooth the top of the mud flat and add a small amount of water before sealing the can if it is to be stored for some time.

Compound can be purchased in 1- or 5-gallon buckets, or in powdered form, which you mix yourself. Unless you are doing a very small job, the 5-gallon bucket is a much better buy. As you are using the mud, scrape the inside wall of the container often to keep residue from hardening and dropping pieces into the compound.

Drywall tape is available in paper tape and in fiberglass tape. Paper tape is precreased and can be used on straight seams as well as for corner taping. Self-adhesive fiberglass tape has the advantage of not needing a coating of mud underneath. This tape is recommended for the novice, except for use on the inside corners, where it is necessary to use the paper tape.

Application

Taping joints is a lengthy project, requiring three applications of mud to each joint. Begin by covering all nail dimples, applying the mud flush with the panel.

If you have chosen to use paper tape at the joints, apply the first layer of mud to the full length of the seam with a 4" mud knife. Apply enough mud to the seams for the drywall tape to adhere and to cover the entire seam. Then soak the paper tape in water for a moment.

Apply the wet tape to the joint (Figure 5-10), smoothing it with a 1½" putty knife. Embed the tape into the mud slightly with the knife. While the mud is still wet, apply a second layer to cover the tape completely, using a 4" taping knife (Figure 5-11). At the same time, draw your blade tightly over the surface to squeeze the mud out from underneath the tape so it is good and flat, being careful not to create any bubbles.

If you are using self-adhesive fiberglass, an undercoat of mud is not necessary. Simply apply the tape over the seam (Figure 5-12), then add a layer of mud over the tape, as shown in Figure 5-13.

Inside corners must be covered with paper tape, because the fiberglass tape will not fold. Again, apply a layer of mud first, covering each side of the corner, then embed the wet folded tape. Use a special corner knife to finish smoothing the mud over and around the corner (Figure 5-14).

Outside corners are easily damaged and require special metal corner beads to provide stability and to protect the drywall (Figure 5-15). Use tin snips to cut the bead to fit the full height of the corner. Fasten it to the framing with screws or nails every 6". Mud over it like any other seam, feathering the mud out from the corner.

Curved corner beads are now available for both inside and outside corners. These new types soften the edges and shadows, and are best suited to smooth wall applications.

Let the first coat of mud dry completely, usually overnight, before you apply the next. If you want to speed the process, a heater with a fan will cut down the drying time considerably. If the first coat is to dry overnight, clean your tools thoroughly and throw away any unused mud. You will need to make up a new batch for the second coat.

To prepare the wall before the second application, use a mud knife to scrape off any dried chips at the seams and nailhead areas. Then sand the first coat smooth with a drywall sander or a sanding block, using 100 grit sandpaper. A pole sander (Figure 5-16) is invaluable for this task. Sand only the mud—be careful not to scuff the surface of the drywall itself. When sanding drywall, always use a paper face mask to avoid inhaling the dust.

Instead of sanding, you can wipe the first coat down with a large wet sponge. Just be careful not to soak the paper or wash away the mud.

Thin the second coat of mud with a little water and apply it with a 6" mud knife. (Each coat you apply should be thinner than the last.) Again, let this coat dry properly, then scrape it and sand or sponge it smooth. Be sure to feather the edges of the layers of mud at the joints so that raised areas don't build up. After the second coat, the tape should not be visible under the mud.

Apply the third and final coat with a 10" mud knife for a smooth, even finish. When it is thoroughly dry, sand or sponge it smooth.

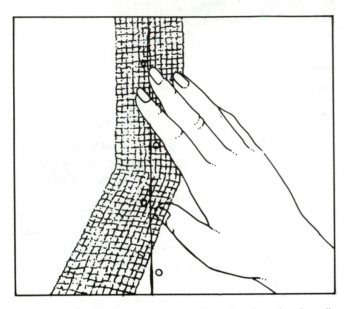

Figure 5-12. Self-adhesive tape is applied directly to the drywall.

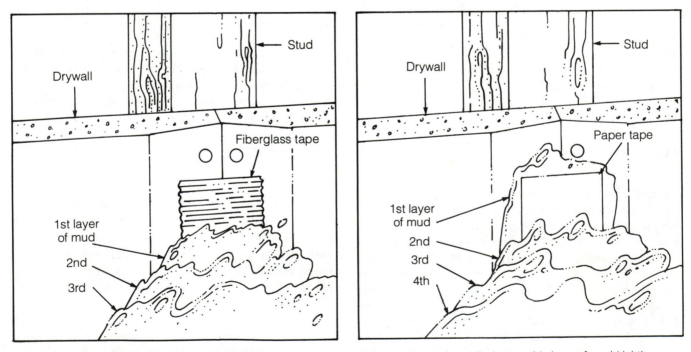

Figure 5-13. Self-adhesive fiber tape is applied directly to the drywall (left); paper tape is applied over a thin layer of mud (right). Note how the edges of the panel are tapered to avoid a bulge at the seam.

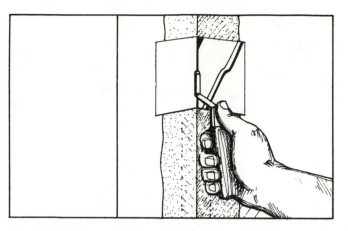

Figure 5-14. Use a special corner knife to smooth the mud over the tape in the inside corners.

If you have decided on a textured finish, only two coats of mud may be needed. Obviously, sanding and smoothing are not as critical as with a smooth wall finish.

Once the final coat has dried and been sanded, use a flashlight to check for blemishes. Hold the light at an angle so that any irregularities cast a shadow. A good smooth finish is essential before applying paint or wallpaper. Always do a final sanding or sponging just before painting or papering the new drywall.

You will need to seal the drywall with a primer-sealer undercoat before painting it. Many primer-sealers are also sizings, a prerequisite to wallpapering. An oil-based primer is recommended for bare drywall, but be sure to check with your dealer for special considerations with the wall covering you plan to use.

Repairs

Small dents and dings in drywall can usually be covered with an application of wallboard compound and smoothed with sandpaper.

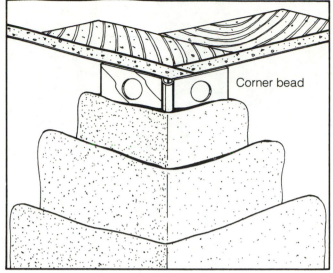

Figure 5-15. A metal corner bead protects outside corners from damage.

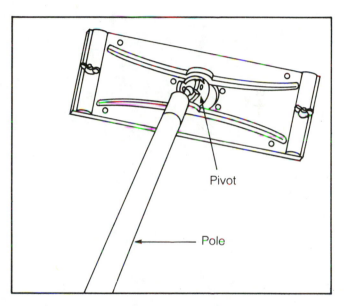

Figure 5-16. With a pole sander, you don't have to stand on a ladder to sand the ceiling and the upper part of the walls.

6 Wall Paneling

PANELING IS A dramatic and easy way to finish your walls. Paneling comes in two basic forms—solid-wood boards in various widths (many of which are tongue-and-groove) and wood-faced 4'x8' panels. In this chapter you will learn how to install both kinds of panels on several different surfaces, with special techniques to fit panels around openings and to custom-cut uneven intersections. You will also learn some shortcuts and useful tips on trimming your new walls, as well as how to construct shelves to complement them.

Before You Begin

SAFETY

Paneling your new walls is not a difficult task. However, it is always a good idea to develop safe work habits and stick to them.

- ☐ Use the appropriate tool for the job.
- ☐ Keep your blades sharp. A dull blade requires excessive force and can easily slip.
- ☐ Be sure that electric tools are properly grounded.
- ☐ Use proper precautions when using power tools.
- ☐ Wear safety glasses or goggles when hammering or sawing, especially if you wear contact lenses.
- ☐ Wear the proper respirator when using adhesives that emit toxic fumes.
- ☐ Wear rubber gloves when using solvents.
- ☐ Be careful to avoid unnecessary strain when lifting heavy panels.
- ☐ Some adhesives are highly flammable. Don't smoke, and extinguish pilot lights and open flames when working with adhesives.

USEFUL TERMS

Furring is strips of wood, usually 1x2 or 2x2, that are attached to masonry or uneven walls to create cavities in which to install insulation or to provide a suitable surface over which to apply paneling or drywall.

A **ramset** is an explosive-powder-activated nailgun.

Scribing is a method of using a compass to transfer the line of an uneven surface to a panel to be cut.

A **shim** is a small wooden wedge used to even out furring strips, or to hold panels in place while attaching them to the wall.

A **vapor barrier** is a sheet of material, usually 6 mil plastic, that is installed between insulation and paneling to prevent the buildup of moisture.

Wood-faced panels are 4'x8' sections of plywood, one side of which is laminated with hardwood veneer.

WHAT YOU WILL NEED

Time. The installation of paneling and trim over bare studs will take 2 to 4 person-hours per 100 square feet. If you must install furring first, allow 3 to 5 person-hours per 100 square feet. When using adhesives, allow 2 to 4 person hours per 100 square feet.

Tools. Paneling a new room can be a very satisfying project, resulting in a warm and inviting new living space. The process requires only tools that are usually found in any home toolbox.

If you are paneling over masonry, you may want to rent a ramset or nail gun, which will make the job of attaching the furring strips much easier. These guns use a .22-caliber powder cartridge to fire a nail into a concrete block or masonry. Though intimidating, they are safe when used properly. As an alternative, there are heavy-duty construction adhesives on the market that will adhere furring strips to masonry. Check with your home center or hardware store.

If you plan to use adhesive as your primary means of attachment, you will also need a caulking gun. You can save yourself time and effort by renting an air compressor with a caulking gun attachment. If you are not familiar with the use of pneumatic tools, read over the information in Chapter 1 before beginning work.

Tools for All Projects
Hammer
Tape measure
Electric drill with various drill bits
Nails
Chalkline
Level
Circular saw
Saber saw
Handsaw

Assorted screwdrivers

Carpenter's pencil

Tools for Paneling

Chalkline

Caulking gun or air compressor with caulking gun attachment

Nail gun or ramset

Compass

Finishing hammer

Finishing or plywood blades

Tools for Trim

Miter box with backsaw

Coping saw

Caulking gun

Tools for Shelves

Orbital sander

Clamps

Chisels and mallet

Materials. To determine the amount of sheet paneling you will need, multiply the length of your wall by its height and then divide by 32 (the area of a 4'x8' panel). For tongue-and-groove paneling, determine the area and consult with your dealer, as widths of this type of paneling vary. For molding, measure the linear feet. To avoid splicing short pieces, purchase extra lengths of paneling from which to cut.

Materials for All Projects

Shims

Screws

Nails

Adhesive

Materials for Wood-Faced Paneling

Wood-faced paneling

Color-coordinated paneling nails

Furring strips

Rigid foam insulation

Vapor barrier

Materials for Tongue-and-Groove Paneling

Tongue-and-groove planks

Adhesive

Color-coordinated paneling nails

Materials for Trim

Quarter-round molding

Caulk

Baseboard moldings

Finishing nails

Carpenter's wood glue

Materials for Shelves

1x2 board

1x4 board

Pole

Wood or plastic pole supports

Supporting pole bracket

Plywood

Quarter-round molding

Adhesive-backed mirror squares

Posts

Tracks and brackets

Shelf boards

Finishing screws

PERMITS AND CODES

In some areas, the installation of wall paneling is governed by local building codes. Contact your local building inspector before beginning work.

DESIGN

Paneling is a good choice of wall covering for casual playrooms or dens, and it can lend an air of elegance to a library or study. Use paneling to pull together spaces that are separate but adjoining, such as a family room/kitchen, or in rooms with cathedral ceilings that expose portions of upper hallways or other rooms. It is important to choose your paneling during the design stage for two reasons. First, it's easy to hide cuts around doors and windows under the trim; and second, the thickness that the paneling adds to the walls will require thicker door jambs.

Properly chosen, paneling and shelves can enhance a room and make it a warm, inviting place. Before you decide on a type of paneling, take the time to become familiar with the variety of colors and textures available and to consider your choice in the light of your particular needs. For example, a pastel panel may be well suited to a dark attic room, while a deeper wood tone will work better in a sunny family room.

The choice between sheet paneling and tongue-and-groove paneling is a matter of personal taste and expense. Solid wood tongue-and-groove is more expensive and more difficult to install. However, many people find the richness of the natural wood to be well worth the extra expense.

WOOD-FACED PANELING

Wood-faced panels, usually 4'x8' sheets with a thin veneer surface, are the most popular wall paneling material on the market. They come in many styles, patterns, and wood types.

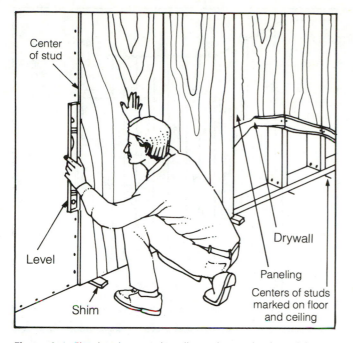

Figure 6-1. Check to be sure that all panels are plumb and that adjacent panels meet over the centers of studs.

Step One
Applying the Paneling

Margin of Error: 1/4" where covered by trim. Exact where exposed.

Most Common Mistakes

☐ Installing windows and door jambs before paneling.

☐ Not taking the time to plan carefully before purchasing the materials for your project.

☐ Failing to fasten the electrical boxes to the frame so that they are flush with the final paneled surface.

☐ Neglecting to furr out an existing wall, if necessary, before installing the paneling.

☐ Not adding insulation or a vapor barrier over an outside or basement wall, where appropriate.

☐ Splintering the veneer panel by cutting panels face up with a saber or circular saw.

☐ Failing to check that each panel is plumb on the wall before applying the next.

☐ Transferring measurements to the panel incorrectly or to the wrong side of the panel.

☐ Not using a finishing hammer and finishing saw blades when working with paneling.

Paneling Over Drywall

If you are starting with exposed stud walls, you will need to cover them with drywall before applying the wall paneling to provide adequate fire safety. Follow the instructions in Chapter 5, Drywall. Your mudding and taping can be rough,

because the drywall will be covered with paneling. However, you must cover the nail or screw heads and fill the joints as part of the flame barrier. Don't forget to get a drywall nailing inspection, if required, before you cover the fasteners.

Like drywall, plywood paneling comes in 4'x8' sheets, and you can special-order it in 4'x10' or 4'x12' sheets. The panels are usually installed vertically, and the edges always nail to a stud or plate. The standard 4'x8' sheet will fit flush against the ceiling of a common stud wall and leave a small gap at the bottom. This gap is hidden under the baseboard. Trim cuts for taller walls should be made at the bottom of the panel, not the top, so the baseboard will cover them. If you must cut the tops to accommodate a sloping ceiling, you can hide the cut edge with molding.

Once your drywall is in place, mark the stud centers on the floor and ceiling. To avoid marring the surfaces, make your marks on small pieces of tape. Begin applying your paneling in an inside corner. Start in the corner (you should have one per wall) where the full sheet of drywall was applied, and work out from there (Figure 6-1). Trim the corner edge so the uncut edge will be plumb and on a stud center when installed. A technique called **scribing** allows you to accommodate walls or ceilings that are not plumb and level, as well as other irregularities such as a fireplace or built-in furniture. For information on how to use this technique, see "Scribing," later in this chapter. When cut, the scribed contour will fit the irregular wall closely, and the uncut edge will still be plumb and centered on a stud.

After the first sheet of paneling is scribed, trimmed as necessary, and installed, the other sheets are applied in sequence to cover the rest of the wall. The last sheet will probably require trimming and/or scribing. Be sure you trim the corner edge and butt the factory edge in the field. For example, if the factory edge of the next-to-last sheet is 30" away from the corner at the bottom and 30 1/2" away at the top, both scribing and trimming will be required. If the wall is straight, this procedure is fairly simple; just trim the panel so it is just shy of 30" at the bottom and 30 1/2" at the top. If the wall is not straight, or if you are terminating the panel at a chimney or a piece of built-in furniture, careful scribing is necessary. In this case you may find it worth the effort to make a paper or cardboard template.

Manufactured paneling usually has flush or recessed lines, simulating separate boards. When the panels are installed vertically, two of these lines in the field and one on each side should line up with the stud center marks on the floor and ceiling. Nail in these darker lines, using nails with colored heads, typically every 8" in the field and 6" on the perimeter. If you are using hardwood plywood paneling, just countersink the finish nails and putty the holes before applying your finish. Thinner panels are more likely to reflect any unevenness in the wall than are thicker panels.

Figure 6-2. Use a ramset to attach 2x2 furring strips to concrete block or masonry walls.

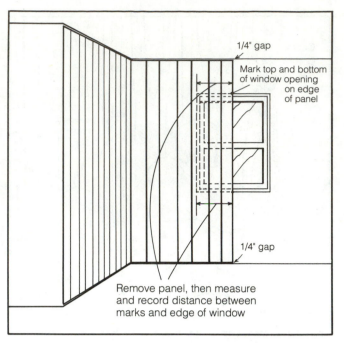

Figure 6-4. Measure paneling to fit around doors and windows.

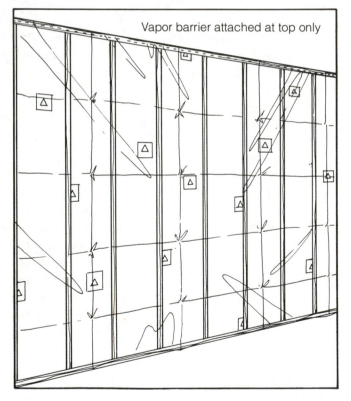

Figure 6-3. Rigid insulation and vapor barrier installed over an uninsulated wall.

Paneling Over Masonry Walls

Because a masonry surface is so hard to penetrate with paneling nails, and because the surface is often uneven, 2x2 furring strips must be attached to such walls (Figure 6-2). It's a good idea to use decay-resistant lumber here.

To attach the furring strips, use adhesive, special concrete shields and lag screws, or a ramset, which can be rented from your local building center. Wear safety glasses and ear protectors when using a ramset, and be sure to use the right size nails and "bullets." Never use a ramset on hollow concrete blocks. Instead, drive the fasteners into the mortar at the joints.

Install horizontal strips at the top and bottom of the wall and vertical strips 16" on center, simulating a stud wall. Use a level on the furring strips and even out the irregularities in the masonry with shims to get the furring surfaces level and even with each other. You are building a sturdy wooden structure that will hold the paneling solidly. If you are working on an uninsulated exterior wall, you should cut rigid foam-core insulation to friction-fit in the spaces between the furring strips. Measure the space between each furring strip separately, at both top and bottom, before you cut the insulation to fit. For full information about installing insulation, see Chapter 4.

Next, add a vapor barrier of 6 mil visqine (a painter's plastic drop cloth) to prevent the buildup of moisture between the insulation and the new paneling. Attach the vapor barrier only at the top (Figure 6-3); gravity and the paneling will keep it in place without puncturing it in too many places. If too many holes are punched in the plastic, its ability to keep moisture out will be destroyed. Now you can attach your paneling over the vapor barrier with nails. Adhesive cannot be used in this situation. Insulated walls that already have a vapor barrier do not require one directly behind the paneling.

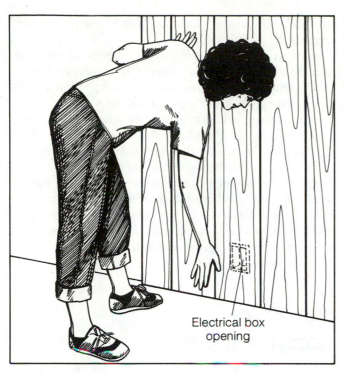

Figure 6-5. Outline edge of electrical box opening with lipstick or colored chalk. Whack the paneling over the box to imprint the outline on the back of the paneling.

Step Two
Fitting Panels
Around Openings

Margin of Error: ¼" where covered by trim. Exact where exposed.

Most Common Mistakes

☐ Cutting window, door, and electrical openings too large.

☐ Failing to complete all electrical wiring and plumbing before installing the paneling.

The easiest way to get an accurate door or window opening measurement is to have one person hold the sheet of paneling in place over the opening while another traces the line of the opening on the back of the panel. This works best for doors. If you are unable to get to the back of the panel, you will need to measure, as described next.

Place the panel in position over the window, butting it tightly up against the previously installed panel. Be sure that the ¼" gap between the floor and the panel is maintained with shims, and use a level to check that the panel is plumb. Mark the edge of the panel to indicate the top and bottom of the window or opening. Remove the panel, then measure and record the distance from each mark to the side of the window (Figure 6-4). Transfer these measurements to the back of the panel, and use a straightedge to connect the points.

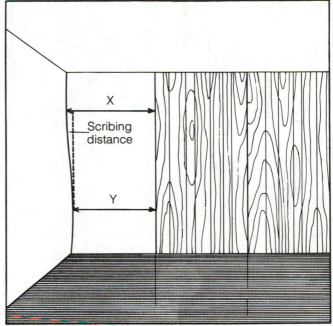

Figure 6-6. Overlap the paneling by the scribing distance. (X - Y = scribing distance.)

For smaller openings like electrical outlets, outline the edge of the outlet with chalk or lipstick. Then position the panel over it (Figure 6-5). Give the panel a whack over the opening so that the imprint appears clearly on the back of the panel. Then make your pencil lines and cut from the back of the panel to avoid splintering the veneer with your circular saw.

Scribing

Now and then a panel must butt up against an irregular surface, such as a fireplace. In these situations, you will find scribing to be the easiest and most effective way of fitting the panel tightly in place.

Begin by measuring from the edge of the last full sheet to the farthest point of the irregularity. Make a note of that distance, and then cut your panel to that width. Next, measure the distance from the edge of the last full sheet of paneling to the nearest point of the irregularity. Make a note of that distance. Subtract the second measurement from the first to get the "scribing distance." Then position the panel you need to trim and fit so that it overlaps the last full sheet of paneling by the scribing distance (Figure 6-6). Use your level to position it plumb and tack it temporarily in place.

Set a compass to the scribing distance. Hold the compass with the tip and the pencil horizontal and ride the tip along the irregular surface while the pencil runs along the panel you wish to trim (Figure 6-7). Trace the irregular line carefully from the top of the panel to the bottom. The result will be a line on the panel that is the exact profile of the irregularity. Cut along this line with a jigsaw and smooth the cut edge with a rasp or sanding block. Now glue or nail the panel

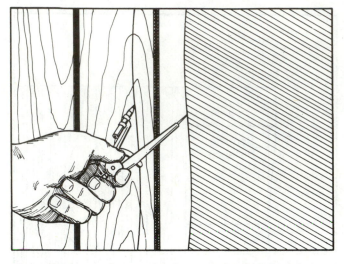

Figure 6-7. Use a compass to scribe a panel to fit an irregular corner.

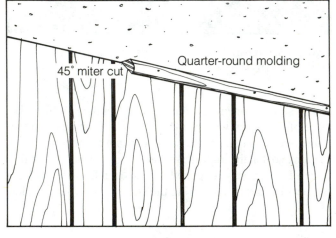

Figure 6-8. Install quarter-round molding where ceiling meets wall.

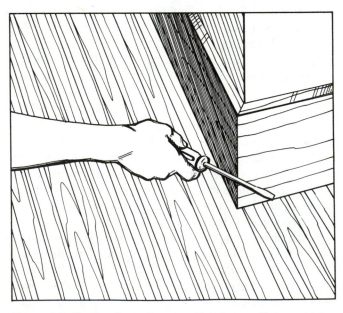

Figure 6-9. Use the shank of a screwdriver to smooth the outside edge of the baseboard.

into place. (A contour gauge can also be used to transfer complex details accurately.)

If you are starting at a corner that is irregular, measure out from the corner 48" or to the center of the farthest stud *under* 48". Snap a plumb chalkline down the center of the stud to establish the position of the edge of the panel. Mark the center on the ceiling and floor for a nailing reference. (Use tape to avoid marring the finished surface.) Place the panel as snug into the corner as possible, using a level on the opposite vertical edge to plumb the panel. Temporarily tack the panel in place at the top and bottom. Remove the panel, then measure from the panel edge to the center line of the stud marked on the floor to determine your scribing distance. This measurement should be the same at the ceiling and at the floor. Scribe and cut with a jigsaw, smooth the cut edge, and install the panel as described above.

Step Three
Applying the Trim

Margin of Error: Exact

Most Common Mistake

☐ Leaving a gap of more than ¼" at the corners.

Trim comes in a huge variety of styles and many materials, including wood, metal, and plastic. Trim is used to cover gaps at inside corners, floor and ceiling joints, and around door and window openings. Trim is the key to an attractive, professional-looking job. And with trim you cover any minor mistakes you may have made in cutting and installing your paneling.

Floor and Ceiling Joints

The basic trim piece for a floor-to-wall or ceiling-to-wall connection is quarter-round molding or baseboard (Figure 6-8). It offers a clean, neat appearance and is easy to install. Simply nail it in place with finishing nails, countersink the nails, fill the holes with matching wood putty, and sand smooth. Or use color-coordinated paneling nails.

Outside Corners

Place your paneling so that the edges meet as tightly as possible at an outside corner. If the intersection of the two pieces is neat enough, it can be left uncovered. Special outside corner molding can also be applied.

Inside Corners

If your walls are straight enough, and your paneling job neat enough, you can sometimes run one sheet tightly into the corner and butt the mate right up to it for a snug fit and a good-looking job. If this is not the case, however, quarter-round molding will work nicely.

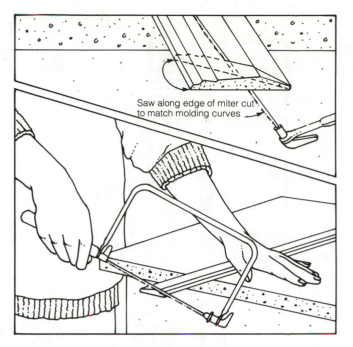

Figure 6-10. Use a coping saw to cut quarter-round molding.

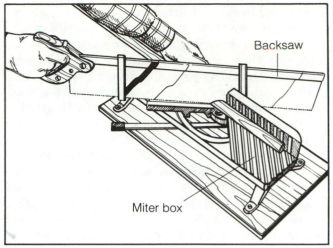

Figure 6-11. Use a miter box and a backsaw to cut the ends of quarter-round molding at a 45-degree angle.

Outside Baseboard Corners

These pieces should first be cut to a 45-degree angle with your miter box and back saw. Nail them into place so they are snug. Then run the round part of your hammer handle or screwdriver shank tightly up the joint to seal any gap that may be left (Figure 6-9).

Inside Baseboard Corners

These corners can be tricky when you are using the types of baseboards that have curves and shapes to them. If you use a miter cut here, the nails will pull the intersecting pieces away from each other, creating a gap. If you are painting, this crack can be filled with caulk and painted over. If you prefer the appearance of the natural wood trim, a process called "coping" will give you a beautifully fitted corner every time.

Begin by butting the first piece of molding up to the wall and nailing it in. Place the second piece of molding in your miter box for a 45-degree cut with the inside wood grain showing on the front of the molding. Then use a coping saw at a 90-degree angle to cut away the wedged portion of the molding, following the outside line exactly (Figure 6-10). This method transfers the perfect profile to the molding, which will fit snugly over the mate at the wall.

Joints Along the Length of the Baseboard

These joints can be ugly and tend to pull apart if they are merely butted up against each other. To avoid these unsightly gaps, miter cut the ends at a 45-degree angle (Figure 6-11) so that the two pieces of molding overlap each other. To keep the joint tight in case the molding shrinks, apply some glue at the miter joint between the two pieces. Allow

the glue to ooze out of the joint and get tacky. Then lightly sand the joint; the glue will mix with the sawdust and conceal the joint.

TONGUE-AND-GROOVE PANELING

Paneling with solid wood tongue-and-groove boards is more difficult than with hardboard panels, but their weight and stiffness mean they require less support. They also offer a real wood appearance. Either special boards for paneling or tongue-and-groove hardwood flooring can be used.

Step One
Applying the Boards

Margin of Error: Exact

Most Common Mistakes

☐ Not adding insulation or a vapor barrier over an outside or basement wall, where appropriate.

☐ Splintering boards by cutting them face up with a saber or circular saw.

☐ Neglecting to check that each piece is plumb on the wall before applying the next.

☐ Transferring measurements to the board incorrectly or to the wrong side.

If you want to install the boards vertically, you need to put up horizontal furring strips so that the boards have something to hold onto. Use adhesive or nails to attach the furring strips horizontally across the studs or masonry wall every 24" to create a solid backing.

If you choose to install this type of paneling horizontally or on the diagonal, furring is not necessary if your drywall is in good shape. Always start the boards in a corner with the groove edge facing the direction in which you are paneling. (The tongue edge of the first board should be in the corner.) The boards can be glued or nailed to the walls, or both glued and nailed. The easiest method is to use a paneling adhesive and toothed trowel, or a paneling adhesive applied with a caulking gun. Follow the adhesive instructions for application. If you are using the cartridge method to apply the adhesive, an air compressor with a caulking gun attachment will save you a great deal of time and effort.

For vertical paneling, apply the boards in a stairstep pattern, being sure that each one is plumb. All butt joints should occur on a furring strip. Use a small piece of paneling board as a pounding board to force two adjacent pieces together. The last piece, next to the intersecting wall, should be cut to size and its tongue slipped into the groove of the adjacent board. It should snap right into place. You may need to make a scribe cut, as explained earlier. However, corner trim often eliminates the need for scribing.

Step Two
Fitting Boards
Around Openings

To panel around large openings, first apply full-size boards as close to door and window jambs as possible. Then measure the distance from the edge of the last board to the edge of the opening. (You will need to notch some boards, and cut others to specific length, above doors and windows and below windows.) Then transfer your measurements very carefully to your board, and just as carefully make your cuts. If you are notching, cut only to within ¼" of the intersection of two cuts with your circular saw. Then finish the cut with a handsaw if the board must butt up against existing trim, since the trim will not cover the cut. Otherwise, use a circular saw with the board face down so the circular blade doesn't cause the board to splinter. This step takes patience and care because you are working with such narrow pieces. Each board must be measured and trimmed separately. To apply trim, see Step Three under Wood-Faced Paneling.

SHELVES

The shelves described here can be applied to both wood-faced and tongue-and-groove wall paneling. Properly planned shelves will enhance the appearance of your new walls, as well as providing you with storage space.

Design

To minimize design and fitting problems, use graph paper to draw plans of your proposed shelves. Take into account the visual effect you want from your shelves, what they will hold, and the structural elements needed. Your plan will be

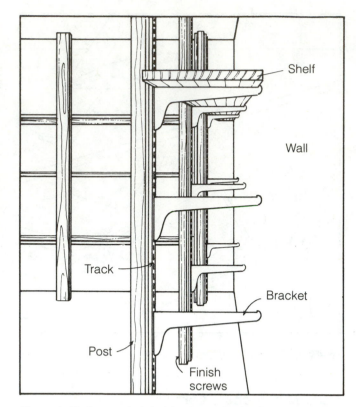

Figure 6-12. Suspended shelving is attached to floor-to-ceiling posts.

helpful in making a materials list. Be sure that you have all necessary materials on hand before you begin building.

Suspended Shelves

Probably the most common shelves are those in which metal tracks are attached to a wall for hanging movable metal brackets. Wood or plastic shelves rest on the brackets. These shelves are very simple to construct. The main installation concern is that the tracks must be attached to the studs behind the wall.

There are several ways to find the studs in a finished wall. Studs are usually located every 16" or 24" on center. Tap along the wall with a hammer until you hear a solid sound; look for seams in the drywall; or use a magnetic stud finder to locate the nails in the studs. Mark the position of the stud on floor and ceiling and snap a chalkline to mark the center of the stud on the wall.

If you don't want to detract from the visual effect of your paneling, or you want more wood and less metal to show, suspended shelves are an attractive alternative to mounting conventional shelving brackets directly to the wall.

Create front supports for the shelves with posts running from floor to ceiling. Space them out from the wall to the depth you want your shelves to be (Figure 6-12). Attach the supports to the floor by drilling holes at the base and securing them with finishing screws. With these supports you can still use the inexpensive track-and-bracket construction. Attach the shelving brackets to the insides of the posts, facing the wall. This hides the tracks and minimizes the amount of metal that is visible.

Closet Shelves

Before building your closet shelves from scratch, you may wish to investigate the many ready-to-assemble closet storage systems that are now available.

To build closet shelves, attach 1x4 ledger boards to the closet wall at the height and length you wish your shelf to be. These ledgers should be level and attached directly to the wall studs for maximum support. The shelf board will rest on the lip of the ledger.

To install a clothes-hanging pole, you will need plastic or wood pole supports that screw into the frame or ledger at ei-ther end of the closet. If the pole is over 5′ long, add a supporting pole bracket in the middle, attached to the ledger.

Recessed Shelves

Many rooms have recessed cubbyhole walls or even closets that will accept shelving. It is a simple matter to measure and cut boards to fit vertically on either side of the alcove. Inexpensive hardware tracks can then be screwed plumb into the boards and adjustable clips installed in the tracks for multi-position shelving.

First measure and cut the shelving from plywood or 1″ stock. Then face the plywood with a 1x2 to cover up the rough edges. If you are using wood boards, sand the shelves with an orbital sander for a fine finish, then paint or stain them as desired.

7 Ceilings

BECAUSE CEILINGS are more "out of the way" than other parts of the interior of the home, such as walls and floors, their impact on the general feel or mood of a house is often underestimated. The floor and ceiling are the largest surfaces in any room, and different ceiling heights, materials, colors, slopes, and angles have a definite effect on the way a room feels to its occupants.

In addition to being an important design feature, ceilings hide the framing of the floor or roof above, plumbing pipes, ductwork, electrical wire, insulation, and so on. Suspended ceilings (ceilings that are hung a set distance from the ceiling joists) work very well for this kind of cover-up because they create a cavity that allows easy access for repairs or further work.

In the past, the most common types of ceilings were lath and plaster, and wood planks. Metal ceilings were also popular because of their light weight and ease of installation. In the past few decades drywall has replaced lath and plaster as a wall and ceiling material, largely because of the ability of drywall to slow the spread of flame. The techniques of working with drywall are presented in Chapter 5. This chapter describes the installation of acoustical ceilings and suspended ceilings.

Before You Begin

SAFETY

☐ Always use the appropriate tool for the job.

☐ Wear the proper dust mask or respirator when sanding or sawing.

☐ Wear safety glasses or goggles whenever you are using power tools, or when hammering overhead, especially if you wear contact lenses.

☐ Watch power cord placement so that it does not interfere with the operation of the tool.

☐ Keep blades sharp. A dull blade requires excessive force and can easily slip.

☐ When using a stepladder, have both pairs of legs fully open and the spread bars locked in place. Never climb higher than the second step from the top. When bracing a ladder against the wall, a safe distance between the feet and the wall is one quarter of the height of the ladder. Do not use an aluminum ladder when working near electrical wires. Consider using scaffolding.

USEFUL TERMS

An **acoustic ceiling** has tiny noise-trapping holes to improve the quality of sound in a room.

Ceiling joists are the horizontal framing elements that support the ceiling drywall.

Ceiling tiles are 12"-square tongue-and-groove tiles that are attached to wood or metal furring strips or tracks.

Cross tees are the elements of a gridwork that connect at right angles to runners.

Furring strips are strips of metal or wood attached directly to an old ceiling (perpendicular to the ceiling joists), onto which ceiling tiles are clipped or stapled.

The **runners** form the main support grid for suspended ceilings. They are installed perpendicular to the joists.

A **suspended ceiling** is a ceiling hung from the original ceiling or from the joists by a grid system, often used to hide exposed joists, rafters, and ductwork.

Tegular panels are two-level panels in which the face is lower than the flange, which rests on the grid.

Tracks are metal furring strips that support the ceiling tiles.

A **valance** is a canopy or covering above a window that creates a decorative effect.

WHAT YOU WILL NEED

Time. Installing either a tile ceiling or a suspended ceiling in a 9'x12' room will require 14 to 20 person-hours, longer if unusual situations are encountered. This job is best undertaken by two people.

Tools and Materials. Suspended ceilings are often hung from the ceiling joists with a metal grid. This creates the cavity between the joists and the ceiling where pipes, wires, and ductwork can be installed and worked on. A tile ceiling is glued directly to a drywall ceiling or onto furring strips that are glued or nailed to the ceiling joists. This type of ceiling works well where height is a consideration and a suspended ceiling would drop too low.

A suspended ceiling isn't hard to install and requires no unusual tools. However, the metal gridwork, especially the 12' runners, requires two people for installation.

Tile ceilings are even easier to install than suspended ceilings. Wood furring strips are nailed to the old ceiling or to the ceiling joists and the new tiles are stapled to these strips. An even simpler system uses 4' metal tracks instead of long furring strips. Instead of staples, clips snap onto the tracks to lock the tiles in place. Everything you need for this method of installation comes in one kit.

Tools for Suspended or Tile Ceilings

20' to 25' metal tape

Straightedge

Framing or combination square

2' to 4' level

Utility knife

Ladder

Hammer

Chalkline

Pencil

String

Putty knife

Nails

Drywall pan

Handsaw

Nail belt

Face mask

Safety goggles

Drill

Miter box

Coping saw

Additional Tools for Suspended Ceilings

Pliers

Aviation snips

Additional Tools for Tile Ceilings

Fine-toothed hacksaw

Screwdriver

Materials for Suspended Ceilings

Eyehooks

Hanger wire

Wall molding

Molding nails

Runners

Cross tees

Panels

Lighting fixtures

Materials for Tile Ceilings

Furring strips

Adhesive

Shims

Tiles

PERMITS AND CODES

Check with your building department to find out about necessary permits.

DESIGN

Ceilings can do many things besides looking nice and hiding structural elements. They can also muffle noise, support lights, and retard flames. An acoustical ceiling with tiny noise-trapping holes or fissures is a wise choice for noisy rooms like entertainment centers.

If you want to put lights in your new ceiling and to be able to relocate them easily, a suspended ceiling is your best bet. You can buy fluorescent fixtures that fit into the grid system in place of a standard-size ceiling panel.

The acoustical ceiling uses space-age technology to create a ceiling that is both lightweight and durable, in addition to absorbing sound. These ceilings come in many different styles, sizes, and colors. You can get tiles or larger panels that look like marble, oak, and other natural materials, with the designs authentically hued, shaded, veined, and striated. If you prefer traditional white, pattern choices include reproductions of bleached wood, sculptured plaster, and rough-troweled stucco.

Most Common Mistakes

☐ Not planning the ceiling layout on paper before beginning work.

☐ Not checking local code for minimum ceiling height and clearance.

☐ Failing to plan grids to avoid running into columns or posts.

☐ Measuring the ceiling height line on the wall from a sloping floor, which creates a sloping ceiling.

☐ Failing to lay out runners so that border tiles will be more than half a tile.

☐ Not installing the runners level.

☐ Soiling the tiles during installation.

☐ Neglecting to have the rough electrical work inspected before installing a suspended ceiling.

☐ Failing to correct any leaks in the roof before installing the ceiling.

☐ Applying loose-filled or roll insulation directly above the ceiling panels rather than in ceiling joist cavities.

THE SUSPENDED CEILING

A suspended ceiling is used where enough height is available to hang it from the ceiling joists and still have enough height between the floor and the new ceiling. A minimum of 7'6" is usually required. The advantage of a suspended ceiling over a tile ceiling is that it allows easy access to pipes, wires, and ductwork. This is very useful if you need to repair or add on to any of these systems. It is also useful in rooms where you want to reduce the ceiling height, either for es-

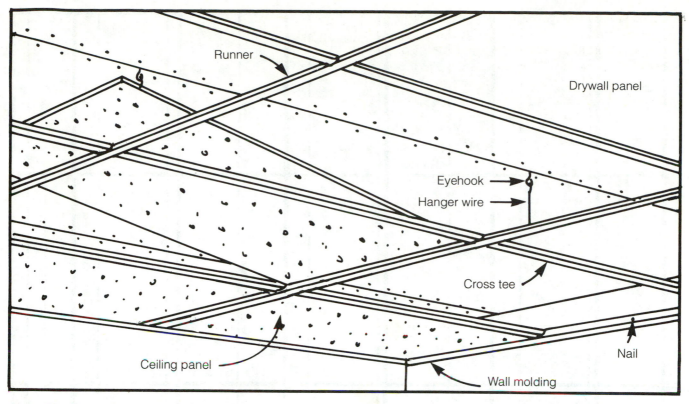

Figure 7-1. The anatomy of a typical suspended ceiling.

thetic reasons or to save energy in rooms where high ceilings allow hot air to gather at the top.

Suspended ceiling systems vary from manufacturer to manufacturer, but the installation techniques are similar. The typical suspended ceiling is formed of a grid and panels. A few simple pieces hook together to form the grid, and the panels are placed in the cells of the grid. The angle molding or wall molding is attached to the wall and supports the runners, which run the long way in the room. These runners are also supported by wires that are attached to the ceiling joists by eyehooks. Cross tees, running perpendicular to the runners, hold the runners together and create spaces or cells into which the panels are inserted. The panels are usually 2′x2′ squares or 2′x4′ rectangles. Figure 7-1 shows how the entire system goes together.

Here are a few important things to remember about how the grid goes together.

1. The runners, not the cross tees, run perpendicular to the ceiling joists.

2. The runners are hung from the joists with wire and eyehooks.

3. The cross tees run parallel with the joists and perpendicular to the runners.

4. The wires supporting the runners are often at an angle, since the holes in the runners into which the wires are threaded occur periodically and are not always directly below the wire.

5. Because the wires are often at an angle, each wire must be bent individually around a reference string to be sure their

bends all occur at the same level. Communities in areas of seismic activity often require diagonal braces, also made of wire, to inhibit movement in these ceilings.

6. The slots in the runners, into which the cross tees interlock, occur at intervals along the runners. These slots must all line up perfectly in the rows of runners so that all of the cross tees will be on line and perpendicular to the runners. To achieve this, you will need to cut the first runner installed in each row to be sure the cross tee slots in each row of runners are aligned.

Step One
Planning Your Ceiling

Margin of Error: Not applicable

Careful planning is essential for a successful ceiling installation. Neglecting or shortchanging this step will cause you great frustration later in the project. Plan well, and the rest of the job will go easily. This section outlines the important issues in planning and ceiling installation.

Border Tiles

Border tiles are the tiles that run next to the walls. Because room dimensions are rarely multiples of exactly 2′ or 4′, these tiles must usually be cut to fit. For appearance' sake, you want the border tiles on opposite sides of the room to be equal and all border tiles to be more than half a tile. You will

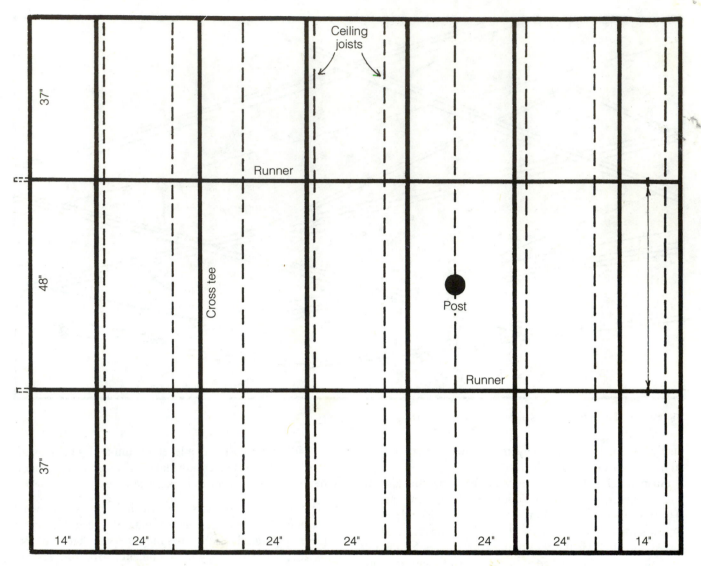

Figure 7-2. A typical sketch for a grid layout.

need to place the cross tees and runners in such a way that you can accomplish this goal.

Using graph paper, make a diagram of where all your runners and cross tees will go. First you must determine the size of all border tiles so that they are more than half a tile and equal in size. To do this, convert the length of the room's short wall into inches. If you are using 2′x4′ panels, divide this measurement by 48 (inches) if the panel length is to run parallel to the short wall. If you are using 2′x2′ panels, or if the panel length will run parallel to the long wall, divide by 24″. Take the remainder (in inches) of this division and add 48″ if the panel length will run parallel to the short wall or if you are using 2′x4′ panels. Add 24″ if the panel length will run parallel to the long wall or if you are using 2′x2′ panels. Half of this final figure equals the border dimensions at each side of the room.

Here's an example. For a room that is 10′2″ wide with the panel length running parallel to the short wall and using 2′x4′ panels:

1. Convert 10′2″ to inches (10′2″ = 122″).

2. Divide 122″ by 4′ = two full panel lengths and a remainder of 26″.

3. Add 48″ to 26″ = 74″; then divide by 2 = 37″.

Thus the border panels at each side will be 37″. There will be one full-size panel and two 37″ border panels (37+48+37 = 122). This dimension of 37″ also equals the distance of the first runner from the sidewall.

Repeat these calculations using the length of the room to find the end border panel size. In our example, the length of the room is 12′4″, or 148″.

Laying Out the Grid

Now that you have determined the size of the border tiles, you can draw a full grid on the graph paper, as shown in Figure 7-2. Indicate the runners on your graph paper by drawing the first and last runners at a distance of one border tile from the sidewalls and perpendicular to the ceiling joists. Add the in-between runners at intervals of 4'. Using a different color pencil, mark the cross tees on the layout sheet. Start at the border tile distance from the end walls (14" in our example); then add the in-between cross tees every 2'. If you are using 2'x2' panels, additional cross tees will be needed, locking into the perpendicular cross tees halfway between the runners.

Columns or Posts. You should take into account any columns or posts in the room that support the floor above. This is a common situation in basements. The grid must be planned so that *no* runners or cross tees run into a column or post. If this does happen, you will need to make slight adjustments, lengthwise or crosswise or both, so that the column falls in the open area of the grid. This adjustment may require unequal border tiles.

Light Fixtures. The location of light fixtures will not require any changes in your grid, but they should be marked on your sketch or grid plan. Remember to do all your rough wiring before installing the grid. Then cut out for the fixtures as you place the ceiling tile.

Estimating the Materials

Wall moldings are available in 10' lengths that are butted together. Measure the perimeter of the room and divide by 10 to find the number of wall molding pieces you will need.

Runners are available in 12' lengths. Tabs at each end of the runners make it possible to join them for lengths longer than 12'. However, no more than two sections can be cut from each 12' length of runner.

Cross tees come in 2' and 4' lengths with connecting tabs at each end. These connecting tabs are inserted into indentations or slots that occur at intervals in the runners and cross tees.

Wire fasteners or eyehooks are necessary at each support point to attach the hanger wire to the ceiling joist.

Hanger wire of 12 to 16 gauge is needed to hang the runners every 4'. The wire should be 6" longer than the distance between the eyehook and the ceiling.

Your graph paper layout will tell you how many ceiling tiles you need to buy. Don't forget to allow for waste on the cut border tiles. Also purchase any lighting fixtures now.

Step Two
Establishing Level Lines and Installing the Wall Molding

Margin of Error: 1/4"

The following installation method may vary from manufacturer to manufacturer, but most methods are similar. Also, the method is usually the same whether you are installing 2'x2' panels or 2'x4' panels.

The first thing to do is to establish level lines on the wall at the height of the new ceiling. Remember that the code may

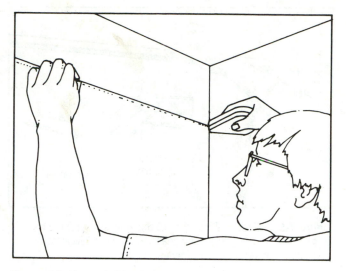

Figure 7-3. Use a chalkline to snap level lines for wall molding.

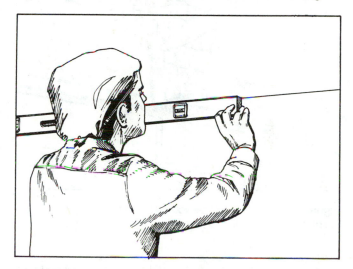

Figure 7-4. Use an 8' level to mark the placement of the wall molding.

require a minimum floor-to-ceiling height, usually 7'6". Try to leave as large a cavity as possible, a minimum of 2" if no lighting fixtures are involved.

Marking the level lines can be simple if your floor is level. In this case, all you need to do is measure up in each corner the height of the ceiling to be installed (in our example, 8'), mark the walls at this point, and snap chalklines connecting these points (Figure 7-3). You now have a level line running around the wall at ceiling height. You will nail your wall molding at this level.

However, if you use this method with a sloping floor, your ceiling will slope to match the floor. If the floor is off level to any great degree (1/4" or more), you will need to determine the difference at each corner and adjust your measurements accordingly. Use an 8' level to determine the dip or rise of your floor. Or you can measure down from the ceiling or joists above, if they are level. You can also simply use an 8' level to draw a level line on all the walls, starting from any point (Figure 7-4).

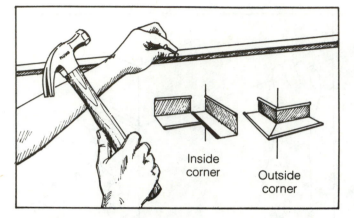

Figure 7-5. Nail the wall molding to the wall, lining up the top edge of the molding with your chalkline. Butt the inside corners and miter cut the outside corners.

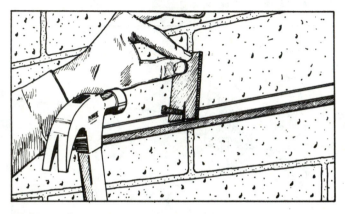

Figure 7-6. Use a scrap of cardboard to hold masonry nails being driven between mortar joints and the edge of the block.

Next you will need to prepunch holes in the wall molding to correspond to the wall studs. You can locate these studs by tapping along the wall with a hammer until you hear a solid sound; look for seams in the drywall; or use a magnetic stud finder to locate the nails in the studs.

Nail the wall molding to the wall around the entire perimeter of the room, lining up the top edge of the molding with your chalkline (Figure 7-5). Butt the molding at the inside corners and miter cut it at the outside corners. If you are fastening the molding to a concrete block wall, use short masonry nails and direct the nail between the mortar joints and the edge of the block. Use a piece of scrap cardboard with a notch cut in it to hold the nail before driving it in (Figure 7-6). If the wall is solid concrete or otherwise unable to accommodate wall molding, hang a section of runner directly next to the wall as a substitute.

Step Three
Snapping Chalklines
for the Runners

Margin of Error: 1/4"

Now you are ready to snap chalklines across the bottom of the ceiling joists to mark where the runners will be. The object of this runner layout is to be certain that no border tile is less than half a tile (24" with 4' tiles). This process was explained in Step One, Planning Your Ceiling. Using your tape measure, snap chalklines perpendicular to the joists. In the example given in Step One, these lines are 37" from either wall, leaving a 48" space in the middle (see Figure 7-2).

Step Four
Installing the Wire Fasteners
and Hanger Wire

Margin of Error: 1/4"

Now you are ready to attach the wire fasteners (eyehooks) and hanger wire that will support the runners. Screw the eyehooks into the ceiling joists where the joists intersect the runner chalklines. Your eyehooks can be placed at 4' intervals; you do not need a fastener at every intersection. Then thread your wire through the eyehooks and wrap it securely around itself three times. The wire should be long enough to extend at least 6" below the level of the new ceiling. Add extra hangers and wire at light fixtures, one for each corner or as instructed by the manufacturer.

Step Five
Stretching Your First
Reference Strings

Margin of Error: Exact

Now you need to stretch some reference strings, which must run exactly at the level of the bottom of the wall moldings. These strings show you precisely where the runners and cross tees will be and serve as guides for cutting the runners and cross tees.

To stretch these strings, choose the corner of the room where you plan to start your installation. As shown in Figure 7-7, you will stretch only two strings: string AB, which will be the border tile distance from one wall (14" in our example); and string CD, which will be the border tile distance from the other wall (37" in our example). Be sure the strings are at the bottom of the wall molding so they will be out of the way while you install the grid. Check your strings with a framing square to be sure they are square. Adjust them until they are square, even if it means that the border tiles must be irregular.

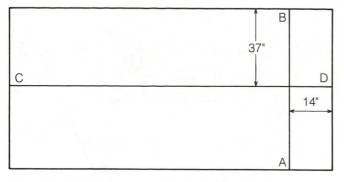

Figure 7-7. Stretch reference strings AB and CD in place at the border tile distances from the walls.

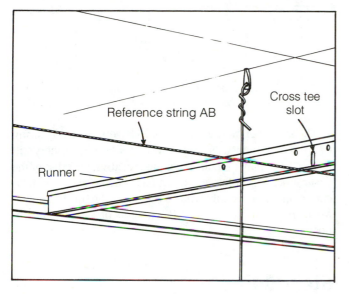

Figure 7-8. Reference string AB aligned with cross tee slots.

Step Six
Measuring and Cutting the Runners and Stretching New Reference Strings

Margin of Error: ⅛"

You are now ready to install the runners. The most important thing to remember is that the runners have to be cut and installed in such a way that the cross tee slots in the runners occur exactly where each cross tee is planned to intersect the runners. The cross tees occur at line AB and then every 24" from line AB (Figure 7-8). You will need to cut the runners' length so that a slot appears exactly along line AB. Slots will automatically be aligned every 24" from there, since they are spaced on the runners every 24". Measure and cut each runner so that the slots are aligned with line AB. Measure each runner; do not use the first runner as a pattern for the rest.

Now hold the cut runner at the level of the strings and next to string CD (Figure 7-9). Locate the wire support hole

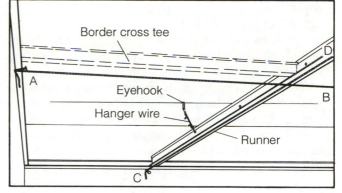
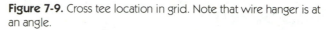

Figure 7-9. Cross tee location in grid. Note that wire hanger is at an angle.

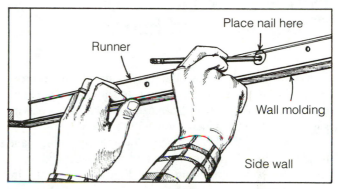

Figure 7-10. Mark location of first wire hanger hole on wall. Drive nail at this point.

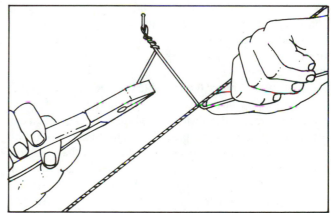

Figure 7-11. Bend wire at right angle around reference string.

(holes on tops of runners that hanging wires are attached to) that is closest to the first wire hanger from this wall. Circle this hole on the runner.

Carry this runner to the long side wall and rest it on the wall molding with the cut end butted against the short end wall. Mark the wall with a pencil or felt-tip pen through the circled hole (Figure 7-10). Remove the runner and drive a nail at this mark to attach another string to. Repeat this procedure on the opposite wall. Then stretch a string tightly from nail to nail. This string is used as a guide to bend your hanger wires at the proper place. Note that the string is aligned with the wire support holes for the first set of wire hangers (although not necessarily with the hanger wires themselves). It is also running level with these holes and therefore indicates where the wire must be bent at an angle of 90 degrees to ensure that the runner is at its proper level.

Align each of the hanger wires to intersect with the string and make a 90-degree bend in the wire where it intersects the string (Figure 7-11). This usually results in support wires that are at an angle in their final position, but the runners are hung perfectly level with the surrounding wall molding.

Step Seven
Hanging the Grid
(Cross Tees and Runners)

Margin of Error: 1/8"

You are now ready to hang the runners and clip in the cross tees. You can run additional strings to show where to bend each wire. Run these strings aligned with each series of wire support holes, into which wires will be inserted.

An easier method is to place a level on the runners and bend the wires as you go. To do this, rest the cut end of the runner on the wall molding. Thread the first prebent wire hanger through the support hole. (This wire hanger has been prebent so that the runner will hang at just the right level; the rest of the wire hangers have not been prebent.) Place a 4' level on the runner and have someone hold it exactly level as you thread the unbent wire hangers through their support holes and bend them so that they keep the runner level. Wrap all wires around themselves three times after threading through the runners.

As you work toward the opposite wall, connect the runner sections together as needed. Be very careful with your measurements. You will need to cut the last piece to fit. (You can sometimes use the excess piece to start the next row.) As you connect and install the pieces, check to be sure that you have cut each runner so that the cross tee slots align exactly with reference string AB. You will have better support if you position an additional wire hanger close to the point where two runner sections are connected. Be sure you are hanging the runners at the right level.

After all the runners are in place, install the cross tees (Figure 7-12). For 24x48 tiles, these 48" pieces are installed every 24" perpendicular to the runners. For 24x24 panels, add a 24" cross tee to the midpoint of the a 48" tee. This process is easy if you have done everything correctly up to here. First install the full-size 4' cross tees in the interior of the room. Once these are in place, lay in a few full ceiling panels to stabilize the system.

Now you must cut the cross tees in the border areas. Most tiles can be cut with a straightedge and a utility knife. Score the tile deeply on the finished surface and flex it on a hard edge, just as you would drywall. Rasp away any unevenness.

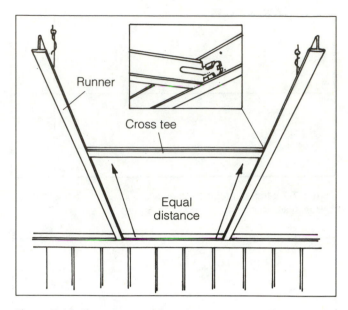

Figure 7-12. Place cross tees into slots on runners. (Slots must be directly across from each other on adjacent runners.)

Measure each border cross tee individually, using string CD, not the runners, as a measuring guide. The runners still have a lot of play in them. To measure, align the edge of the first runner with reference string CD. Then make your measurement from the side wall to the near edge of the runner. Measure and cut accurately. Repeat this process on the opposite wall.

Step Eight
Installing the Panels

Margin of Error: Not applicable

Installing the full panels is as easy as just slipping them into the grid from below and dropping them into place. Make sure your hands are clean, or wear clean gloves, so you don't soil the white panels.

The border panels will need to be cut to size. The larger 24x48 flat panels usually require only a straight cut with a sharp knife or saw to fit snugly between the grids and the wall molding.

If you are using tegular 24x24 panels, you will have to cut in a flange on the freshly cut edge of the border tiles so they will fit the grid (Figure 7-13). (Tegular means two levels; the face of the tile is lower than the grid level.) To cut in the flange, measure the size of the opening plus the flange. Place the cut panel in position in the grid. The cut side without the flange should rest on the wall molding. Draw a pencil line where the wall molding meets the border panel. Be sure the opposite end of the panel is centered in the grid.

Remove the panel and lay it face up on a flat surface. Cut along the pencil line so that your utility knife only penetrates half the thickness of the panel. Then, laying your utility knife flat on the table, cut into the side of the panel, halfway

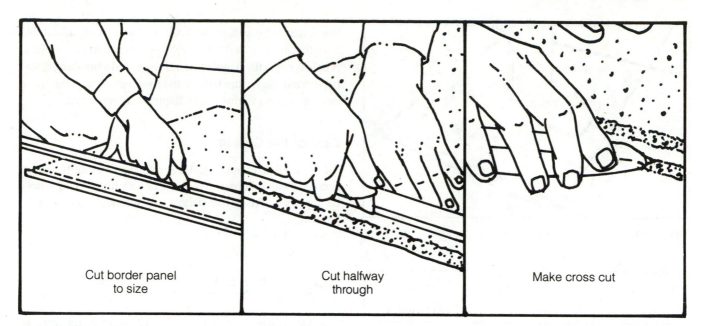

| Cut border panel to size | Cut halfway through | Make cross cut |

Figure 7-13. Three-step process for cutting border tiles to size and cutting flange.

through its thickness, to meet your original cut, thereby creating the flange. Use special paint, available where you bought the tile, to restore the surface that you cut. Now install the panel in your grid.

Step Nine
Special Situations

Margin of Error: Not applicable

Boxing Around Basement Windows

To install a suspended ceiling around basement windows, build a three-sided valance around each window, as shown in Figure 7-14. Use ¼" plywood for the top and 1x6 pine for the three sides. Be sure to build the valance wide enough to allow the window to open and long enough to allow open drapery. In most cases, 9" on either side of the window, for a total of 18", is sufficient for open drapes.

Attach the top of the valance to the bottom of the ceiling joist and install the wall molding for the ceiling panels at the desired level. Curtain rods can be attached to the inside of the valance.

Boxing Around Iron Support Beams and Ductwork

Many basements have horizontal iron support beams that support the first floor. To box around them, follow these steps (Figure 7-15).

Construct a wooden lattice to attach to both sides of the support beam. Use 1x1½ wood strips (1x3 ripped in half) and 1x3 center supports spaced every 16" to build the lattice. Nail the lattice to the floor joists that run on top of the iron beam.

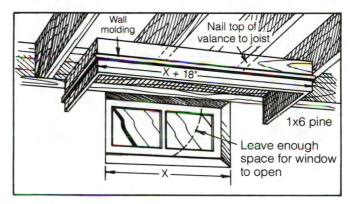

Figure 7-14. Boxing around a basement window.

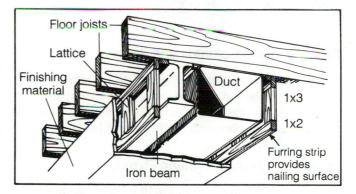

Figure 7-15. Boxing around a beam and duct.

Enclose the support beam by nailing a finishing material, such as drywall or paneling, to the lattice. Attach the same material to the bottom of the lattice to cover the bottom of the beam. Attach the outside corner molding. Now snap a chalkline onto this finished box at the height of the new ceiling and nail the wall molding along this line. This method can also be used to box around ductwork.

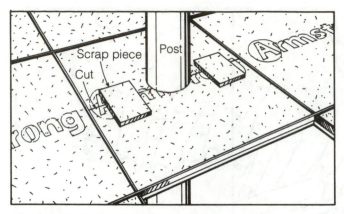

Figure 7-16. Cut tiles to fit around a post or column.

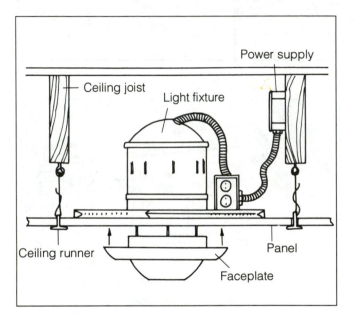

Figure 7-17. Lighting fixture installed in suspended ceiling.

Fitting Around Columns and Posts

Cut the panel in two at the midpoint of the column. Then cut semicircles to the size required so that the rejoined panel will fit snugly around the post, as shown in Figure 7-16. Make all cuts with a very sharp utility or fiberboard knife.

Installing Electrical Lighting Fixtures

Lighting fixtures are easy to install in suspended ceilings (Figure 7-17). It is best to install all your rough wiring before you begin the project. There is often a cavity between the panels and the joists, and the panels can be removed, so it is possible to install fixtures later. However, it takes considerably more effort after the ceiling has been put up.

You can use either incandescent or fluorescent fixtures. Fluorescent fixtures often come with a translucent panel that fits directly into a panel cell. Incandescent fixtures are either flush-mounted or recessed. You need to be more careful with incandescent fixtures, because they get much hotter than

fluorescent. Incandescent fixtures come with adjustable arms that are attached to the ceiling joists to carry the weight. A hole is cut in the panel for the fixture, and a finishing collar fits around the fixture to hide the rough-cut hole. (For more information on wiring, see Chapter 2, Electricity.)

Care of the Ceiling

Caring for a suspended ceiling is an easy matter. If a panel becomes water damaged, marred, or very dirty, it can simply be replaced. Also, the panels are washable and can be painted.

THE TILE CEILING

Standard ceiling tiles are usually 12" square and come in many patterns and colors. They attach directly to wood or metal furring strips, and leave a large cavity as do suspended ceilings. Unless you use the clip method described in Steps One through Seven, following, the tiles are permanently attached; unlike suspended panels, they cannot be easily removed. However, they are quick and easy to install and work well in rooms where you do not want to lower the ceiling height.

The method of installation described here is a new method that uses metal furring strips and clips. These strips, or tracks, are attached to the ceiling joists and support the tiles. The clips make it possible to remove ceiling tiles without damaging them in order to correct minor mistakes, insert light fixtures, or reach wiring and pipes between the joists. You merely slide the clip back along the track to release the tile. This system reduces nailing by two thirds. Since the metal tracks don't have to be spaced precisely 12" apart as do wood furring strips, this system gives you a greater margin of error. And it doesn't require that you saw the tracks; they simply overlap at the end wall.

This simple system comes in a kit with all the materials and instructions you will need, except for the tiles. Steps Seven through Ten, following, discuss installation using conventional wood furring strips.

Step One
Preparation

Margin of Error: Not applicable

Leave the tiles in open boxes in the room where they will be installed for at least 24 hours, so they can become acclimated to the temperature and humidity. Also, repair any leaks or moisture problems before you begin.

Step Two
Laying Out the Ceiling

Margin of Error: 1/4"

The layout for ceiling tiles is somewhat simpler than that for a suspended ceiling. The main thing you are planning for is the border tiles, the rows of tiles that run along the walls of a room. You want to plan these tiles so that they are never less than 6" (half a tile). Rarely do room dimensions work out exactly in multiples of 12".

For example, assume that the width of the room between two of the walls is 9'8". If you made no adjustments, there would be nine full-size tiles and two border rows of 4" each. To correct for these small border rows, covert 9'8" (116") into 8'20" (116"). Now you can have eight full-size courses and two border rows of 10" each. Work out a similar layout in the other direction (in our example, 12'4" coverts to eleven full-size tiles and two 8" border tiles). In this way, all four border rows of a rectangular or square room are more than 6", and the two opposite border rows are equal.

Remember to make cuts for light fixtures and parts.

Step Three
Installing the First Row
of Metal Furring Strips

Margin of Error: 1/2"

The metal furring strips or tracks need to be nailed to something solid in order to hold the ceiling and prevent it from sagging. The ceiling joists will work fine when the furring strips are nailed perpendicularly across them. These strips usually come in 4' sections. There are a few things to remember about installing the strips. They must be well secured to the ceiling joists, level, and parallel.

Nail the first row of metal furring strips 1" away from the wall. Nail at each joist with the nails provided in the kit. Give the strip a tug to be sure it is well secured. Use two nails for every 4' of track nailed into the joists to prevent it from sagging after the tiles are up. Continue placing the 4' strips 1" from the wall. It is not essential that the ends of the strips butt right up against each other; there can be a gap of as much as 1/4" between the 4" strips. Also, the joints do not need to meet over a joist. Just be sure that the tracks are in line, since you may need to attach a clip over the junction of two tracks.

When you reach the other end of the wall you may need to cut a section of the 4' strips to fit. This can be done with a fine-tooth hacksaw.

Step Four
Installing the Remaining Rows

Margin of Error: 1/2"

After the first row of furring strips is in place, proceed with the second row. This second row of furring strips should be placed a distance from the wall that is the size of the border tile less 2". In our example, where we have 10" border tiles, this second row would be placed 8" (10"-2"=8") from the wall.

Measure as you go, being sure to keep a constant 8" from the wall. Nail this row up in the same manner as you did the row next to the wall, being sure to stagger the joints. (The joints between two 4' sections of strips should not occur at the same place in two adjacent rows, but rather should be staggered. A series of joints in a row across the furring strip could cause a noticeable dip in the ceiling.)

After the second row is installed, go on to the remaining rows, which are all placed 12" apart. Again, the next to the last row should be at a distance from the wall equal to the size of a border tile less 2" (8", in our example). The last row should be 1" from the wall.

Step Five
Squaring the Ceiling
with Strings

Margin of Error: Exact

If your walls meet at true right angles so that the room is a perfect square or rectangle, you can omit this step.

Unfortunately, this is often not the case. In this instance you must set up strings that are at true right angles and lay the tiles according to these strings. The strings will serve as guides for installing and cutting the border tiles. If you omit this step, the tile ceiling will look out of line with the walls.

You need to set up two strings that run at the level of the new ceiling and out from each wall the width of the border tiles at that wall, similar to those shown in Figure 7-7. The two strings are attached to nails driven temporarily into the walls, and intersect near a corner. The strings outline the edges of the two intersection border rows.

For example, let's say that one row is a 10" row and the intersecting row is 8". Set up one line so that it is at the level of the ceiling and running 10" from the wall. Do the same with the intersecting string so that it is running 8" from the wall. Once the strings are in place, use a framing square to be sure that the two strings are square. Remember, if they are just a little off square over the 2' width of the tile, the walls could be a few inches off over the distance of the whole wall. Therefore, you need to be sure that both lines are running exactly along the arms of the square. If they are not, adjust one of the strings (preferably the one that outlines the border row that will be least noticeable from below) until the lines are

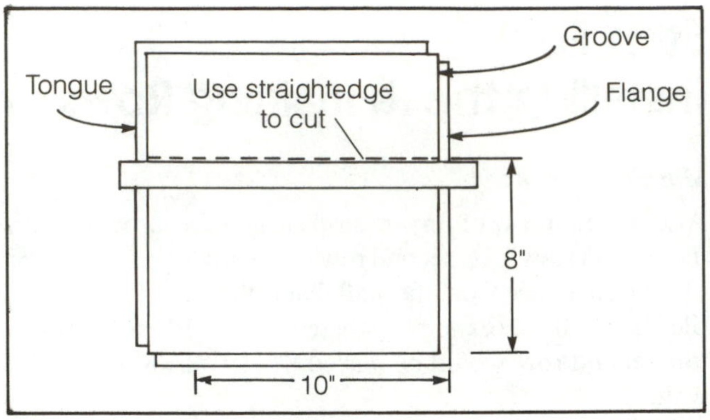

Figure 7-18. Cutting border tiles.

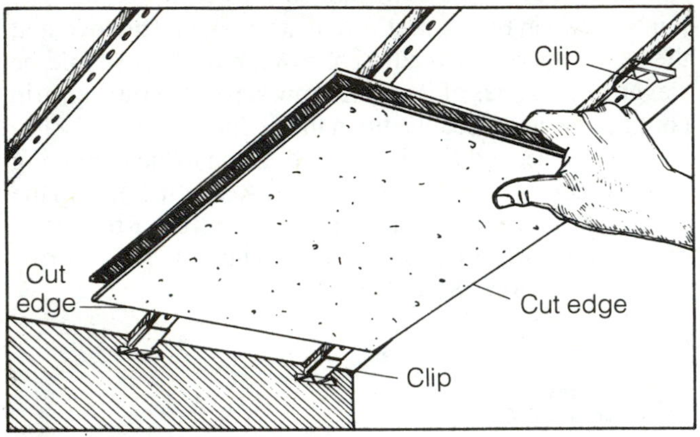

Figure 7-19. Installing the first border tile. Note that the cut edges are against the wall.

exactly at right angles. You now have a square reference from which to start installing the tiles.

Step Six
Installing the Tiles

Margin of Error: 1/8"

Begin installing your tiles in the corner of the room where the two strings intersect.

You will need to cut border tiles to fit. Cut the tile face up with a sharp utility knife. Cut the tile so that the edges next to the wall are the cut edges with no tongues or grooves. All the edges pointing toward the interior of the room should be factory edges (Figure 7-18).

After cutting the first few tiles, snap a clip into each of the first two tracks and push the clips flush against the wall, as shown in Figure 7-19. Place the first tile in the corner and push the cut edge of the tile into the clips. Secure the other edge of the tile by snapping clips into the tracks and pushing them onto the flange. Be sure your hands are clean, or wear clean gloves, so that you don't soil the tiles.

Install the next three tiles that surround your first corner tile. Make sure your tiles fit snugly into the corner and line up with the border reference string lines. This is very important, so take your time. Adjust them until they are perfectly aligned.

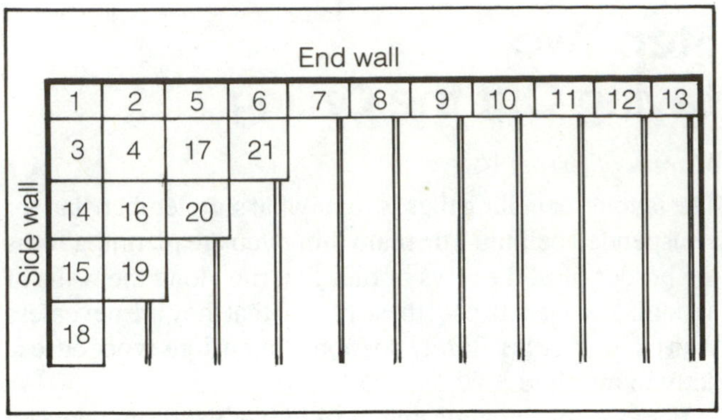

Figure 7-20. Install ceiling tiles in a pyramid pattern.

Once these first four tiles are in place, continue with the installation pattern shown in Figure 7-20. When you reach the opposite side wall, cut the border tiles 1/2" short of the wall to leave a gap for expansion due to moisture. Install the remaining tiles diagonally across the room, in the pattern shown shown in Figure 7-20.

To install the last tile in a row, snap a clip on the end of each track and push it flush up against the wall. Cut the last tile to fit so that it is 1/2" short of the wall. Position the tile in place, then slide the clip into the edge of the tile with a screwdriver, as shown in Figure 7-21.

Finally, nail on the molding. (Paint or stain the molding before installing it.) Be sure to nail the molding every 24" into the wall studs, not into the ceiling (Figure 7-22).

Step Seven
Installing a Tile Ceiling with Wood Furring Strips

Margin of Error: 1/4"

Tile ceilings can also be installed using wood furring strips; in fact, some manufacturers require this type of system. Preparing for installation and calculating the border tiles are the same as for the clip method (Steps One and Two).

The furring strips are nailed perpendicular to the joists. If you are installing 12x24 tiles, furring strips must be installed on 12" centers. When stapling 24" tiles to furring strips, make sure that the tiles run lengthwise along the furring strips, not perpendicular across them.

Use two 8-penny nails at each joist to keep the strips from warping. You need to penetrate into the joists at least 1"; don't forget the drywall thickness. Use a 4′ to 8′ level to be sure the strips are level, shimming as needed.

The first furring strip is flush up against the wall, as shown in Figure 7-23. The second strip is positioned so that its center is the same distance from the wall as the width of the border tile that butts against the wall plus 1/2" to allow for the

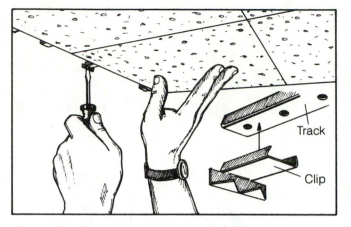

Figure 7-21. Slip the clips onto the last tile with a screwdriver.

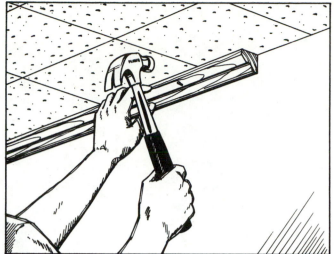

Figure 7-22. Be sure to nail molding into the wall studs, not the ceiling.

stapling flange of the tile. For example, if the width of the border tile that butts against the wall is 10", add ½" to the 10" width and position the second strip so that its center is 10½" from the side wall.

After installing the second strip, work across the ceiling, nailing furring strips spaced 12" on center. Be exact. Nail the final strip flush against the wall.

When two furring strips are joined, the butt joint should always be over the center of a joist. Never allow these joints to fall in between joists where they cannot be nailed. Also, stagger the joints so that joints in adjacent rows do not fall on the same joist.

Step Eight
Squaring the Ceiling
with Strings

Margin of Error: Exact

Same as explained in Step Five for the clip method.

Step Nine
Installing the First Row of Tiles

Margin of Error: ⅛"

After your lines are in place, you can cut the border tiles. Cut them face up with a sharp utility knife. Be sure to include the face and flange of your tile in your measurement. Each border tile should be cut and measured individually. Cut them ¼" shy of the actual measurement to make them fit easier. The gap between the wall and the tile will be covered by molding.

Cut the tiles so that the cut edge is against the wall and the factory edge points toward the interior of the room. The out-

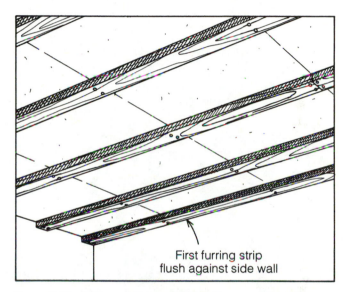

First furring strip flush against side wall

Figure 7-23. First wood furring strip is flush against the wall. The center of the second is the width of the border tile plus ½".

side edges of the flanges should line up exactly with your reference strings. Fasten each tile with four ½" or 9/16" staples, two in each flange (use six staples for 12x24 tiles).

Work across the ceiling, installing two or three border tiles at a time, filling in between with full-size tiles. When you reach the last row, measure and cut each tile individually. If the stapling flange isn't large enough for stapling, face-nail the tile in place near the wall where the nailhead will be hidden by the molding.

Finally, nail on the molding as described in Step Six for the clip method.

8 Doors and Trim

DOORS ARE DIVIDED into two classes, interior and exterior. Their installation differs slightly, because exterior doors must be windproof and watertight. **Prehung doors,** for either interior or exterior application, are already installed in their jambs when you purchase them. Some exterior doors have a threshold in place, some do not. Interior doors also come in two types. Some come fully installed in their jambs and some come partly assembled, their hinge jambs attached to the door and the head and strike jambs attached to the hinge jamb temporarily. (It is also possible to buy just the door and build your own jambs. However, this chapter describes installing prehung doors.)

All of these prehung varieties are a vast improvement over the old labor-intensive types, which required a great deal of fitting work. Prehung doors are prehinged, with holes for locksets and deadbolts already drilled, and with their jambs cut to exact dimensions. Installing a prehung door is a fairly simple task that requires little physical effort. However, accuracy and precision are essential. If the door is not hung properly, it will be too tight or too loose, and it may open or close by itself.

This chapter also discusses trimming windows and doors. As with hanging doors, accuracy is crucial. A sloppy trim job is highly visible. If you plan to stain your trim or finish with varnish or polyurethane, your work needs to be exact, because every crack will be visible. If you plan to paint the trim, you don't have to be as exact, because any cracks will be filled with painter's caulk. For information on applying trim to wall, ceiling, and floor joints, see Chapter 6, Wall Paneling. For information on installing thresholds, see Chapter 14, Weatherizing. And for information on putting locks in your doors, see Chapter 15, Home Security.

Before You Begin

SAFETY

☐ Use the appropriate tool for the job.

☐ Keep blades sharp. A dull blade requires excessive force and can slip and cause accidents.

☐ Be careful when lifting, to avoid unnecessary strain.

☐ Be sure that electric tools are properly grounded.

☐ Use safety glasses or goggles when hammering, sawing, or drilling, especially if you wear contact lenses.

USEFUL TERMS

The **casing** is the outer trim of the door that covers the gap between the door jamb and the drywall or paneling.

The **head jamb** is the upper portion of the door jamb.

A **reveal** is a small portion of jamb left as a visual detail or to provide clearance for hinge barrels when applying the casing.

The **rough opening** is the hole framed into the wall where the door will be installed.

A **shim** is a small, usually tapered piece of wood used to fill in the space between the door jambs and the surrounding framing studs.

The **side jamb** is the inner portion of the door trim on either side of the door. One side is called the **hinge jamb,** the other the **strike jamb.**

The **stop molding** is the portion of the door trim that stops the door's swing when it is being closed.

WHAT YOU WILL NEED

Time. It takes about two hours to hang a prehung door. The amount of time required for trim work depends on the difficulty of the project and on your familiarity with this work.

Tools

Level

Hammer

Drill and bits

Nailset

Tape

Square

Circular saw

Handsaw

Miter box

Pencil

Electric screwdriver or drill

Materials

Prehung door

Screws

Finishing nails

Trim material

PERMITS AND CODES

The fire code requires that exterior doors in dwellings must be at least 32" wide, and no interior door may be under 24" wide. The code also requires a solid core "one hour" door between the living space and the garage for fire safety.

DESIGN

These days, doors come in a huge array of styles and materials. Modern manufacturing techniques have brought costs down, and modern materials have greatly improved security and reduced maintenance.

Doors make a highly visible design statement; it's a good idea to purchase the best you can afford. Your main design decision is the type and material of prehung door to install. Solid core doors are recommended over hollow core because they offer greater sound reduction and security. Besides wood, doors are made of materials ranging from fiberglass to metal. Foam-filled doors with fiberglass or steel skins look like painted wooden panel doors but are much tougher. These doors also deaden sound and provide some insulative value. In fact, many communities now require insulated exterior doors.

When you purchase prehung doors, you will need to specify the direction in which you want them to swing and on which side you want them to be hinged. This subject deserves a lot of consideration, because the way a door swings can have a large effect on the way a room feels. Most prehung doors are built to fit walls made with 2x4 studs and drywall on each side. If your walls are thicker than that, you will have to order wider jambs and trim them to the proper width.

Trim also makes a statement about your house. Carefully chosen, it can highlight the best features of your home and draw attention away from the less attractive ones.

If you plan to paint your door jambs and trim, they can be of inexpensive "finger jointed" wood—several small pieces of wood joined together to make a long piece of trim or casing. If you plan to stain the wood or simply seal it with varnish or polyurethane, you should order solid jambs and trim. When you order your doors, you will also need to indicate the size and style of your door trim.

HANGING AND TRIMMING A PREHUNG INTERIOR DOOR

Most Common Mistakes

- ☐ Installing the door off plumb.
- ☐ Installing the door in an opening that is too small and lacks shim space.
- ☐ Dinging the casing, trim, or jamb while hammering.
- ☐ Shimming improperly or insufficiently.
- ☐ Ordering the door with the wrong direction of swing or hinged on the wrong side.

Step One
Inspecting the Door and Opening

Margin of Error: 1/4"

Hanging doors can be frustrating because there are so many things that can go wrong. The trick is to approach the process one step at a time, in the proper sequence.

All doors are made in standard sizes. The dimensions of your rough opening are determined by the size of the door to be hung. Door sizes are designated in feet and inches; a 3'0" door is 36" wide. Figure 8-1 shows the anatomy of a typical prehung interior door.

First, remeasure your rough opening to be sure that the prehung door will fit. The opening should be 1" to 1½" wider and ½" to 1" taller than the prehung door and its jambs. Also measure diagonally in both directions across the opening. If the diagonal measurements are equal (within approximately 1/4"), then the opening is square. However, this

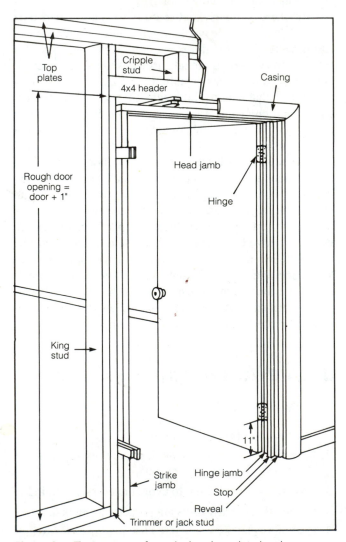

Figure 8-1. The anatomy of a typical prehung interior door.

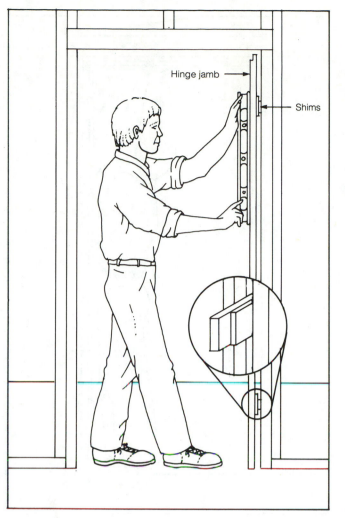

Figure 8-2. Use shims and a level to plumb the hinge jamb.

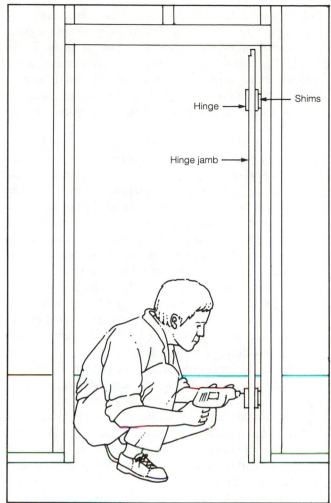

Figure 8-3. Before installing the door, secure the hinge jamb with screws or nails through the jamb and shims into the trimmer stud.

is seldom the case. If the opening is not square, or if it is too large or too small, it must be corrected before you proceed. If the opening is too small, it will have to be reframed; or you can use a smaller door. If it is too large, 1x4s or 2x4s can be added to make it smaller. With wide casing this should not present a problem. With narrow casing, however, there may be gaps that need to be filled in with drywall. Also check the area around the door opening on both sides where the trim will be attached to be sure the area is flat.

As you hang the door, bear in mind that the clearance between the door and the jambs may need to be increased if you are going to paint the jambs and the door itself. One coat of primer and two coats of enamel are about 1/32" thick. A total of 12 coats are applied to the two jambs and two door edges, so the layers of paint approach 1/8" in thickness. On the other hand, if your gaps are too large, weather-stripping becomes a problem on exterior doors, and interior doors don't look right. Ideally, when all varnishing or priming and painting are completed, a gap of 1/8" is left on both sides and at the top of the door.

Step Two
Installing the Hinge Jamb

Margin of Error: Within 1/16" of plumb and flush with the wall surfaces on each side

Remove the blocks that temporarily attach the jambs and casing to the door. Mark the door bottom on the hinge jamb. Take off the hinge jamb by removing the hinge pins, *not the hinges themselves.*

The height of the door off the floor is determined by the length of the hinge jamb. Therefore you should check the floor for level, not only where the door will be placed, but where it will swing as well. The distance the hinge jamb protrudes below the door is the distance between the bottom of the door and the floor. If you plan to install thick carpet or wooden finish flooring later, now is the time to take the thickness of the material into account. If you have a forced air furnace, leave a 3/8" gap at the bottom of the interior doors, to allow warm air into closed rooms and to allow cold air to cycle back to the furnace.

The hinge jamb, cut or shimmed to the correct length, is the first piece to be installed. Traditionally, the hinge jamb was secured with finish nails through small shims. These days, bugle-head drywall screws are often used instead of finish nails because of their superior strength. Shims are necessary because all buildings settle over time, and the space provided by the shims allows adjustment to accommodate this settling.

If your king stud and trimmer on the hinge side of the door are perfectly plumb, you can use small pieces of plywood as shims. Otherwise, use two tapered shims, slid past one another, to adjust the hinge jamb to plumb, as shown in Figure 8-2. The shim thickness should be roughly half of the difference between the rough opening measurement and the total width of the door plus its jambs and gaps. Always shim under the hinges, since this is where the weight is borne.

The edges of the hinge jamb must line up with the wall surface on each side. Hold the jamb in place with your knee and screw or nail through the center of the jamb into the trimmer stud, where the screws will eventually be covered by the door stop trim piece (Figure 8-3). Install the screws with an electric screw gun or a reversible drill.

For increased durability, place additional screws under or through the hinge plate. Tighten the screws enough to compress the shims. If the jamb is not perfectly plumb after the shims are compressed, just back the screws out a little, adjust the shims, and resecure the screws. To put a screw under a hinge, simply remove the hinge jamb plate and screw into the mortised part (but not in the hinge screw holes), and then replace the hinge plate.

Once the hinge jamb is plumb and secure, install the door by mating the door's hinge plates to the jamb's hinge plates and inserting the hinge pins. Make sure that the door doesn't swing on its own.

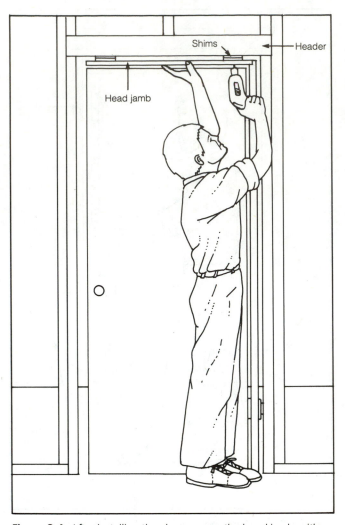

Figure 8-4. After installing the door, secure the head jamb with screws or nails through the jamb and shims into the header.

Step Three
Installing the Head Jamb

Margin of Error: Within 1/16" of level and flush with the wall surfaces on each side

Some head jambs have grooves, called **dadoes;** some have notches, called **rabbets;** and some are simply butt jointed, depending on the manufacturer. The distance above the hung door is determined by the manufacturer with the grooved and notched models, and by you with the butt-jointed models. Some flexibility is possible, even with the notched types. Shims are used to provide appropriate gaps on the butt-jointed types.

With the door in its closed position, stand on the side opposite the swing. Set the head jamb in place and shim the gap from the top of the door as necessary. Use additional shims on top of the head jamb in two places, near the ends, and line up the edges with the wall surfaces. Holding the head jamb in place with one hand, push the door open and screw or nail

through the jamb and shims where the doorstop will cover the screw heads, as shown in Figure 8-4. Now close the door and check the gap at the top. It should be even, and about the same size as the gap on the hinge side. Don't use a level or square to set the head jamb; instead, make the jamb conform to the door itself.

Step Four
Installing the Strike Jamb

Margin of Error: Within 1/16" of plumb and flush with the wall surfaces on each side

Like the head jamb, the strike jamb is installed to conform to the door and not to plumb, although if your hinge jamb is plumb and your gaps are even, the strike jamb will automatically be plumb. Be sure to install any premortised strike plate notches on the correct side, as described in Chapter 15, Home Security, and line up the jamb edges with the finished

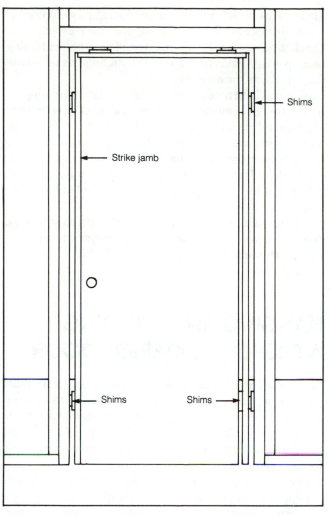

Figure 8-5. Finally, install the strike jamb as you did the hinge jamb.

wall surfaces. By opening and closing the door, you can check the gaps and adjust as necessary (Figure 8-5).

Use shims and screws to straighten all the jambs and perfect the gap widths. For more durable and better-sounding operation of the lockset, it's a good idea to put at least one screw near the strike plate location.

Step Five
Installing the Lockset

Margin of Error: 1/16"

Prebored and premortised doors and jambs make the locksets easy to install. Simply follow the manufacturer's directions, which are included with the hardware.

If you don't have this prebored and premortised type, then you can follow the detailed instructions given in Chapter 15, Home Security.

Step Six
Installing the Door Stops

Margin of Error: 1/16"

After installing the lockset, close the door and mark the location of the door's edge in pencil on the jamb. Now open the door and use small finish nails to install the top piece of stop, lining up the edge of the stop with your pencil mark. If you intend to paint the door and jamb, remember to leave a suitable gap to allow for the thickness of the paint. Be sure to maintain this gap as you install the stops on the side jambs.

Step Seven
Trimming Out the Door Jamb
with Beveled Casing

Margin of Error: 1/16"

Before trimming out the door jamb, you will need to cut off all the shim ends that are sticking out. Try to cut them even with or below the drywall surface. A handsaw works best for this, but you may have to use a chisel for shims that are close to the floor.

If your casing is premitered, you should adjust the length by trimming the bottom, not the mitered end. Start at the hinge side, remembering that the hinge barrels and pins require a certain amount of clearance from the jamb edge. This clearance is known as a **reveal,** because it exposes the jamb

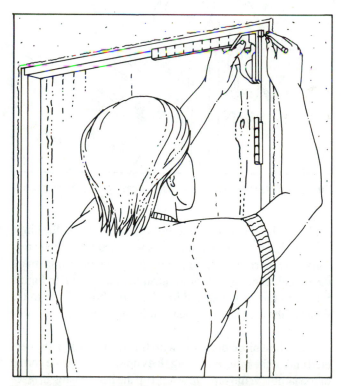

Figure 8-6. Use a combination square to mark the reveal.

Figure 8-7. Secure the head casing with finish nails.

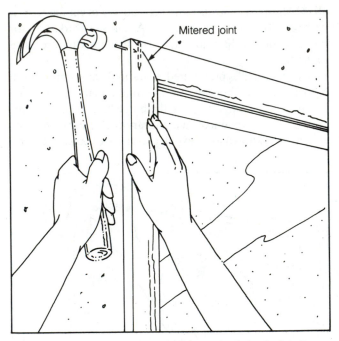

Mitered joint

Figure 8-8. Nail the mitred joints of the casing in both directions.

slightly. The reveal is needed so that you can get the hinge pins out later, and it is sometimes widened for esthetic reasons. To determine the length of this piece of casing, mark the reveal, using a combination square, as shown in Figure 8-6. Add the height of the inside of the hinge jamb to the width of the reveal, and measure this distance from the *inside* of the mitered corner to determine the cut at the bottom. Install this first piece of casing with finish nails so that the beveled end of the mitered casing lines up with the inside corner of the jambs, at the top. Now hold up the head casing in place and check the mitered joint. Plane as required for a tight fit.

Make a mark on the opposite inside edge, again including the reveal distance of the side jambs, and miter this end cut. Check to be sure that the new mitered edge of the head casing lines up with the interior corner of the jamb and secure it with finish nails, as shown in Figure 8-7.

Now check the mitered corner of the strike jamb casing for fit with the head jamb trim and adjust the length if necessary. Maintaining the reveal, secure the last piece of casing. Nail each mitered corner in both directions, as shown in Figure 8-8, to prevent the joints from opening up. Finally, go to the other side and repeat this process. It's a good idea to predrill before you nail the mitered corners to avoid splitting the wood.

Casing that is not premitered is installed in the same way, except that you must make all the miter cuts. Butt-jointed casings are much easier to cut and install, although they are less attractive.

HANGING AND TRIMMING A PREHUNG EXTERIOR DOOR

Hanging an exterior prehung door is generally easier than hanging an interior door, because most exterior doors come completely assembled in their jambs, with thresholds already in place. The whole unit is set into position, leveled and plumbed, and secured through shims to the adjacent framing in one operation.

Exterior doors have their stops built into their jambs. Although this makes them more weatherproof, it means that you can't conceal the screws under the door stop trim. Screws are still a better choice than nails, however; just use small wood plugs or putty to cover the visible ones.

The interior casing of exterior doors is the same as for interior doors, but the outside trim work must be weatherproof. Some manufacturers ship exterior doors with the outside casing already installed. All you need to do is caulk the back of this casing, and under the threshold, before pushing the whole unit into position and securing it with screws.

Many communities now require that the space between the jamb and the frame be insulated. If the code requires this in your area, be sure to insulate this cavity before you trim out the interior.

INSTALLING WINDOW TRIM

As with doors, casing for windows is available in a wide variety of styles, sizes, and shapes.

Beveled casing, the same kind that is commonly used on doors, must be mitered to fit together on the ends (see Figure 8-8). The plainness of beveled or thin flat casing focuses attention on the view, not on the window itself.

Butt-jointed styles closely resemble exterior window casing but are usually smaller in size and are often embellished

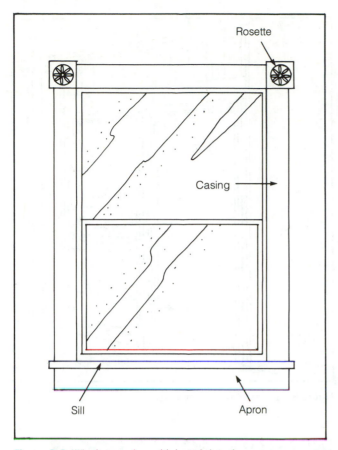

Figure 8-9. Window casing with butt-jointed corners, decorated with rosettes.

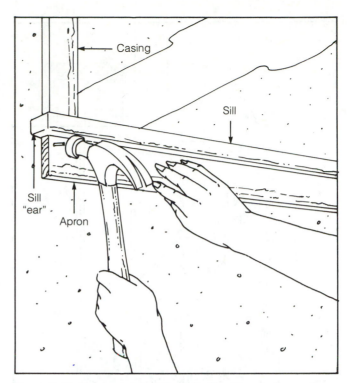

Figure 8-10. The apron is installed last, after the window casing and sill.

with routed edges or decorative corner blocks, called *rosettes* (Figure 8-9).

Both types of casing usually butt against the interior window sill and a small piece of trim, called an *apron,* is nailed below the sill to cover any gap between the drywall and the bottom of the sill.

All casing is installed with finish nails to minimize puttying work later. Number 4 finish nails are fine for attaching the inside casing to the jamb, but at the outside edge the nail must go through the drywall and penetrate about 1" into the trimmer stud. The length of nail needed depends on the thickness of the casing and the wall-covering material. Pilot holes are often required for larger nails.

The first piece of trim to be installed is always the sill. An "ear" extends out from the sill on either side so the casing on the sides can butt to the sill. The depth of the sill is up to you, but these ears must be at least as wide as the side casing.

Level the sill in the rough opening with shims and secure it with finish nails. Next install the side casing, as described in Step Seven for doors, with the sill acting like a floor. Adjust the miter joints and reveals as you work. The last piece to be installed is the apron, below the sill. The apron is usually the same length as the width of the casings and window together; the apron's edges line up with the casing edges, as shown in Figure 8-10.

For a simple, modern appearance, some people prefer no casing or sills at all on their windows. In this case, drywall is applied where the jamb would be. Metal corners are installed around the opening and finished with drywall compound. However, the drywall "sill" lacks impact resistance, and may be damaged if you leave the window open on a rainy day.

INSTALLING SLIDING GLASS DOORS

Sliding glass doors require careful placement of the rough opening during the framing process. Most are designed to be installed over the exterior siding with a small nailing flange, as shown in Figure 8-11. These doors come in precut kit form, and the jamb is assembled on the floor with screws provided in the kit. Some manufacturers recommend installing the jamb first, and some recommend installing the fixed glass panel in the jamb before placing the jamb in the rough opening.

To install a sliding glass door in your rough opening, you must first flash (waterproof) the opening according to the manufacturer's directions. Then run a bead of caulk along the outside edge of the bottom of the opening and, with a helper, tilt the jamb into position. Split the shim space equally at each end so you can plumb the sides later. Using your level, shim at the bottom to adjust the bottom to level. These jambs are flexible, so sight down the exterior edge to

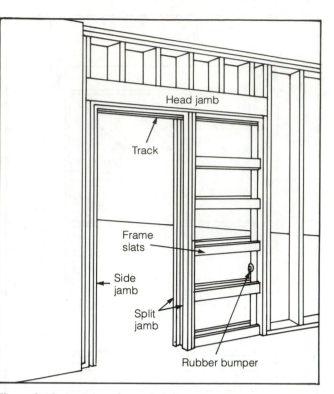

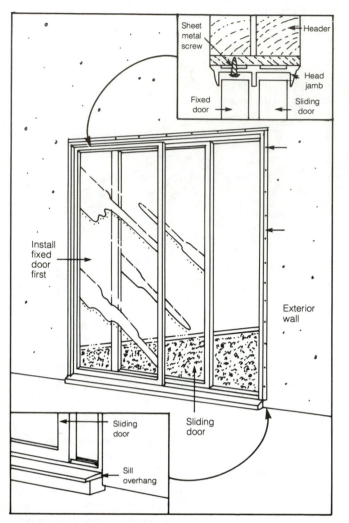

Figure 8-11. Anatomy of a sliding glass door.

Figure 8-12. Anatomy of a pocket door.

be sure it is also straight. Now nail or screw the flange to the siding about every 12". Use galvanized nails or screws to secure the flange. Use your level and shims to plumb the side jambs, and secure these flanges to the siding.

If the fixed panel is not already in place, install it now. This will help to make the head jamb straight. Be sure to sight down the edge and verify that the head jamb is straight before you secure it. Now install the movable panel and its frame. Two holes, one on each end of the bottom of the door panel, provide adjustment access for the door rollers. Insert a #2 phillips head screwdriver into the hole to engage the adjustment screw. Turn the screw clockwise to raise the door or counterclockwise to lower the door, as necessary. Adjust the rollers so the door clears the bottom jamb and slide the door almost closed. Adjust the rollers to make the strike jamb and door edge parallel, then close the door and check the latch operation.

Follow the manufacturer's directions for exterior trim, caulking and flashing as necessary to waterproof the door. Interior jambs are usually provided with sliding glass doors, so only casing is usually required to finish off the interior side.

INSTALLING POCKET DOORS

Like sliding glass doors, pocket door openings require careful placement during framing. Pocket doors, which come in various sizes, are usually hollow core, to reduce the weight borne by the overhead track. They are prehung in a carefully sized lightly built "pocket," which is basically a box, as shown in Figure 8-12. The box is 3⅝" wide, the same width as standard framing. The rough opening is much larger than the door itself—twice as large. Unlike other doors, pocket doors are always installed *before the drywall is applied*.

To install a pocket door in a suitable rough opening, first remove all the packaging, but *not* the wood braces and blocks. The wood cleat near the bottom is left in place to hold the strike jamb, and the block across the door keeps the assembly square. Place the closed door unit in the rough opening. Make sure the jambs and sides of the box are flush to the framing and adjust the door opening and jambs to the desired location laterally.

Level the bottom if necessary and drive nails through the bottom of the pocket portion into the subfloor. Plumb the pocket side jamb and shim between the frame and the back of the pocket portion. A nail or screw here will keep the pocket side jamb plumb. Shim and screw or nail the head jamb to the header above it. Be sure that the nails are long enough to penetrate the frame. Remove the block holding the door shut, and remove the cleat on the strike jamb. Pull out the door and shim and secure the jamb to provide a good fit with the door edge. When the door is fully pulled out, the door is slightly narrower than the opening itself. These small gaps will be covered with the doorstop that comes with the door, which prevents the door from swinging in the opening. The doorstop is nailed in on both sides of the door. Use only as many nails as needed to hold the stops in place. To renew the door rollers, or to paint a pocket door, remove one set of stops, swing the door out of plumb, and disengage the rollers and door from the track.

Finally, drywall is applied over the pocket "box" and brought flush with the jambs. Use drywall screws, but be sure they don't go through the box sides and into the door. Casing is applied just as with a prehung door.

9 Vinyl Floors

This chapter describes the kinds of vinyl flooring materials on the market today and the techniques used to install them. Vinyl is an easy, affordable way to customize your floors, offering a huge variety of patterns, colors, styles, and installation choices.

This chapter also discusses floor preparation, template use, cutting and installing sheet vinyl flooring, the application of perimeter bond materials and full-spread adhesive floors, installing a self-adhesive tile floor, and the application of vinyl flooring over concrete.

Before You Begin

SAFETY

☐ Some adhesives are toxic. Be sure to provide adequate ventilation with window fans when using them.

☐ Some adhesives are flammable. Turn off gas valves on appliances in your work area.

☐ Wear the proper respirator when using substances that give off toxic fumes.

☐ Wear rubber gloves when using solvents.

☐ Keep blades sharp. Dull blades require excessive force and can easily slip.

☐ Wear safety glasses or goggles whenever you are hammering, prying, or cutting.

☐ Use the proper protection, take precautions, and plan ahead. Never bypass safety to save money or to rush a project.

USEFUL TERMS

Full-spread adhesives require the application of the adhesive with a trowel under the entire vinyl floor.

Ledging is a situation where one side of a seam rises up higher than the other.

A **perimeter bond** sheet vinyl floor is attached only at walls and seams, where flooring shrinks after installation.

A **subfloor** is a layer of plywood or boards that covers the floor joists. An underlayment is sometimes added over the subfloor if a perfectly smooth surface is needed over which to install a vinyl floor.

A **template** is a paper pattern used to ensure accurate, error-free installation.

An **underlayment** is a layer of thin particle board installed over the subfloor that gives a smooth, level surface over which the vinyl floor is applied.

WHAT YOU WILL NEED

Time. Most vinyl floor installations can be completed in one or two days by a single worker. For a 9′x12′ room, using perimeter bond sheet vinyl or self-adhesive tiles, plan on 7 to 9 person-hours. Full-spread adhesive will require 9 to 11 person-hours.

Tools. Vinyl floor installation requires very few tools that are not in every home owner's toolbox. In addition to the tools listed below, a hair blow drier may come in handy to heat up tiles before making complicated cuts.

Tools for Perimeter Bond Sheet Vinyl or Full-Spread Adhesive

Scissors

Pencil or ballpoint pen

1"-wide ruler

Notched trowel

Notched blade or utility knife

Rolling pin or seam roller

Staple gun (for perimeter bond sheet vinyl)

Tools for Self-Adhesive Vinyl Tiles

Scissors

Pencil or ballpoint pen

Utility knife

Chalkline

Carpenter's square

Materials for Perimeter Bond Sheet Vinyl or Full-Spread Adhesive

Craft or butcher paper

Do-it-yourself installation kit (for perimeter bond sheet vinyl)

Masking tape

Sheet vinyl

Adhesive

Seam sealer kit

Staples (for perimeter bond sheet vinyl)

Materials for Self-Adhesive Vinyl Tile

Craft or butcher paper

Tiles

Vinyl wall base

PERMITS AND CODES

Laying a new floor may be regulated by local building codes, and a permit may be necessary. Check your local building code before beginning work.

DESIGN

The color you choose for your new floor is likely to be determined by the predominant color of the room. Neutral tones and single-color rooms will make your decision easy. For a multicolored space you will need to decide which color you prefer to emphasize.

In selecting a pattern, keep in mind that the most effective way to combine patterns in a room is to use one large pattern, one medium pattern, and one small pattern distributed among walls, fabrics, and flooring. Of course, these patterns should be color-coordinated.

If your floor offers a wide expanse of uninterrupted space, you may wish to use a large pattern. However, if the space is broken up, has alcoves, or is interrupted by counters or appliances, a more pleasing effect will be accomplished with a smaller pattern.

You can use the pattern to create a visual span from one space to another by repeating like shapes in regular sections both vertically and horizontally.

Most Common Mistake

☐ The single most common mistake in any vinyl flooring project is applying the flooring over an improperly cleaned or prepared surface, such as a basement floor that has a moisture problem.

SHEET VINYL FLOORING

Step One
Preparing the Subfloor
or Underlayment

Margin of Error: The subfloor or underlayment should be level within $1/8$", with no gaps larger than $1/4$"

Most Common Mistake

☐ Not leveling the floor or applying an underlayment if needed.

If your subfloor is level and structurally sound, with an even finish, simply fill any holes or cracks with floor filler and be sure no splinters or nailheads are protruding. Then sweep and vacuum thoroughly and mop the floor with a mild cleaner.

If any areas slope or dip badly, fill them with leveling compound, allow it to dry thoroughly, then install an underlayment of $1/4$" paraticle board to create a smooth, level surface. Plan the seams of the underlayment so they do not match those of the subflooring beneath. Over an open joist system, first apply a layer of $3/4$" tongue-and-groove plywood as a subfloor. Check local code for specific recommendations for your area.

Nail the underlayment with 6-penny ring-shank nails every 4" to 6" around the edge and every 4" in the middle. Be sure all the heads are slightly below the surface. Leave a $1/2$" gap between the plywood and the wall all the way around, and $1/16$" between sheets, to allow for expansion and contraction of the wood in cold, wet, or humid regions. In temperate regions, it is common to fill these joints with joint filler and then sand them smooth.

Step Two
Making the Template

Margin of Error: Exact

Most Common Mistake

☐ Neglecting to make a template when working with sheet vinyl.

A template or pattern is essential for accurately cutting your vinyl floor (Figure 9-1). Craft paper, butcher paper, and the paper that comes in the do-it-yourself installation kits all work equally well. The template will enable you to transfer

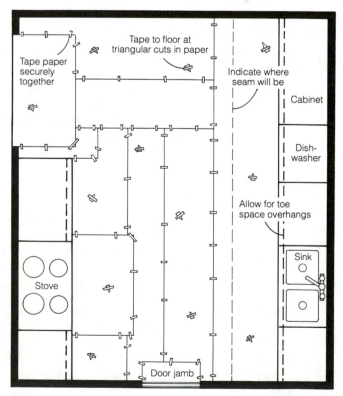

Tape paper securely together

Tape to floor at triangular cuts in paper

Indicate where seam will be

Cabinet

Dish-washer

Allow for toe space overhangs

Sink

Stove

Door jamb

Figure 9-1. A typical paper template.

accurate measurements to the vinyl flooring without making unnecessary or awkward cuts during installation.

To keep the pattern from shifting while you work, cut little triangles in various areas of the paper. You can then tape the pattern to the floor with masking tape pressed over the cutouts (Figure 9-2).

If you need a bigger piece, tape overlapping edges of the paper together, keeping the pattern smooth and flat as you progress. Flooring usually comes in 12′ widths. If you are working with a floor large enough to require two pieces of flooring (over 12′), you will need to follow special steps for seam fitting, pattern matching, and seam sealing. If at all possible, it is best to lay out the flooring so that the seam will fall in a low-traffic area.

Many floors have irregular, odd-shaped, or just plain hard-to-fit objects like pipes or built-in cabinets. Use smaller pieces of paper to make templates for irregular sections of the floor, and attach them to the main template with tape. Finally, check to be certain that the template is an exact fit, and make any necessary corrections.

If you are using an installation kit, the accompanying roller disk will aid you in marking your pattern. When using this roller, leave a gap of about ½" between your template and the wall. The roller disk is designed to transfer the wall line to the pattern paper, leaving a space of exactly 1" between the pencil line and the wall (Figure 9-3). In other words, this line on the template is actually one full inch shy of the wall everywhere you use the roller disk. With this method, when you transfer your template to the vinyl, you must use a 1"-wide straightedge placed along your outline mark to put that inch back onto the flooring when you mark it. Whether you use an installation kit with a disk roller, a makeshift marker, or just press the paper up to the wall, creasing it for your outline, it is best to work a short distance at a time. Don't try to mark a wall in one continuous line.

Note on the pattern the position of any object you had to fit around, so that you can check its fit and its relative location one last time before you complete the installation. When you have finished your template, you will have a paper floor with all of its "landmarks" clearly indicated. If there are any holes for registers for the heating system, just ignore them when making your template. These holes can be cut after the flooring is laid. Now you are ready to get an accurate transfer of your paper pattern onto the vinyl material.

Step Three
Cutting the Vinyl

Margin of Error: Exact

Most Common Mistakes

☐ Laying out the template on the wrong side, causing you to cut the floor backward.

☐ Not lining up the template seamline with a pattern (grout) line on the flooring material.

Unroll the new flooring face up on a clean, smooth surface. (Otherwise, small stones or dirt can become embedded in the back, eventually wearing through or tearing the new floor.) The basement, garage, attic, or driveway is often the best place for this. However, if you are working outside, don't expose the vinyl to direct sunlight.

Overlap the vinyl pieces where the seams will fall. Check the two sections for pattern match all along the overlap and at each corner of the pattern. if you are working with a pronounced design that calls for a perfect match, keep both pieces running in the direction they came off the roll.

Tape the two vinyl sections securely together after they are matched so they won't move when you cut them. Then cut straight through the overlapping edges of the two pieces so that they fit together perfectly (Figure 9-4). (It's a good idea to practice on a piece of scrap flooring before making the actual cut.) Getting a good-looking seam is not difficult if you make your cut in a simulated grout line or other pattern feature that can serve as camouflage. Be sure to keep a sharp blade in your utility knife.

After you have made your cut, double check the pattern match before continuing. Then tape the seam together.

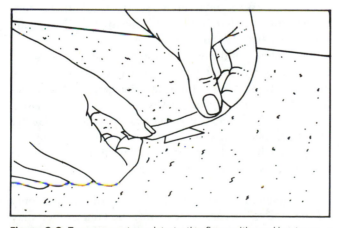

Figure 9-2. Tape paper template to the floor with masking tape over triangular cutouts.

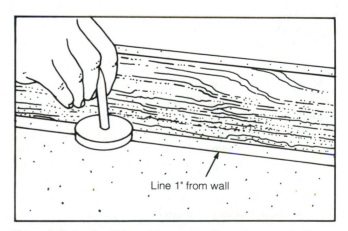

Figure 9-3. A roller disk enables you to draw a line exactly 1" from the edge of the wall onto your paper template.

Line 1" from wall

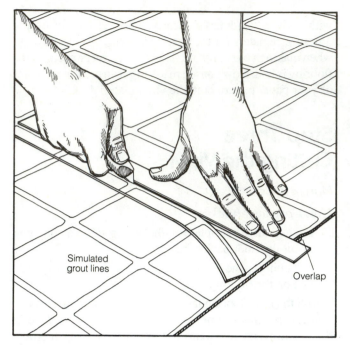

Figure 9-4. To match the pattern at a seam, overlap the two pieces until the pattern matches. Then tape the two pieces together and cut through both.

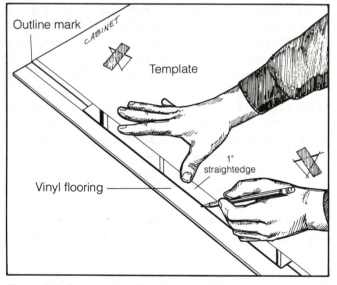

Figure 9-5. If you used a disk roller, you will need to transfer the "lost" 1" back onto the vinyl.

Now lay out your paper pattern or template over the flooring material, making sure that the seam falls in a low-traffic or low-visibility part of the room. Be sure that you are not positioning the template upside down and that you are cutting the flooring as you want it. Compensate on both sides for any out-of-line walls by shifting the template in a direction that will split the difference of the error. If possible, don't position a line in the vinyl pattern too close to the out-of-line wall, where it will be more obvious.

Once you have the template situated where you want it, tape it to the vinyl through the triangular slits, just as you taped it to the subfloor.

As mentioned earlier, if you used a roller or a 1" marking guide, remember to transfer the "lost" 1" back onto the flooring material, using a pencil or ballpoint pen (Figure 9-5). After you have transferred the dimensions to the flooring material, remove the template.

Use a notched blade knife or a utility knife to trim the vinyl. Many kits include a notched blade knife. Always make sure the blade is sharp. Cut very carefully and true along your line for a precise fit.

Once the floor has been cut out, roll it up with the pattern showing on the outside and any narrow protruding areas on the outside end of the roll.

Step Four
Installing the Flooring

Margin of Error: Within ¼" at edges, exact at seams

Most Common Mistakes

☐ When estimating the amount of sheet vinyl or perimeter bond material, forgetting to allow for pattern matching at seams.

☐ Unrolling perimeter bond sheet vinyl too early, or waiting too long to lay it, so that it shrinks before it is permanently laid in place.

☐ Failing to use flooring materials with the compatible adhesive and appropriate trowel at seams.

PERIMETER BOND
SHEET VINYL FLOORING

Carry your roll of cut vinyl flooring into the room in which it will be installed. Carefully unroll and position it over the clean, dry subfloor, matching up the landmarks you indicated on your template.

Carefully assess your cutting job. If any additional trimming needs to be done, now is the time to do it—before any adhesives have been applied.

The first part of the new floor to be secured is the seam. This is done by applying the adhesive along the floor between the two sections of flooring. First, gently fold one section back and tape it out of the way. Draw a pencil line along the edge of the other section to mark the seamline. Gently fold the second section back and tape it out of the way.

Apply a band of adhesive to the subfloor along the seamline, using the recommended notched-tooth metal trowel (Figure 9-6). Check the manufacturer's recommendations about the width of the adhesive. Some require only a 3" band (1 ½" on either side of the pencil line); others may require as much as 6" of adhesive (3" on either side of the seam).

Apply the adhesive all along the pencil line to about 1 ½" away from any cabinets. You want to stop the adhesive here so that, after the seam is pressed together and rolled, you will be able to fold back the flooring under the cabinets to apply adhesive there. You can't get a staple gun under the cabinet overhang, so you have to glue the areas under the cabinets.

Lay one piece of the flooring into the adhesive, and then the other. Make sure the edges of the vinyl are tight against each other. If you don't, you'll get a condition called "ledging," where one side rides up higher than the other. Dirt can build up here and draw attention to the seam.

Now go over the seam with a rolling pin or seam roller, to press the vinyl into the adhesive and eliminate ledging.

To prevent moisture from getting under the vinyl along this seam, use a special seam sealer kit. Read and follow the instructions carefully. When applying solvent, hold the bottle at the proper angle and don't wipe up any of the excess. It will evaporate, and you won't see it after a short time. Give the seam a few hours to set up before walking on it.

Use the adhesive, as instructed, on the perimeter areas that will not be covered by molding and in areas where you are unable to use your staple gun. Roll the edge of the flooring back, apply the adhesive in the proper amount with the notched trowel or manufacturer's suggested applicator, and press the flooring into place with the roller.

For the edges that will be covered by quarter-round trim or baseboards, staples applied with a staple gun work best. They are fast and easy to apply and they provide great holding power. In addition, if the flooring material shrinks or expands with temperature and humidity, staples will cause fewer problems than will adhesives. Staple close to the wall, so that the molding will cover the staples (Figure 9-7).

Perimeter-bonded vinyl flooring will contract slightly, tightening like a drumhead, over the 24 to 48 hours after installation. You should wait until the floor has contracted to its final tension before moving the furniture and appliances onto it.

Most vinyl floors today are "no-wax." Once the floor has contracted, all you have to do is damp mop. As always, follow the manufacturer's suggestions for cleaning and care.

FULL-SPREAD ADHESIVE SHEET VINYL FLOORING

Full-spread adhesive is fast becoming the least popular type of vinyl flooring. It is more difficult to install than perimenter bond, and it cannot be removed as easily as other floorings if you want to install another floor in the future. One advantage of full-spread adhesive flooring is that coved (curved) edges can be obtained around the perimeter of the room, eliminating the need for baseboards. Properly sealed, these coved edges can greatly improve water-proofing in bathrooms and kitchens. However, this type of flooring is difficult to install. If you choose coved edges, consider calling in a professional. Check around to see if your pattern is available in a perimeter bond application before you opt for

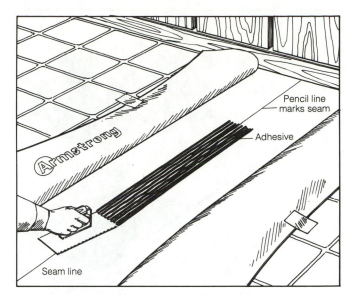

Figure 9-6. Tape vinyl back and trowel adhesive over penciled seamline.

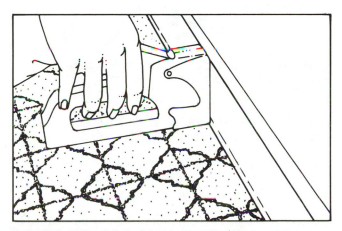

Figure 9-7. Perimeter bond flooring requires stapling at the edges only. Staples will be covered by the quarter-round trim.

the full-spread. If your pattern is available only in a full-spread application, try to limit its installation to small rooms. It is much too cumbersome to try to align on larger floors that are already spread with adhesive.

1. Full-spread adhesive must be applied on a surface that is smooth and free of grease, dirt, and any irregularities. Clean the subfloor well. See Step One, Preparing the Subfloor, earlier in this chapter.

2. Follow the template procedure described in Step Two.

3. Roll up the material and carry it into the room. Place the roll against a wall and unroll it as you work toward the opposite wall (Figure 9-8).

4. One of the most important things about working with adhesives is to use the correct type of applicator or trowel and adhesive. This information is included in the manufacturer's instructions. The adhesive should be applied to enough of

Figure 9-8. For full-spread adhesive application, spread adhesive with a toothed trowel and unroll the vinyl as you go.

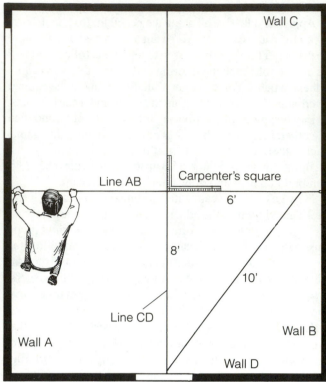

Figure 9-9. Use a 3-4-5 triangle to be sure your layout lines are square.

the floor at a time to allow you to place the sheet vinyl and give you some working and adjusting room.

5. If you are applying a seamed floor, lay the smaller section first. Follow the instructions for seams as described for perimeter bond vinyl flooring.

6. If you have done a careful job of outlining the odd and irregular shapes of the floor, and of transferring the template to the right side of the flooring, getting the sheet to fit should present no problems.

7. Once the flooring is in place, you should go over it with a rolling pin or a 100-pound roller to ensure a good bond between the floor and the adhesive. Roll from the center of the floor out toward the edges to get rid of all the air bubbles and waves.

SELF-ADHESIVE VINYL TILES

Self-adhesive vinyl tiles are the easiest type of floor to put down. Because of the sticky backing, there is no need to mess with gooey adhesives and seam sealers. You need only acclimate the tiles by storing them there overnight in open boxes in the room in which they will be installed. This is especially important when installing floors over concrete. You will need to buy about 10 percent more tile than the total area you plan to cover, to allow for border tiles.

Step One Preparation

Margin of Error: Subfloor should be level within 1/8" and with gaps no larger than 1/4"

Most Common Mistake

☐ Not purchasing about 10 percent more tile than the total area you plan to cover, to allow for border tiles.

When laying a tile floor, you will have a more balanced floor if you work from the center of the room outward. You will need to establish layout lines and find the center of the floor. You must also be sure that the seams in the tiles do not line up directly over seams in the subfloor.

First, measure to find the midpoints of two opposite walls (wall A and wall B in Figure 9-9). Snap a chalkline between the midpoints of these walls (line AB). Measure to find the midpoints of the other two opposite walls (in this case, wall C and wall D).

Before snapping the second line (line CD), place a carpenter's square in the center where the two lines intersect. If necessary, adjust the second line (line CD) so that the two lines intersect at a 90-degree angle. These lines must be perfectly square. You can easily check for square with the 3-4-5 triangle technique, as follows.

Start at the intersection of the two layout lines and measure 6′ along line AB. Then measure 8′ along line CD. If the lines are perfectly square, the measurement between the two

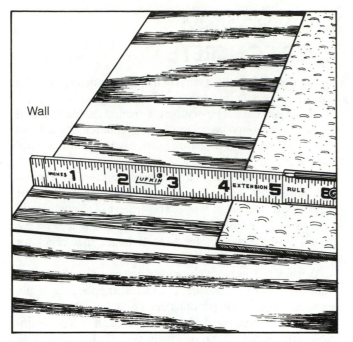

Figure 9-10. If the space between the last tile and the wall is less than half a tile (6" with 12" tiles), move the center line over half a tile space.

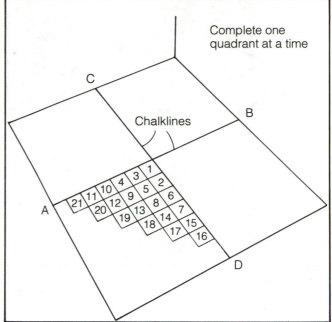

Figure 9-11. Pattern for laying tiles.

points will be exactly 10'. (Of course, you can use any multiples of 3-4-5, but it is best to use the longest possible measurements to ensure the greatest accuracy.)

If the lines are not perfectly square, adjust line CD until they are square. Do not adjust line AB! Lay loose tile from the center point along line AB to the wall. If the space between the last tile and the wall is less than half a tile, move line CD half a tile (6" with 12" tiles) closer to one wall and snap a new line CD (Figure 9-10). Repeat this process by laying tiles along line CD and adjusting line AB. This will ensure equal borders on opposite walls, and all borders will be more than half a tile.

Step Two
Laying the Tiles

Margin of Error: Exact

Most Common Mistakes

☐ Not laying out and squaring your working lines when placing square tiles.

☐ Placing a pattern line too close to an irregular wall, thereby accentuating the out-of-line wall.

☐ Neglecting to lay the floor tiles in the direction indicated by the arrows on the backs of the tiles.

After making sure that your subfloor is clean and free of debris and dirt, begin laying the tiles. Vinyl floor tiles should be installed in a certain direction, indicated by an arrow on the back of the tile. The tiles have a paper backing that is peeled off to expose the adhesive.

Beginning at the intersection of the working lines, the first tile goes down along the first working line (line AB), with the second along line CD, as shown in Figure 9-11. Work out toward the borders, completing one quadrant at a time. When each tile is in place, press it firmly onto the subfloor. Be sure the tiles are snug so that they will end up properly at the wall with a good finished look.

Vinyl tiles are easily cut with a utility knife or scissors, and are even easier to cut if they are first warmed with a blow drier. This technique is especially helpful in making a cut to fit around an intricate shape. In the case of a complex cut, a template of butcher paper or craft paper is needed as well. Cut the paper to fit around the obstacle, then trace the pattern onto the tile.

A consistently accurate method of cutting a border tile for a perfect fit at an outside corner, even though the wall may be slightly out of line, is shown in Figure 9-12. Lay the tile you want to cut squarely on top of the tile that is already in place on the row adjacent to the border row. Take another loose tile and butt it up against the wall so it overlaps the tile you want to cut. The second loose tile thus becomes a straightedge for marking the border tile. Repeat this procedure on the other side of the corner. Then score the border tile with a sharp utility knife to outline the portion of the tile to be removed. Make a diagonal cut across the back from the inside corner. The tile should break cleanly along the scored lines, leaving you with an L-shaped piece that will fit perfectly into place.

When fitting border tiles along irregular or curving walls, you will need a paper template. Place the template in position and push it into the corner or curve as tightly as you can,

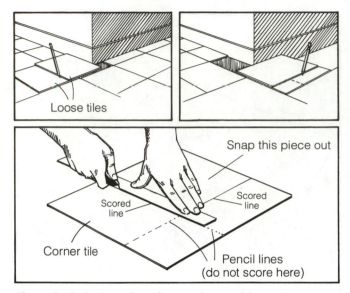

Loose tiles

Snap this piece out

Scored line

Scored line

Corner tile

Pencil lines
(do not score here)

Figure 9-12. Cutting a tile to fit around an outside corner.

creasing the paper as you go. Mark the crease with a pencil as accurately as you can manage. Transfer the pattern to the tile (making sure the tile is facing in the proper direction) and make your cut very carefully along the line with a utility knife.

DRY TILES

Dry-backed flooring tiles that need an adhesive can be laid the same as sticky-backed tiles, but they are messier and more difficult to lay. Follow the manufacturer's instructions for specific preparation, adhesive and trowel use, and drying time. This type of flooring, like full-spread adhesive sheet vinyl, can be difficult to remove later.

APPLYING VINYL OVER CONCRETE

If you plan to apply sheet vinyl or tiles over concrete, note the following special considerations.

The concrete must be dry. New concrete should be cured to a hard, dry, nonpowdery finish. New concrete should also have at least a 4 mil moisture barrier between the ground and the concrete slab.

To be on the safe side, test all concrete subfloors for moisture, preferably during the rainy season. This test can be done in three different ways. The easiest is to completely tape down 2'x2' polyfilm squares in several places on the floor. Leave the squares for 24 to 48 hours, then check for condensation under the plastic.

A second test involves chipping small sections of concrete from the floor in several areas. To each chipped area, apply a solution of 3 percent penophalene in alcohol. This solution can be purchased at most drugstores. A red color reaction indicates the presence of moisture in your floor.

The third test involves the use of calcium chloride crystals, also available from a druggist. Make a 3"-diameter putty ring on the slab, place ½ teaspoon of the calcium chloride in the circle, then cover the crystals with a water glass to seal them off from the air. If the crystals dissolve within 12 hours, the slab is too wet to use adhesives.

To carry an applied floor, a concrete subfloor should have a density of 90 pounds per cubic foot or more. A lighter slab tends to hold moisture longer, and to retain a scaly or chalky surface. Either moisture retention or concrete dust can lead to problems.

10 Hardwood Floors

A HARDWOOD FLOOR is perhaps the most beautiful and durable floor you can install. Earlier in this country's construction history, hardwoods were the most common of all flooring materials. With the advent of vinyl and linoleum flooring, and later with the widespread use of carpeting, they fell out of favor. In recent years, however, they have regained some of their lost popularity.

Part of the reason for their comeback has been the introduction of new types of hardwood flooring. These new types are as beautiful and as durable as the earlier tongue-and-groove plank flooring, and they are so easy to install that their application is a fairly simple project. It may surprise many people to learn that a parquet or a plank floor can easily be installed in a weekend.

This chapter discusses installing both parquet floors and prefinished plank (strip) floors, and finishing unfinished hardwood floors. For the most part, this chapter deals with installing prefinished floors. These floors are already stained and have a protective top coat. However, you can also install unfinished hardwood floors that will need to be finished by sanding, staining (if you choose), and application of a protective finish.

Before You Begin

SAFETY

☐ Wear safety glasses or goggles whenever you are using power tools, especially if you wear contact lenses.

☐ Always unplug your power tools when making adjustments or changing blades, drill bits, or sandpaper.

☐ Be sure your tools are properly grounded.

☐ Watch power cord placement so that it doesn't interfere with the tool's operation.

☐ Wear ear protectors when using power tools, because some operate at noise levels that can damage hearing.

☐ Be careful not to let loose hair and clothing get caught in power tools.

☐ Wear the proper respirator or face mask when sanding, sawing, or using substances that give off toxic fumes.

☐ Some adhesives are toxic. Be sure to provide adequate ventilation with window fans when using them.

☐ Some adhesives are flammable. Turn off gas appliances in the vicinity.

☐ Wear rubber gloves when using solvents.

☐ Use the appropriate tool for the job.

☐ Keep blades sharp. A dull blade requires excessive force and can easily slip.

☐ Seal all heating and air conditioning ducts and electrical outlets when sanding.

☐ To prevent spontaneous combustion, dispose of oily rags correctly.

☐ Use the proper protection, take precautions, and plan ahead. Never bypass safety to save money or to rush a project.

USEFUL TERMS

Baseboard is the trim that is used where walls and floors meet. Also called shoe molding.

A **floor register** is an opening in the floor, usually covered by a grate, that brings heated or cooled air into a room.

Glazier's points are small metal triangles that are used to hold glass panes in their frames.

A **penetrating sealant** is a finish that soaks into the wood as well as providing a hard finished surface.

Polyurethane is a synthetic rubber polymer sealant for wood.

Reducer strips are prefabricated door thresholds for use where two rooms with different floor levels come together.

A **surface finish** is a finish that provides a hard surface coat without penetrating the wood.

A **subfloor** is a layer of plywood or boards that covers the floor joists. An underlayment is sometimes added over the subfloor if a perfectly smooth surface is needed over which to install a finished floor.

An **underlayment** is a layer of thin particle board installed over the subfloor that gives a smooth, level surface over which the finished floor is applied.

PERMITS AND CODES

Laying a new floor may be regulated by local building codes, and a permit may be necessary. Check your local building code before beginning work.

WHAT YOU WILL NEED

Because the tools and materials lists for the various projects are so extensive, they appear at the beginning of each section in this chapter: Installing Parquet Floors, Installing Strip Flooring, and Sanding and Finishing Hardwood Floors.

INSTALLING PARQUET FLOORS

Some people look at parquet floors, with all their small beautiful inlaid pieces, and think, "What patience and skill that person must have had!" Actually, patience and great skill are no longer required to install this beautiful flooring. In fact, this is now a fairly simple project because all of those little pieces have been prefabricated into larger tiles. These days, a prefinished parquet floor is no more difficult to install than vinyl floor tiles.

WHAT YOU WILL NEED

Time. Plan on approximately 10 to 15 person-hours to complete a 9'x12' room. This can be a one-person task.

Tools for Installing Parquet Floors

Ear protectors

Respirator/face mask

Eye protection

Carpenter's pencil

Hammer

Utility knife

Heavy-duty shop vacuum

Fan(s)

Tape measure

Carpenter's square

Pry bar and wood wedge

Extension cords (heavy duty)

Chalkline and chalk

Jigsaw

Notched trowel

150-lb. roller

Handsaw

Radial arm saw or table saw

Materials for Installing Parquet Floors

Mastic or adhesive

Parquet tiles

Plywood

Reducer strip

Adhesive cleaning solvent

Rags

Step One
Preparing the Subfloor

Margin of Error: Within 3/16" of level

Most Common Mistake

☐ Not leveling the floor or applying an underlayment if needed.

If your subfloor is level and structurally sound, with an even finish, simply fill any holes or cracks with floor filler and be sure no splinters or nail heads are protruding. Then sweep and vacuum thoroughly and mop the floor with a mild cleaner.

If any areas slope or dip badly, fill them with leveling compound, allow it to dry thoroughly, then install an underlayment of 1/4" plywood to create a smooth, level surface. Plan the seams of the underlayment so they do not match those of the subflooring beneath. Over an open joist system, first apply a layer of 3/4" tongue-and-groove plywood as a subfloor. Check local code for specific recommendations.

Nail the underlayment with 6-penny ring-shank nails every 4" to 6" around the edge and every 4" in the middle. Leave a 1/4" gap between the plywood and the wall all the way around, and 1/16" between sheets, to allow for expansion and contraction of the wood.

Step Two
Locating Your Layout Lines

Margin of Error: 1/4"

Most Common Mistakes

☐ Not using layout lines.

☐ Not adjusting the border tiles correctly.

As with vinyl floor tiles, you need to mark your floor with layout lines that will guide you in installing the parquet floor tiles. The two layout lines cross approximately in the center of the floor and divide your room into four quadrants that are roughly equal in size. The tiles are then laid out from the center, where the lines cross, toward the corners. This process needs to be done precisely, because it affects the final outcome of the project considerably.

First, find the center of the room and establish your layout lines. In Figure 10-1, walls A and B are 20'6" and walls C and D are 14'8". Wall D is the most visible wall, having a wide opening into another room, so you will want a full tile at this opening for appearance' sake. Using increments of a full tile (usually 12"), measure along walls A and B from wall D approximately half the room—in this case, about 10'. Snap a chalkline AB between these midpoints. Now find the midpoints of walls C and D and snap your second line (in Figure 10-1, the dotted line).

You may need to make some adjustments to these lines. You want the border tiles along walls A and B to be equal in

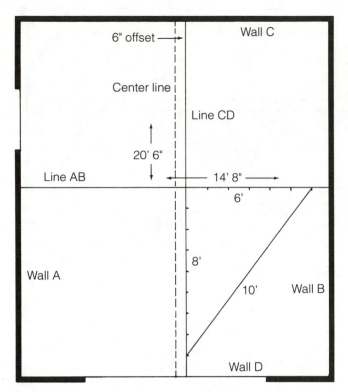

Figure 10-1. Layout lines for a parquet floor.

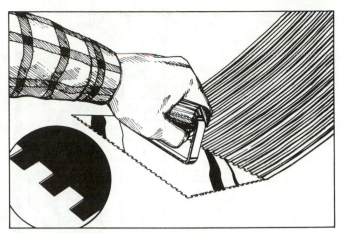

Figure 10-2. Use a toothed trowel, held at a 45-degree angle, to apply the adhesive.

width and more than half a tile. To do this, calculate the length of line AB in inches (14'8" = 176"), divide that number by 2, then divide the result (88") by the size of the tile (12"). If more than half a tile remains along walls A and B, you will not need to adjust your chalkline. In our example, however, the remainder is only 4", less than half a tile (88" divided by 12" = 7'4"). In this case, you would end up with two rows of 4" border tiles and 14 rows of full-size tiles. Remember, you want border tiles that are 6" or more in size. To accomplish this, move the center chalkline (line C/D) by half a tile (6"). This becomes your second layout line CD (in Figure 10-1, the solid line), which will leave border tiles of 10" along walls A and B, and 13 rows of tiles in between. (It's a good idea to check your calculations by dry-laying your tiles to see how they work out.)

Before proceeding, you must check to be sure that your two layout lines, AB and CD, are perfectly perpendicular to each other. If all the walls were perfectly parallel, the lines would automatically be at right angles. However, this is rarely the case; the walls are usually a little off parallel.

Use a 3-4-5 triangle to check your right angle. Start at the intersection of the two layout lines and measure 6' along line AB and then 8' along line CD. Mark these points and measure the distance between them. If the lines are perfectly square, the distance between the two points will be exactly 10'. (You can use any multiple of 3-4-5, but it is best to use the longest possible measurements to ensure the greatest accuracy.) If the lines are not perfectly square, adjust line CD until they are. Do not move line AB or you will have odd-cut tiles at the highly visible doorway.

Step Three
Applying the Adhesives

Margin of Error: Not applicable

Most Common Mistakes

☐ Using the wrong adhesive.

☐ Applying the adhesive when it or the room is too cold.

☐ Using the wrong trowel.

Clean and vacuum the subfloor thoroughly and be sure there are no protruding nails, screws, or splinters. Be sure to provide good ventilation, such as a window fan, because adhesive fumes can be toxic. Turn off nearby gas appliances; some adhesives are highly combustible.

Be sure you have chosen the proper adhesive for the flooring, and follow the manufacturer's instructions closely. Most adhesives should be stored in a room heated to 70 degrees for 24 hours before applying, and the wood tiles should be stored loosely in the room for at least 24 hours so they can acclimate to its temperature and humidity. If you are not able to store the adhesive in a heated room before applying it, you can place the unopened can in warm water to heat it up.

Use a toothed trowel to spread the adhesive in the area you will be working in. Hold the trowel at a 45-degree angle to get even ridges (Figure 10-2). Spread up to, but do not cover, your layout lines. Be careful not to spread a larger area than you can cover in 2 to 3 hours. A little experimentation will show you the proper amount of adhesive. Too much adhesive will squeeze up between the tiles; too little will not allow the tiles to adhere properly. Ridges 1/8" high are about right. Let the adhesive thicken and become tacky before laying the tiles. Most adhesives take about an hour to set up properly, but there are some variations. Follow the manufacturer's instructions.

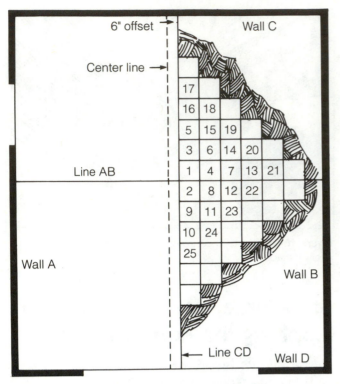

Figure 10-3. Installation pattern for parquet floor tiles.

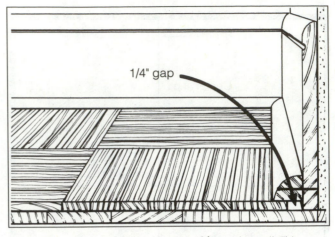

Figure 10-5. Leave an expansion gap of ¼" at the wall. This gap will be covered by quarter-round molding. Be sure to nail the molding to the wall, not to the floor.

Figure 10-4. Use a plywood board to distribute your weight over freshly laid tiles.

Step Four
Laying the Tiles

Margin of Error: ⅛"

Most Common Mistakes

☐ Not leaving a ¼" expansion gap between tiles and the wall.

☐ Not allowing the adhesive to set up properly.

After your adhesive has set up, you can start laying the tiles. This is finish work, and you'll be living with it for a long time, so go slow and do a good job. Lay the tiles in the pattern shown in Figure 10-3, or as instructed by the manufacturer. Do one side of the room and then the other in the same pyramid fashion. Place the tiles exactly up to your layout lines. Here is where your earlier accuracy will pay off.

Take special care in laying your first 10 or 12 tiles, because they will determine the appearance of the entire floor. Check to be sure there is no debris lifting the tiles. Engage the tongues and grooves of the tiles as you lay them next to each other, but don't slide them into place. Occasionally you may need to use a mallet or hammer and a block of wood to force them together.

Every few tiles, stop and tap the tiles with your mallet or hammer and wood block to be sure they are properly seated. If any adhesive gets on the tiles, clean them immediately with a rag soaked in solvent. Never apply the solvent directly to the tiles; it could mar the finish.

Don't step on the tiles for 24 hours after they are laid. To avoid putting your weight directly on any one tile, place a sheet of plywood as a kneeling board over the newly laid tile as you continue to work (Figure 10-4). Be sure there is no adhesive between the board and the tiles.

You will need to cut the border tiles to fit. This is best done with a fine-tooth handsaw, although a table or radial arm saw is easier to use. Don't forget to leave a ¼" expansion gap between these border tiles and the walls, as shown in Figure 10-5. Many manufacturers recommend placing a cork expansion strip in this gap.

Step Five
Rolling the Floor

Margin of Error: Not applicable

Most Common Mistake

☐ Omitting this step.

Figure 10-6. After the floor is completed, roll it with a 150-pound roller to ensure proper adhesion.

After you have finished laying the floor, or a section of the floor, go over it with a rented 100- to 150-pound floor roller (Figure 10-6). If you can't get a roller, use a kitchen rolling pin, putting all your weight on it. To ensure proper adhering, this step must be done within 4 hours of when the adhesive was originally spread.

After you have installed and finished the entire floor, and the adhesive has set, nail your molding in place. Be sure to nail the molding into the wall, not the floor, to allow the flooring to expand. Reducer strips may be needed if your new floor meets another floor that is either higher or lower. These reducer strips are the same color and material as your flooring, and are nailed to the subfloor where the two floors meet.

INSTALLING STRIP FLOORING

Laying a hardwood strip or plank floor used to be a good deal more difficult than it is today. Strip flooring came only in rather thick (¾") boards that had to be nailed to the subflooring. This process, which requires a special nailing gun, takes considerably more work than gluing. Although this flooring is still available, the new, thinner (⅜" or 5⁄16"), prefinished floorings are much easier to install. They are glued instead of nailed, and they come prefinished, so no sanding and finishing are required. Like parquet flooring, strip flooring comes in many colors and styles.

WHAT YOU WILL NEED

Time. Plan on 10 to 15 person-hours to complete a 9'x12' room. This can be a one-person task.

Tools for Installing Strip Flooring
Ear protectors
Respirator/face mask
Eye protection
Carpenter's pencil
Hammer
Circular saw
Jigsaw
Handsaw
Utility knife
Heavy-duty shop vacuum
Fan(s)
Tape measure
Carpenter's square
Straightedge board
Pry bar and wood wedge
Extension cords (heavy duty)
Chalkline and chalk
Notched trowel
150-pound roller
Materials for Installing Strip Flooring
Mastic or adhesive
Tongue-and-groove planking (glue-down type)
Plywood
Reducer strip
Adhesive cleaning solvent
Rags

Step One
Prepping and
Repairing the Floor

Margin of Error: Within 3⁄16" of level

Most Common Mistakes
☐ Not leveling the floor or applying an underlayment if needed.

This step is the same as Step One under parquet flooring.

Step Two
Planning the Floor

1. Strip flooring installation traditionally begins at the most visible wall of the room.

2. Strip flooring is usually installed parallel with the long wall of the room, perpendicular to the joists.

3. The piece of flooring next to the most visible wall should be a full-size piece. If you are using random-width boards,

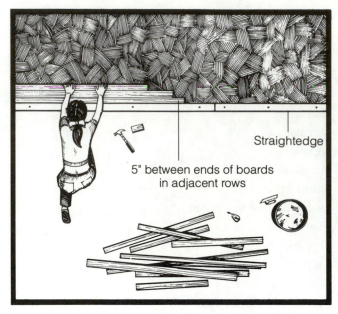

Figure 10-7. Nail down a 2x4, at a distance of 30" to 32" from the wall, to use as a straightedge.

this should be a wide board. The piece next to the wall opposite this most visible wall can be a special-cut piece.

4. When installing flooring in adjacent rooms and halls perpendicular to the main room, you may want to turn the direction of the plank. However, don't lay the flooring in the short direction of a long hallway; this creates an unpleasing "ladder" effect.

5. To ensure a good blending of color, work out of several cartons at once.

6. Don't use boards that have a substantial bow.

To ensure that the most visible wall has a full-width board, and that the planks are installed straight, use a layout line. This is a chalkline snapped on the floor approximately 30" to 32" from the most visible wall and running in the direction in which the flooring will be laid. Its exact distance from the wall depends on the width of the boards you are laying. Again, your object is to have a full-size plank against the most visible wall.

The following example uses both 3" and 5" planks, so eight planks will equal 32" (four 3" planks and four 5" planks). You therefore measure out from the wall 32 ¼" at each end, mark these spots, and snap a chalkline between them. (The additional ¼" is for the expansion gap between the flooring and the wall.) Then install a straight 2x4 as a straightedge to act as a guide when laying the floor (Figure 10-7). Be sure the straightedge is temporarily nailed to the subfloor perfectly straight and exactly on the layout line. This straightedge will determine the appearance of the entire floor.

Step Three
Applying the Adhesive

Margin of Error: Not applicable

Most Common Mistakes

☐ Using the wrong adhesive.

☐ Applying the adhesive when it or the room is too cold.

☐ Using the wrong trowel.

Apply the adhesive between the straightedge and the most visible wall, 30" to 32" away. Never cover an area with adhesive that cannot be laid within 4 hours. Other than that, the adhesive is applied as discussed in Step Three under parquet flooring.

Step Four
Laying the Planks

Margin of Error: Exact

Most Common Mistakes

☐ Not wiping off excess glue.

☐ Not laying a full-size board next to the most visible wall.

☐ Not achieving a tight fit between boards.

☐ Using bowed boards.

☐ Not leaving a ¼" expansion gap between all walls and flooring.

Your first row of flooring will be laid tight up against the straightedge. Install it so that the tongue is against the straightedge. If you are using random-width boards, the piece next to the wall should be the widest piece.

Make sure that this first board is good and straight, and install it tight up against the straightedge. If you are using flooring that has fake pegs, cut the end of the first plank in each row so that all the pegs don't line up next to a wall. Also be sure that there is at least 5" between the ends of the planks in adjacent rows (see Figure 10-7). Leave a ¼" expansion gap between all walls and the flooring.

As you lay the planks, use a hammer or mallet and a scrap piece of flooring to force the planks tightly together and ensure a snug fit. Remember to let the adhesive set up to a sticky feel before you apply the flooring. Don't slide the planks into place, because this will cause the adhesive to ooze up between the boards. Rather, insert the tongue into the groove and adjust it into final position. If any adhesive gets on the planks, wipe it off immediately with a rag wet with solvent. Never apply the solvent directly to the plank; it could mar the finish.

Work toward the most visible wall until that section is completed. You can use a pry bar against the wall to force the last piece snug up against its adjacent course.

Don't kneel or walk on the newly laid planks. Use a clean piece of plywood as a kneeling board to spread your weight out. Be sure there is no excess glue on the planks before placing the plywood on top. As you cover each section, go over it with a 150-pound floor roller rented from your supplier.

After you have done the first area, remove the straight-edge and continue laying the floor, using the first plank as a straightedge. Your final piece, across from the most visible wall, may need to be cut to fit.

After you have installed and finished the entire floor, install the molding or baseboard, nailing it into the wall, not the floor, to allow the floor to expand.

SANDING AND FINISHING HARDWOOD FLOORS

Unfinished hardwood floors must be sanded to a smooth, even finish, free of ridges, dips, and irregularities, before they are stained and/or finished. Sanding involves several passes with a large drum sander and a smaller edge sander with progressively finer grades of sandpaper. Sand with the grain wherever possible.

WHAT YOU WILL NEED

Time. Finishing a 9'x12' hardwood floor may take anywhere from 8 to 18 person-hours. Remember, however, that more time will be needed between steps to allow coats of finish to dry.

Tools. Except for a few specialty tools, most of the tools you will need to finish hardwood floors are common ones. Specialty tools that you will probably need to rent include a drum sander, an edge sander, a floor buffer, and a heavy-duty vacuum cleaner. The drum sander is a large sander used on the main body of the floor. The edge sander is designed to sand the floor where it meets the wall, where the drum sander will not reach. The floor buffer is used for very fine sanding and for polishing. The shop vacuum is needed to remove as much dust as possible before you apply the stain and protective finish.

Tools for Repairs

Variable-speed drill

Drill bit stop

Drill bits

Nailset

Chisel

Putty knife

Pry bar

Caulking gun

Screwdriver

Tools for Finishing

Putty knife

Drum sander

Edge or disk sander

Block sander

Orbital sander

Coarse-, medium-, and fine-grit sandpaper

Nailset

Paint tray and roller

Lamb's wool mop

Tack cloth

Cheesecloth

Floor buffer

Materials for Repairs

Graphite (tube)

Wood dough

8-penny finishing nails

3/16" round-head wood screws

3/4" hardwood flooring strips

Subflooring adhesive

2x4, 2x6, or 2x8 for bridging

Rags

Materials for Finishing

Duct tape

Plastic sheets

Wood stain

Wood sealer

Polyurethane

Paint stick or coat hanger for stirring paint

#2 steel wood machine disks and pads

Step One
Repairing Squeaky
or Cupped Boards

Margin of Error: Not applicable

Most Common Mistake

☐ Not fixing any problems before sanding.

Before you sand your newly laid floor, some prep work will probably be in order. Make a careful survey of the floor. You will need to repair any squeaky areas or ridged or cupped boards before sanding.

Squeaky boards are annoying, but they can often be easily fixed. The first thing to try is tapping the squeaky area with a hammer and a 2x4 wrapped in a towel. Another simple technique is to insert a shim from below the floor, between the floor joist and the area where the floor is squeaking. If that doesn't work, try squirting some lubricant such as graphite, talcum powder, floor oil, or mineral oil between the boards. Next, you can try forcing metal glazier's points between the boards every 6" to separate the boards.

If these simple techniques don't work, try drilling a pilot hole through the board, nailing from above with a finishing nail, and then countersinking the nail and filling the hole

Figure 10-11. Use a putty knife and wood dough to fill cracks.

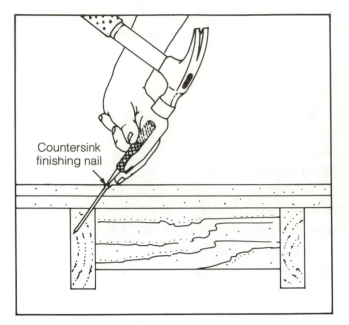

Figure 10-8. To fix a squeaky board, nail it from above into a joist.

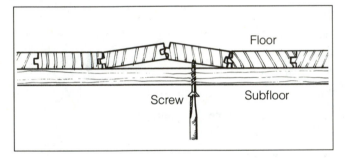

Figure 10-9. Use a screw to pull down a warped floorboard.

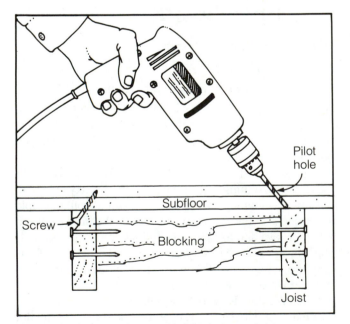

Figure 10-10. A wood or metal bridge between joists may stiffen the floor enough to eliminate a squeak.

with wood dough (Figure 10-8). This technique also works for repairing cupped or warped boards.

If the floor joists are exposed from below, you can drill a pilot hole up through the floor joist and/or subflooring and 1/4" into the squeaky board (Figure 10-9). Use a drill bit stop to prevent drilling through the floor surface. Wrap masking tape around the bit as a drill guide. Then you can grab the board from below with a 3/16" round-head wood screw with a large washer. This technique of screwing the board from below also works for repairing cupped or warped boards. Another possible solution is to add metal joist bridging or wood blocking between the joists near the squeak (Figure 10-10). This will often stiffen the floor and eliminate the squeak.

If there are any small holes or cracks in your new floor, now is the time to fill them. Use a putty knife to fill cracks thoroughly with a wood dough that matches the color of your unfinished floor (Figure 10-11). Allow the wood dough to dry thoroughly before sanding.

Step Two Preparing the Room for Sanding

Margin of Error: Not applicable

Most Common Mistake

☐ Neglecting to prepare the room.

After you have prepared the floor, you will need to take a few additional steps before sanding. Remove the floor registers, if they have been installed, and seal the openings with plastic. Also seal any heating or air conditioning ducts. Search out any protruding nailheads and countersink them with a nailset. Sanding produces a very flammable dust, so turn off all gas and electrical appliances and seal off all electrical outlets. Seal the room off tightly from the rest of the house to avoid dust problems. However, you should open a window and use a window fan to provide adequate ventilation while sanding. After all this is done, sweep the floor well and vacuum with a heavy-duty shop vacuum.

Step Three
Sanding the Floor

Margin of Error: Everything level within ⅛"

Most Common Mistakes

☐ Allowing sander to gouge floor.

☐ Leaving high spots or ridges.

☐ Not using an edge sander.

☐ Not sanding with fine paper.

Most oak floorings are ¾" thick and can be sanded a number of times. Thinner floors—½", ⅜", or 5/16"—must be refinished with caution to avoid sanding through to the subfloor. If your floor is thinner than ¾", consult a professional floor refinisher.

You are now ready to begin sanding. This is the only difficult part of the process; you need to be very careful or you can gouge the floor past repair. This happened to a friend of mine who had not bothered to learn to use the drum sander properly. Fortunately, his gouge was in an area covered by a sofa; but you don't want to have to arrange your furniture according to your gouges.

When you rent the drum sander, be sure to get a manufacturer's instructional manual and some hints and a demonstration from the store where you rent it. Be sure that the sander is in good shape and functioning well, and check to be sure you have all the dust bags, special wrenches, and attachments. The drum sander is a powerful machine. Although it does not require any great strength to handle, you should practice on a piece of plywood, or with fine sandpaper, until you get the hang of it. Always use a dust mask and ear protection when you are working with a drum sander.

Purchase several grits of "open face" sandpaper. You will use the coarse grits for rough sanding and the finer grits at the end to provide a smooth finish. If you need to sand cupped boards, start with a 20-grit paper. For the second sanding, use a medium, 80-grit paper. The final finish sanding requires a fine, 100-grit paper, or even finer for certain woods. The number of sanding passes, two or more, depends on the condition of your floor.

Be sure to buy enough sandpaper. The average room requires about ten sheets of each grade for the drum sander and ten sheets of each grade for the edge sander. Get a surplus and return what you don't use. Be sure the paper is properly installed in the sander, and remember to change it regularly.

In your first sanding, with rough-grit sandpaper, you will be removing any stains or discolorations and leveling the floor to a smooth surface. If there are warped boards or ridges that you were not able to repair earlier, you will need to sand diagonally across the floor in those areas with a rough-grade sandpaper until the floor is smooth. Then sand

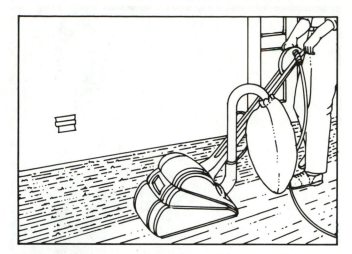

Figure 10-12. Use a professional drum sander to sand the floor.

with the grain of the floor to get out the sanding marks left by the diagonal sanding. Except for these badly cupped areas, always sand with the grain of the floor.

Never turn the sander on while the sandpaper and drum are touching the floor. Tilt the sander back by the handle until it is out of contact, start the sander, and when it reaches full speed slowly lower it until the sandpaper touches the floor (Figure 10-12). Begin to move the moment the drum touches the floor. Let the sander pull you forward at a slow, steady speed. You can sand both forward and backward, but always keep the sander in motion. Never allow it to stop while it is in contact with the floor. Sand in straight lines with the grain of the floor. As you approach the end of your run, lift the sander while it is still moving forward.

You should sand about two-thirds of the floor in one direction and one-third in the other, as shown in Figure 10-13. Whenever you need to reposition the sander, make certain the drum is off the floor. Overlap your passes to be sure you are sanding all areas thoroughly, and to ensure an even finish with no sanding marks. Go forward and then return over the same area as you go backward. Move sideways in 3" to 4" increments to overlap each pass.

After you have done your first pass on the main body of the floor, use an edge sander, with the same coarse-grit paper, where the floor meets the wall and in other areas missed by the drum sander (Figure 10-14). Follow the manufacturer's instructions with this machine. It can also gouge the wood, although not as easily as the drum sander.

After the first sanding, fill any dents, gouges, or cracks with wood dough and allow it to dry. Then repeat the sanding process with both the drum and edge sanders with medium-grit paper.

Before you begin the final sanding, use a hand sanding block to get to any areas the power tools could not reach, such as under radiators and in corners. Then repeat the sanding process a final time, using a fine-grit paper.

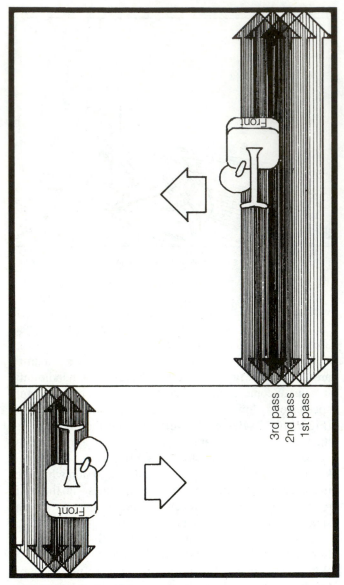

Figure 10-13. Recommended pattern of sanding with a drum sander.

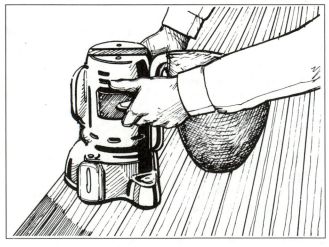

Figure 10-14. Use an edge sander where the floor meets the wall.

Step Four
Applying the Stain

Margin of Error: Not applicable

Most Common Mistakes

☐ Not removing all the sanding dust before staining.

☐ Staining unevenly.

It is best to finish the floor and apply a protective sealant as soon as possible after sanding the floor, preferably the same day. This protects the floor from moisture and other problems that could cause the wood grain to rise and create a rough surface. Before you begin finishing the floor, you need to be sure that it is perfectly clean and free of dust or debris. Also check carefully for any flaws or imperfections.

Fill any remaining cracks or holes with wood dough, allow it to dry, and then sand it smooth. Sand off any swirls or sanding marks. Vacuum the floors well and rub them with a tack cloth to pick up all the fine dust. Finally, rub your entire floor well with cheesecloth.

Staining the floor is optional. You may want to just put on a protective finish and let the natural color of the wood show through. If you decide to stain the floor, it's a good idea to test the color on an area that will be hidden before applying it to the entire floor. The color may appear quite different from the small sample you saw at the store.

Before staining your floor, you may want to apply a wood sealer, especially if you have installed a softwood floor. This is not the heavy-duty protective finish that you will apply last, but rather a light-weight sealer that seals the open pores of the wood, making it easier to apply the stain evenly. Some

Figure 10-15. Use a professional buffer with a steel wool pad to sand between coats of stain and between coats of polyurethane.

wood sealers are colored and stain and seal the floor in one application.

Applying stain can be tricky; follow the manufacturer's instructions carefully. It takes concentration and some skill to get a good even finish with no blotchy areas where the stain is unevenly applied. The sealer will help, because the pores will be sealed and the stain will not penetrate as deep or as quickly.

Pour all the stain you will need into one container and mix it thoroughly to ensure even color. You can use rags, brushes, or a roller to apply the stain. Go carefully and be sure that the stain is penetrating to give an even color. The pigments of the stain are in suspension, not in solution, so the stain must be stirred regularly during application. Apply a generous coat; after 5 to 10 minutes, wipe vigorously with a rag to remove the excess. The amount of time you allow the stain to set on the floor will determine the darkness of the color. After wiping off the excess stain, buff the floor with a professional buffer and a #1 steel wool disk (Figure 10-15). As always, follow the manufacturer's instructions. Vacuum the floor thoroughly before applying the final coat.

Keep rags handy to wipe up any excess stain. To avoid the danger of spontaneous combustion, never store oily rags together or in a closed container.

Step Five
Applying the Protective Finish

Margin of Error: Not applicable

Most Common Mistakes

☐ Not sanding after every coat.

☐ Not stirring the finish properly.

There are several types of protective finishes. The two most common types are penetrating sealers and surface finishes, including polyurethane, varnish, and shellac. Penetrating sealers (mentioned under staining) may be clear or tinted. They penetrate the pores of the wood, so the finish wears as the wood wears and can be retouched with wax in heavy-traffic areas. These penetrating sealers are often used as an undercoat with surface finishes. However, make sure that the two finishes are compatible before you begin.

Surface finishes provide a tough, clear coating over stained or sealed wood. Polyurethane has largely replaced varnish, shellac, and lacquer. A heavy-traffic wax is often applied over the polyurethane.

Finishes come in a clear gloss finish (high gloss) and a satin finish (low gloss). The satin finish shows dust less.

Applying Polyurethane

Be sure to buy the slower-drying air-drying polyurethanes, rather than the faster-drying moisture-cured types that professionals use. Make sure that whatever type you use is compatible with any undercoat you may have applied.

Always stir polyurethane well before you apply it. The hardeners settle to the bottom, and if the polyurethane is not well stirred the floor will not dry evenly. Use a paint stick or install a bent coat hanger in a variable speed drill. Stir at a low speed, being careful not to create bubbles in the polyurethane. Ventilate the room well and wear a mask made for use with toxic fumes. In ventilating, however, be careful not to create a situation that will allow dust particles to settle on the wet floor.

It is best to apply the finish with a lamb's wool applicator and a paint tray. Use a brush at the walls and in hard-to-reach areas. Apply the polyurethane evenly, moving the applicator in the direction of the grain.

Allow the first coat of polyurethane to dry completely (Drying time will vary with the temperature and humidity.) When the floor is completely dry, with no tacky feel, sand it with a buffer equipped with a #2 steel wool disk. This is much easier than using a hand sander, although you will still have to sand hard-to-reach areas by hand. Vacuum after sanding, and then go over the floor with a damp mop to remove all the dust.

The second coat of polyurethane should be applied across the grain. When the second coat is completely dry, repeat the sanding process. Three or four coats are usually applied. the final coat, which is applied with the grain of the wood, does not need to be buffed. For one final layer of protection, you may apply a coat of heavy-traffic wax.

You can move in as soon as the final coat is dry. the protective finish may give off unpleasant fumes, but the odor should not be noticeable after a week or so.

11 Ceramic Tile

INSTALLING CERAMIC TILE in your bathroom or kitchen is one of the most satisfying projects you can undertake around your home. That's because the result is so beautiful—no other surface combines the colorful appeal of tile with its practicality and durability. Properly installed, a tile floor can retain its easy-to-clean good looks for a lifetime.

Tile comes in a bewildering array of sizes, shapes, colors, and finishes. Larger, thicker tiles are usually used for floors; smaller, thinner ones are used for walls, countertops, and shower stalls.

Vitreous tile and **glazed tile** both resist water absorption through their finished surface, and are a good choice for areas where water will be present. Unglazed tiles absorb water, and are a poor choice for wet areas. Unglazed tile has a dull surface; glazed tile is satin or shiny; and the vitreous type is available in dull, satin, and shiny finishes. All tiles have dull backs so the adhesive has something to stick to.

Tiles are available in shapes like squares, rectangles, hexagons, thin strips, and thick strips, and in many sizes. Standard wall and counter tiles are about 4" by 4" and of uniform thickness. Smaller sizes, called **mosaic tiles,** are often glued to a fiber backing. Mosaic sheets are available in solid colors and in patterns.

You will need color-matched trim pieces to complete your installation. Trim for countertop edges, backsplashes, and wall accents can be quite elaborate; trim for the larger format floor tiles is usually limited to bullnoses for doorways and baseboard pieces.

A trip to a tile showroom can be overwhelming with the variety of shapes, sizes, colors, and glazes of tile available. Unless you have a firm idea of what you want, plan to visit the showroom at least twice before you make up your mind; you'll be living with your selection for a long time.

Until about 30 years ago, tile was set into mortar—a difficult job that was best left to a professional. These days, tile is set with a strong adhesive on top of backer board, a much easier task.

This chapter describes the process of installing ceramic tile on kitchen and bathroom walls, floors, and counters, from putting up the backer board through grouting and sealing the tile. The job requires patience and precision, and it can be messy, but it's not really difficult once your layout lines are in exactly the right place.

Before You Begin

SAFETY

- ☐ Wear safety glasses or goggles when cutting tile to protect against flying chips.
- ☐ Cut or broken tile edges are very sharp. Use a tile sander to smooth these edges.
- ☐ Wear ear protectors when using power tools. Some tools operate at noise levels that can damage hearing.
- ☐ Be careful not to let loose hair and clothing get caught in tools. Roll your up sleeves and remove jewelry.
- ☐ Wear the proper respirator or face mask when sanding, sawing, or using substances that give off toxic fumes.
- ☐ Keep blades sharp. A dull blade requires excessive force and can easily slip.
- ☐ Always use the right tool for the job.
- ☐ Don't drill, shape, saw, or cut anything that isn't firmly secured.
- ☐ Don't work with tools when you are tired. That's when most accidents occur.
- ☐ Read the owner's manual for all tools and understand their proper use.
- ☐ Keep tools out of the reach of small children.
- ☐ Unplug all power tools when changing settings or parts.

WHAT YOU WILL NEED

Time. The time you will need depends on the size and complexity of your tiling job. Allow yourself plenty of time—laying tile is a painstaking process.

Tools. Most specialty tile tools can be purchased inexpensively. You can probably rent or borrow an electric tile saw from your tile dealer.

Tape measure

Tile cutter

Tile nippers

Tile sander

Combination square

Carbide rod sawblade

Framing square

Notched trowel

Level

Hammer

Rubber mallet

Floor scraper

Caulking gun and caulk

Chalk line

Screwdriver or can opener

Putty knife

Utility knife

Large sponge

Grout mixing tray

Grout trowel

Margin trowel

Materials. Field tiles, including mosaic sheets, are purchased by the square foot. Trim tiles, such as counter edges, backsplashes, and edge detail pieces, are figured in linear feet. Before you order your tile, you should make accurate measurements of the space you want to cover with tile and draw your plan out on graph paper. To allow for cuts and damage, order about 5 percent more tile than you need, or even more for complicated jobs. The color of the glaze will vary from shipment to shipment, so if you have to go back to the store for more tile, you may find that the color does not match very well.

Self-spacing tiles have small tabs cast into their back edges, in the corners. These tabs typically produce a very narrow grout line. If you are not using self-spacing tiles, you will need to buy small plastic spacers to maintain proper alignment and grout spacing. Plastic spacers come in the form of X's, Y's, and T's, with legs in widths varying from $1/16$" to $1/2$". The width of the leg determines the width of the grout line. Spacers are made of a flexible material that can be compressed slightly so that you can make minor adjustments.

Grout comes in many colors. If you decide to use a colored grout, be sure that it won't stain the tile you've selected. In choosing kitchen tile, keep in mind that a dark grout does not show dirt like a white grout.

Tile

Backer board or underlayment (for floors)

Grout

Roofing nails for backer board

Nails for underlayment (for floors)

Mastic

Spacers

Wood for battens

Grout sealer

Grout fortifier

USEFUL TERMS

Backer board is a thin sheet of concrete sandwiched between pieces of thin fiberglass mesh and made into sheets like plywood. It is used as a backing for tile.

A **batten** is a straight piece of wood nailed to the wall or floor as a guide.

Mastic is a generic name for cement mortar *or* tile adhesive.

A **rod saw** is a small wire encrusted with carbide chunks that fits into a hacksaw. Small holes are best cut in tiles with a rod saw.

A **spacer** is a piece of plastic or wood that is used to keep uniform spaces between the tiles.

Thinset is a cement-based adhesive.

Tile adhesive is a solvent-based adhesive that is used to stick tiles to backer board or drywall.

An **underlayment** is a piece of heel-proof plywood installed over the subfloor to provide a base for installing tile.

Most Common Mistakes

☐ Cutting tile with equipment and blades not designed for that purpose.

☐ Not using the proper backing or underlayment as a base for the tile.

☐ Not having the tile and underlayment at the proper temperature. Follow the manufacturer's directions.

☐ Not sealing the joints of the backing well.

☐ Not laying out the tiles correctly, and therefore ending up with very narrow tiles on the ends of the rows.

☐ Misaligning the tiles, so the job looks sloppy and out of level.

☐ Not using waterproof mastic when applying tile where it will get wet.

☐ Poor adhesion of tiles to the mastic, allowing the tiles to pull away from the wall.

☐ Not applying silicone caulk around the lip of the tub or shower pan.

☐ Not allowing the mastic to dry long enough before applying the grout.

☐ Not wiping the grout off before it sets up.

☐ Not sealing the grout with a silicone sealer a few days after installation, when the grout has had time to cure.

TILE WALLS

Step One
Installing the Backer Board

Margin of Error: $1/4$"

Before you begin, cover any drains with tape so that debris won't fall in and clog them. Line the tub, shower, and/or sink with cardboard to avoid scratching them. In bathrooms, kitchens, and other areas that are exposed to moisture, the basic wall surface should be greenrock (moisture-resistant drywall).

For the best tiling surface, a mortar-based backer board is installed over greenrock. Backer board is easy to apply and compares in quality to the traditional but difficult method of doing a mortar bed.

Backer board is made of a concrete core that is coated on both sides with a thin fiberglass mesh. It comes in plywood-like sheets that are 7/16" thick, and is applied in much the same way as drywall. It is installed with the smooth side out if you plan to use adhesive and the rough side out if you plan to use epoxy or acrylic mortar.

The height of the backer board determines the height of the tile job. Once the tile has been laid, a line of quarter-round or other trim tiles will cover up the rough edge of the backer board.

If the tile is not going all the way to the ceiling, you will need to make some level layout lines at the correct height so that you have a line to run the backer board to. In laying out these lines, make sure that there is at least one row of tiles above the shower head. Use a level to establish an accurate line all the way around the surface to be tiled.

Determine the height of the backer board by measuring carefully so that when the tiles are installed up the wall you won't have to cut the tile for the top row. Also check to make sure that the tub is level. If you are working around a tub or shower pan that is not level and cannot be adjusted, cut your backer board so that the cut edge is along the lip of the tub or shower pan and is at the same angle as the tub, before cutting the top.

If your tub can be adjusted to be level, do so by placing shims under the tub before you put up the backer board. If you are tiling around a shower, be sure that the shower pan is correctly seated so that it is level and will drain well.

Start with the back wall, because the backer board that goes on there requires the fewest cuts. Mark the locations of the studs on small pieces of tape on the floor and ceiling. Later, when you are putting the backer board up, you can snap a chalkline from floor to ceiling on the backer board along the center of the stud to show you where to nail. (There are several ways to find the studs in a finished wall. Studs are usually located every 16" on center. Tap along the wall with a hammer until you hear a solid sound; look for seams in the drywall or mud over fasteners; or use a magnetic stud finder to locate the nails in the studs. Drive a finish nail into the wall in an area that will be covered by tile to verify the location of the stud behind the drywall.)

If you plan to use a floor and wall tile adhesive, install the backer board with the smooth side out. If you plan to use an epoxy or acrylic mortar, install the textured side out. If you are using epoxy or acrylic, make sure that the room is very well ventilated.

Cutting the backer board is easy. Make careful measurements, and mark them with chalk on the front of the backer board. Use a straightedge and a utility knife to score along your chalkline. The backer board will crack along that scored line when it is bent, just like drywall. Then turn the piece over and score the back to cut through the mesh.

Use galvanized roofing nails to hang the backer board. The nails must be long enough to go through the backer board and the drywall and penetrate 1" into the studs. Nail at 6" intervals around the edges and in the center over the studs. Nailheads should be flush with the surface but not counter-sunk. Countersinking the nails can cause the backer board to crack or break. Joints should be close together but not tight. Some backer board manufacturers recommend the use of a nail and a large washer at the edge for better holding. Check the manufacturer's instructions.

Position 1/4" spacers along the rim of the tub to hold the backer board up slightly. After all the backer board is up, but before you lay the tile, fill the gap with silicone caulk to form a water-tight seal.

When making the holes for the faucets and shower head, measure very accurately. Remember the cardinal rule of building: Measure twice, cut once.

Cutouts and holes for plumbing pipes and fixtures can be made by breaking through the fiberglass mesh with the edge of a hammerhead. For neater cuts, use a saber saw with a carbide blade or a masonry hole saw attachment for a drill.

Step Two
Taping the Joints of the Backer Board

Margin of Error: 1/4"

After the backer board is nailed in position, all the joints—including the gaps between dissimilar materials, such as backer board and greenrock—must be filled, much like the procedure for taping drywall (see Chapter 5, Drywall).

For the seams and corner, a 2"-wide coated fiberglass mesh tape is embedded in a dry-set or latex portland cement mortar. The gaps and cracks, including the one along the top of the tub, are filled with a thin coat of the same mortar.

When this mortar is dry, it needs to be waterproofed. Coat the entire backer board surface with a waterproofing sealer.

Step Three
Laying Out the Tile

Margin of Error: 1/8"

You have more leeway in laying out the tile for walls than for floors or countertops, because the finished tile surface doesn't have to go all the way to the ceiling. For appearance' sake, it's best to use full-sized tiles at the top and bottom of the walls and avoid having to cut tiles for top and bottom. This means you must add up the dimensions of all the field tiles, accent and trim strips, and grout lines to determine the height of the finished wall. Around the shower, the height of the finished surface will determine the height of the backer board, so measure and add carefully.

The following explanation of a tile wall installation assumes that you are using standard square tiles. If you are using prealigned mosaic sheets, adjust your layout lines to

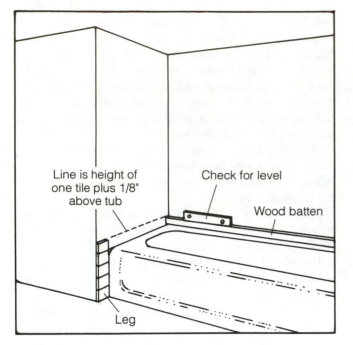

Figure 11-1. Horizontal working lines for tile layout.

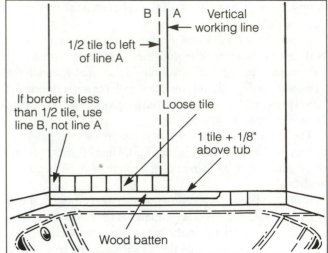

Figure 11-2. Vertical working lines for tile layout.

reflect the sheet format. Although these sheets are uniform squares, their sizes vary by manufacturer and style.

Before you roll up your sleeves and go to work, you want to make sure that you have everything you're going to need. Double check your supplies carefully.

Do the colors of the tile match? There is often some discrepancy in tile color from box to box. It's a good idea to pull tiles out of different boxes as you work so that any slight color difference is blended in.

Horizontal Working Lines

It is crucial that you make accurate layout lines. These lines are the map you follow in installing your tile, so be sure they are bold and easy to see.

The horizontal lines come first (Figure 11-1). The way you lay them out depends on whether or not your tub or shower pan is level.

For a Level Tub or Shower Pan. If the tub or shower pan is level to ⅛", measure and mark your horizontal line from the high point of the tub. A difference of ⅛" is easy to disguise at the bottom. Measure up from the lip of the tub the width of the tile plus ⅛". If you are using standard 4 ⅛" square tile, measure up 4 ¼" and make a level line, using a level, along the back wall and the two end walls.

For an Out of Level Tub or Shower Pan. If the tub or shower pan is not level to ⅛", mark your horizontal line from the low point. If you don't do this, the gap along the edge of the tub and tile will show. Determine a level line in the same way as for a level tub, and then run a batten along the bottom of the line so you have a level line to work off of. To do this, nail a straight wooden batten so that the top of the

batten is set to the horizontal line. This provides an exactly level surface on which to begin laying the tile. After all the tile is laid, remove the batten and install the bottom row of tile. In this case, you will need to custom-cut the bottom row of tiles to fit.

Vertical Working Lines

When you lay the tiles out, adjust them so that the border tiles (the tiles on the vertical edges) are more than half a tile in width, and so that the the tiles on each edge are the same size.

To do this, first locate the midpoint of the back wall and mark it on the horizontal line (Figure 11-2). Then line up a row of loose tiles along the back of the tub, making sure that a joint matches up with the center mark. If your tiles are not self-spacing, use plastic spacers. The distance that is left at either end gives you the dimension of your border tiles.

If the end tiles turn out to be larger than half a tile, mark the vertical center line all the way up the wall, using a level and straightedge. The edge of the tile will be set to this line (line A in Figure 11-2).

If it turns out that the end tiles are smaller than half the width of a tile, move the center line exactly one half the width of a tile to the left or right (line B in Figure 11-2). By making this adjustment you avoid having narrow tiles on the borders. Very narrow tiles are unattractive and hard to cut.

The vertical layout lines for the end walls are usually marked after the back wall has been tiled. Just position the vertical working lines to minimize the number of tiles to be cut, and locate any cut tiles in the corners. Also decide whether you want to align the joints between the tiles or to stagger them so that they fall in the middle of the tile in the rows directly above and below them. In this case you will need to develop vertical layout lines so that no row has edge tiles that are less than half a tile.

Determine where you are going to put the towel rods and the soap dish or any other special accessory tiles, and mark

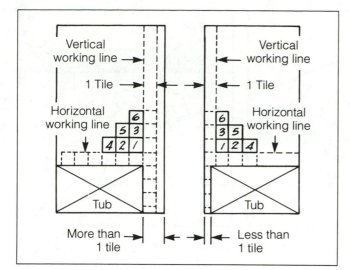

Figure 11-3. Tile layout on side walls.

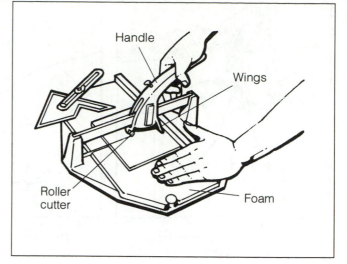

Figure 11-4. Use a tile cutter for straight cuts.

their locations. These will be installed last, and usually take up the room of ½, 1, or 1 ½ tiles.

If your soap dish fits into the wall, cut your hole before you spread the adhesive, and position it to minimize or even eliminate the need to cut any tiles to go around it.

Step Four
Spreading the Adhesive

Margin of Error: Not applicable

For a tub or shower enclosure, you should start with the back wall, unless you are also tiling the ceiling, in which case you should start there.

It is very important to use waterproof mastic in areas that are exposed to moisture. Before you apply the adhesive, read the manufacturer's instructions and note the drying time. Don't spread any more adhesive than you can work with before it sets up. Generally it's best to spread enough for 30 to 40 minutes work.

When applying the adhesive, be careful not to obscure your working lines. Also, be sure to leave blank spaces where you plan to install accessories.

Use the flat side of your trowel to spread the adhesive over a wide area of the wall. Then run the notched side through the adhesive at a 45-degree angle to create grooves. The peaks of the grooves should be nearly as thick as the tiles; the valleys should be only a thin film.

Step Five
Laying the Tile

Margin of Error: ⅛"

When laying the tile you can either align the joints in the tile of each row or stagger the joints. If you stagger the joints, the joints of one row will fall in the middle of the tiles in the row directly above and below. This is an esthetic decision; staggering the joints slightly is easier, but aligning the joints is not difficult. The tabs on self-spacing tiles do not align if you stagger the joints. Use plastic T's to space staggered joints.

Set the first tile along one side of the vertical and horizontal working lines (Figure 11-3). When setting the tile, use a gentle twisting motion. Don't slide the tile into place or you will squeeze the adhesive to one side.

If you are working with a batten, make sure that the tiles are firmly seated on it. If you are not working with a batten, be sure to line the top edge of the tile up along the horizontal line. If necessary, use two spacer legs underneath the tiles along the lip of the tub to hold the tile up along the line.

Lay the tiles row by row in a triangular pattern, using the spacers at the intersections, as shown in Figure 11-3. Keep a watchful eye out for correct alignment along the working lines. Tap the tiles with a rubber mallet and a block of padded wood as you go.

On inside corners, the tiles are laid up to the corner, leaving a small gap for grout. Outside corners may be treated with a bullnose tile; or you can use a special outside corner tile that has a curved lip. As you work, keep checking with your level to be sure that you are staying plumb and level, and adjust your tiles as needed. Also check to be sure the tiles are flush and are not pushed out from the wall.

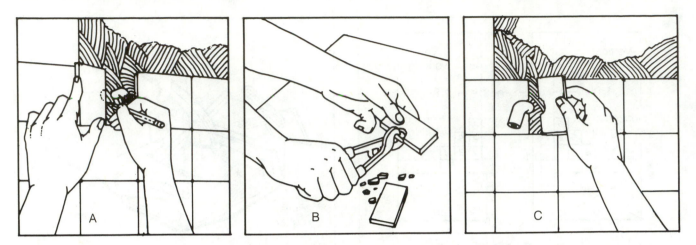

Figure 11-5. Use tile nippers for irregular shapes. A: Draw outline of pipe on tile. B: Nibble out small bites of the tile with nippers. C: Position tile around pipe.

Step Six
Cutting the Tile

Margin of Error: Exact

You may need to cut the border tiles to fit. Many tile dealers will loan you a simple tile cutter; or you can rent a wet saw.

Measure carefully, allowing for the grout line. Transfer your measurements to the tile to be cut.

Some tiles have small parallel ridges on their backs. Whenever possible, make your cuts in the same direction as these ridges.

When cutting with a nonpower tile cutter (Figure 11-4), score the tile only once. Multiple scores will dull the blade and create jagged edges on the tile. Place the breaking wings, located at the bottom of the handle, about 1/2" from either edge of the tile and slowly but firmly press down on the handle until the wings break the tile along the scored line. Smooth rough edges with a tile sander.

Cut tiles to fit around pipes and faucets after all the field tiles are laid. Remember to allow for the grout lines when taking your measurements.

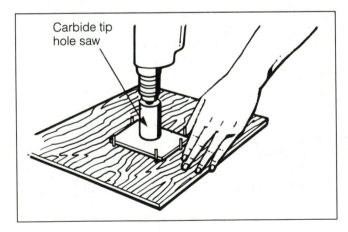

Figure 11-6. Use a carbide tip hole saw to cut holes in tiles for plumbing pipes.

There are several ways to make complicated cuts. To fit a tile around a pipe, first cut the tile in two and draw on the tile the outline of the cut you need to make. Score the line with a micro cutter (a small sharp wheel with a handle). Score all over the area to be cut away, then "nibble" the area out with tile nippers (Figure 11-5). Use a tile stone to smooth the edges of the cuts you made with the nippers. To cut small holes for plumbing pipes, you can use a rod saw with a carbide blade, or you can get a tile-cutting attachment for your drill (Figure 11-6).

Step Seven
Trim Tiles and Final Adjustments

Margin of Error: 1/8"

All the edges of the tiled area need to be finished off with edge and corner trim. Simply butter the adhesive on the back of the tiles and stick them onto the wall in the correct position, aligning the grout joints carefully.

Before the adhesive sets up, make any adjustments needed for correct alignment and remove any spacers you have used. Check to see if the tiles are fully set by trying to pull one up. Then clean off any adhesive on the face of the tile. Allow the adhesive to dry for 24 to 48 hours, depending on the type of adhesive.

Step Eight
Grouting

Margin of Error: Not applicable

Grout comes in many colors, to match or contrast with your tile. In addition to highlighting the tile, grout seals the gaps between tiles and keeps out water and dirt. It must be properly applied, or water can get behind the tile and cause rot.

There are many types of grout. Some include sand and some do not. Mix the grout with water, according to the

Figure 11-7. Spread grout with a grout trowel or squeegee.

Figure 11-8. Remove excess grout with a grout trowel or squeegee.

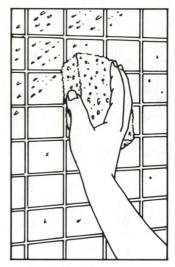

Figure 11-9. Remove remaining grout with a damp sponge.

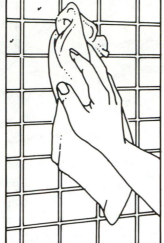

Figure 11-10. Remove film with a soft clean rag.

manufacturer's instructions. A latex additive is often used to make the grout spread easier and bond better and to reduce shrinkage. The grout should be thick enough to be easily troweled into the joints, not soupy.

For standard 4 ⅛" tiles, where the joints are very narrow, use a nonsanded grout. For wider grout joints, with other types of tiles, use a sanded grout, which holds up better.

The easiest way to apply grout is with a grout trowel (a rubber-faced float) or a squeegee, although you can do it with your fingers and a large sponge. Spread the grout on the surface of the tile, forcing it into the joints (Figure 11-7). It is crucial that the joints be completely filled, so that there are no bubbles or gaps. Grout only a small area at a time, because the grout begins to harden as soon as it is spread.

Scrape off the excess grout by wiping diagonally across the tiles with your grout trowel or squeegee (Figure 11-8). With a clean, damp sponge, wipe away any remaining grout (Figure 11-9). Wipe the grout away as you go. Grout a small area, then wipe it down; don't wait until you have grouted the entire area. Rinse the sponge frequently in clean water. Continue to rinse and wring out the sponge until the joints are smooth and level with the tiles.

Allow the grout to dry about 30 minutes, until a hazy film appears. Wipe the film away with a soft clean cloth (Figure 11-10). Use a margin trowel or the end of a toothbrush handle to tool the joints and clean the intersections. To tool the joints, run the trowel or toothbrush handle down the grout line to push the grout in and to remove excess grout.

Step Nine
Installing the Soap Dish and Other Accessories

Margin of Error: ⅛"

After you have laid your field tiles and the adhesive has dried, it's time to install the soap dish (Figure 11-11) and towel rack. Simply butter the back of the accessory and place it in the space you left open for that purpose. To hold the accessories in place until the adhesive dries, tape them tightly to the wall with duct tape. Just be sure that the adhesive behind the field tiles is completely dry, or the tape may pull the tiles off the wall.

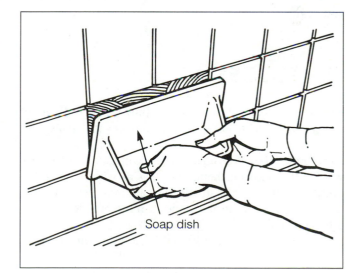

Soap dish

Figure 11-11. Remember to leave untiled spaces for the soap dish and other accessories.

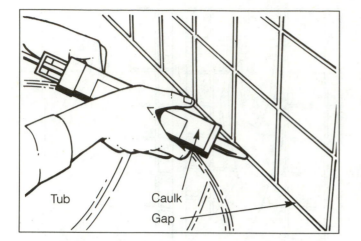

Figure 11-12. Caulk the gap between the tub and the wall.

Step Ten
Caulking and Sealing

Margin of Error: Not applicable

The final step in tiling your bathroom wall is to run a bead of silicone caulk around the edge of the tub, along the top where it meets the wall, and at the base where it meets the floor (Figure 11-12). Also caulk around the plumbing pipes and around the rims of the soap dish and towel rods. Wait until the grout is completely dry before caulking. It's also a good idea to fill the tub with water before caulking to maximize the size of the gap to be filled. Leave the water in the tub until the caulking has cured.

After the grout has completely dried and cured, it needs to be sealed with a silicone-based sealer, painted on according to the manufacturer's instructions. Drying time ranges from three days to two weeks, so be sure to read the label before you begin.

TILE FLOORS

Although the general rules for installing tile on walls apply to any tile job, there are specific techniques that apply only to floors.

Before you begin, cover any drains with tape so that debris won't fall in and clog them. Line the sink with cardboard to avoid scratching it. You should tile your floors before the toilet and cabinets are installed; never try to lay tile around a cabinet or toilet.

Before you order your materials, determine what you will need to finish the exposed edges properly. For example, if your finished floor level is going to be higher than the adjoining room or hallway, you should get bullnose tile to create a smooth transition. If the floor will meet a carpeted edge at the same level, then a regular square-edged tile will work.

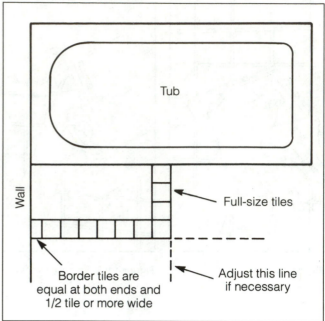

Figure 11-13. Layout for tile floor.

Step One
The Underlayment

Margin of Error: 1/4"

Proper backing for the tile floor is very important. The backing may consist of exterior-grade heel-proof plywood, luan underlayment panel, or mortar-based backer board. Don't use particle board, flakeboard, or masonite as underlayment for ceramic tile. The total floor sheathing should be at least 1 1/4" thick over the floor joists on 16" centers. Otherwise, flex may cause tiles to pop out of place. If your subfloor has been seriously dented and roughed up during construction, or if you need added stiffness, you may want to add a layer of underlayment over the original subfloor. (For information on installing an underlayment, see Chapter 9, Vinyl Floors.) If you do install a new underlayment over the subfloor, staple polyethylene plastic on top of the subfloor to protect it from water.

When applying a plywood underlayment, leave a slight gap between panels and about 1/4" along the edges to allow for expansion and contraction. Fill low areas and seams with a quick-drying latex patching compound, using a wide application blade to create as flat a surface as possible.

Stagger the joints of the underlayment in a brick-joint fashion, and be sure that underlayment seams do not fall directly over existing subfloor seams. With whatever underlayment you use, except for backer board, countersink all nails slightly.

If you use a mortar-based backer board, cover the joints and seams with joint compound and then seal them with a moisture-resistant sealant.

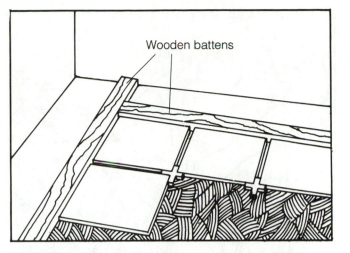

Figure 11-14. Nail battens at a right angle so you will have a square corner from which to start laying your floor tiles.

You can lay tile over concrete, but it must cure for at least 28 days first.

Step Two
Establishing the Layout Lines

Margin of Error: 1/8"

It is crucial that you establish accurate working lines. You want a layout in which there are full-size tiles in areas of high visibility, and in which all edge (border) tiles are at least half a tile wide.

Many floor tiles have matching baseboard pieces, and some baseboard tiles are coved. If you use coved baseboard, be sure to take it into account when making the layout lines.

Begin by making a dry run. Lay the dry tiles out from the two most visible walls to see which layout will work best in your room.

If the tiles at the end of each row (border tiles) are less than half a tile wide, adjust the row by moving it the width of half a tile to either the left or the right. This will ensure that all the cut tiles are more than half a tile in width (Figure 11-13). (See Step Three under Tile Walls.)

Next, check to be sure that the corner that you are working off of is square. If it isn't, tack battens to the floor a tile's width away from the wall along both walls. Then snap another line parallel to the first and outside of it by the thickness of two grout lines (to allow for the grout lines along the wall between the first and second rows of tiles).

Nail battens made from 1x2s or 1x3s along the second (working) line so that you have a firm position to start running your tiles (Figure 11-14). Make sure your battens are straight and form a right angle, and use your spacers.

Once the tiles are laid in the field, remove the battens and lay your tile along the edges, cutting the tiles as necessary. When you are cutting tiles, always remember to leave room for the grout line.

Step Three
Spreading the Adhesive, Laying and Cutting Tiles, and Grouting

Margin of Error: 1/8"

These steps are basically the same as those outlined earlier for installing tiles on walls.

Instead of laying the tiles in a pyramid fashion, as for walls, lay them row by row, cutting them as needed when you get to the end of a row. Use spacers at each joint. Then, with your eye close to the floor, sight down the edges and adjust the tiles if necessary.

TILE COUNTER TOPS

For counter top backing, you can use either backer board or exterior grade plywood. Be sure to cut out all openings for your sink and fixtures before applying the tile, and then cut the tile to fit around these openings. When you are ordering your tile, be sure to take into account all the trim and backsplash tile you'll need, and allow about 10 percent extra.

Step One
Laying Out the Tile

Margin of Error: 1/8"

If you are tiling around a sink, mark the center point of the sink. If there is no sink, mark the center point of the counter top. Make a dry run of the tiles along the edge to see whether the center line needs to be moved half a tile's width so that you don't end up with less than half a tile on the ends. (See Step Three under Tile Walls.)

It's a good idea to make a dry run of how all the tiles will go around the sink and then label them so that you will know where each tile goes after you have cut them. Use a full tile along the front of the counter top, even if that means the tile along the backsplash will be less than half a tile wide.

Step Two
Setting the Tile

Margin of Error: 1/8"

Set the front edge pieces first, before spreading the adhesive for the field tiles. Butter the back of the edge tiles with adhesive and place them along the front edge of the counter top (Figure 11-15). Use spacer legs to maintain your grout line layout.

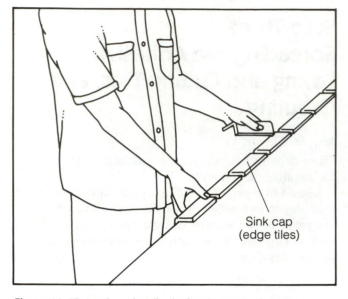

Figure 11-15. Lay the edge tiles before laying the field tiles.

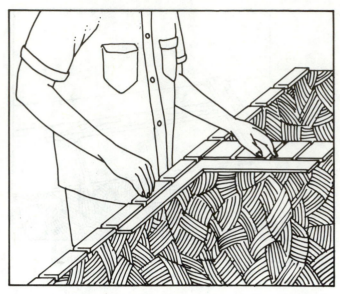

Figure 11-16. Use a framing square to install the first row of field tiles.

Unless the sink is mounted to be on top of the tile, lay the sink trim next. Be sure to caulk between the sink and the plywood backing before setting the sink trim.

If you are using quarter-round tiles, you can either miter the corners or use specially molded quarter-round corners.

Now you are ready to set the field tiles (Figure 11-16). Use a framing square to make sure your lines are straight. Lay each row of tile from front to back, starting either at the center or from the sides of the sink. Cut the tile as needed.

Install the backsplash last (Figure 11-17). The backsplash is usually made of bullnose tiles that can be applied directly above the back field tiles. Use spacer legs to maintain your grout line space at the bottom of the backsplash. Butter the back of the bullnose tiles and stick them to the wall. You can also apply adhesive on the wall; just be sure to stay below the top of the tile so that adhesive does not show above the tile. After grouting, you will need to caulk this joint.

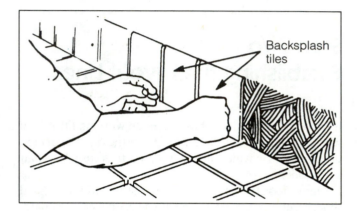

Figure 11-17. The backsplash is made of bullnose tiles.

Step Three
Grouting and Finishing

Margin of Error: Not applicable

These steps are the same as those described earlier for applying tiles to walls.

12 Painting and Wallpapering

PAINTING AND WALLPAPERING are simple projects, and with the information in this chapter they can be enjoyable and effective as well. You will learn how to prepare a wall, estimate materials, and use your tools correctly.

Neither painting nor wallpapering demands a lot of you physically. The toughest part is painting or papering the ceiling. The key thing is proper preparation. You may be tempted to take shortcuts here. Don't.

Before You Begin

SAFETY

It's important to understand, develop, and adhere to proper safety practices for any project you undertake. For both painting and wallpapering, safety precautions include the following.

☐ Always use the appropriate tool for the job.

☐ Keep blades sharp. A dull blade requires excessive force, and can easily slip.

☐ Always wear the proper respirator or face mask when sanding or working with chemicals.

☐ Wipe up spills immediately.

☐ Don't smoke or allow open flames, such as pilot lights, around solvents or solvent-based paints.

☐ Store and dispose of rags properly to avoid spontaneous combustion.

USEFUL TERMS

Booking the wallpaper means to loosely fold presoaked wallpaper, pasted side to pasted side, to allow a few minutes for curing (expansion of the adhesive) before applying it to the wall.

Cutting in means to use a 3" or 4" brush to paint corners and edges that cannot be covered by a roller, such as where wall meets wall, where wall meets ceiling, and next to the trim.

Feathering is a series of light strokes with brush or roller, lifting the applicator lightly at the end of each stroke to blend in the paint.

A **sash brush** is a 1 ½" angled brush made for detail painting of windows and narrow trim pieces.

Sizing is a liquid that is painted on the wall before papering. Sizing dries to a tacky feel, ensuring proper adhesion of wallpaper. It also makes it easy to remove the wallpaper in the future.

A **trim brush** is a 2" brush for painting door trim and other wide moldings.

TSP (trisodium phosphate) is an industrial cleaner.

PERMITS AND CODES

Some areas require permits whenever you are spending more than a certain amount of money on construction, repairs, or remodeling. Check with your local building inspector to see if you need a permit. Usually only a small fee is required, and this ordinance is often not enforced. Other than this, no permits or inspections apply in either painting or wallpapering projects.

PAINTING

WHAT YOU WILL NEED

Time. Preparation time will depend on the extent of the problems encountered. Painting (including cutting in) takes approximately 30 to 60 minutes per 100 square feet.

Tools for Painting. Figure 12-1 shows some of the tools you will need for your painting project.

For the most part, it is best to use paint rollers for the large areas, brushes for smaller areas, and specialized tools for corners and trim. For tight areas like small bathrooms and closets, where there may be lots of trim and little room to maneuver a roller, consider using a paint pad instead. Always purchase high-quality tools, or you will regret it later. Cheap rollers, pads, and brushes can cause uneven application of the paint and an unprofessional looking result.

Rollers come in many different types, with naps that differ according to their use. A good synthetic roller cover will work as well as a lambswool roller. Read the package and be sure to buy the proper types for your application. The roller you purchase should have a handle with nylon bearings, a comfortable grip, a threaded hole for an extension, and a beveled end. A fairly new option on the market, the electric roller, supplies the roller with a continuous flow of paint. An air compressor with a painting attachment can also save you time and effort (see Chapter 1, Tools).

You will also need to purchase a pan to hold the paint and a metal or plastic grid, or screen, to go in the pan. The screen ensures that the roller is properly loaded with paint.

Roller | Roller cover | Large brush | Small brush | Angled trim brush

Figure 12-1. Tools for a typical painting project.

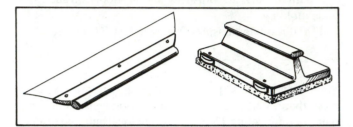

Figure 12-2. The paint guide and paint edger are used for cutting in—painting the corners where ceilings meet walls and where walls intersect.

Brushes come in two types, with synthetic or natural bristles. Natural bristles are recommended for oil-based paints but not for water-based paints. Synthetic filament brushes (nylon or polyester) must be used for water-thinned paint, although they work with solvent coatings as well. Polyester brushes should not be used with shellacs and lacquers. Always purchase high-quality brushes. Most jobs require a 4" brush for cutting in, a 2" brush for baseboards and trim, and a 1 ½" to 2" angled sash brush for windows and smaller trim. Paint pads should have beveled edges and a curled rear edge.

You may also need some specialty tools, such as a paint guide and edger, shown in Figure 12-2.

Materials for Painting. There are two types of paint: alkyd (oil-based) paint and latex (water-based) paint. Latex paints are generally used in areas that don't require frequent washing. Cleanup with these paints requires only water and is much easier than with oil-based paints, which require a solvent for cleaning up.

Oil-based paints are applied in areas that require frequent washing. They are resistant to damage, and are often applied over metal or wood.

Paints also come in several finishes: primers, gloss, and flat. Primers (undercoats and sealers) are used as bases or undercoats beneath the finish coat. Flat paints with no gloss are often used on walls and ceilings. Gloss finishes (from low to high gloss) are used on woodwork and in bathrooms and kitchens because of their water-repellent nature.

Tools for Prepping Walls

Safety glasses or goggles

Respirator or face mask

Ear protectors

Rubber gloves

Paint scraper

Fan

Hand sanding block

Orbital sander

Screwdriver

Putty knife

Sponge

Cap or scarf

Old clothes

Materials for Prepping Walls

Primer

Sizing (for wallpapering)

Tools for Painting

Drop cloths

Ladders

Buckets

Paint edger

Brushes, 4", 3", and 1½"

Angled sash brushes, 1½" and 2"

Roller pan with screen

Roller covers with appropriate naps

Roller handle

Roller extender

Paint guide

Materials for Painting

Masking tape, 2" wide

Newspaper

Adhesive pad or primer

Paint

Paint thinner (for oil-based paints)

Aluminum foil

Rags

Estimating Paint

To estimate the amount of paint you will need, first calculate the area of the walls and ceiling in square feet. Multiply the perimeter of the room by the height of the walls. For the ceiling, multiply the length by the width. Add these two numbers together to determine the number of square feet you will need to cover. After you figure the square footage, add a little more for touch-up. A gallon of base coat will cover 350 to 450 square feet. Purchase all the paint you will need in one order; it's difficult to match colors exactly in a second batch.

Most Common Mistakes

The single most common mistake in any project is failure to read and follow the manufacturer's instructions for tools and materials. The most common mistakes in painting include the following.

- ☐ Not preparing a clean, sanded, and primed (if necessary) surface.
- ☐ Failing to mix the paints properly.
- ☐ Applying too much paint, or not enough paint, to the applicator.
- ☐ Using a water-logged applicator.
- ☐ Not solving dampness problems in the walls or ceilings before painting.

Step One
Prepping the Walls

Margin of Error: Not applicable

Most of us believe that we know everything we need to know about painting. This assumption often leads to poor quality work, both in preparation and in the actual paint application. You need to understand—and use—the proper procedures to ensure a high-quality painting or papering job.

If a job is worth doing, it's worth doing right the first time; and proper preparation is the key. Because it seems to lead to more work, preparation is a step that is too often left out, and the final result reflects this omission. It's too easy just to start painting or papering, without going through the necessary preparatory steps. The paint job may even look pretty good for a while. But sooner or later, the poor quality will show up.

Prepping the wall for a new covering is much the same whether you are papering or painting, although prepping the wall for papering involves a few more steps.

1. Turn the electricity off and remove everything from the walls and ceilings, including electrical wall and ceiling light fixtures, switch plates, and outlet plates, if these have already been installed. After you have safely wrapped all disconnected light fixture wires, you can turn the electricity back on.

2. Vacuum and/or mop the floors and all ledges to remove dust and debris. Cover the floor with a drop cloth.

3. A primer coat is recommended in many cases. For example, drywall must be well sealed with a primer before it is painted, or it will absorb the paint. Or you can apply an adhesive pad to the wall. This is a liquid just like a primer, but it dries to a tacky consistency. Ask your paint supplier for recommendations for your particular job.

4. Always apply a coat of liquid sizing to the surface before hanging wallpaper. The sizing gives a better adhesive to the wallpaper and also makes removal easier in the future.

5. Mask off windows (and the woodwork and trim, if they have been installed) with newspaper and masking tape that is at least 2" wide.

6. Before you begin, assemble all the ladders, buckets, brushes, paints, and everything else you are going to need.

Prepping the Trim and Woodwork

If your woodwork and trim are already installed, you will paint them last. But you need to prep them before beginning to paint, or else the debris from prepping will settle on the new paint. First, fill all dents and gouges with wood putty or patching compound. Don't use fast-drying compound, which is hard to sand. If the gouge is over 1/8" deep, use two layers. Woodwork and trim are usually painted with an enamel or glossy paint, which is both durable and easy to clean.

Getting Ready to Apply the Paint

Properly applying the paint is the final step in a professional-looking paint job. You have prepped the surfaces and chosen the right paint and applicators; now the fun starts.

Before you begin applying the paint, be sure that it is properly mixed. Professionals use a system called "boxing," which ensures that there are no mismatches among different cans of paint. Mix all your paint into one large container until the color and consistency are uniform. It is important to mix enough paint to cover all surfaces; matching can be difficult if you run out.

Air often causes a scum on the surface of oil-based paints. If this happens, you will need to strain the paint through a nylon stocking to remove this "skin." When thinning paint with either a thinner for oil-based paints or water for water-based, thin slowly to avoid overthinning.

After you open each can of paint, use a nail and hammer to punch holes in the rim of the can so that excess paint will drip back in (Figure 12-3).

Plan to paint your room in the following sequence.

1. Ceilings

2. Walls

3. Trim (if installed), windows, door, then baseboard

Paint the ceilings first so that any drips that fall on the walls will be covered later. When painting the walls, always paint from the top down, and do the trim last, again so that any paint that drips down can be covered.

Needless to say, you should wear old clothes. Unless you want to try some unusual hair coloring combinations, wear a hat and scarf or hooded sweatshirt while doing the ceilings.

Step Two
Cutting In

Margin of Error: Not applicable

Cutting in is the process of applying paint to all the places shown in Figure 12-4—all corners where ceilings meet walls and where walls intersect, and next to all molding,

Figure 12-3. Use a nail to punch holes in the rim of the paint can to let excess paint drip back in.

Figure 12-4. Cut in these areas before painting the large surfaces.

trim, and baseboards. Because rollers and sprayers cannot neatly reach these areas, use a 3" or 4" brush to paint all these edges before doing the large surfaces. You can also use a paint edger, a sponge-type brush with a small set of wheels on the side that enable it to make an even close cut. Use a paint edger or straightedge next to trim or baseboard to be sure that no paint gets on the wood. Do all necessary cutting in before painting the large surfaces.

Step Three
Painting the Large Surfaces

Margin of Error: Not applicable

After finishing the cutting in, you are ready to paint the ceiling and then the walls. Be sure the area is well lighted so you can see any ridges or drips. Painting the ceilings is physically difficult. Painting overhead can cause back and neck strain and an occasional eye full of paint. Safety goggles (and yoga) are a must when painting ceilings. Use a high-quality roller with an extension so that you can easily reach all areas of the ceiling. With such a roller, you won't need a ladder, except for touch-ups and cutting in. Use the same roller with extension for the high parts of the walls. If your ceilings are especially high, you may want to erect a low scaffold, using sawhorses or ladders with a 2x12 board between them.

To use a roller, pour the paint into the roller tray or paint pan so that the paint in the reservoir is ½" deep. This amount of paint will enable you to load the roller fully without underloading or overloading it. You can save on cleanup time by lining your tray with heavy-duty aluminum foil before pouring in the paint.

Roll or dip your roller into the paint reservoir and roll it around until the paint saturates the roller. Then run the roller a couple of times over the washboard area of the tray to remove excess paint so that it won't drip. You may be surprised at how much paint the roller holds, so be careful to saturate it thoroughly.

To avoid splattering, apply the paint slowly on the ceiling and walls. In the beginning, use overlapping V-shaped strokes, as shown in Figure 12-5. Begin at a corner and work across the wall or ceiling, covering about 3 square feet at a time. After you have made your V-shaped zigzag patterns, fill in the unpainted areas with parallel strokes without lifting the roller from the surface. Increase the pressure on the roller as you work to deliver the paint smoothly.

When you are rolling into unpainted areas, feather the paint in with a series of light strokes, and lift the roller at the end of each stroke. When you need to remove the roller to reload, begin the next section, rolling in a zigzag into the outer border of the area you just completed. Then lightly roll the area between the two sections. Paint the entire surface. Don't allow the paint to dry on part of the wall or ceiling.

Figure 12-5. Spread paint in unpainted areas with zigzag V-shaped strokes.

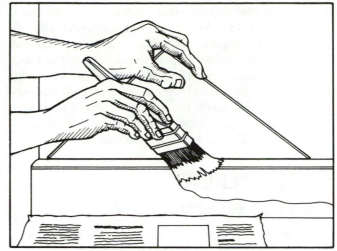

Figure 12-6. When painting baseboards, use a paint guide or masking tape on the walls and cover the floor with newspaper.

Step Four
Painting the Trim and Woodwork

Margin of Error: Exact

After you have finished all the large surfaces, you are ready to paint the trim and woodwork, if they have been installed. To do this successfully, you need to change your mental set about painting. Until now, you have been working on large surfaces, and detailing has not been important. Now you are changing from rough work to finish work. Attention to detail and care at this stage means the difference between a job that is professional-looking and one that is sloppy.

You will also be using different tools. During this stage you will use the smaller angled brushes and a metal paint guide. Use a 1½" angled sash brush on narrow molding, and a 2" trim brush on wider trim. As you apply the paint to the trim and woodwork, keep a supply of clean rags nearby to immediately wipe off any paint that gets on the previously painted surfaces. With oil-based paints, use a little mineral spirits or paint thinner. With water-based paints, use a mild detergent and water. Oil-based paints are most often used on trim because they give a surface that is both durable and easy to clean.

Always paint horizontal surfaces first and then vertical surfaces. Begin with the trim closest to the ceiling and work down. Do the baseboards last. Paint the top edge of the baseboard first, then the floor edge, and finally the center, using a larger brush. Be sure to cover the edge of the wall with a paint guide or masking tape (Figure 12-6).

Paint the inner sections of doors and windows before the outer portions. Windows especially require great care and patience. Apply the paint right down to the glass, so that the paint creates a seal between the wood and the glass. You can either tape the glass or remove the excess paint later with a razor-blade knife. If you are applying masking tape to the panes, leave a hairline gap of glass exposed between the tape and the wood to be sure you have a good paint seal between the wood and glass. Remove the tape as soon as the paint is completely dry.

When painting double-paned windows, you need to follow a certain order. You will need to be able to raise and lower the sashes to reach all areas. Begin by painting the exterior sash. Paint the horizontal side pieces, then the vertical, and then the muntins (the pieces that divide the window into small sections), as shown in Figure 12-7. Paint the lower part of the sash first, then raise the window and do the upper part. Repeat this process with the interior sash. Finally, paint the frame and trim, first the top sides and then the sill.

Raise and lower the sashes a few times while the paint is drying to be sure they don't dry stuck. Don't paint the jambs (the area where the window slides) unless absolutely necessary. To help the window move more smoothly after painting, rub a candle or a bar of soap over the jambs after the paint is completely dry.

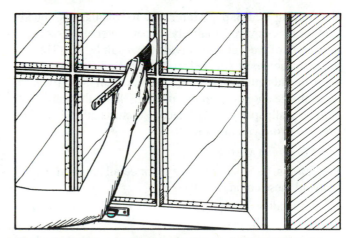

Figure 12-7. Use an angled trim brush to paint the muntins. Paint slightly onto the glass to ensure a good seal between wood and glass.

Doors are best painted when removed from their hinges and set on sawhorses. Flat doors are easily painted with rollers; panel doors require much greater care. First remove all hardware. With panel doors, paint the molding and the inside edges of the panel cavities first, and then the panels. Finally, paint all the horizontal and vertical pieces around the panels. If the door opens into the room, paint the door's latch edge, the jamb, and the door side of the door stop as well. When the door is dry, replace the hardware and rehang the door.

WALLPAPERING

WHAT YOU WILL NEED

Time. Wallpapering averages 10 to 20 minutes per sheet, longer if you must work around trim.

Tools for Wallpapering

Steel tape measure

Wallpaper level

Water tray

Seam roller

Wallpaper brush

Razor knife with lots of blades

Broadknife

Large sponge

Bucket

Pencil

Ladder

Materials for Wallpapering. An enormous number of different types of wall coverings are available. Consult your supplier or a book on wallpapering for complete information. Just be sure to purchase the prepasted type with adhesive on the back.

Wallpaper

Wallpaper paste (if needed)

Paint remover or mineral spirits

Estimating Wallpaper Materials. To calculate the square footage to be covered, multiply the perimeter of the room by the height of the walls and divide the result by 30. (The average roll covers 36 square feet, but there will be some waste for trim and pattern matching.) Subtract half a roll for each normal-size door or window opening. This is the number of rolls of wallpaper you will need. Purchase all rolls in one order to avoid variations in stock.

Most Common Mistakes

Preparation, patience, and an eye for detail are all you need to avoid these common mistakes.

☐ Not sanding, cleaning, and sizing the walls before applying the wallpaper.

☐ Failing to soak the prepasted wallpaper long enough.

☐ Failing to allow the wallcovering to cure the proper amount of time after soaking.

☐ Letting the adhesive dry on the woodwork.

☐ Not positioning the strips of wallpaper level and plumb.

☐ Not getting air pockets out when smoothing the covering on the wall.

☐ Not planning for pattern match-up and extra on top and bottom before cutting each strip.

☐ Underestimating the amount of wallpaper needed for the job.

☐ Not allowing the sizing to dry.

☐ Not overlapping the wallpapers that have a tendency to shrink.

☐ Using a seam roller on embossed wallpaper.

Step One
Planning Your Project

Margin of Error: Not applicable

Proper planning is essential to a professional-looking paperhanging job. Planning involves understanding where the rolls will be applied and where they will meet at seamlines. Once you start to hang the paper, you must also make adjustments so that the patterns match.

First, you have to decide where to start. This decision will determine the location of the point of mismatch—where odd-shaped pieces will need to be cut. You want these mismatch points to be in the least visible locations. This consideration is more important when you are working with a design with a large pattern. With a neutral or nondirectional pattern, you can begin in an inconspicuous corner or area of the room.

Step Two
Prepping the Walls

Margin of Error: Not applicable

Follow the prepping in Step One for painting. The following additional steps are also recommended for a professional-looking job.

It is important for the walls to be very clean and free of any dust or debris.

When working with an untreated new wall, apply an oil-based primer before papering.

Check to see if your new wallpaper requires a sizing. (With cloth-backed vinyl hung over drywall that has never been sealed, you need to apply a vinyl-to-vinyl primer before hanging the paper.)

Now apply the sizing. This step is sometimes skipped, but it is worth the effort. Sizing is a liquid, applied like paint, that dries tacky. It ensures good adhesion and allows the paper to be easily removed in the future.

Step Three
Marking a Level Line

Margin of Error: Exact

Starting at an inconspicuous corner, measure to a point that is a distance from the corner of 1" less than the width of the wallpaper roll. Make a mark at this point. For example, if your wallpaper rolls are 20" wide, make a mark 19" from the corner.

At this mark, you will make an exactly plumb (vertical) line. There is a good chance that the corner is not plumb, so this process guarantees that you will be working from a plumb line. A common, and drastic, mistake in hanging wallpaper is to hang it out of plumb.

You can use a chalkline, a 4′ level, or a wallpaper level (a straightedge with a level bubble) to mark this line on the wall. Be sure that the level bubble is reading true level, and then mark the line from the ceiling to the floor.

Step Four
Cutting the Wallpaper

Margin of Error: Exact

You are now ready to cut your first piece of wallpaper. You need to cut the paper so that there is a 2" overlap at the ceiling and floor. This excess will be trimmed away later. Also, you will want the pattern to break at the ceiling line. This pattern break line can be whatever you find most attractive. Hold each piece up against the wall before you cut it, and mark where it will meet the baseboard and ceiling line.

Use a straightedge and scissors or a utility knife to cut the paper. Change the blade often to avoid ripping the paper.

Step Five
Soaking the Wallpaper

Margin of Error: Exact

Unlike the older types of wallpaper that needed paste spread on the back, most wallpapers today are prepasted—the adhesive is already applied. You simply soak the wallpaper in water and hang it. However, be careful to follow the manufacturer's instructions closely. Not only is there a set period of time you need to let the paper soak in the tray, there is also a set period of time during which it must cure after it is removed from the tray and before it is applied. This time varies, but it is usually several minutes.

Most professionals apply paste even to prepasted wallpaper, for added insurance that it will adhere properly. With high-quality paper, applied on a properly prepared wall, additional paste is not needed. If you are in doubt, consult your supplier.

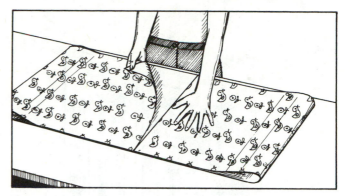

Figure 12-8. "Booking" the wallpaper after it has been soaked. Be careful not to crease the folds.

The paper is placed in a tray of lukewarm water, rolled up, with the pattern side in. Place the tray next to the wall directly below the area to be hung. Upon removing the wallpaper from the tray, fold it, pasted side to pasted side, so that it comes out flat, as shown in Figure 12-8. Be sure to fold the paper loosely and not to crease it at the folds. This is called "booking." Allow the paper to cure to its maximum width before hanging it. Be sure that no dust or debris settles on the paper while it is curing.

Step Six
Hanging the First Sheet

Margin of Error: Exact

You are now ready to hang your first piece of wallpaper. Apply it so that one edge is exactly vertical and aligned with your plumb mark. Leave the bottom fold folded and work at first only with the upper part of the sheet. Be sure the mark for the ceiling is aligned so that there is a pattern break at the ceiling line. If you are working at an inside corner, as is often the case, wrap the 1" overlap into the corner. (See the section on inside corners in Step Eight.)

Use a wallpaper brush to work out any bubbles, stroking the brush from the inside to the outside to push the air out. Start at the top and work your way down the paper. Keep working with the brush until all the bubbles are out and the paper is perfectly smooth on the wall. Be sure you stay aligned with your plumb mark as you work with the brush. Gently lift the bottom edge of the strip to free the sheet of any wrinkles.

When the upper part is smooth, release the bottom fold and position it, using the palms of your hands. Then use the smoothing brush as you did above (Figure 12-9). Be sure that no debris on the wall is poking through. You will trim the paper after the next sheet is hung.

Figure 12-9. Applying the first sheet. Note the 2" overlap at top and bottom.

Step Seven
Hanging the Second and Subsequent Sheets

Margin of Error: Exact

Before cutting the second sheet, be sure that you have allowed for the pattern matching at the seamlines. If your wallpaper has a large pattern, alternate between two different rolls to avoid waste.

The second sheet butts snugly against the first. Do not overlap seams. Apply this sheet as you did the first and maneuver it against the first with your hands. After this sheet is in place, you can go back and trim the first one with a straightedge or broadknife. To ensure a good trim job, change the razor blade for each strip of wallpaper.

After the sheets are in place, go over them with a large damp sponge to get out all the small bubbles and paste. Wipe up any excess paste at the seams and ends with the sponge before it dries. After 20 to 30 minutes, use a seam roller, as shown in Figure 12-10, to be sure that the seams are well secured. Press the roller lightly to avoid glossy areas. If you are working with raised or flocked wallpaper, omit this step.

Step Eight
Corners and Openings

Margin of Error: Exact

Corners, both inside and outside, are the most demanding part of hanging paper. In and of themselves, they are not too difficult. However, the corners are seldom true plumb (ver-

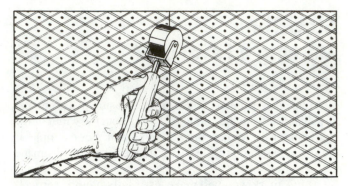

Figure 12-10. Use a seam roller at the seams 20 to 30 minutes after hanging the paper. Do not press too hard or you will gloss the paper.

tical), and this is where the difficulty lies. You need to hang your wallpaper plumb, even if the corners are not. Go slowly here; this is where your skills will be challenged the most.

Inside Corners

At both the top and the bottom of the wall, measure the distances from the strip next to the corner to the corner itself. Add 1" to the greater of the two measurements and cut a sheet lengthwise to this measurement. (If this measurement is within 6" of your full sheet measurement, use a full sheet.) If there is a sheet next to the corner, its edge can be used as a plumb line. (That's why it's so important to install that sheet plumb.)

If there is no sheet at the corner, simply measure out from the corner the dimensions of a wallpaper roll less 1" (for corner overlap) and draw a plumb line. This line will be your guideline in hanging your first sheet.

Now simply hang the sheet as described earlier and wrap the excess into the corner. Since few corners are perfectly plumb, you will need to strike a plumbline on the adjacent wall, again at a distance from the corner of 1" less than the dimension of the roll. Then apply another sheet and wrap the excess so it overlaps the first sheet. Finally, use your broadknife and razor knife to cut the overlapping sheets in the corner and peel away the two excess pieces.

Outside Corners

If the outside corner is exactly plumb (although they seldom are), you can simply wrap the paper around the corner and begin from its edge on the other side of the corner. If the corner is not plumb, a little more attention is needed.

As with inside corners, measure at the top and bottom of the wall the distance from the last sheet to the corner. Add 1" to the longest measurement and cut a sheet that size. If the measurement is within 6" of a full sheet, use a full sheet.

Hang this sheet, cutting a diagonal slit at the corner at the top so it will bend around the corner. Hang it so that it is smooth and fold it smoothly around the corner. Now strike another plumbline on the intersecting wall. The plumbline should be the width of the roll from the corner. Now simply

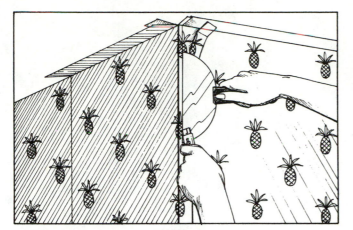

Figure 12-11. Mark a plumb line ¼" to ½" from the outside corner. Cut the paper at this line with a broadknife or razor knife. Remove the excess paper.

hang your intersecting piece to that plumbline. After both pieces are in place, make a new plumbline ¼" to ½" from the corner on the side of the corner. At this line, cut through both pieces of paper and peel away the excess, as shown in Figure 12-11.

Windows and Doors

Openings for windows and doors, fireplaces, and built-in bookshelves and cabinets offer a challenge to the novice. In these areas, don't try to cut the paper first and then apply it. Cut it after it is in place. If you are having trouble with a complex area, take the time to step back and think about it before proceeding.

To work around window openings, simply hang your paper so that it is aligned with the adjacent piece and press it loosely against the window trim. Now cut along the sides of the opening, leaving a 2" excess, which you will trim away later. Using a sharp razor, cut a 45-degree slit at the cor-

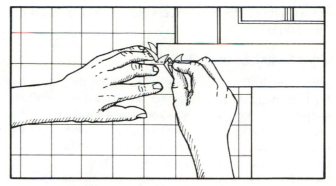

Figure 12-13. Make small cuts to fit the paper around sills.

ners, both top and bottom, to the outside edge of the molding, ending exactly at the molding's edge (Figure 12-12).

Press the paper against the molding with the wallpaper brush and use your broadknife and razor knife to cut away the excess. Leave a hairline gap between the molding and the paper.

As shown in Figure 12-13, you will need to make a series of small diagonal cuts around the sill area to fit all the little corners. Go slow and make small cuts to avoid over-cutting. Press the paper tightly against the molding and trim it where needed.

Finally, you will need to paper the area above and below the window with short strips. Be sure the vertical patterns below the window are aligned with those above, and that the patterns match where they meet the paper hung to the sides

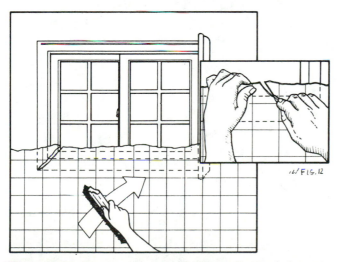

Figure 12-12. Use a razor to cut a 45-degree slit at both the top and bottom corners of the molding. Cut away excess paper.

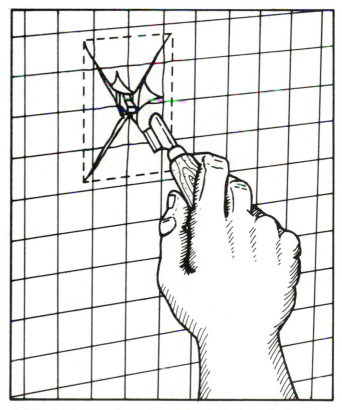

Figure 12-14. Cover over light switches and electrical outlets. Make diagonal cuts in the paper and trim the excess.

of the windows. Wipe any excess glue off the woodwork before it dries.

Light Switches and Outlets

After turning off the electricity and removing the plates from the light switches and outlets (if they have been installed), simply cover over the holes as you hang the wallpaper. Then use your razor knife to make two diagonal cuts across the outlet or switch, about 3" long, to expose the switch or outlet (Figure 12-14). Cut away the excess. You can cover the plates by tucking the wallpaper into the wall and replacing the cover.

13 Kitchen Cabinets and Counter Tops

COMPLETING A KITCHEN is one of the more difficult tasks the owner-builder faces. Aside from installing the cabinets, it involves the electrical, plumbing, gas, and venting systems, as well as many specialized tasks, such as installing flooring and trim. This chapter explains how to install kitchen cabinets and both laminated and preformed counter tops. An overview outlines the basics of installing sinks and appliances; however, these tasks are different in each home, and you will need to gather more information before installing your appliances and plumbing.

You will need to use many of the techniques you learned in other chapters for such tasks as installing finish flooring and drywall and completing the plumbing and electrical systems. Refer to these chapters as necessary.

Before You Begin

SAFETY

☐ Work patiently. If you become frustrated or try to hurry a job like installing cabinets, the chances are great that you will make a mistake.

☐ Unplug tools when making adjustments or changing blades.

☐ Keep work surfaces and traffic areas free of scraps and debris.

☐ If an object such as a cabinet or appliance is too heavy or awkward to lift easily, get help in moving it. Bend from the knees when picking up large or heavy items.

☐ Turn off all utilities before beginning work on them. Remember that pilot lights must be relit.

☐ Use the proper protection, take precautions, and plan ahead. Never bypass safety to save money or to rush a project.

WHAT YOU WILL NEED

Time. The time you will need to install your kitchen depends entirely on the scope of the task; it is not possible to make a meaningful general estimate.

Tools

Hammer
Level
Tape measure
Standard and phillips head screwdrivers
Cordless electric screwdriver
Electric drill
Plane
Crowbar
Dolly
Wrenches
Plumber's wrenches
1" to 1½" pipe wrench
Pry bar
Putty knife
Saw
Nailset
Circular saw
Chalkline
Plumb bob
C-clamps or handscrews
Compass
Router with carbide-tipped laminate trimming bit
Saber saw with fine-tooth blade
Vacuum cleaner
Sanding block and sandpaper
Fine-cut file
Carpenter's square
Combination square
Ladder
Mud tray
Mud knives
Vacuum cleaner

Materials. Aside from such major items as the cabinets and counter top materials, you will need fixtures, flooring materials, paint, and materials to complete the plumbing and electrical hookups.

Materials for Preparation

Newspaper

Wire mesh

Drywall

Spackling/patching plaster

Cement filler

Plywood

Drywall tape

Drywall compound

Primer/sealer

Paint

Rollers and brushes

Materials for Installation

New cabinetry (custom or ready-made)

Counter top material: laminate, end splash, and 1x2 ledger board

Scrap wood (2x4) for jacks

Paper for templates

Shims

Silicone sealant

Wood screws/self-drilling screws

Natural bristle paintbrushes

Brown wrapping paper

Rolling pin

Sanding block and 80 grit sandpaper

Laminate adhesive/contact cement

Masking tape

Plumber's putty

PERMITS AND CODES

It's important to check your local building code to find out which phases of your kitchen installation need to be inspected.

It is assumed that you submitted detailed drawings to indicate all structural, wiring, and plumbing work intended, and that these areas have been inspected during your rough inspections.

DESIGN

In many homes, kitchens are multiuse centers, designed as much for entertainment as for cooking and eating. This book is geared toward construction rather than design. However, many fine books on kitchen design are available to help you plan your new kitchen and to meet your family's needs. Magazines, home centers, and home shows are other sources of inspiration.

One of the major considerations in designing your kitchen is the "work triangle"—the arrangement of the stove, refrigerator, and sink (Figure 13-1). For maximum efficiency, these major workstations should be placed 4′ to 7′ from each other, for a total of no more than 21′. If more than one person

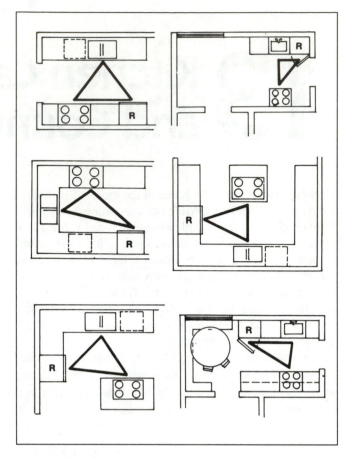

Figure 13-1. Sample kitchen layouts and work triangles.

works in your kitchen at a time, plan your new work area so that you won't get in each other's way.

One of the most important elements of an efficient kitchen, one that is a pleasure to work in, is plenty of counter space for preparing food, cooking, and cleaning up. Your plan should also make efficient use of storage space, with plenty of cabinets, drawers, and shelves.

Step One Preparation

Margin of Error: 1/4"

Most Common Mistakes

☐ Not marking location of studs.

☐ Neglecting to have all electrical and plumbing systems in place and inspected.

Walls

Before you install your new cabinets and appliances, the walls must be painted. Counter tops will be installed after the cabinetry is in place.

You will also need to locate and mark the wall studs on the floor and ceiling as a reference for attaching the new cabinetry. There are several ways to find the studs in a finished wall. Studs are usually located every 16" on center. Tap along the wall with a hammer until you hear a solid sound; look for seams in the drywall; or use a magnetic or density-type stud finder to locate the nails in the studs. Mark the position of the stud on floor and ceiling and snap a chalkline to mark the center of the stud on the wall; or make your marks on small pieces of tape at floor and ceiling if you don't want to put chalk on the wall.

Floors

Ceramic tile floors are usually laid before the cabinets are installed, while vinyl flooring can be laid either before or after the cabinets are in place. Prepare the subfloor as described in Chapter 9, Vinyl Floors. Fill any holes or gouges, and nail down protruding boards. Remove any glue or paint that may have spilled. Countersink nail and screw heads that are sticking up above the surface.

Sequence of Installation

Here is the sequence in which the kitchen is put together. The first step is preparation: primer and paint on the walls, and ceramic tile or hardwood on the floors. (Ceramic tile and hardwood flooring are always laid before cabinets are installed, while vinyl flooring can be laid either before or after the cabinets are in place.) Second, install the cabinets: wall cabinets, then base cabinets and islands. After the cabinets are in place, install the doors, drawers, and hardware. Third, install the plywood base (for tile counter tops), the recessed sink, and the counter top itself. (If you are using a surface-mounted sink, it goes over the counter top.) Faucets and other fittings come next. Fourth, install the appliance—disposal, dishwasher, over the range hood/vent, wall oven, range, etc. Finally, install lighting fixtures and trim.

Step Two
Installing Cabinets

Margin of Error: $1/16$" gap between cabinets; level and plumb within $1/8$"

Most Common Mistakes

☐ Not installing cabinets level and plumb.
☐ Not attaching cabinets to studs.
☐ Damaging or marring cabinets.
☐ Not aligning cabinet doors.
☐ Damaging the walls during installation.
☐ Not cutting sink opening to proper dimension.
☐ Not properly fitting and installing drop-in appliances.
☐ Not making exact measurements and cuts.
☐ Not installing all needed utilities.

Accurate measurements are crucial to ensure a snug fit when installing stock cabinets. Custom-made cabinetry is usually

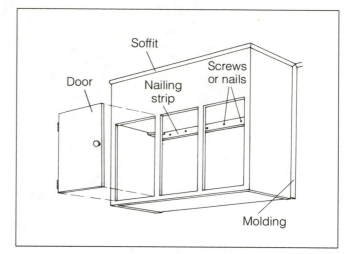

Figure 13-2. The anatomy of a wall cabinet.

sold with a warranty conditional on having the cabinets installed by the dealer. In fact, the dealer will probably send someone to your house to take the measurements.

Both standard and custom cabinets are usually made to uniform sizes. This is a help in designing kitchens, and ensures that sinks, dishwashers, and counter tops in standard sizes will fit.

Inside the cabinets, and sometimes on the top and bottom, are pieces called **nailing strips**. This is where you secure the cabinets to the studs. Rather than attaching the cabinets with nails, however, 3" buglehead screws, installed with a drill or screwgun, are much stronger and easier to install. If you can't get to the nailing strip of the lower cabinets, toenail the sides of the cabinets to the floor, through the shims.

The most important thing to remember about installing cabinets is to begin from the highest level of the floor to set your cabinet heights. It's easy to raise a cabinet with shims, but trimming off all the bottoms is a nightmare. Check the floor level carefully to find the highest point over which a cabinet will go, and determine your level lines from there.

Most ready-made cabinets come with a scribe allowance on their sides to allow you to scribe them to irregular walls. To scribe a line, set the cabinet in position against the wall and plumb the front. Stick a strip of masking tape along the side of the cabinet to be scribed. Set the points of a compass to the width of the widest gap between the side of the cabinet and the wall. Run the compass along the wall and the irregularities will be marked on the tape. Now you can plane or sand down to the line so the cabinet will rest flush against the wall. If the scribe edge is not included on your cabinets, or if your cabinets go all the way to the ceiling, plan on trimming the edges with molding.

Install the upper wall cabinets first so that the lower ones aren't in your way. (Figure 13-2 shows the anatomy of a wall cabinet.) These cabinets have no support except for their attachment to the wall, so they must be securely attached.

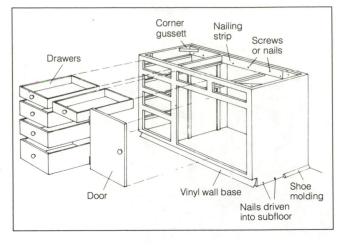

Figure 13-3. The anatomy of a base cabinet.

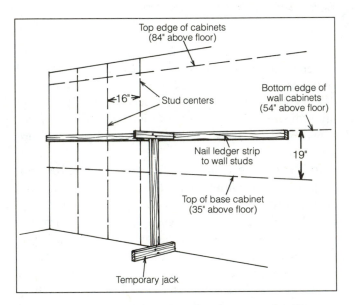

Figure 13-4. Marking reference lines for placement of wall cabinets.

Before installing any of your new cabinets, remove all the drawers, doors, and hardware and label them carefully for easy reassembly. This will make the units much lighter and more manageable.

Installing Wall Cabinets

The first step in installing wall cabinets is to measure the height of the base—usually about 35". (Figure 13-3 shows the anatomy of a base cabinet.) Measure this distance up from the floor and draw a horizontal line across the walls. (If your floor is not level, measure from the highest point.) Now add the thickness of your finished counter top above the first mark and mark this level as well. Work carefully; this line must be true horizontal, because it indicates where the surface of the counter top will be.

Above this second line, measure up to the point where the bottom of the upper cabinet will be (usually 18" to 19"). Use a level to draw another horizontal line across the wall. This

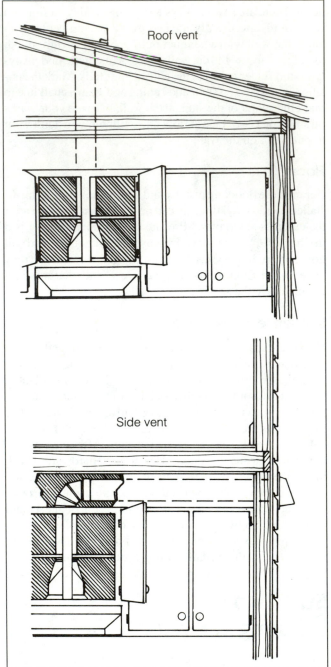

Figure 13-5. Ranges must be vented to the outside. These openings need to be cut before upper cabinets are installed.

line (approximately 54" above the floor) must also be true horizontal and parallel to the line for the counter top.

Screw a temporary 1x2 ledger board to the wall so that the top of the board is even with the line for the bottom of the wall cabinets (Figure 13-4). Be sure you are screwing into the studs. Now mark the cabinet widths along the length of the ledger strip. You want the joints of the upper cabinets to be directly over the joints of the lower cabinets. Mark the position of the base cabinets on the wall and use a level to make sure the upper cabinets are plumb at the joints. Don't forget to add or subtract any scribe or trim differences.

Figure 13-6. Once the upper cabinet is level and plumb, attach it with screws through the nailing strip and into the wall studs.

Figure 13-7. Check base cabinets for level and shim as necessary.

You will need to make some temporary jacks to support the wall cabinets while you attach them to the wall. The jacks should reach exactly from the floor to the bottom of the upper cabinets. Wide blocks of wood nailed to both ends of a 2x4 work well for this purpose. Put the jacks in position near the ledger (see Figure 13-4). Shim to adjust for uneven floors.

Before you begin installing your upper cabinets, you need to cut openings for any hoods, ducts, or vents (Figure 13-5). With the cabinet upside down on the floor, center the hood upside down on the bottom of the cabinet. Trace the outline of the vent hole you plan to cut out along the line for the opening. Also cut out the hole where the duct will leave the cabinet and enter the wall or ceiling. The manufacturer's instructions will guide you in this process.

You are now ready to hang the cabinets. Mark the location of the wall studs on the hanging cleats of each cabinet. Then drill pilot holes for screws at these points; or use self-drilling bugle-head screws. These require no predrilling except when they are used at face frames. Start in a corner if possible, or at one end. Work out or across from this cabinet to install the rest.

Lift the first cabinet into position onto the ledger board and the temporary jacks. Check to see that the cabinet is both level and plumb. If necessary, shim the back of the cabinet to bring it into plumb. Screw 3" No. 8 flat-head wood screws or self-drilling bugle-head screws through the nailing strip at the back of the cabinet and into the wall studs (Figure 13-6). Use two screws at the top and two at the bottom, if possible. Use longer screws if necessary to ensure that they penetrate at least 1¼" into the studs. Each unit should be attached to

at least two studs. If only one stud is located behind a unit, use a toggle bolt as an additional fastener.

Attach all of the upper cabinets in this manner. Then go back and screw the cabinet fronts together. When connecting adjoining cabinets, it may be necessary to loosen the wall screws to allow the faces of the cabinet to be attached flush to each other. Use handscrews or a C-clamp with soft wood scraps between the jaws of the clamp and the face frames of the cabinets to hold the units flush while you screw them together. Many prefabricated cabinets have predrilled holes in the face, top, and bottom.

When all cabinets are attached, check them once again for level and plumb. Then remove the jacks and the ledger board.

Installing Base Cabinets

Position your lower cabinets in place and level them with shims. If your lower cabinets have separate bases, set the bases in position, shimming as necessary to keep them level. Where the cabinet bases meet in a corner, square the intersection with a framing square. Then anchor the bases to the floor and place the cabinet units on top of them. Cabinets that do not have freestanding bases must be leveled and anchored in position individually (Figure 13-7). Again, start in a corner, if possible, or on an end. You will work off this first cabinet, so if it is not level and plumb at the right height, the others won't be either. Be sure to measure and leave room for your appliances, adding ¼" for clearance—more if you will be adding end panels (plywood pieces that will cover the exposed ends of the cabinets). Check the position of your base units against the horizontal line that you drew on the wall, making sure the tops are uniformly on the line you made for the cabinet height.

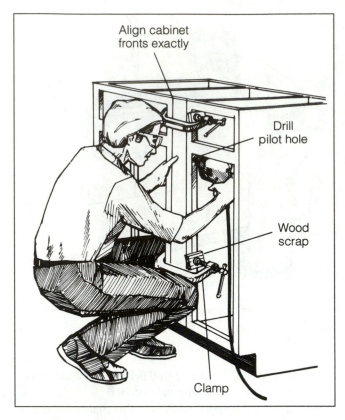

Figure 13-8. Align cabinet fronts exactly and clamp them in place before screwing them to the wall.

As you join the cabinet units together (Figure 13-8), slide a level down the entire length of the cabinets, adding shims to bring them up to level. Place your level front to back on the top of the cabinet to check for level, again shimming if necessary. As with the upper cabinets, use clamps to hold the units in place while you screw them together. Then screw the cabinet into the wall with 3" screws through the top nailing strip and into the wall studs. If the wall is uneven, there will be gaps between the back of the cabinet and the wall. To avoid pulling your cabinets out of plumb as you secure them to the wall, shim the gaps at the fastening point (where the stud is located) before screwing the cabinet into place. Carefully saw or chisel off the ends of the shims.

Repair any holes you have made in the walls that will show. If your cabinets are not prefinished, now is the time to finish or paint them.

Installing Island Cabinets

Island cabinets must have all of the individual units screwed together into one big piece and placed into position before leveling and plumbing on all four sides. If the base is separate, level and plumb it. Then fasten it to the floor with countersunk screws, toenails, or sheet metal angles. Anchor the cabinets to the base. Units with built-in bases are also screwed together before leveling. Long screws are available to secure the level island to the floor, through the base. When installing an island unit, it is important to square it to the cab-

inets along the wall and to the wall itself, as well as lining the unit up properly with the overhead fixtures (stove vent or lighting). Measure on both ceiling and floor to determine the exact location.

Step Three
Installing Laminate
Counter Tops

Margin of Error: Level within 1/8"

Most Common Mistakes

☐ Not scribing counter tops to the contours of the wall.

☐ Not applying the finish surface accurately.

☐ Not cutting the sink opening to the proper dimensions.

☐ Scratching the counter top while installing it.

☐ Puncturing the counter top surface with screws while fastening it from below.

☐ Not checking the corners and ends to be sure they are square before cutting the counter top.

☐ Not providing adequate ventilation when using contact cement to adhere laminates.

☐ Not spreading enough adhesive when laminating the counter top, causing the laminate to lift up in the corners or along the edges.

The two common types of counter tops are preformed laminate and laminate custom-built at the site. Preformed tops come assembled from the manufacturer, while custom tops are built at the job site using raw materials (laminates and plywood or particle board). Other common counter top materials include tile and butcher block.

Preformed Counter Tops

Preformed counter tops are available only in standard sizes, so you usually have to purchase one that is a little longer than you need and cut it to length. These counter tops are available with mitered corners, and have a built-in backsplash with a 1/2" scribe lip to accommodate irregularities in your walls. A flush end trim piece with a heat-sensitive adhesive backing is literally ironed in place. The backsplash end is glued and nailed into position.

1. To measure for your counter, add the counter overhang (usually between 3/4" and 1" in front and on open ends) and add it to the length of your base cabinets.

2. If an end splash is to be included (Figure 13-9), subtract 3/4" from the length of the counter top on that side. Plan your cut carefully for an end splash. Mark the cut on the bottom and cut out from the bottom with a circular saw fitted with a fine-tooth plywood blade to protect against chipping. Cut the excess off with a handsaw. Smooth the edges of the cut with a file or sandpaper.

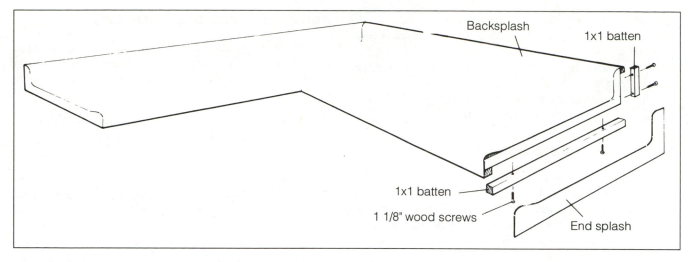

Figure 13-9. Components of a preformed counter top.

3. The end splash is screwed directly onto the edge of the counter top or into wood battens previously attached to the edge. Apply silicone sealant to all surfaces to be joined and hold the end splash in place with C-clamps while driving in the screws. The end splash, a preshaped strip of matching laminate, is glued to the end of the counter top. The end splash usually requires filing or trimming with a router, so install it before you install the top itself.

4. U- and L-shaped counter tops need to be ordered mitered to order; it is difficult to accurately miter these sections at home. These premitered sections have small slots for draw bolts cut into the bottom edges. Coat the edges with silicone sealant before aligning the edges and tightening the bolts.

5. Like cabinets, counter tops rarely fit perfectly against the back or side walls. They come with a scribing strip (Figure 13-10) that can be trimmed to the exact contours of your irregular walls, as described earlier. After scribing, you can plane or sand down to the line so the counter top will rest flush against the wall. The scribing provides a counter top lip that is parallel to the cabinet face, as well as accommodating any unevenness in the wall. This will ensure that your prefabricated miter joints will fit if you installed the base cabinets square. Make all scribe adjustments before trimming the square ends. Once your contours are correct, position the counter top on the cabinet base. Check that all is level, and shim where needed. Check also that drawers and doors open freely.

6. Fasten down the counter top by running screws up from below through the top frame and corners. If there are no corner brackets, install them on the base units. This will allow you to install the counter top easily. Self-drilling bugle head screws work well for this job. Round-head screws work best here. They will not be seen, and so do not have to be counter sunk, and they bear more weight than do other kinds of screws. Use screws that are long enough to penetrate ½" into the backing material. Be careful; one screw that is too

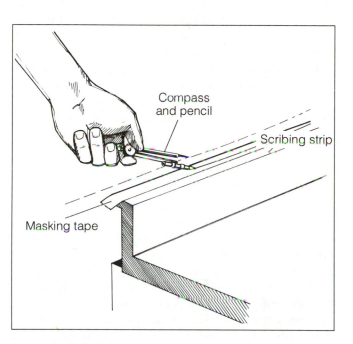

Figure 13-10. Scribing allows you to trim your counter top to the exact contours of your wall.

long can ruin the laminate by penetrating the surface or by making a small lump in the surface.

Custom Laminate Counter Tops

You can also create your own laminate counter top. This option is somewhat more difficult, but it offers greater variety in design and color. Most dealers stock 4'x8' sheets that are ¹⁄₁₆" thick, but they can be special ordered in widths from 2' to 5' and in lengths from 6' to 12'. Store the laminate in your kitchen for at least 48 hours before installing it to allow it to adjust to the temperature and humidity.

The laminate is applied to a base of ¾" particle board, which extends out to form a lip in front of the cabinet. The lip is often made thicker by screwing and gluing on a thin additional strip of particle board under the front edge before laminating.

Roller-nose or flush-cutting router bits are used to trim the laminate edges and joints.

Make certain that the surface upon which you will be applying the laminate is even and smooth.

Applying Laminate to Counter Edges

1. When planning your cuts, try to reserve the factory edges for the places you won't be able to reach with a router, such as where counter top meets backsplash. Cut the laminate with a saber saw fitted with a fine-tooth blade. Leave a margin of ½" on all sides except for the factory edge.

2. Use a soft paintbrush or a vacuum cleaner to completely remove any dust from the counter and the back of the laminate strip being applied. Spread contact cement onto the counter edge with a ¾" natural bristle brush, covering the entire surface. Then brush the contact cement onto the back of the strip of laminate and allow both pieces to set for about 15 minutes. The contact cement is ready for bonding when a piece of brown paper will not stick to it. When working with contact cement, make sure your work area is very well ventilated.

3. Drape strips of brown wrapping paper over the edge of the counter so that the two cement-covered surfaces won't come in contact with each other. Position the strip of laminate close to the counter edge so that the ½" margin extends evenly above and below the edge of the counter. This may be a two-person job. If one end of the strip is to meet an inside corner, start by butting that end into the corner, pulling out the first piece of brown paper and pressing the strip onto the counter's edge. Work your way along the edge of the counter, removing one strip of paper at a time and pressing the laminate into position. Be sure the laminate is exactly where you want it. Once the entire strip is in position, roll over it several times with a rolling pin or a hand roller, using firm, even pressure to ensure a good bond.

4. Trim the laminate with a router fitted with a carbide-tipped flush-cutting bit. Hold the router in position with the lower part of the faceplate flat against the newly laminated strip and the bit held just above the excess. Slowly lower the router until the bit meets the counter top, then move the router along the strip, trimming flush with the counter top. Trim the excess laminate on all sides of the edge, moving in a counterclockwise motion.

5. After laminating all of the counter edges and trimming them with the router, smooth the top edges with a sanding block fitted with 100 grit sandpaper or with a file. Then dust thoroughly. Don't touch the sandpaper to the laminate surface; it will leave permanent scratches. Smears or globs of cement should be allowed to dry and then rubbed off the surface with a rag. Solvent will clean up any spills.

Applying Laminate to Counter Tops

1. Mark all corner miters on the particle board. Scribe a factory edge to fit your wall and transfer these miter marks to the laminate, leaving ½" or so overhanging in front and on the end.

2. Cut the laminate with a straightedge and a circular saw fitted with a fine-tooth plywood blade, a saber saw, a router, or a laminate cutter. (A laminate cutter is a blade made to fit your utility knife.)

3. All scribing, fitting, and adjustments need to be made before you begin gluing. You should dry fit all the pieces together before installing them. If you have a complicated shape, a cardboard template can be helpful. Always begin in a corner and work out from there as you apply the laminate.

4. The easiest way to spread the adhesive for the counter top is with a paint tray and a mohair-covered paint roller. Spread newspapers on the floor. Lay the plastic laminate upside down on top of the newspapers and roll the contact cement on, covering the entire surface. Apply a slightly thicker coat of cement near the edges. Next cover the counter surface with adhesive and allow both pieces to dry for about 15 minutes, or until brown paper will not stick to the adhesive.

5. Dowels or wood strips work better than brown paper to keep the laminate from sticking to the cemented counter surface (Figure 13-11). Place the dowels at intervals of 1'. Then lay the laminate, adhesive side down, on the dowels. Put the factory edge against the backsplash and set the tip of the diagonal cut into the corner. This corner is where you will begin.

6. Pull out the dowel nearest the corner, while pressing the laminate into position. Be sure the laminate is exactly where you want it. Use a sweeping motion so that no air bubbles are trapped beneath the laminate. Work along the counter, pulling out strips of wood and pressing the laminate down. Then immediately roll the surface with your rolling pin or hand roller, applying extra pressure near the edges. When placing the second piece of laminate, make certain the diagonal seam at the corner is very tight and roll the seam thoroughly.

7. If the laminate fails to bond, or if a bubble forms at some point, place a piece of the brown wrapping paper over the spot and place a hot iron (set for cotton) on top of the paper until the laminate feels hot to the touch. The heat will soften the contact cement enough to regain some of its stickiness. Then use the roller again with a firm, steady pressure until the laminate has cooled.

8. Before router-trimming the counter top, put masking tape around the newly laminated edges to avoid marring them. Router off the excess as you did with the edges, moving the router steadily from left to right. Then replace the bit with a 22-degree bevel bit and bevel the seam at the top of the counter, again moving from left to right (Figure 13-12). It's

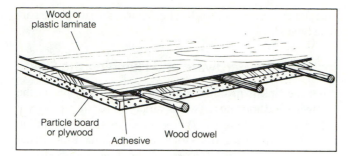

Figure 13-11. Dowels or wood strips keep the laminate from sticking to the particle board base while you position it.

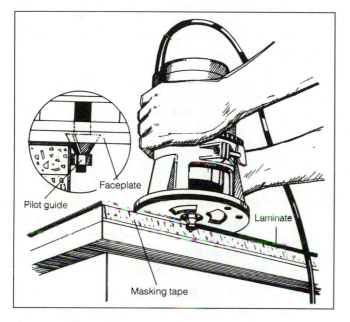

Figure 13-12. Use a router with a 22-degree bevel bit to bevel the seam at the top of the counter.

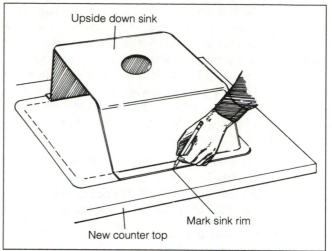

Figure 13-13. Outline the sink and then draw another line ½" inside of the first line to show you where to cut.

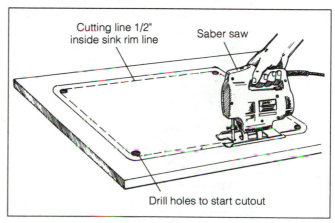

Figure 13-14. Cut along the inside pencil line with a saber saw.

best to practice this technique on scrap before doing the actual project.

9. Finish the bevels with a ¼" single-cut mill file, applying pressure on the downward stroke. Check each angle with your finger to be sure there are no rough edges that could result in cracks later. Inside corners are particularly likely to crack if they are not filed smooth.

Step Four
Installing the Sink
and Dishwasher

Most Common Mistakes

☐ Not cutting the sink opening to the proper dimensions.

☐ Not lining up the opening with the sink base cabinet.

No matter what material you have chosen for your counter, some general rules apply to the installation of sinks. Surface-mounted sinks and self-rimming stainless steel sinks are generally installed with caulking and clamps, while self-rimming porcelain sinks need only caulk. Recessed sinks, where the unit is set on the plywood base, are most commonly used with tiled counter tops; porcelain and cast iron sinks are recommended for recessed installation. Stainless steel sinks are not recommended for use with tile because the steel and the tile expand and contract at different rates. However, a double-walled stainless steel sink may work with tile.

1. Position the sink upside down on the newly laminated counter top or the plywood base. Try to center it, but leave at least 1½" and not more than 3" from the front edge of the counter. Draw a pencil line around the edge of the sink, as shown in Figure 13-13; then remove the sink. (If you are using a metal rim for a sink that is not self-rimming, use the rim's outside edge as a template rather than the sink itself.) Now measure inward and draw another line ½" inside of the first line. Be sure of your marks.

2. Drill a hole large enough for a saber saw blade to the inside of each corner of the inside line. Cut along the inside pencil line with your saber saw while another person supports the cut from below (Figure 13-14). Lift the waste piece out.

3. Run a bead of caulk along the entire bottom edge of the upside down self-rimming sink. Position the sink carefully over the opening and press it down firmly until the excess caulk oozes out along the edges. Follow the manufacturer's instructions for any additional hardware that comes with the sink. Typically, a clip or a small metal stud fits in a small

channel on the bottom, and a clip secures the rim to the particle board base.

Installing the Hardware and Plumbing the Sink

After the sink is installed, all that remains is to install the hardware and hook up the water supply and drain pipes. (See Chapter 3, Plumbing.) This chapter gives a general outline rather than full instructions for plumbing a sink. Refer to the manufacturer's instructions, or to a book on plumbing.

1. Faucets are mounted through the prepunched holes in the back of the sink, using an adjustable wrench and plumber's putty. Faucets must be installed so that the valves work the right way. The left-hand valve is always connected to the hot water supply and the right-hand side to the cold. Follow the manufacturer's instructions.

2. Supply line connector kits are available that contain everything you need to connect the water supply line—flexible copper pipe, hardware, shutoff valves, and instructions. You will need to specify the diameter and material of the supply line and whether or not you will be adding a dishwasher. The dishwasher requires a special T-shaped shutoff valve.

3. After connecting the water supply line, install the basket strainer. Pack the rim of the hole in the sink with plumber's putty and push the strainer down into place. From beneath the sink, slip on a rubber gasket and metal ring, as shown in Figure 13-15. Then slip on the lock nut and tighten it until the putty oozes out. Clean off all excess putty.

4. Next, install the P-trap. Connect the tailpiece to the basket strainer, using a slip nut over a washer. Then connect the P-trap to the tailpiece with another washer and slip nut. Attach the P-trap to the wall stub-out with a curved drain expansion pipe (see Figure 13-15).

Installing the Dishwasher

The three main connections of a dishwasher are the electrical cord (which will plug into an outlet under or near the dishwasher), the rubber drain hose, and the hot water supply line. An air gap is often needed as well to prevent waste material from backing up into the dishwasher. The waste line for a dishwasher leads up to the vent and drains into a line leading to the disposal.

1. Drill a hole, large enough to accommodate all three connections, through the cabinet wall between the sink and the dishwasher compartment.

2. Thread the black rubber drain hose, the electrical cord, and the water supply tubing through this opening. Leave enough supply tubing in the dishwasher compartment to reach the connections at the front of the dishwasher.

3. You will need to remove a knockout from the disposal collar to attach the drain hose. Fit the hose to the collar with the adjustable hose clamps provided.

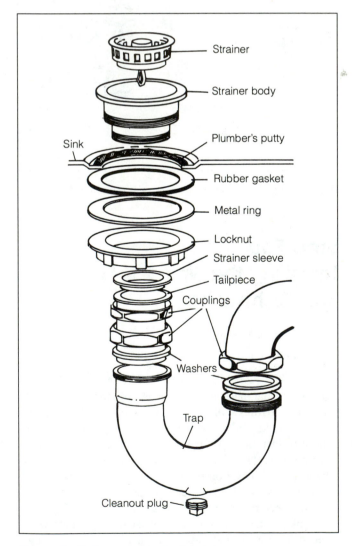

Figure 13-15. Components of a sink drain.

4. If you are adding an air gap, attach the dishwasher hose to the longest of the two hoses in the air gap, using hose clamps. Hook the shorter hose in the air gap to the collar of the disposal unit, again removing a knockout and attaching with hose clamps.

5. Attach the hot water supply line. The tubing must fit snugly to the fitting on the front of the dishwasher and to the shutoff valve. Secure it with the hose clamps provided.

Step Five
Installing Other Appliances

Hood/Vent

Install the hood/vent before the range or cooktop so that you can reach all connections easily (Figure 13-16).

1. Connect a section of 6" or 7" metal ducting to the duct pipe entering the cabinet and to the hood. If these holes are too close for a turn, you may need to have a sheet metal box with nailing flanges made to your specifications. Connect the hood collar or transition fitting to the duct by tightening the metal collar provided, or by wrapping duct tape around both collar and duct.

2. Lift the hood into position and trace the holes for attaching it to the underside of the cabinet, if you did not do this earlier. Drill pilot holes and attach the unit with the screws provided.

3. Connect the wiring in accordance with the manufacturer's instructions.

Ranges and Ovens

Drop-in ranges and ovens are connected in much the same way as their freestanding counterparts. However, they do not simply slide into place, but must be installed on top of a low base cabinet unit for support (Figure 13-17). These can be hung from flanges from the counter level or screwed to the base cabinet below and/or to adjacent units.

1. The electric range/oven has its own pigtail cord that plugs into a separate 220-volt circuit. Attach the unit according to the manufacturer's instructions.

2. Hook up the gas supply line with flexible tubing, adding dope putty and nuts at either end. A range with a pilotless ignition system must also be plugged into a 110-volt circuit. You must call the utility company to check your range hookup before you position it permanently.

Built-In Ovens

Gas and electrical connections for built-ins are the same as for drop-in types. These are most commonly located in an adjacent cabinet. Duct attachments are the same as for hood/vents. The oven will be attached to the surrounding cabinetry.

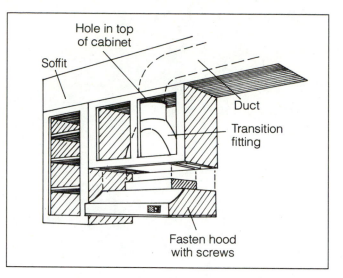

Figure 13-16. The hood/vent is installed before the range or cooktop.

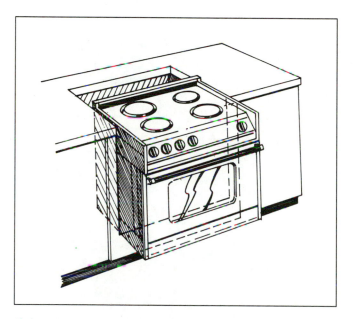

Figure 13-17. A drop-in range is installed on top of a low base cabinet unit.

1. Lift the unit into place and tighten the screws into the sides, top, or bottom of the cabinets. The model you have purchased will dictate whether the face flanges will overlap the cutout edges of the cabinet or whether you will need to install special trim pieces.

2. A microwave oven simply plugs into any grounded 110-volt circuit; it may not even need to be trimmed or attached.

14 Weatherizing

WEATHERIZING A HOME is a two-part process. The first part, which must be completed before the walls are enclosed, includes insulating, ventilating, and installing vapor barriers, as described in Chapter 4, Insulation and Ventilation. The second part, which is done after the house is completed, includes caulking, installing weatherstripping, and other forms of energy conservation. This second step is the subject of this chapter.

Some manufacturers these days install weatherstripping on their doors and windows. If you feel that the manufacturer's weatherstripping is inadequate, you can add more of your own. With today's high energy costs, every leak that can be sealed will save you money.

However, it may be possible to seal your home too tightly. Recent studies have called into question the quality of the air inside tightly sealed homes. You may want to allow in a certain amount of fresh air just to make sure that your indoor air-pollution level is not too high. And you should check the radon level in your basement or crawlspace. Inexpensive radon testing kits are available at many home supply centers and hardware stores in areas where this is a concern.

Before You Begin

SAFETY

Although weatherstripping your new home doesn't sound like a dangerous way to spend a weekend, simple carelessness can lead to potentially harmful situations.

☐ Wear gloves when working with fiberglass.

☐ Wear safety glasses or goggles when hammering.

☐ When sealing your house weather tight, provide adequate ventilation. Ventilation prevents the unhealthy build-up of moisture and fumes from materials used in building the home.

☐ Do not extend the insulation of the gas water heater to the floor. If you do, you will cut off the air supply to the pilot light and the burner.

☐ Do not tape or insulate too close to the vent stack on top of a gas water heater.

USEFUL TERMS

Bulb vinyl weatherstripping is composed of a rounded piece of vinyl (the bulb) attached to a piece of stiff aluminum that is nailed to the inside of the door or window frame.

Caulk is a flexible seal applied with a pressurized applicator to seal cracks and gaps.

A **door threshold** is a piece of wood or metal placed beneath the door to shed water and seal out drafts.

A **downspout** is the portion of a rain gutter that drains from the roof to the ground.

Glazing compound is a type of putty used to seal glass into window frames.

A **jalousie window** is a window formed of horizontal glass slats.

Oakum is a loose, stringy hemp fiber made from old ropes that is used as a caulking material for deep cracks.

A **soffit** is the underside of an enclosed eave on a roof.

Weatherstripping is material added to the movable parts or the jambs of doors and windows to seal them against air infiltration.

Window film is a 6 mil plastic covering that is stapled or adhered to the window in lieu of storm closures.

A **window sash** is the framework that holds glass panes in a window.

WHAT YOU WILL NEED

Time. The amount of time needed to weatherstrip your home depends on the extent of work needed. Most door and window caulking and weatherstripping can be accomplished by one person in a weekend.

Tools. Weatherizing your home requires only the most basic tools found in any home toolbox.

Hacksaw with fine-tooth blade

Pry bar

Circular saw

Drill

Hammer

Tack hammer

Nailset

Caulking gun

Screwdrivers

Steel tape measure

Scissors

Tinsnips

Plane

Putty knife

Utility knife

Hair drier

Because caulking is a major part of weatherstripping, an air compressor with a caulking gun attachment will make this job go more smoothly and easily.

Materials. The materials you need will of course depend on the kind of weatherizing you plan to do. The following list should cover most of your needs.

Thresholds

Caulk

Finishing nails

Galvanized shingle nails

Wood dough

Sandpaper, grades 100 through 180

Stain

Sealer

Weatherstripping materials

Door-bottom seals

Window glazing compound

Fiberglass or oakum

Window film

Programmable thermostat

Masking tape

Insulating jacket for hot water heater

Duct tape

Pipe insulating tape

Pipe insulating sleeves

Insulating fireplace baffle

Glass fireplace doors

Once you have decided which materials best suit your situation, you'll want to make a complete list before you go shopping. Take measurements of all the doors and windows that need weatherstripping and estimate the amount of caulking you will need. Note the number and sizes of openings you want to cover with window film. Also write down any specialty items, such as thresholds, a programmable thermostat, or a water heater blanket.

PERMITS AND CODES

Most weatherizing tasks are simple enough that they don't require permits.

Most Common Mistakes

☐ Neglecting to do a thorough weatherizing audit of your home.

☐ Neglecting to insulate properly in conjunction with weatherizing.

☐ Applying caulk, sealants, and weatherstripping in temperatures too cold for the material being used.

☐ Not providing for adequate ventilation and air circulation when making your home weather tight.

☐ Sealing off the room that houses the thermostat control.

☐ Neglecting to save receipts for materials and labor used in making your home more energy efficient, which may entitle you to state and federal tax credits. Check with your local energy supplier.

Step One
The Weatherizing Audit

Margin of Error: Not applicable

Although insulation reduces heat loss, heated or cooled air can still leak out through seemingly inconsequential cracks. In fact, these "inconsequential" cracks can add up to the equivalent of a 2-square-foot hole!

There are a number of ways to go about tracking down and sealing these leaks. You can contract for an energy audit (a scientific, thermographic audit, conducted by a professional, that produces a comprehensive report on the leaks in your home). Usually, however, your local utility company will conduct an audit at your home free of charge. You may not get the detail in the free audit that you would in one you paid for, but it will provide you with useful information and a place to begin. The utility company may also suggest improvements that would make you eligible for energy tax credits. A third option is to do your energy audit yourself, following the guidelines in this chapter.

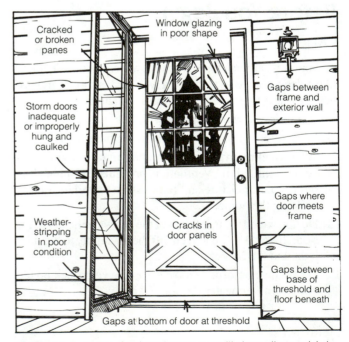

Figure 14-1. Areas of a door that are most likely to allow cold air to enter and heated air to escape.

Doors

The first step in weatherizing your home is to gather information. Begin by checking each exterior door for the following most probable leaks (Figure 14-1).

1. Are there any noticeable cracks at areas where the door meets the frame?

2. Is there any space at the joint between the frame and the interior and exterior walls of the house?

3. Is there a gap between the threshold and the bottom of the door?

4. Is there space between the base of the threshold and the floor underneath?

5. If your door has glass panes, are they properly glazed?

6. Are any of the panes cracked or broken?

7. Do the doors have weatherstripping?

8. If you live in a cold region, does your home have adequate storm doors? Are they properly hung and caulked?

Take the same approach to interior doors. Keeping them properly sealed helps reduce room-to-room infiltration and makes it possible to control more precisely the heating and cooling of individual rooms. However, if your home has a forced air heating system, leave a 3/8" gap at the bottom of interior doors to allow the air to return to the furnace.

Windows

Next take stock of all the windows.

1. Do any of the moving parts allow air to leak?

2. Are there any gaps or flaws in the construction around the frame?

3. Are the seams around the window trim caulked?

4. Do any windows that are not covered with draperies, shades, or blinds have any insulative value?

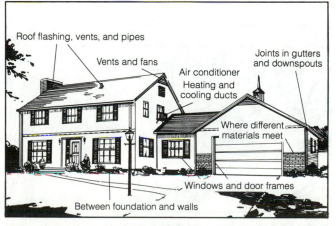

Figure 14-2. Areas of the house that are most likely to allow energy leakage.

5. Do the windows have weatherstripping?

6. Are storm windows installed? If so, are they properly fitted and caulked, to eliminate gaps where the window meets the framing?

Other Openings

Once you have covered all the conventional openings to your home, begin looking for other, not so obvious ones (Figure 14-2). Are there any air leaks in the following places?

1. Foundation cracks or cracks in basement walls?

2. Separations between any two elements of the house, such as chimney and roof?

3. Utility pipes?

4. Phone and electric cable lines?

5. Mail slot?

6. Clothes dryer vent?

Energy-Saving Maintenance Tips

Energy can leak from your home in ways other than through openings. How do you and your home rate on energy conservation?

1. Keep your furnace clean and well-tuned for maximum efficiency.

2. Check the furnace, air-conditioning, and range filters frequently and clean or replace as necessary.

3. Keep your heating and cooling registers clean and unblocked.

4. Set your thermostat a little lower in the winter and a little higher in the summer.

5. Turn your thermostat down when you are out of the house.

6. Make sure your thermostat is clean and in good repair.

7. Consider installing a programmable thermostat.

8. Make sure your thermostat is properly located. A thermostat that is located too near a heat or cold source or on an outside wall can waste a lot of energy.

9. Don't routinely heat or cool seldom-used rooms.

10. Check annually for leaks in heating and cooling ducts.

11. Make sure your water heater is functioning well, and set it at an efficient temperature.

12. Insulate your hot and cold water pipes and heating and air-conditioning ducts.

13. Turn the water heater off and extinguish other pilot lights when you go away on vacation.

7. Outside light connections?

8. TV antenna entry?

9. Electrical outlets?

10. Cracks and splits in siding?

11. Gaps or loose mortar between any blocks, bricks, or stone facing?

12. Air ducts for heating and cooling systems?

13. Window air conditioning units?

14. Leaking basement windows?

15. Roof flashing?

16. Split or loose roof shingles?

17. Poor drainage around the house?

18. Damaged, blocked, or poorly connected downspouts?

Don't try to make your garage air tight. Because of the possibility of gasoline leaks, codes require one 6 x 14 vent per car in the garage, within 18" of the floor. Your garage may be cold in the winter, but it will be safe all year round.

Step Two
Caulking

Margin of Error: Not applicable

Caulk is a material that forms a flexible seal to stop air and moisture infiltration. The better types of caulk will last up to 20 years. Although these may cost more, they will save you the time and expense of recaulking frequently.

There are no practical alternatives to caulking. If you weatherstrip and caulk in addition to insulating your home, you will reduce your energy bill considerably. Also, caulk-ing is your first line of defense against insect invasions and fungus.

Caulk is used on window and door frames, siding, corner joints, foundations, and almost any area where you may find a seam or crack.

Take another look at your weatherization audit. It's likely that many of the places you noticed are prime targets for caulking.

There are many types of caulk for various uses, so check with your home center to find out what type will work best for your particular needs. Generally, you apply caulk from a tube with a caulking gun or from a pressurized can, as shown in Figure 14-3. A standard cartridge of caulk will give you approximately 25' of ¼" bead. You can also purchase rope caulk, which comes in a coil and is simply unwound and stuffed into cracks and crevices.

The trick to a good caulking job is learning to draw an even bead. This may take a little practice. Be sure to hold the caulking gun at a consistent angle of about 45 degrees and draw the bead consistently, rather than in a stop-and-start fashion. Always release the trigger before pulling the gun away to prevent excess caulk from oozing out.

Since caulking is a major element of weatherizing, access to an air compressor will come in very handy. Fitted with a caulking gun attachment, the air compressor allows a smooth, almost effortless application in all areas needing caulk (Figure 14-4).

Be sure the seam or crack you are filling is free from any debris. Use a putty knife or a large screwdriver to scrape the

Figure 14-3. Use a pressurized can to caulk between interior window or door frame and wall.

Figure 14-4. If you have a lot of caulking to do, an air compressor fitted with a caulking gun will make your task easier.

opening clean. Also, the crack should be dry before you apply the caulk. Any moisture in the crack will be trapped inside once the caulk sets up.

If you are covering both sides of a crack or seam with a single wide bead of caulk, make sure it adheres to both sides. The caulk needs to be inside the crack, so if the bead you draw is on the surface of the material, use a putty knife to force it into the crack or seam and smooth it out. With a little practice you will learn the proper angle at which to hold the can or gun so that the caulk is forced immediately into the crack as it comes out of the tube.

The gap between the door frame and the exterior and interior walls can be ⅜" or even more. This space must be carefully and completely caulked to seal it against energy loss in cold regions.

Cracks in the foundation or basement walls can be terrific energy losers. Before caulking them, be certain the crack is very clean. Remove any loose mortar, dirt, and moisture. You may want to paint the area with a primer if the material is porous.

Smaller cracks can be sealed off with a liberal bead of caulk, forced smoothly into the crack. Extra deep or wide cracks should be stuffed with polyethylene foam, fiberglass, or oakum to within 1/2" of the surface. Then caulk over this material to provide a seal.

Where dissimilar materials meet—at wall and foundation, wall and roof, chimney and house, or porch and house—a seal of caulk will reward you with lower energy bills.

Where utility pipes, vent pipes, exterior plumbing, and electrical or phone connections enter the house, caulk the separation. If any of these openings penetrate the ceiling below an unheated attic or the wall to the garage, caulk there as well.

Keep all gutters, downspouts, soffits, and eaves clean and in good repair. Caulk wooden gutters to prevent decay. Tie the downspouts to storm drains, or otherwise divert runoff water away from the foundation, to avoid wet basements, decay problems in crawlspaces, and cracks and settling in the foundation.

Step Three
Window Treatments

Margin of Error: Not applicable

Properly sized and placed, snug-fitting windows can save a significant amount on your heating and cooling bills. Casement windows offer almost 100 percent of their sash opening for ventilation, while double-hung and sliding types offer only 50 percent. A well-placed sliding door will give up to three times the ventilation of an average window.

Energy-efficient sash and frame windows with double-pane insulating glass have low infiltration rates and will easily pay for themselves in energy saved.

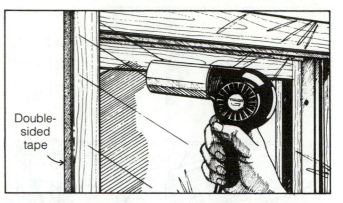

Figure 14-5. Use a blow drier to shrink the window insulation film to fit.

Storm Glazing

If you live in a cold area, storm doors and windows, specially fitted with heavy-duty weatherstripping and sealed glass inserts, go a long way in sealing up a house. There are many do-it-yourself storm window and door kits available. Never caulk the little openings in storm windows. They allow moisture to escape rather than condensing on the glass.

If you don't want to go to the expense of providing storm windows for all of your windows, consider the option of adding window insulator film on the inside. This clear plastic film is used with double-sided tape to shrink around your window, window grouping, or glass door. Application of window film is quite simple.

1. Make sure that your interior window molding is clean and dry.

2. Measure and cut the double-sided tape and apply it to the outside edges or faces of the window molding.

3. Unfold the film and cut it to the size of the window (including trim), allowing 2" extra all around.

4. Starting at the top, press the film securely to the tape. The film will have wrinkles.

5. Now shrink the film with a hair blow drier set on the highest setting, being careful not to touch the film (Figure 14-5). Just aim the hot air evenly over the entire covering. This takes the wrinkles out and leaves you with a clear "pane."

6. Trim the excess film with a sharp utility knife or scissors.

This film reduces air leakage by approximately 97 percent, thus reducing frost build-up on windows. The film and tape can be removed at the end of the season.

Window Coverings

Window treatments—draperies, roller shades, venetian blinds, roman shades, louvres, quilts, sunscreens, and exterior awnings—are another prime area for home energy management. Window treatments can offer greater energy savings at less cost than storm windows or double-paned glass. The combinations are almost endless, ranging from

Figure 14-6. Common types of weatherstripping.

Figure 14-7. Apply caulk before installing the threshold.

simple sew-it-yourself, install-it-yourself window quilt systems through professionally installed, passive solar gain controls that can turn your house into an efficient heat pump. Many of these good-looking and energy-efficient offerings are inexpensive as well.

Step Four
Weatherstripping

Margin of Error: Not applicable

Weatherstripping products are numerous, and some are quite specialized. All are designed to seal a gap or space where heated or cooled air is leaking away, most often around doors and windows (Figure 14-6). Modern materials and designs have resulted in a great number of effective, durable, inexpensive, and easy-to-install products. Whatever type of weatherstripping you choose to apply to your doors and windows, it must be applied to a clean, dry surface and in temperatures above 50°.

Weatherstripping Door Bottoms

The first step in weatherstripping your doors is to assess each doorway carefully and plan accordingly. Don't overlook doors that lead to unheated rooms, the basement, or the garage. They can drain off just as much energy as doors to the outside. If you heat your garage, even occasionally, it will be worthwhile to seal that door as well, to minimize cross drafts from required ventilation. Special sweeps and shoes are made to keep rain as well as cold air out at the door bottom. If the weatherstripping that you buy does not come with its own fasteners, use appropriate galvanized fasteners placed 3" apart.

Installing Thresholds

The threshold seals the door at the bottom and is most effective when used in conjunction with a door shoe or door sweep.

Wooden thresholds add warmth in appearance as well as energy efficiency, but they are a bit more costly than aluminum. Bronze and stainless steel are considerably more expensive. All types come in standard door widths. Choose your threshold to match your floor.

Wooden Thresholds. To install a wooden threshold, follow these steps.

1. Trim the threshold to the length between the door jambs. Use a template to mark the door stop notches and cut them out. Be sure that water running off the door will drip on the sloping portion of the threshold, to drain outside.

2. Thoroughly clean the door sill and spread a generous amount of caulk on it (Figure 14-7) to ensure an airtight seal between the sill and the threshold.

3. Use your hammer to tap the new threshold gently into place.

4. Drill pilot holes slightly smaller than the finishing rails you will use to secure the threshold. Then nail the threshold into its permanent position.

5. Countersink the nails with a nailset and fill the holes with wood dough. Sand lightly when dry.

6. Apply a stain if you like. Then apply a water-repellant finish or two coats of a penetrating sealer.

Aluminium and Other Metal Thresholds. Metal thresholds are installed in the same way as wooden ones, except that you will need a hacksaw if it is necessary to cut the threshold to fit, and a metal file to smooth the resulting rough edge. Predrill pilot holes in the floor to make it easier to install the screws.

Figure 14-8 shows a **thermal threshold**, an aluminum threshold with a vinyl gasket that presses against the bottom of the door for a tight seal against drafts.

Interlocking Thresholds. The interlocking threshold shown in Figure 14-9 is recommended in cold climates. Although

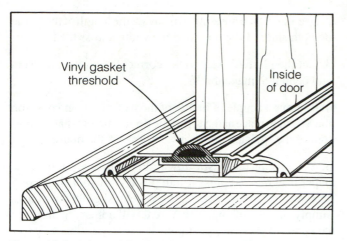

Figure 14-8. A thermal threshold is an aluminum threshold with a vinyl gasket.

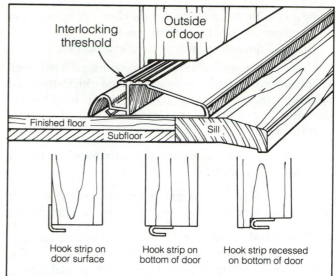

Figure 14-9. Interlocking thresholds are very efficient, but are difficult to install.

it is very efficient when in good condition, the interlocking elements are difficult to install and easily damaged. Special tools are required, and complicated adjustments are often necessary.

Half Thresholds. Half thresholds are used where two floors of different heights come together. They are available in metal, or they can be made by adapting a wooden threshold (Figure 14-10).

Door Bottom Seals

These seals, or sweeps, are either self-adhesive or fastened with screws. They are used to close the gap between the threshold and the bottom of the door (Figure 14-11). It is not usually necessary to remove the door to install them. They are easy to apply, inexpensive, and are sized for standard doors. Look for products that have clear instructions and, if they are attached with screws, slotted screw holes for easy adjustment.

Self-adhesive door seals are applied to the bottom of the interior side of inward-swinging doors.

Storm/entry door seals, which can be used on either the inside or the outside of the door, require a drill and a screwdriver for application. First cut the seal to fit. Then remove the paper backing from the adhesive side and press the seal against the door, positioning it for maximum contact with the floor. Drill pilot holes and secure the seal with screws (see Figure 14-11).

Door Shoes

Installing door shoes (Figure 14-12) and automatic door bottoms requires that the door be removed. For effectiveness, durability, and appearance, door shoes rate about the same as door bottom sweeps. If the clearance between door and threshold is between 1/2" and 3/16", application should be no problem. If the clearance is less than that, you'll need to trim

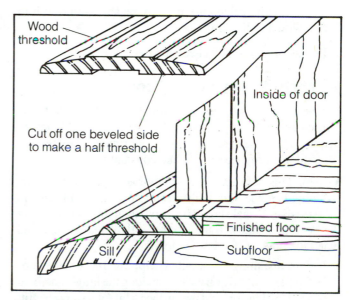

Figure 14-10. A half threshold is used where floors of different heights come together.

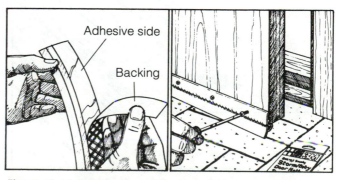

Figure 14-11. Door bottom seals may be either self-adhesive (left) or fastened with screws (right).

some off the bottom of the door. If the clearance is more than ½", you can install a thicker threshold.

To install door shoes, follow these instructions.

1. Measure the length of the door to determine if it will need to be trimmed. The door shoe should come with instructions specifying proper clearance. Once the shoe is installed, the door must be able to open and close easily, yet still fit tightly against all the frame elements.

2. Remove the door and lay it across a couple of sawhorses or on a sturdy work table.

3. Clamp a 2x4 or other straightedge to the door bottom to act as a cutting guide. Then saw or plane the door, if necessary.

4. Measure and cut the door shoe to the width of the door and notch the outside drip edge so that it clears the doorstops. For this you will need a hacksaw or a jigsaw with a metal-cutting blade.

5. Attach the shoe to the bottom of the door with the screws provided.

6. Slip the vinyl ridge into place in the shoe and trim it to length with a utility knife.

7. Rehang the door and check the fit.

Weatherstripping Around Doors

The best products for door treatments are of the plastic V-seal variety or of spring metal. Unlike windows, doors are opened and closed frequently all year round. They require something sturdy enough to take constant use.

V-Seal. This self-adhesive, sticky-back type of weatherstripping is made of durable plastic. It is easy to install and inexpensive. V-seal should be installed in the seams around the door or window frame so that a tight seal is achieved when the door or window is closed.

1. Before installing the weatherstripping, be sure the door does not fit too tightly on the top or along the hinge side. You may need to plane or sand the surface a bit for a smoother fit.

2. Use a steel tape measure to measure the length of the frame on both sides of the door and the width across the top.

3. Cut the plastic V-seal to the correct length with scissors and bend it to make the V.

4. Remove a couple of inches of the paper liner and position the V-seal in place at the top of the door frame so that the bottom of the V-shape points inward toward the house.

5. As you bring the plastic down, simultaneously pull off the paper backing and press it into place with your finger or a screwdriver (Figure 14-13). If you get it slightly out of line, simply pull it back up. The V-seal will adhere again when you press it back into position.

6. Run the V-seal all the way down to the bottom of the door frame. Do the same on the opposite side of the frame and at the top.

Spring Metal. Although it is one of the more expensive weatherstripping materials, spring metal is very durable and is virtually invisible when the door is closed. This type of weatherstripping is a bit more difficult to install than V-seal, and requires a tack hammer and awl or screwdriver.

1. Spring metal weatherstripping is installed on the door jamb next to the door stop. Measure along the sides and the top of the door jamb and cut the spring metal to the correct length with tinsnips.

2. Begin with the hinge side of the doorway, then do the latch side above and below the latch plate. Install the top piece last, miter-cutting the corners.

3. Position the spring metal so that the edge does not quite contact the stop.

4. Tack each strip at the ends to align it and stretch it flat against the jamb before nailing along its length.

5. Some manufacturers provide a strip to fit behind the strike plate. You can also trim a piece to fit.

6. When all the strips have been installed, use an awl or a screwdriver to score along the outside edge to spring the metal into position (Figure 14-14).

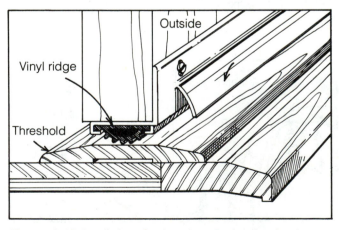

Figure 14-12. Installation of a door shoe requires that the door be removed.

Figure 14-13. Use your finger or a screwdriver to press the V-seal into place.

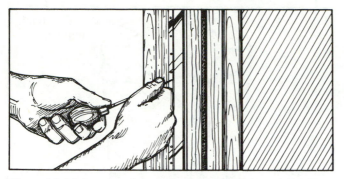

Figure 14-14. Run an awl or screwdriver along the outside edge to spring the metal into place.

Weatherstripping Around Windows

Double-Hung Windows. V-seal and spring metal weatherstripping are most effective and durable on double-hung windows. Different manufacturers require different fastening techniques; some types are pressure sensitive, others require tacking. For durability, spring metal is the best, although plastic V-seal runs a very close second.

A double-hung window is the most complicated kind of window to weatherstrip; but once you've done one, you can handle other types of windows easily. Figure 14-15 shows where to apply weatherstripping on a double-hung window.

1. As with any weatherstripping job, begin by cleaning the surfaces thoroughly.

2. Measure from the base of the inner channel to 2" above the top rail of the upper sash. Cut four strips to that length for the inner and outer vertical sash channels. You can easily cut the plastic with scissors, but you will need tinsnips for the metal.

3. Next, bend the plastic V. Lower the top sash and slip the weatherstripping materials down into both channels with the point of the V facing toward the house, or the springy part of the metal toward the outside. You will have to secure the top weather stripping, move the top sash back up, and then secure the bottom.

4. Be careful not to cover the pulleys, and be sure that the sash cords or chains can run free. This may require a bit of custom trimming.

5. Place the weatherstripping full length along the top of the upper sash rail and along the bottom of the lower sash rail.

6. The midsection of the window calls for extra care. The sashes can travel past each other far enough to catch one leg of the V and jam or crumple it. Thin, self-adhesive dacron fuzz weatherstripping eliminates this problem. It is applied to the top rail of the bottom sash, so it can't be seen.

Casement Windows and Awning Windows. Casement and awning windows cannot normally be sealed by placing weatherstripping outside. Adhesive-backed foam weatherstripping works best on the interior frame where the sash makes contact. Self-adhesive foam rubber weatherstripping

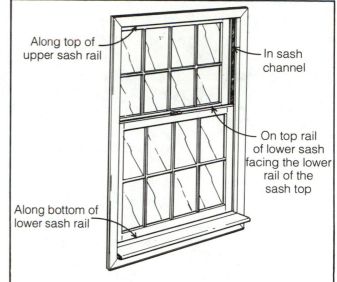

Figure 14-15. Location of weatherstripping on a double-hung window.

is easy to install, widely available in various sizes, and quite inexpensive. Its major drawback is that it wears quickly and cannot be used where friction occurs, such as in the sash channel of a double-hung window.

Sliding Windows. Weatherstripping for sliding metal windows is best installed by a professional glazier or weatherstripping contractor; in fact, it is difficult to find anything on the market for home installation. Sliding wood windows are best insulated with V-seal or spring metal, but adhesive-backed foam or bulb vinyl can also be used effectively if you are closing windows down for the winter and do not plan to open them until warm weather returns. Tubular or bulb vinyl weatherstripping is reusable season after season. This type is especially good for sliding glass doors. Simply cut it to the proper length and press the flanged protrusion into the gap to be sealed, either inside or out. Some types must be secured with nails or staples spaced 4" to 6" apart. You should never paint tubular or bulb vinyl weatherstripping; paint stiffens the vinyl and diminishes its sealing ability.

If both sashes move, weatherstrip them as you would for a double-hung window. If only one sash is movable, use spring metal in the channel where the sash closes against the frame and bulb vinyl on the top, bottom, and where the sashes join.

Jalousie Windows. The design of jalousie windows makes them nearly impossible to weatherstrip. A clear vinyl strip installed across the bottom of each pane is a partial solution, but these make the side gaps larger. You might consider replacing these windows. If that is not an option, storm windows are recommended.

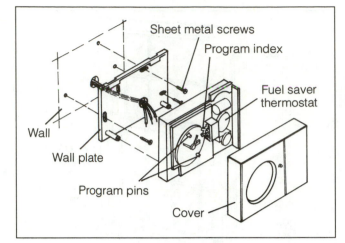

Figure 14-16. Components of a programmable thermostat.

Step Five
Energy Conservation

Margin of Error: Not applicable

The following conservation measures can help you reduce your energy costs significantly.

The Thermostat

The location of your thermostat does make a difference. If it is too near a heat or cold source, or on an outside wall, it can waste energy and cause unnecessary problems.

When weatherizing the interior doors of your home, you don't want to seal off the room with the thermostat. The purpose of tightening interior doors is to avoid heating or cooling unused rooms.

Turn the thermostat down at night when you are sleeping and during the day when the house is unoccupied and use the heat or air conditioner only in the morning and evening. An easily installed programmable thermostat (Figure 14-16) can also help you save energy. To install a programmable thermostat, follow these steps. (Also see Chapter 3, Electricity, for information on working with electrical fixtures.)

1. Turn the power off at the furnace or by removing the fuse or pulling the circuit breaker that runs the furnace fan.

2. Lift the cover plate off the old thermostat. Carefully write down which numbered or lettered wire is connected to which wire on the existing thermostat, and tag each wire with masking tape.

3. Remove the thermostat and inspect the wiring. If it is discolored, or if the insulation is cracked, cut back the insulation to a solid material and rewrap the wire with electrical tape to within 1" of the end.

4. Pull the wires through the opening of the new programmable thermostat wall plate and fasten the wires into place with the color-coded screws provided.

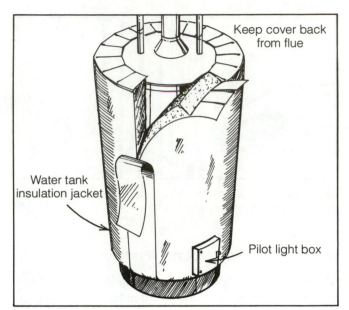

Figure 14-17. Insulating jacket for gas water heater.

5. Screw the thermostat into the wall and install the cover plate.

6. Restore the power to the furnace and then relight the pilot light. Program the thermostat according to the manufacturer's directions.

The Water Heater

Turning down the water heater to 110° will save you energy and prevent accidental scalding. If a hotter temperature is needed, as for a dishwasher, you can get a small water heating booster, which is installed in the plumbing system just before the appliance it serves.

Wrap your water heater in an insulating jacket to improve its heat retention (Figure 14-17). This insulation will also keep the heating element from working so hard to keep the water hot. If you have a gas hot water heater, be careful not to install the jacket too close to the floor. The pilot light and the burner require combustion air.

When you leave home for a vacation, turn off all pilot lights, including the one in the water heater. Check with your local gas company first about turning off and relighting gas pilot lights.

Tune-Ups and Maintenance

It pays to have your furnace and central air conditioner tuned up every couple of years before the heating or cooling season. Although these are jobs for a professional, you can take measures to add to the efficiency of these appliances.

Carefully examine all ducts and flues and seal any leaks with duct tape. Leaks usually occur at a bend in the duct. Replace filters regularly on furnaces and air-conditioning units. Keep heating/cooling registers clean and free from blockage. Window air conditioners should be removed and

Figure 14-18. Wrap the air conditioner in plastic and seal it with duct tape if it will not be used for several months.

cleaned in winter, and the space between the air conditioner and the wall should be sealed with insulating material. During the cooler months you can wrap the air conditioner in plastic and seal it with duct tape (Figure 14-18).

Fireplace chimneys allow warm air to drift right up and out of your home. Reduce this loss by installing a fireplace damper, if you don't have one already. This must be custom-fitted in your chimney by a professional, and it can be expensive. Remote cable-controlled dampers are available that mount atop the chimney. Be sure to mount the cable locking gate where you can adjust it while a fire is burning. Glass fireplace doors work well for the fireplace that is used only occasionally. These doors, which seal against the opening, provide good protection against infiltration.

There are kits available to help you seal off infiltration through electrical outlets. These nonflammable foam pad inserts fit right over the outlet under the plate. Cap the sockets when not in use.

Don't overwork your utilities. Insulating hot and cold water pipes as well as heating and cooling ducts can prevent sweating on hot days and freezing on cold days. Condensation can reduce the effectiveness of your subfloor insulation and cause many other moisture-related problems.

Pipe insulating sleeves are available for most size pipes, as well as one-size-fits-all foam tape. The sleeves are slit on one side to pop over the pipe like a long hot dog bun.

If you have air conditioning, you will find two lines running from the central unit to the condenser outside. The larger line is called a vapor line; this is the coldest portion of the whole system. If the vapor line is not insulated, the efficiency of the system may be reduced by 20 percent or more. The smaller line is the liquid return line; it carries heat from the central unit, and should not be insulated.

15 Home Security

WHETHER YOU LIVE in the city, the suburbs, or the country, home security is probably an important issue for you. There are no guarantees against crime. But with a relatively small investment of time, energy, and money, you can implement home security measures that will decrease the chance that your home will be broken into and increase the chance that stolen items will be recovered. Unfortunately, it's easy to overlook these measures and feel secure—until something happens.

This chapter will introduce some effective security measures you can implement around your home. You will learn how to install deadbolts and entrance locks in exterior doors. Other issues of home security addressed in this chapter include windows, safes and hiding places, alarm systems, and fire security.

Before You Begin

SAFETY

Safety is not directly addressed in this chapter because home security is, in itself, safety. Keep in mind, however, the general safe use practices for any tool you use in making your home secure.

USEFUL TERMS

A **deadbolt**, or **deadlocking latch**, is a 1" steel bar that, when engaged, extends all the way through the jamb.

Door lights are windows in or immediately adjacent to a door.

A **double-cylinder lock** is a lock for which a key is needed to unlock both inside and outside. These locks may violate the fire code in residential buildings.

A **hole saw** is a drill accessory used to create the big hole in which to insert the lockset or deadbolt cylinder into a door. Common sizes are from 1" to 2 ½".

A **mortise** is a notch or square hole cut out specifically to fit a full mortise lock or a hinge.

Polycarbonate is a shatterproof plastic that is up to 250 times stronger than regular glass.

Safety glass is two-ply glass with an adhesive plastic core. It is almost as strong as tempered glass, and unlike tempered glass, it can be cut to size.

A **spade bit** is a drill accessory used to create a hole in the door edge in which to insert the latch set.

A **spring latch** is a throw that has no hardened insert and so is easily jimmied with a credit card.

Tempered glass is four to five times stronger than regular glass. It is made by heating glass almost to the melting point and then chilling it rapidly, causing a tough skin to form around the glass. It cannot be cut without shattering.

WHAT YOU WILL NEED

Time. Making your home secure is not something you can set a time limit on; the process involves different amounts of time for every home. One person can install a deadbolt or a lock set in 2 to 4 hours.

Tools and Materials. The tools and materials you need will depend on what you plan to do to make your home more secure. The following lists should cover most of your needs.

Tools

Electric engraver

⅜" drill

Hole saws

Spade bits

Pencil

Utility knife

Chisel

Hammer

Wood rasp

Pry bar

Screwdrivers

Wrenches

Materials

Sheet metal

Glazing

Polycarbonate (shatterproof plastic)

Solid wood door

Metal door

3" flat head wood screws

Set screws

Sheet metal screws

Dead bolt

Key-in-knob lock

Full-mortise lock

Rim-mounted lock

10-penny nails

Keyed window locks

Bolt-action window locks

Lever-type sash locks

Hasp

Window bars

False book, soft drink can, etc., for hiding valuables

Push-button combination deadbolt

Plywood

Battery-operated alarm

Self-contained alarm

Smoke detector

PERMITS AND CODES

Permits are not usually required for improving security around the home. However, some areas require a permit if more than a certain dollar amount of work is being done. Replacing windows and doors may fall into this category. Also, electrical work for exterior lighting and alarm systems will require permits and inspections.

Codes do not allow the use of double-cylinder deadbolts in most areas, because they can prevent a quick exit in case of fire if you can't find the key.

The Home Security Survey

The best start for a home security program is to have a security survey done by a professional. In many areas, the police department will send a security expert out to your home to walk the house and grounds with you. If this service is not available in your community, the police department may provide pamphlets and other materials that will help you to make your own survey. Several excellent books are available on this subject. If you plan to have a professional install an alarm system, the company will often perform the survey. Be careful, though, because the company may have a hidden agenda—to sell you a more expensive security system than you really need.

To do the survey correctly, you need to think like a burglar. Imagine that you want to break into your own home without getting caught. Where would you enter? When? How? What do you think would give you away? A little imagination will lead you to the following conclusions. Almost all home security is focused on these two facts.

1. Your points of entry—doors and windows—are where you are most vulnerable.

2. Burglars fear two things: being heard and being seen.

A walk around your home, preferably with a professional, will quickly highlight your weaknesses in home security (Figure 15-1). If you, like most of us, lock yourself out from time to time, you already know these points of vulnerability.

You probably also know just how easy it is to break into most homes.

Windows are the most vulnerable points of entry. The standard types of screens and window latches do little to deter a burglar. The common window screen can be opened from the outside with a butter knife in just 5 seconds; the traditional window latch requires a penknife and about 5 seconds more.

Many doors are equipped with simple spring locks; these can be opened with a credit card or a knife. Even if the door is equipped with a deadbolt, a forceful shove can often break the wooden jamb and trim around the door.

As you walk through and around your home, make a list of all vulnerable areas, especially those easily accessible from the ground, including the basement windows and doors. Also check out second-floor entry points that are easily accessible with a ladder.

Ask yourself, What would make my house a house that a burglar would not want to hit? (Park the Jaguar in the back, the Volkswagen in the front.) Are there high bushes for burglars to hide in? Are some areas of the house hidden? Is the lighting adequate? Are valuable items visible through first-floor windows?

If burglars believe they would be in full view of the neighbors, you can be sure they will avoid your home. You may need to cut back some shrubs. If you live where there are no neighbors close by, a noisy alarm system is your best deterrent. At night, motion-sensitive lighting is recommended out of doors.

Are your exterior doors hollow core, or the more durable solid wood or metal doors? Do any trees offer easy access to second-story windows? Are sliding-glass or garage doors vulnerable? What type of windows do you have? Are they vulnerable?

After you complete your security survey, you are ready to make some decisions about what security measures you want to implement. This chapter discusses ways of installing these measures yourself.

Doors

Because windows are usually easier to penetrate, doors are not always the preferred entrance for a burglar. However, doors are usually their preferred exit.

Sixty percent of all home burglars enter through doors. The common key-in-knob lock can be opened in a matter of seconds by a professional with a credit card or a screwdriver. However, there are simple things you can do to make this technique unusable.

First, let's look at the door itself (Figure 15-2). There are many different types of entrance doors, and some are more secure than others. Many include a window or a glass panel directly adjoining the door (a door light). Unless your door locks with a key from the inside, a burglar can break the

Tree leading
to open window

Valuables visible
through window

Broken light
fixture

Screen can be
easily cut

Glass near
door locks

Uncollected
mail

Open basement window

High bushes
offer hiding places

Hinges on
outside of door

Uncollected newspapers

Figure 15-1. A security survey will reveal any vulnerable areas around your home.

glass, reach around to the inside, and open the door. If the panel is large enough, he or she can simply crawl in.

If you have such a door, and don't want to replace it, you can replace the glass panel with tempered glass. This glass is many times stronger than common plate glass, and should deter any intruder. Many doors already have tempered glass, since local codes often require it. If yours does not, take the exact measurements to a glass company and order a replacement pane. It may be fairly expensive. This glass has to be special ordered because it must be heat-treated (tempered) by the manufacturer and shipped to the glass company.

If your door has standard glass in it or near it, and you don't want to replace it with tempered glass just yet, you might consider replacing it with frosted glass, or setting a mortised bolt in the door bottom instead.

Study the door itself. Is it sturdy and well built? Some newer homes have doors that have a hollow interior (hollow-core doors). These are very easy to break. You may want to

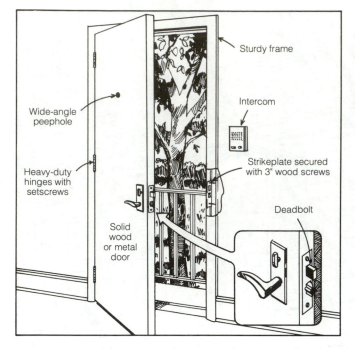

Figure 15-2. Features of a secure entry door.

Wide-angle peephole

Heavy-duty hinges with setscrews

Solid wood or metal door

Sturdy frame

Intercom

Strikeplate secured with 3" wood screws

Deadbolt

Figure 15-4. Insert screws into the top track to prevent sliding doors from being lifted off the track.

Sheet metal screws

Bar or pipe to prevent door from opening

Door

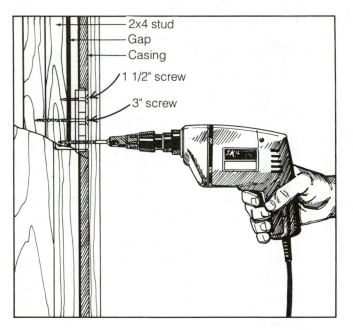

Figure 15-3. Screws that are 3" long penetrate deep into the studs.

2x4 stud
Gap
Casing
1 1/2" screw
3" screw

replace the door with a new metal or solid-core door. Although replacing a door may seem intimidating, it is actually quite simple. You can buy doors in all standard sizes with the hinges and hardware preinstalled. Simply remove the pins from the hinges of the old door, remove the door, slip the new door on, and replace the hinges. Just be sure that the hinges, handles, locks, and strikeplates match up. For more information on hanging doors, see Chapter 8, Doors and Trim.

Hinges are another area of possible vulnerability. If the hinges are exposed to the exterior, you have a problem. This is why residential exterior doors always open toward the interior. Burglars can simply pop out the hinges and remove the door, even when it is locked tight! This situation is a burglar's dream, and it was some carpenter's mistake. In this case, you need to reinstall the hinges so they are exposed to the inside, or to replace them with hinges that use fixed pins that cannot be removed. You can also buy kits that allow you to retrofit existing hinges with these setscrews to make them nonremovable.

Even a high-quality metal or solid wood door may not be secure if the frame around the door is not sturdy. In that case, the door can be penetrated with a pry bar, or even with a good shove. The jamb (the exposed frame around the door) is made of 1"-thick wood, which is easy to break through. However, the jamb is attached to a 2x4 framing member. If all hinge screws, strikeplate screws, and bolts penetrate into this thicker member, the door is much more secure. Replace all the screws in the hinges and strikeplates with high-quality 3" screws, which will penetrate deep into this frame, as shown in Figure 15-3. Also be sure to use a long deadbolt.

You may want to replace not only the door but the surrounding frame (jamb, trim, and molding) as well. Test to see if the frame is movable (if there is a gap between the frame and the wall stud). If it is, a burglar can simply push on the frame with a crowbar and pop the door open. Metal stripping can be installed around existing doors to make the door more secure. Although replacing both the frame and the door is somewhat complex, it is easier than you may think. You can buy doors "prehung." This means that the door is hung in its new frame with all hardware and hinges in place. You simply take out the old door and frame and replace it with a new,

Figure 15-5. The four most common types of locks.

more secure one. Depending on the type of siding and interior finish, this can be anywhere from a two-hour to a two-day job. Remember, you are not concerned just with the quality of the door itself, but also with the way it is attached to its frame.

There are a few other things to consider about doors. For one thing, you should install a door viewer or peephole that has a 180-degree viewing area—and use it. If you have sliding glass doors, check to see if they can be lifted off their tracks from the outside. If so, screw some screws in at the top that protrude into the track but do not obstruct the door from sliding (Figure 15-4). You can also fit a bar or pipe into the inside track so that the door can't be slid open when it is in place. These bars are available in any hardware or home center; or you can cut dowels to length yourself.

Small pin locks are available for sliding glass doors in keyed and spring-loaded styles. Be sure to install the spring type far enough in from the edge that a burglar can't get at it.

Deadbolts and Entrance Locks

Regardless of the strength of your doors, an intruder can always gain entry if your locks are not adequate. There are several standard measurements for locking mechanisms, so the bored holes on your door and frame may not match the new lock to be installed. Try to match the holes, or enlarge the existing holes. You can buy hardware that aids in adapting to existing holes. If all this fails, you will need to install a new door.

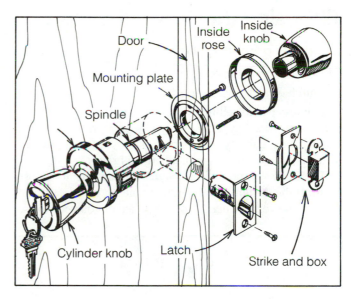

Figure 15-6. Components of a typical key-in-knob lock.

Four commonly used lock systems are described below and illustrated in Figure 15-5. The key-in-knob and the deadbolt are the most often used and the easiest to install.

1. Key-in-knob locks (Figure 15-6) are the most common exterior door locks, but they can be easily jimmied. The better ones have a hardened steel pin with a beveled latch.

2. Deadbolt locks are an excellent way to make your entry door secure. Look for a bolt at least 1" long; a rotating steel pin within the bolt to resist hacksaws; and a free-spinning brass cover over the outside cylinder to resist wrenches.

3. Full mortise locks almost always have to be installed by a professional locksmith. They offer double-lock protection, including a deadbolt.

4. Rim-mounted locks are sometimes called "mortised-in" bolts. They mount to the interior surface of the door and make a good second lock because of their ability to resist prying. They're always mounted on the lower half of the door so that smoke will not obscure them.

Installing a Deadbolt or Entrance Lock

Installing a deadbolt or entrance lock is a simple project that requires only a few special tools and should take no more than 2 or 3 hours. The main thing is to be sure of the exact location of the holes before you start to drill. If the hole is improperly drilled, it can ruin the door. Also be sure to use long (3") screws for the strikeplate so that they will penetrate deeply into the frame behind the jamb.

Step One
Choosing the Proper Lockset

Margin of Error: Not applicable

Most Common Mistake

☐ Purchasing an inadequate lockset.

The first step in installing a new lock is to choose your hardware. It pays to buy a nationally known brand, one whose quality and reliability you can trust. This is not an area where you want to cut corners with a bargain brand.

There are several different styles and designs to choose from. If the design is a decorative feature, it is a matter of taste. However, you need to decide whether you want to use

a double-cylinder, double-keyed lock or not. The advantage to these locks is that you can lock the door on the way out and no one can open it from the outside *or* the inside without a key. This stops burglars from carrying things out the door. The disadvantage is that they can hinder your escape in case of fire. You may want to use an entrance lock that only key locks from the outside, combined with a mortise bolt in the threshold. In case of fire, you will be able to get out quickly without fumbling for the key to open a keyed deadbolt.

Latch bolts come in varying lengths. It's best to choose the longest available. If it's ever needed, it will be worth the extra money.

Step Two
Using the Template

Margin of Error: Exact

Most Common Mistakes

☐ Marking the location of the hole incorrectly.

☐ Locating the new latch at the same level as the previous strikeplate.

In the package with your new entrance lock or deadbolt you will find a small paper template that shows you exactly where to drill the two holes you need install the system. You need to drill a hole through the door face for the lock or deadbolt and one through the edge of the door for the latch. These two holes must be perfectly aligned so that the mechanism will fit together properly. The template is your guide to this alignment.

First, decide how high on the door you want to install the lock. Entrance locks are usually 36" above the floor. The main thing to watch for here is the location of the old strikeplate. Even if you are not reusing this strikeplate (and usually you will not), be sure to center the new strikeplate directly on top of the old one.

Instructions on the use of the template are provided in the package. Generally you simply bend the template and wrap

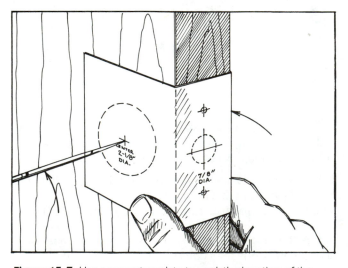

Figure 15-7. Use a paper template to mark the location of the holes you will drill on the edge and face of the door.

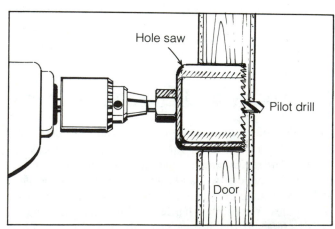

Figure 15-8. Use a hole saw to drill a large hole for the lock.

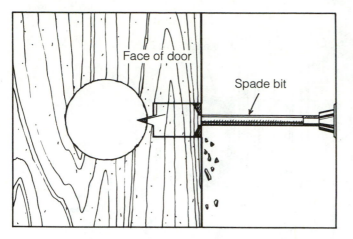

Figure 15-9. Use a spade bit to drill a hole for the spring latch.

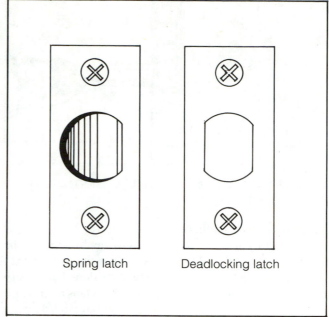

Spring latch   Deadlocking latch

Figure 15-10. Typical latch plates.

it around the door so that the specified side is on the face of the door and the other side is on the edge. The hole center should be directly across from the center of the strike plate opening (Figure 15-7). Two holes in the template show you where to make your marks on the edge and on the face. Use a sharp instrument or a nail to mark the door at these two points. Double-check your work; you don't want to have to scrap a good door because a hole was drilled in the wrong place.

Step Three
Drilling the Holes

Margin of Error: Exact

Most Common Mistakes

☐ Drilling in the wrong place.

☐ Not drilling straight.

☐ Using the wrong size drill bits.

☐ Drilling all the way through both faces of the door in one pass.

☐ Using a dull drill bit.

☐ Using a small (¼") drill.

You are now ready to start drilling. Use a ⅜" drill to provide adequate power to drill cleanly through the solid door. Metal doors usually come predrilled. Use the bit size specified by the manufacturer (often 2 ⅛"). You will need a long spade bit to drill through the edge of the door for the hole for the latch, and you will need a hole saw for the hole through the face for the lock or deadbolt itself.

When drilling the larger lock hole through the door face, it is important to get a clean cut with no unsightly splinters. To do this, you need to use a hole saw, which has a small pilot drill in the center. This pilot drill has two functions. First, it allows you to exactly line up the center of the hole saw when you start to drill. Second, it will poke out the other side of the door before the hole saw itself penetrates all the way

through. As soon as you see the pilot bit pop out the other side, stop drilling immediately (Figure 15-8). Remove the hole saw and start drilling again from the other side of the door. This will create a clean, splinter-free hole. After the hole is drilled in the face, you are ready to drill the latch hole in the edge. Don't drill this hole first.

To drill the latch hole on the edge of the door, use the spade bit specified by the manufacturer. Drill this latch hole until it meets the larger hole you just drilled, as shown in Figure 15-9. To ensure a straight hole, always be careful to hold the drill level as you work.

Step Four
Installing the Spring Latch Plate

Margin of Error: Exact

Most Common Mistakes

☐ Chiseling the hole sloppily or too deep.

☐ Not drilling pilot holes before inserting screws.

After both holes are drilled, you are ready to install the spring latch (Figure 15-10). This is a simple task and should come out perfectly if you take your time and do it accurately. You will need to mortise (inset) the plate into the edge of the door so that it is flush with the surface of the edge.

Place the latch so that the hidden part goes in the hole you drilled in the edge of the door. It is a good idea to actually install the spring latch first, to be sure that the plate is properly located.

When you are sure the plate is properly placed, hold it snug or screw it against the edge of the door. With a sharp

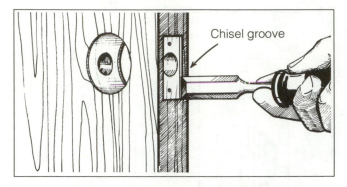

Figure 15-11. Chisel out the area where the spring latch plate will be installed.

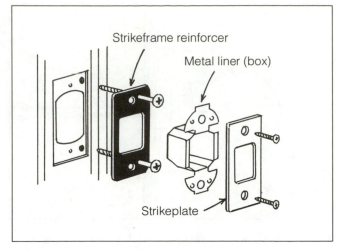

Figure 15-12. Components of the strike plate.

pencil or a utility knife, outline the plate on the door. Now chisel out this area to a depth equal to the thickness of the latch plate (Figure 15-11). This will allow the latch plate to sit flush with the surface of the edge of the door. Use a sharp chisel the same width as the plate. Use light taps of the hammer so you don't gouge out too much wood and sink the plate too deeply. Work slowly and carefully to create a tight fit.

When you are satisfied with the fit, install the latch with the two screws provided. It's best to drill pilot holes first with a bit that is slightly thinner than the shank of the screw. The pilot holes ensure that the screws will go in straight and not split the wood. After the pilot holes are drilled, hold the plate firmly against the door and install the screws.

With the spring latch in place, you can install the lock mechanism. This comes in two pieces, inserted from either side of the door. Needless to say, be sure the keyed knob is pointing out. Slip in the keyed knob, threading it through the latch piece, and then the interior sections. These two are usually joined together by two screws that insert through the interior section and screw into the exterior section, tightly sandwiching the door and holding the lock firmly in place. Now place the cover plate over the interior section. Finally, slip on the knob. There is usually a spring clip that you must press down to slip on the knob. When you release this clip, it fits into a groove and secures the knob.

Step Five
Installing the Strikeplate

Margin of Error: Exact

Most Common Mistakes

☐ Not aligning the strikeplate with the spring latch.

☐ Installing the strikeplate in the old holes if they are in poor condition.

☐ Not using long enough screws.

When your entrance lock is in and functioning properly, you can install the strikeplate in the frame of the door. Don't install this in the holes created by the previous strikeplate screws, or the screws will not have good wood to bite into. Of course, it's a little late to be thinking about this now, since

the plate must align with the spring latch of the lock you just installed. Just be sure that this alignment is exact so that the latch can be easily inserted into the plate and metal liner.

The strikeplate is usually a three-part assembly made up of a strikeframe reinforcer, metal liner (box), and finished strikeplate (Figure 15-12). The metal liner often requires a fairly deep hole. To create this hole, locate the exact center of the strikeplate on the frame and drill two holes with a $7/8$" bit, one $3/8$" above the center point and one $3/8$" below (refer to the manufacturer's instructions). Then chisel out the wood between the two holes and in the corners to create one hole that the metal liner will fit into tightly. Before installing the metal liner, install the strikeframe reinforcer, using two long (3") screws to penetrate into the wall frame. (Be sure to drill pilot holes first.) Now insert the metal liner and screw in the finished strikeplate. Test your lock. If it works smoothly, pat yourself on the back. If it doesn't, you may need to chisel out more wood or slightly adjust the location of the strikeplate.

Windows

Windows are almost as popular as doors as entry points for burglars. Unfortunately, they are much harder to secure than doors, because the glass can always be broken. There are several things you can do to reduce the threat of entry through your windows. Attaching them to a central alarm system is one of the best ways. Also, the glass can be replaced with tempered glass or polycarbonate, although this is a costly alternative. Metal bars can be installed over the windows, but they don't enhance your view, and they can be a real threat to life in case of fire, unless they are fitted with the required emergency releases. And of course, be sure to keep foliage in front of windows well trimmed so that burglars can't hide there. Aside from these techniques, the best way of making your windows secure is to install security latches and other such devices. They are inexpensive, easy

Figure 15-13. Be sure your casement windows are well secured by removing the crank and installing a lock.

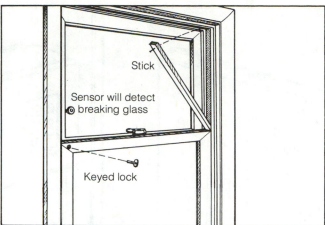

Figure 15-14. Three ways of securing windows.

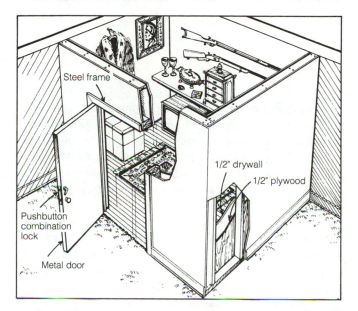

Figure 15-15. A closet can be converted into a small vault.

to install, and will usually deter burglars, unless they are willing to break the glass despite the noise.

You may think that your window locks are effective, but this is often not the case. Clasp locks can be opened with a butter knife inserted between the two windows. There are several different types of window locks on the market, all of which are relatively easy to install. Some locks even allow you to leave the window locked in a partially opened position. Battery-operated alarms are also available for individual windows.

Keyed locks for windows are available, but they can be hard to open in an emergency, such as a fire. Casement windows, which have cranks, can be secured by simply removing the handle (Figure 15-13). Leave the handle in an accessible place in case of fire. You may need to secure only the windows on the first floor, if you feel that your second- and third-floor windows are not vulnerable (Figure 15-14).

Air conditioners or fans installed in windows can also be vulnerable points. They can often be removed by a burglar. Be sure the units are bolted to the house in such a way that they can't be removed from the outside. Also make sure that the window can't be raised.

Safes and Hiding Places

After you have taken all possible precautions to keep burglars from breaking into your home, you may want to take further measures to keep them from locating your valuables if they do break in. This might mean either hiding valuables or placing them in safes so that they can't be removed even if they are located. Some very simple, inexpensive, and clever hiding devices are available. For example, you can buy a small container that looks like a head of lettuce. You put your valuables in it and place it in the refrigerator. Unless the burglar is aware of the gimmick, or decides to make a salad, your jewels are safe. Similar containers are available

as soft drink cans, hollow books, or false electrical boxes. If you have wide (6" to 12") baseboards, you can remove a section, hollow out the areas between the studs, put small valuables in, and tack the baseboard back in place.

An imaginative tour of your home will reveal many other effective hiding places. Remember, burglars don't usually have much time to search, so they grab whatever is handy.

If you feel it's worth the effort, you can strengthen a closet to serve as a small vault (Figure 15-15). Simply install a metal or solid wood door and a couple of deadbolts or a pushbutton combination lock. It is a good idea to line the interior with plywood, since drywall can be easily broken through.

Many models and sizes of residential safes are available. Although somewhat more expensive than the other devices described here, they can be effective if properly installed. Smaller onces cemented into place are an excellent deterrent. But remember, a safe will also alert a burglar to what's inside, so be sure it is well secured.

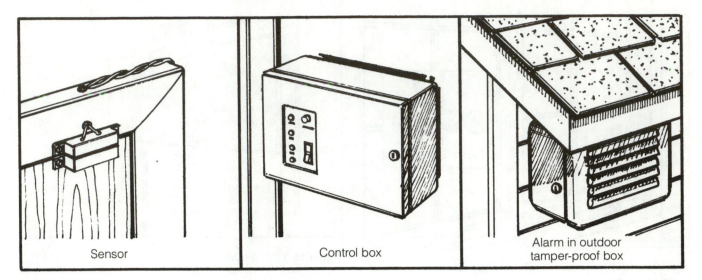

Sensor

Control box

Alarm in outdoor
tamper-proof box

Figure 15-16. The three basic components of an alarm system.

Alarm Systems

Electronic alarms have become very popular in the last decade. Their popularity is well earned; they are both effective and affordable. However, you should not put too much faith in them. When combined with the other safety measures discussed in this chapter, they will make your house relatively secure. But if you rely totally on alarm systems, you will still be vulnerable.

Professional burglars know how to silence or incapacitate even the most complicated alarm systems. Remote alarms—alarms that ring only at the police station or at a private security office—often allow burglars time to get away before help arrives. Also, false alarms are becoming so common that alarms are often ignored.

There are several different types of alarm systems on the market. Some of them are easy to install—you simply screw the sending units into doors and windows. If the door or window is opened or broken, an alarm sounds and a signal is sent to a main receiving unit. Other types are best installed by a professional alarm company. In choosing an alarm system, you need to consider your family's lifestyle. Motion-sensing detectors will be self-defeating if you have pets. If you have several children or frequent overnight guests, alarm systems that demand that you enter a code when entering and leaving the house may not work. I remember arriving at my sister's house alone late one night. I let myself in, and immediately heard the soft buzzer on the alarm system, indicating that I had 10 seconds to enter the code before the alarm would blast. I had forgotten the code and stood there helplessly in the hallway as the alarm woke my sister, her family, and all the neighbors.

Once you've decided which type of alarm system will work best for you, be sure to buy a high-quality system. With luck, and with all the other precautions you've taken, you may never need it. But if you do, you will want it to work properly.

All systems have three basic components, as shown in Figure 15-16: the sensor that senses the intrusion, the control that sounds the alarm once the intrusion has occurred, and the alarm itself. These systems may operate off a battery, off the home's electrical current, or both. Although they are easy to install, the battery-operated units are often not sophisticated enough to satisfy all your needs.

Self-Contained Alarm Systems

Self-contained alarm systems have the alarm, control, and sensor all in one unit (Figure 15-17). They are most commonly used in small houses, offices, and apartments that have a limited number of doors and windows. They can be as simple as a cigarette-box-sized alarm that hangs on the door or chainguard. Others can be plugged into any wall outlet and have a simple motion detector. The more sophisticated models are activated by a change in air pressure, as when a door or window is opened, or work off of high-frequency sound waves. These units are less expensive and easier to install than some others. Their drawbacks are that burglars can quickly locate and disable them because the alarm is with the control. Also, the ones that work off of air pressure or sound waves often give false alarms in response to noise upstairs or high winds.

Alarm Systems
with Separate Components

The best alarm systems separate the sensor from the control and from the alarm; these work well if you want to guard several rooms at once. Individual sensors, such as a magnetic contact, are placed on the windows and doors, and the wires

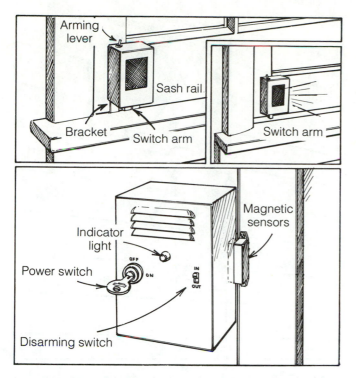

Figure 15-17. Three typical self-contained alarms.

to the alarm control are hidden in the framing. This makes it much more difficult for the burglar to dismantle the system.

These units often have several control stations around the house so that you can activate or deactivate all or part of your sensors. Some units even tell you which doors and windows are open or closed. They also have panic buttons that can be used when you hear someone prowling around outside. These systems are usually activated and deactivated by a code and can sound an alarm at the house, at the police station or security office, or both. Also, some alarms can be wired to dial a number automatically and give a recorded message. You can change the number so that the system will reach you wherever you are, in case the house is burning or you are being robbed.

When you install an alarm, put decals on your doors to let burglars know that your house is equipped with an alarm. They will probably go away.

Neighborhood Watch Programs

As mentioned earlier, burglars fear being observed. Many communities have neighborhood watch programs. Watching out for your neighbors is one of the most effective deterrants to burglars. Your police department will probably give you advice on organizing your block or neighborhood, and may even send an officer out to address your group. They may also provide "Crime Watch" stickers for your windows and doors.

In some areas the police department will loan you an electric engraver with which you can permanently mark your

driver's license number on your television, stereo, and other valuables. This will make it possible for the police to return your possessions to you in case they are stolen and retrieved.

Fire Security

Most of this chapter has been devoted to securing your valuables against theft. It is even more important to secure your home itself, and its occupants, against the threat of fire. This section of the chapter is shorter than the sections on home security, not because fire security is less important (in fact, it is much more important), but because fire alarm systems do not require detailed installation instructions. All you have to do is screw the smoke detectors to the walls at the right places.

Fire security is extremely important. To lose your valuables is one thing; to lose a family member is something else altogether. In the United States, almost five thousand people die in fires each year.

Fire safety begins with a thorough investigation of every room in the home to locate possible trouble spots. It is a rare home that does not have at least one of the following fire safety problems.

☐ Overloaded or undersized electrical circuits
☐ Too many electrical appliances plugged into one outlet
☐ Electrical cords running under carpet or rug
☐ Frayed wires
☐ Defective appliances
☐ Oversized fuses
☐ Flammable liquids stored
☐ Gas leaks
☐ Accumulation of grease in stove
☐ Accumulation of grease in range hood
☐ Bare light bulbs, especially in closets
☐ Built-up soot in chimney or wood stove flue
☐ Improperly installed fireplace or wood stove
☐ Inadequate screen in front of open fireplace or wood stove
☐ Outdoor barbecue grease build-up
☐ Children playing with matches
☐ Sloppy workshop area
☐ Smoking in bed
☐ Double cylinder deadbolts
☐ Security bars without an emergency release

The Christmas season poses the following special dangers.

☐ Dry tree
☐ Plastic tree that is not fire retardant
☐ Tree placed near heat source
☐ Children playing with candles

Visit your local fire department and pick up their pamphlets on fire safety. A fire department representative may even visit your home for a security tour.

After you have evaluated all the possible problems and corrected them, you are ready to take some offensive, as opposed to defensive, tactics.

Clean your chimneys and flues as needed to prevent soot, or hire a chimney sweep to do it. As soot accumulates, oily tars leach to the surface. These flammable tars are the source of many residential tars.

Discuss the location and operation of the gas main valve and electrical main breaker with your family. Keep a wrench of appropriate size near the gas main valve.

Plan fire escape routes. Be sure that each bedroom has at least two possible ways out. Teach the entire family, especially children, what to do in case of fire. Make sure they know that most deaths are caused by smoke inhalation, not by the fire itself. Learn how to protect yourself against smoke inhalation. Decide on a meeting place outside your house or at a neighbor's home so you can quickly determine if anyone is missing. Tape the fire department number to all phones. Remind your family to forget about their possessions, just escape. Determine if any special fire escapes or rope ladders are needed for quick escape from the second floor (Figure 15-18). Put a few fire extinguishers, the multipurpose (ABC) type, around the house, especially in the kitchen (Figure 15-19). And finally, conduct a fire drill.

Above all, install smoke detectors. These simple devices are inexpensive and can be installed in just a few minutes. They run off either household electricity or batteries. Experts estimate that half the lives lost in home fires could be saved with these detectors.

Install the detectors between the sleeping areas and the rest of the house. In multilevel homes, codes require at least one on each floor. In a two-story house, install one on the ceiling at the bottom of the staircase. Put one at the bottom of the basement staircase as well. Don't install them near an air supply, open duct, or vent, which can pull the smoke away from the detector. And don't place them near safe sources of heat or smoke, such as a fireplace, which will activate them unnecessarily.

Figure 15-18. A rope ladder is a good idea for second-story bedrooms, especially if there is only one stairway.

Dry chemical extinguisher   Water extinguisher   Carbon dioxide extinguisher

Figure 15-19. Three types of fire extinguishers. The multipurpose ABC type is recommended.

16 Decks

BUILDING A DECK is a fairly complex project that can be demanding both physically and mentally. However, decks don't have to be leakproof or perfectly built, the work goes quickly, and the reward is an enjoyable living area for a small price.

There are two key things to remember in building a deck. First, because the deck is completely exposed to the weather, you must use the proper materials and construction techniques to avoid decay. And second, be sure that your deck is level, plumb, and solidly constructed.

Before You Begin

SAFETY

☐ Always use the appropriate tool for the job.

☐ Keep blades and bits sharp. A dull tool requires excessive force, and can easily slip.

☐ Wear safety goggles and glasses when using power tools, especially if you wear contact lenses.

☐ Always unplug your power tools when making adjustments or changing attachments.

☐ Be sure your electric tools are properly grounded.

☐ Watch power cord placement so it does not interfere with the operation of the tool.

☐ Wear ear protection when operating power tools; some operate at a noise level that is high enough to damage hearing.

☐ Be careful that loose hair and clothing do not get caught in power tools.

☐ Be careful when carrying long boards at the work site.

☐ Wear heavy-soled, sturdy work boots.

☐ To avoid back strain, bend from the knees when lifting large or heavy objects, and be careful when digging post holes.

USEFUL TERMS

All-heart grades are grades of wood that contain no knots or blemishes.

Band joists are 2"-thick top-quality boards that are nailed around the outer joists of the deck and across the end of the joists to form an attractive border.

The **bow** is the deviation from straight and true seen when looking down the edge of a board.

Checking is the tendency of wood to split across the grain as it dries.

Construction common is a grade of redwood that contains sapwood.

The **crown** is the highest point of a warped board seen when looking down the side of the the board; the convex side.

The **cup** is the warp of a board seen from the end of the board; the concave side.

Decking is the boards that make up the surface of the deck.

The **footing** is the concrete base on which the foundation wall or pier rests.

A **girder** is a horizontal support member of a deck framing system that rests on the piers. It is usually 4" wide and the same depth as the joists. The girder is most often parallel to the ledger and supports the opposite end of the joists.

Hot dipped galvanized (HDG) is a rustproof coated metal that is less expensive than aluminum or stainless steel. It is used for nails, bolts, screws, and other metal fasteners.

Joists are a system of floor framing that commonly uses 2x6 lumber or larger, depending on the span.

A **lag screw** is a long screw with a hexagonal head.

A **ledger** is a board of the same size as the joists, attached to a wall, to which the joists are attached perpendicularly.

A **pad** is a cast concrete base designed to spread the load of a pier block over a larger area.

Pier blocks are concrete blocks that support the posts several inches above ground to avoid decay.

Piers are holes dug to below the frost line and filled with concrete to provide a firm footing for the foundation pier blocks.

A **plumb bob** is a heavy object suspended on the end of a string for the purpose of establishing a true vertical line.

Posts are the upright members, usually 4x4, that support the deck.

Pressure-treated lumber has been infused with copper salts that greatly reduce the ability of insects and fungi to grow in the wood. Always wear a mask when cutting this material.

Sapwood is the portion of the tree between the heartwood and the bark. This material is much weaker than heartwood, and should not be used for decking.

Toenailing is nailing at an angle that reduces the chance of nails loosening under stress.

A **torpedo level** is a level 8" or 9" in length with vials to read level, plumb, and 45 degrees.

WHAT YOU WILL NEED

Time. A 12′x12′ deck with a simple foundation and railing can be completed by two people in a few days. Allow 64 to 85 person-hours to completion, longer for complex railing and foundation designs.

Tools. Most deck projects require only common framing tools; no specialized tools are necessary, although you may want to consider renting a pneumatic tool for nailing on the decking. Be sure to use high-quality tools that are capable of doing the job without strain. This is especially important in your choice of power tools.

Safety goggles

Ear plugs

Framing hammer

Torpedo level

4′ level

Plumb bob

Pencil

Nail pouch

Framing square

Combination square

Tape measure

Sawhorses

Shovel

Wheelbarrow or pan for mixing concrete

Cement hoe

Trowel

Pry bar

Caulking gun

Extension cords

Socket or crescent wrench

Power saw

Handsaw

Materials. Your choice of decking and fastener materials is very important. All materials must be chosen for their ability to resist decay and rust. Use only hot dipped galvanized (HDG) nails, bolts, screws, and metal fasteners. Double hot dipped is even better. These galvanized fasteners won't rust quickly. Aluminium and stainless steel nails won't rust either, but HDG is more commonly used and less expensive. Don't use electroplated galvanized (EG); galvanized plating often chips.

Many types of galvanized sheet metal fasteners are commonly used in deck construction. These fasteners simplify your project and strengthen your construction. They can be used in many areas of deck construction, including the following attachments.

☐ Joist to ledger (joist hanger)

☐ Girder to post (post cap)

☐ Joist to girder (right-angle bracket)

☐ Post to foundation (post anchor)

All wood used on the deck must be decay resistant. These woods include redwood, cedar, cypress, and pressure-treated wood. Redwood is perhaps the most attractive and durable wood to use, especially in exposed areas such as the decking and railing. It is decay resistant, dimensionally stable, and relatively straight. It is easy to saw and nail and has little or no pitch. It resists warping, checking, and cupping, and is strong for its light weight. It comes in several grades. Construction common, which contains some sapwood, is acceptable for deck boards. The more expensive all-heart grade is better.

Pressure-treated wood is also commonly used. It is treated to resist decay, and is often green in color. For the best decay resistance, use a pressure-treated frame with redwood decking and railings.

Deck joists are usually 2x6, 2x8, or 2x10 stock, depending on the span. The decking boards are usually 2x4 or 2x6; 2x8 stock is too wide and will cup if used as a decking board. Girders are 4x4, 4x6, or 4x8, or built up with 2x material. Ledgers are 2x6, 2x8, or 2x10, like joists. Posts are usually 4x4 or 4x6.

Your materials list is likely to include the following items.

Pier blocks

Decking

Girder stock

Joist stock

Post stock

Ledger board

Band joists

HDG nails

HDG lag bolts

Joist hangers

Joist hanger nails

Right-angle brackets

Post caps

Post anchors

Railing stock

Flashing

Butyl caulk

Water-repellent sealer

Nylon string

Ready-mix concrete

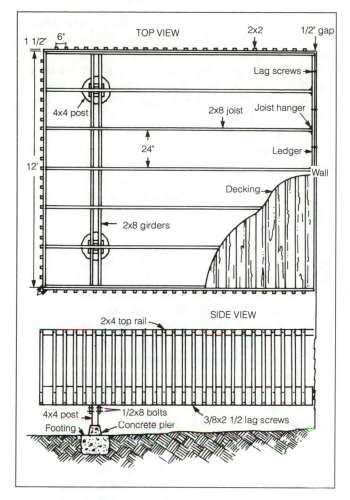

Figure 16-1. A typical set of deck plans.

ESTIMATING MATERIALS

Estimating materials for your deck is fairly simple and straightforward. Use your plans, as shown in Figure 16-1, to determine the following information.

☐ Number of square feet of decking

☐ Size and length of joists, bands, decking, posts, girders, and railings

☐ Number of joist hangers

☐ Number of piers

☐ Amount of concrete for footings

☐ Number and kind of nails, washers, nuts, and bolts

☐ Amount of water-repellent (The California Redwood Association recommends that you treat all the wood with water repellent before the deck is built.)

PERMITS AND CODES

In most areas a permit is required before you begin to build a deck. If the deck is not attached to the house, or if you live in a rural area, you may not need a permit. Check this out before you begin to build.

The permit office will probably require a set of plans. These need not be elaborate, and you can draw them yourself, buy a set, or have a set prepared by a draftsperson or architect. The plans need to specify the following information, as shown in Figure 16-1.

1. Location of the deck. The deck must be far enough away from neighboring property lines, utility easements, and gas, water, and sewer lines.

2. Space between railing pickets. Usually the pickets must be spaced no more than 6" apart.

3. Railing height. If the deck is under 18" high, no railing may be required. Over that, a railing is usually required, and a minimum height of 36" to 42" is usually specified.

4. Foundation piers. The local code will regulate the size, spacing, number, and method of construction of your piers. It will also regulate the depth of your pier holes, depending on the frostline in the area and on the pad width in more temperate climates.

5. The girder. The code will specify the size and location of the girder.

6. Joists. The code will specify the size and spacing of the joists, depending on the type of wood you are using. Joist charts are available at the code office for each type of wood.

7. Fasteners. Many codes detail nailing and fastener requirements for decks.

8. Decking. Your plans must specify the size of deck boards and the type of wood to be used.

9. Posts. Your plans must specify the size of the posts.

10. Bracing. Unless the girder is directly supported by its piers, you will need some sort of diagonal bracing. If applied to the posts, these braces will restrict access under the deck. Some codes allow you to "let in" braces diagonally, in the top or bottom of the joists, to avoid obstructing the access.

11. Earthquakes. In earthquake and hurricane areas, there may be further requirements on how the piers are fastened to the footings, the girders to the posts, and the joists to the girders. The code may also specify the type of metal fasteners that must be used. Additional (or larger) diagonal bracing is often required in areas where hurricanes or earthquakes are common.

DESIGN

There is much to say about the design of a deck, and many books are available on the subject. This chapter provides you not with a primer on deck design but rather with a few design parameters to consider. This is not to understate the importance of design. How well you are pleased with your handiwork and how much you will enjoy using it depend on design more than on construction. Your answers to the following questions will help you to think through your design requirements.

1. At what time of day during each season of the year does the deck location get sun and shade?

2. How much privacy will the deck have from the neighbors? Will this change when the trees lose their leaves or grow taller?

3. What kind of access will there be from the deck to the house? To the yard?

4. How large should the deck be? How much yard must be sacrificed?

5. How should the railings be designed? With planters? With seats?

6. Where should the stairs be placed?

7. Are there any utility lines overhead or below?

8. Should the deck be covered?

9. What will be placed on the deck? A barbecue? A table and chairs?

10. Will the deck block the light or the view from any windows of the house?

11. How should the deck be positioned to take advantage of the views?

12. How much money do you plan to spend?

Step One
Determining the Level and Length of the Ledger

Margin of Error: 1/4"

Most Common Mistakes

- [ ] Choosing the wrong height or location for the deck.
- [ ] Using badly bowed boards.
- [ ] Not using redwood, cedar, cypress, or pressure-treated stock.
- [ ] Not following code.

If you are attaching the deck to your house, as shown in Figure 16-2, you will probably use a ledger board. This board is bolted to the house and the deck is hung on it. If you plan a freestanding deck (not attached to the house), you will not use a ledger. In some areas a deck attached to a house will be taxed, but if it is separated from the house by even an inch or two it will not. This chapter considers the more common approach of attaching the deck to the house. If your deck is freestanding, everything discussed here will still apply, except that the ledger is not bolted to the house. Added bracing may be needed to stabilize a freestanding deck.

The Level of the Ledger

The level, or height, of the ledger determines the height of the deck. The top of the ledger will be 1 1/2" below the final top surface of the deck, because 1 1/2" decking boards will be nailed on top. The deck joists, which support the decking, or surface of the deck, are sometimes installed so that they sit on top of the ledger, as shown in Figure 16-3, rather than hanging from it. In that case, the top of the ledger will be considerably lower than the final level of the deck (by the width of the joist plus 1 1/2"). Before installing the ledger, you need to decide whether to hang the joists from the ledger or to rest them on top. It is stronger to hang them from the ledger with joist hangers, and that is the method described in this chapter and illustrated in Figures 16-16 and 16-17.

No matter what approach you use, you need to be sure that the ledger is low enough so that the level of the finished deck will be at least 1" below the level of the finished floor inside the house (Figure 16-4). This is necessary because you want to step down from the house to the deck. Also, if the deck is higher than the floor, water can run from the deck to the house. If you don't plan to have a door from the house to the deck, the height of the deck is not so important.

To determine the height of the deck, you must first determine the level of the interior finished floor and transfer this level to the outside of the wall where the deck will be built. To do this, measure on the inside and outside from a common reference point, such as a windowsill. (If the sill slopes toward the outside, be sure to adjust your measurements.) Another method is to measure up from the foundation wall, accounting for the floor joist, subfloor, and finished flooring material. Once you have determined the level of the interior finished floor, mark it on the exterior wall. Make a second mark a minimum of 2 1/2" below this first mark. This will allow you to install 1 1/2" decking and still place the level of the deck 1" below the level of the interior floor. You should place the top of the ledger on this second mark.

The Length of the Ledger

As shown in Figure 16-5, the length of the ledger equals the total width of the deck less 3" (6" if a band joist is used on each side). This 3" is so that the joists at either end of the deck will overlap the ledger and be nailed to it. The joists are 1 1/2" thick, hence the 3" reduction in length so that the finished deck will be the designated length. If possible, the ledger should be one long piece of stock. However, if the length is over 16', it may be hard to find a straight piece that long. In this case, two pieces will work. Always use pieces that are at least 6' long, and preferably longer.

Location on the Wall

It is important that the ledger be securely attached. The lag screws that attach the ledger to the wall need to penetrate something solid, such as wall studs or floor joists. The ledger is often placed at the same level as the floor joists of the first floor, which automatically solves the problem. In this case, the lag screws will penetrate the existing rim joist, behind the siding.

If you are installing the ledger at some other level, secure the ledger with lag screws to the wall studs.

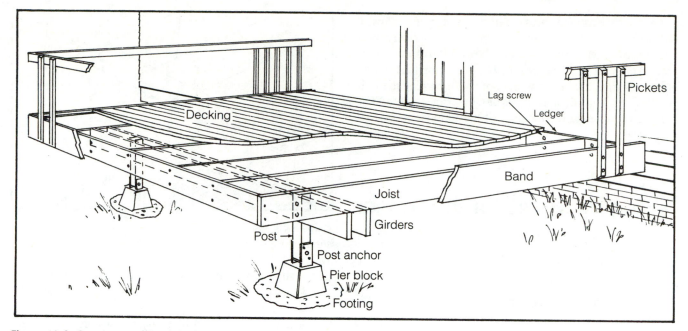

Figure 16-2. Components of a typical deck.

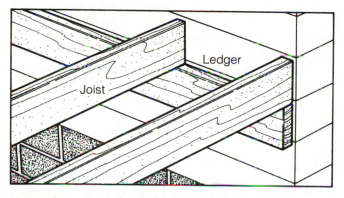

Figure 16-3. An alternate method of installing joists, in which the joists are set on top of the ledger rather than hanging from it.

Choosing the Ledger

Select a straight board for the ledger, one that is the same size as the joists and has little bowing. If the ledger is bowed, the deck will have a corresponding curve upward or downward. Some minor bowing can be forced out as you install the board, but anything greater than about ½" of curve over 12' of board will throw the deck off. The ledger, like all decking materials, should be of redwood, cedar, cypress, or pressure-treated lumber.

At this point you have selected your ledger board and decided on its final placement in regard to both its height and its location on the wall. Now check to see if there are any obstructions, such as hose faucets, dryer vents, gas or water pipes, or electrical wires. Such obstructions may have to be relocated; or perhaps you will have to break the ledger, leaving a gap where the obstruction occurs. Remember that everything below the ledger will be underneath the deck and not easily accessible. You may need to call an electrician or

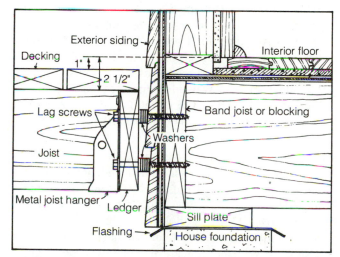

Figure 16-4. The ledger is installed 2½" below the level of the interior finished floor. Be sure it is bolted or screwed into something solid, such as a band joist or blocking.

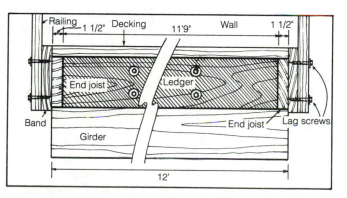

Figure 16-5. The length of the ledger equals the width of the deck less 3" if there is no band, or 6" if a band is used.

a plumber to rearrange wires or pipes. Don't try to work with the electrical or gas system unless you know exactly what you are doing. Mark on the ground the location of any underground pipes or wires before you begin digging the foundation holes so that you can be sure of not disturbing them. If you cannot locate all of the pipes or wires, dig slowly and be prepared to change the location of the foundation piers if necessary.

Step Two
Drilling the Holes for the Ledger

Margin of Error: 1/4"

Most Common Mistakes

☐ Using a badly bowed board.

☐ Not using rustproof lag screws or bolts.

☐ Not installing the ledger at the proper height or location.

☐ Not caulking the bolt holes in the wall before installing the ledger.

☐ Drilling holes where joists will be attached. (If you are bolting the ledger to an existing rim joist, lag screw placement is flexible. If you are bolting the ledger to the wall studs, accurate placement is much more critical. In either case, the lag screw holes and the joist locations should be marked to avoid placing the joists over the lag screws. The joists can be offset if necessary, as long as they remain properly centered, so that the deck planks always break on the center of a joist.)

Now you are ready to install the ledger. First, cut your ledger board to the proper length—the total length of the deck less 3" (6" if band joists are to be used). Next, you will drill holes in the ledger for the lag screws or bolts that will hold the ledger to the house. Drill these holes with a bit that is 1/8" larger than the actual screws so that you will have a little play for adjustments. With the ledger resting on sawhorses, begin at one end and mark the lag screw locations. These holes are usually drilled in pairs, one above the other, every 32", or staggered singly every 16". Drill a pair of holes 12" in from either end, or on the end studs, then drill the rest of the holes. Drill all holes at least 2" in from the edge of the board. (You should check the local code to see if there are any regulations concerning the size and location of these lag screws.)

You are now ready to attach the ledger temporarily to the wall, mark the corresponding holes on the siding, remove the ledger, and drill the holes in the siding. If there is a slight bow, or crown, in the board, remember to turn it up toward the sky.

Place the top edge of the ledger at the mark on the wall that represents the top of the ledger, and nail one end temporarily in place. Then place a 4' or 8' level on the board, get it exactly level, and nail in the other end. The ledger is now temporarily nailed in its proper place. Check once again to be sure it is exactly level before marking the holes. Then, with a felt-tipped

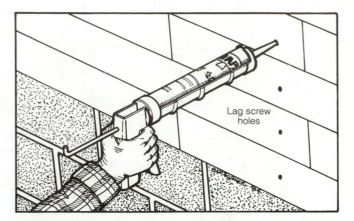

Figure 16-6. Squirt butyl caulk into lag screw holes before attaching the ledger.

pen or sharp pencil, mark on the wall the location of the lag screw holes that you drilled in the ledger. Now remove the ledger.

You are now ready to drill the lag screw holes in the wall. Do not use the same size bit that you used on the ledger. Use a bit that is one size *smaller* than the shank of the lag screw. This will ensure that the lag screw gets a good bite into the wall. Drill all the holes, being sure to hold the drill straight so the lag screws will go in straight. Be sure that you are drilling into solid wood.

Before you attach the ledger permanently to the wall with lag screws, squirt some butyl caulk into the holes in the wall (Figure 16-6). This will keep rainwater from flowing into the structure through the lag screw holes.

Step Three
Attaching the Ledger Permanently to the Wall

Margin of Error: 1/4"

Most Common Mistakes

☐ Not leaving a space between the wall and the ledger.

☐ Not screwing the ledger into something solid.

☐ Not using rustproof lag screws.

☐ Using galvanized washers with aluminum siding.

☐ Not caulking the holes in the wall before installing the ledger.

There is still one crucial detail you must attend to before you attach the ledger to the wall. If the ledger were attached directly against the wall, with the back surface of the ledger tight against the wall, rainwater running down the wall would get trapped between the wall and the back surface of the ledger and promote decay. To avoid this, you need to leave a small space (1/2" to 3/4") so that water can run down to the ground.

The easiest way to provide this space is to install washers on the lag screws between the ledger and the wall (see Figure

16-4). These washers should be rust-proof HDG. If your wall is aluminum siding, use aluminum washers. Galvanized metal touching aluminum causes corrosion. Stack these washers to leave an adequate gap. If your siding is not flat but has different surface levels (beveled siding, aluminum siding, or shingles), more or fewer washers can be installed on the top screws than on the lower ones, to compensate for any unevenness. You want the ledger to be installed plumb.

After you have squirted caulk into the holes, threaded the lag screws into the ledger, and installed the proper number of washers on each screw, lift the ledger into place, tap the screws into the wall, and tighten the screws with a socket or crescent wrench. Be sure that the screws are biting solidly into the wall, especially the last 2". You are now ready to install the two end joists and to locate your pier holes.

If you are using pressure-treated lumber or a decay-resistant lumber that is not all heart, you should paint the cut ends of the ledger with a water-repellent at this point.

Step Four
Attaching the Two Outer Joists

Margin of Error: 1/4"

Most Common Mistakes

☐ Joists not set at right angle to the wall.

☐ Joists not placed level.

☐ Joists not nailed to cover exposed ends of the ledger.

☐ Crown not pointing skyward.

Once the ledger is permanently attached to the wall, you can install the two outermost joists at either end of the ledger. These joists will be used as reference points for locating the foundation pier holes. The outer joists are set in place, and lines are drawn on them at a prescribed distance from the wall. A string stretched between these lines determines the location of the foundation pier holes. The distance from the house to the supporting girder will depend on the size of your deck, the type of wood being used for the joists, and the size and spacing of the joists.

There are several techniques for locating your pier holes, including one that involves setting up batter boards and layout lines. However, unless your lot slopes steeply, the following method—using the two outer joists as reference points—is the simplest and easiest.

Choose two of your straightest joists to install at either end of the ledger. As you look down the joists you will notice that they have a small bow, or crown. Almost no piece of wood is ever perfectly straight. When the board is installed, this crown should always point up toward the sky (Figure 16-7) to allow gravity to straighten it out. This is called "crowning" the joist. Don't worry about cutting the joists to the proper length at this time; you will cut them after you apply the decking.

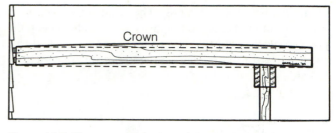

Figure 16-7. The crown of the board should always point up.

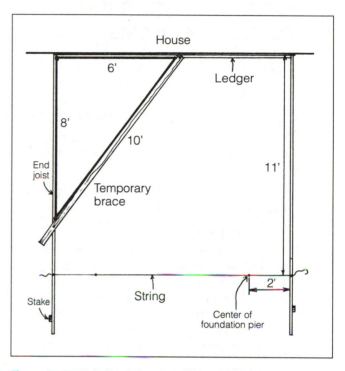

Figure 16-8. Use a 3-4-5 triangle to be sure that the two end joists are exactly at right angles to the ledger.

Nail these outer joists to the ledger with the joists covering up the exposed ends of the ledger. One person nails the joist to the ledger, using three or four 16-penny HDG nails, while another person supports the other end of the joist in a level position. After the end is nailed to the ledger, drive a temporary 2x4 stake into the ground to hold the "floating" end level and at a right angle to the ledger. To position this stake, after nailing the joist to the ledger and while another person is supporting the other end, place a framing square at the intersection of the joist and the ledger. Adjust this intersection to approximately 90 degrees, drive a stake in the ground to support the joist there, place a 4' or 6' level on the joist to be sure it is level, and nail the joist to the stake. At this point none of these measurements need to be too accurate. The next step, using a 3-4-5 triangle, will ensure that these two outside joists are at a true right angle to the ledger (Figure 16-8).

Measure 8' along the end joist on the outside edge and mark that point. Measure along the back of the ledger 6' and mark there. Now measure between these two marks. If that line is exactly 10' long, then you have a true right angle. If it is not, then adjust your stake and joist until the line between the marks is exactly 10′ long. Then nail some temporary braces from the ledger to the joists at an angle to keep the joists in place. Your two outer joists are now level, at true right angles to the ledger, and temporarily supported by stakes.

Step Five
Locating and Digging the Foundation Pier Holes

Margin of Error: 1″

Most Common Mistakes

☐ Locating a pier hole on top of an underground pipe or wire.

☐ Not checking the plans for the exact locations of the holes.

☐ Not digging deep enough for local codes and frost lines.

☐ Not digging until you find stable, undisturbed soil.

The location of the pier block holes is unique to each deck project. Local building codes will have some say here, and design is also a factor. Piers are often inset from the sides of the deck to hide them from view. The girder that is supported by these piers is often inset from the end of the deck a foot or two, because of the visual appeal of a cantilevered or overhanging deck. Since the cantilevered portion is not directly supported by posts, codes specify how far it may extend be-

yond the nearest post. A maximum overhang of one quarter of the total span is common.

At this point, with the two outer joists in place, you have a clear outline of the edges of the deck. From this outline you can locate your foundation pier holes. Check your plans to determine their exact locations. For example, say that your plans call for two holes, the centers of which are exactly 11′ from the wall and 2′ in from the outer edges of the sides of the deck. Measure along each of the two outer joists 11′ from the wall, mark the joists, drive nails at those points, and tie a string from joist to joist between the two nails. Now measure 2′ from the outside edges of the joists along the string and mark the string at those points by tying on a short length of string (Figure 16-9). Make the knot tight so the marker string won't slip. If decorative band joists are to be added over the two side joists just installed (see Figure 16-2), be sure to allow for them in your measurements. The string markers locate the centers of the two pier holes. Now use a plumb bob to transfer these marks to the ground. Drive in two small stakes (Figure 16-10), then mark out for the radius of the pier holes and begin digging.

How to dig a hole may seem obvious, but there are a few things to keep in mind. The size of the hole is important. The diameter of a pier hole is usually about 16″, but check your local code. The depth of the hole is often regulated by code as well. Required depths range from 12″ to 60″, depending on the frost level in your area. (The colder the climate, the deeper the hole needs to be.)

Once you have determined the necessary diameter and depth, simply dig your holes, being sure to dig good, straight

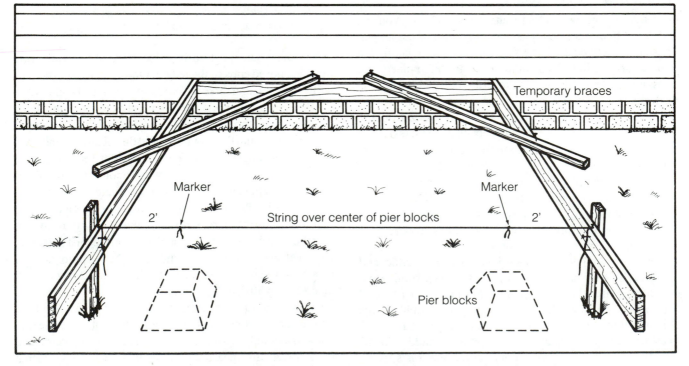

Figure 16-9. The two end joists are installed level and square to the ledger. The string is stretched exactly over the centers of the pier blocks.

(not sloping) walls. Dig until you hit stable, undisturbed soil. Never backfill a hole with loose dirt before pouring concrete. Loose dirt will compact and cause settling.

In many warm, temperate areas, pads are often used instead of piers to support the pier blocks. Piers are used in these regions when the ground slopes, or near a drop-off.

Step Six
Pouring the Footings and Setting the Pier Blocks

Margin of Error: ½"

Most Common Mistakes

☐ Tops of pier blocks not level.

☐ Pier blocks not properly aligned.

☐ Not using metal connectors where required.

☐ Failing to reinforce piers with steel, if required by code.

☐ Neglecting to have reinforcement inspected before concrete is poured, if required by code.

Now you are ready to mix up some concrete, pour it in the hole, drop a pier block in the fresh concrete, and level and align it.

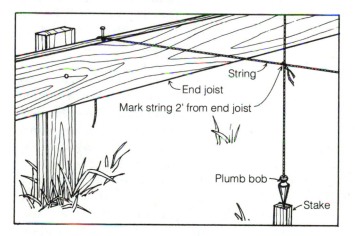

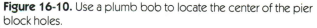

Figure 16-10. Use a plumb bob to locate the center of the pier block holes.

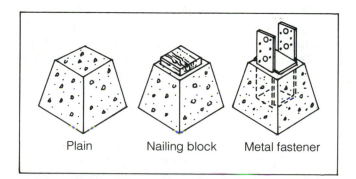

Figure 16-11. Three types of pier blocks. The one with the metal fastener is used for extra strength in earthquake areas.

A few words on mixing concrete are in order here. For small deck jobs, you can buy ready-mixed concrete with all the ingredients in one bag. Simply mix in some water and pour the concrete in the hole. Be sure to buy enough bags to fill all your holes; you don't want to run short and have to rush back to the store to finish off a hole. You will be surprised how many bags it can take to fill a hole. As a rule of thumb, a 60-pound bag of ready-mixed concrete will fill about ½ square foot, or a hole 6"x12"x12".

Mix the concrete with water in a wheelbarrow with a cement hoe, following the instructions on the bag. Pour the concrete in the hole to within an inch or so of the top and smooth it out with a piece of 2x4 or a trowel until it is fairly level. Now you are ready to place the pier blocks.

Pier blocks serve as a transition from the concrete foundation footings to the posts supporting the girder. They can be built at the site, and are also available at building centers and hardware stores in a range of styles and sizes (Figure 16-11). It really isn't worth the hassle of pouring them yourself.

The most common type of pier is a truncated concrete pyramid on top of which the wooden post sits. The weight of the deck keeps the post in contact with the pier block. Another version has a small piece of redwood or pressure-treated lumber embedded in the top so that the post can be toenailed to the block. Metal fasteners are often used in areas where there are earthquakes. They are embedded in the pier blocks and the posts are bolted to them to prevent the posts from shaking off the pier blocks in an earthquake. Other metal anchors are intended to be placed in wet concrete piers. They have corrugated metal tangs that are gripped by the concrete as it sets, and are often required where earthquakes or hurricanes are likely. Be sure that the metal anchors are the correct size for the posts you plan to use.

After the hole has been filled with concrete, and the concrete leveled and smoothed, drop the pier block into the fresh concrete and work it down until at least 3" or 4" of the base

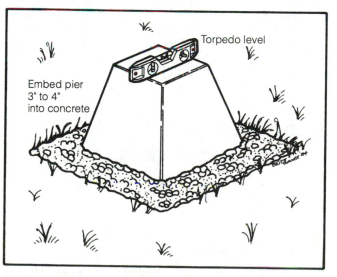

Figure 16-12. Use a small torpedo level to level the pier blocks.

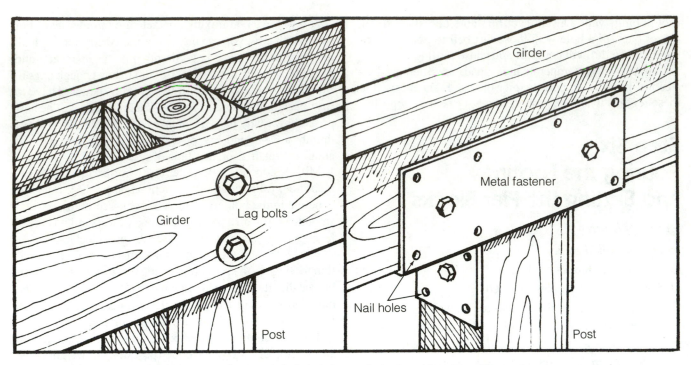

Figure 16-13. Two types of girder/post attachments. Left, 2x6 girders are bolted to either side of the post. Right, 4x6 girder rests on top of the post and is attached with metal fasteners.

of the block is embedded. As you set the blocks, be sure of two things: that they are properly aligned and that they are level. Some regions require up to 12" clearance from the post bottoms to grade, to avoid pest and decay problems. In this case, heavy paper tubes are placed on the top of the pier or pad. These tubes are filled with concrete, and the metal anchors worked down into the top while the concrete is fresh.

To check alignment, simply drop the plumb bob from the mark on your string to be sure the tip of the plumb bob is in the center of the pier block. To check level, place a small torpedo level in both directions as well as diagonally across the top of the pier blocks (Figure 16-12). Tap and move the blocks around until the tops are level. After your pier blocks or metal anchors are properly set, allow the concrete to harden—this can take anywhere from 8 to 24 hours. For a strong footing, keep the concrete damp while it is hardening. You can do this by sprinkling water on the pour as it dries, or by laying wet cloths across the top.

Step Seven
Installing the Girders

Margin of Error: 1/4"

Most Common Mistakes

☐ Using badly bowed girder stock.

☐ Not installing the girder level.

Now you are ready to install your girders. You can do this in one of two ways. One way is to prebuild the girder/post sys-

tem, bolt or nail the entire thing together, and then move it into place as one large piece. The other way is to build it in place piece by piece. If the posts and girders are not too long and heavy, the first procedure is recommended.

There are several different girder/post variations. As shown in Figure 16-13, two girders can sandwich the posts and be bolted or nailed to them; or the girder can rest on top of the posts, attached with metal fasteners. As long as it passes your local code, either system will work. The former method, which uses two girders, one on either side of the post, is the method described in our example.

To build your girder/post system, first cut the wooden posts to the proper height. In our example, the height of the posts is the same as the level of the bottom of the joists. Note that the bottoms of the joists rest on top of the girders and that the tops of the girders are at the same height as the tops of the posts.

To determine this post height, go back to your two outer joists and check to be sure they are still exactly level. Now move the string that is on top of the joists so that it is connected on the bottoms of the joists. The level of the bottoms of the joists is the same level as the top of the posts you are about to cut. Now measure from the top of each pier block (or metal fastener) to the string, as shown in Figure 16-14, and cut the posts to correspond to each of these measurements. It's that simple; just be sure you are accurate and that you make good straight cuts so the posts will sit smoothly on the pier blocks. To make these cuts, mark around the circumference of the post, cut one side, then rotate the post and cut the side opposite the first cut.

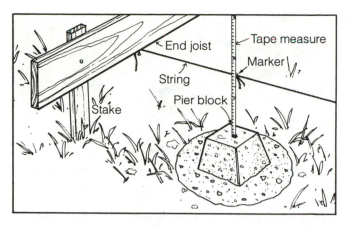

Figure 16-14. To determine the height of the post, measure from top of pier to top of post, as indicated by the strings attached to the bottoms of the end joists.

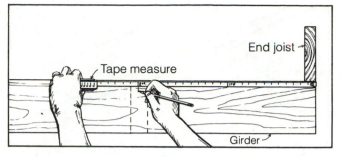

Figure 16-15. Hook tape to nail at center of first joist and mark ledger every 24".

After the posts are cut, cut your pieces of girder stock to the specified length—the length of the ledger plus 3". If possible, use one continuous piece of girder stock for each piece; but if the deck is too long, and you have to use two pieces, be sure that the pieces meet at a post so they can both be attached to it. If the girder is made of pieces, the proper cantilever must be maintained. At least three posts must be used to piece in a girder. Your girder stock must be completely straight. Select these pieces yourself at the lumber yard. The deck joists sit on top of the girders, so if they are bowed, the entire deck will rise or fall. If there is a slight bow, or crown (no greater than ½" in 12'), point it up toward the sky and it will settle down in time.

Once all your posts and girders are cut, you can assemble them into one unit, if the girder is to be bolted or nailed to either side of the posts rather than resting on top of the posts. This is usually done with bolts, nails, or nails and metal fasteners. For most decks, bolts are the recommended method of assembly. If you are resting a single girder on top of the posts, use metal fasteners as shown in Figure 16-13. Remember to use HDG fasteners, bolts, or nails so they won't rust. If you are bolting the deck together, drill your holes good and straight so the bolts will go through straight. Use a bit that is ⅛" larger than the bolt, to allow for making final adjustments.

Once the entire unit is assembled, move it into place under your two outer joists. If you are assembling the pieces in place, the application is pretty much the same. Before toenailing the outer joists to the top of the girder, measure out from the wall to be sure the girder is the proper distance from the wall, and check the posts for plumb. Once you have ascertained this, check once again to be sure that the joists are still at right angles to the ledger and still level. Then nail the joists into the girders with 16-penny galvanized nails; or use L-shaped metal fasteners, called framing clips, and nails.

Step Eight
Laying Out the Joists on the Girder

Margin of Error: ¼"

Most Common Mistakes

☐ Nailing the joist hanger on the wrong side of the mark.

☐ Improper layout.

Now that your girder is in place, you are ready to install your remaining joists. To do this you need to make marks, called layout marks, on the girder to show where each joist will be located. These marks reflect the ledger joist layout marks, and are easily transferred.

Joists are usually located so that their centers occur exactly every 16" or 24". This is called their "on center" distance. The distance between joists depends on several important factors:

1. Size of the joists

2. Length of span from ledger to girder

3. Type of wood used for the joists

4. Any heavy loading, such as planter boxes or snow

The size and spacing of the joists are among the few crucial dimensions specified in deck building. If you undersize or overspace the joists, the deck could collapse, and the building inspector will stop the project. You should talk to a building code officer about the proper sizing for your joists and span. Joists placed 24" on center are usually adequate.

After you have determined the joist spacing layout on the girder, make a second mark ¾" to one side of the center line, so that you will know on which side of this line the joists will sit (Figure 16-15).

After you have made all your marks, begin nailing the metal joist hangers on the ledger, using the special stubby joist hanger nails that are provided with the hangers. Nail only on one side of the hanger, allowing the other side to float free until the joist is inserted. Nail the hangers so that the *interior* edge is nailed along the line you drew to mark the side of the joist, as shown in Figure 16-16. As you go along, be

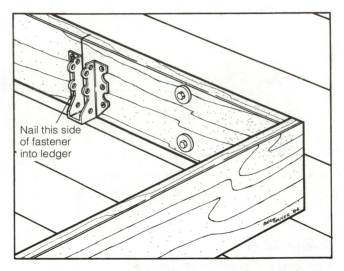

Figure 16-16. Nail one side of hanger to the ledger. Align the edge of the joist hanger with the line that marks the side of the joist.

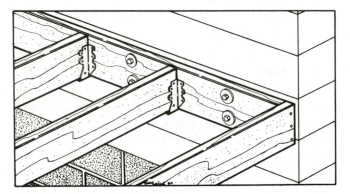

Figure 16-17. Joists are installed and nailed to joist hangers.

sure that you are clear about which side of the mark the joist hanger and joist should be nailed to, to ensure proper spacing. Even a seasoned professional can accidentally put the joist hanger on the wrong side of the mark.

Step Nine
Installing the Remaining Joists

Margin of Error: 1/4"

Most Common Mistakes

☐ Not crowning the joists.

☐ Placing a joist on the wrong side of the layout mark.

Installing the remaining joists is fairly simple. Some builders cut the joists to length before installing them. However, it is generally better to cut the joists after almost all of the decking boards are in place. The reason for this will become clear later on. Now, simply insert the joists into the joist hangers, as shown in Figure 16-17. As you do this, be sure that you crown each joist, pointing the bow skyward. Insert the joist in the hanger, then nail the loose side of the hanger

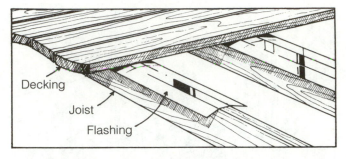

Figure 16-18. Galvanized metal flashing is sometimes installed over the joists.

tightly into the joist and into the ledger. Then use two 16-penny HDG nails to toenail the other end of the joist to the girder. Special HDG sheet metal fasteners can be used here instead of just nails. These fasteners are especially recommended in earthquake and hurricane areas.

Step Ten
Applying the Deck Boards

Margin of Error: 1/4"

Most Common Mistakes

☐ Not leaving a gap between the deck boards.

☐ Not using enough nails.

☐ Not forcing the bow out of crooked boards.

You are now ready to start installing your deck boards. This part of the job is quite satisfying because it goes so quickly and easily and you really start to see your deck coming together. You need to consider individually each board you apply, since they will all be seen. Examine each piece and put the most attractive pieces in the high-visibility areas. Also look at each side of each board to see which side you want exposed. Check to see how badly the boards are bowed. Reject any very bad pieces, because they will look crooked once the decking is down.

Some builders, especially in areas of heavy rain or snow, place aluminum or galvanized metal flashing on top of each joist before the deck boards are applied, as shown in Figure 16-18. This flashing helps keep water from getting trapped between the decking and the joists, causing rot. You will need to find out whether this is a good idea in your area.

Begin applying your decking from the wall and work toward the yard. Be sure that the first course you apply next to the wall is made of good, straight pieces, because this course is used as a guide, and if it is crooked it affects all the other courses. Also be sure to leave a gap between the first course and the wall, so that water can drain down the wall.

If possible, purchase boards that are long enough to span the entire width of the deck. If the deck is too wide, this may not be possible. Lengths over 14' are often very crooked. If two pieces are needed, the pieces must always join directly over the center of a joist, to provide a bearing surface for each

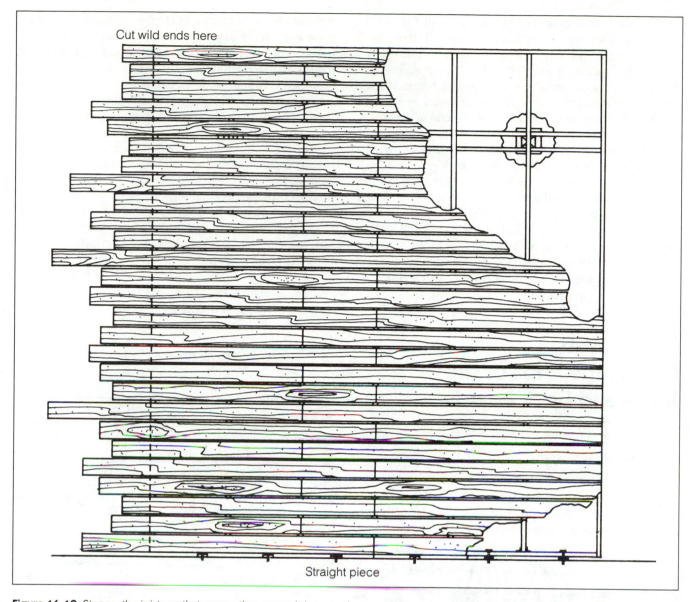

Cut wild ends here

Straight piece

Figure 16-19. Stagger the joists so that every other course joins over the same joists.

end. Don't join all the courses over the same joist; the joints will look like a big suture running down the deck. Stagger the joints so that every other course joins over the same joists, as shown in Figure 16-19, or place them randomly.

Use double-dipped HDG 16-penny nails rather than finishing nails in deck construction. Stainless steel or aluminum nails work even better because they do not stain the wood, but they may be hard to find. Do not use electroplated nails, which often rust. Except with redwood, it is best to use two nails in 2x4 boards and three nails in 2x6 boards, at each point where the board crosses a joist. For 2x4 and 2x6 redwood boards, two nails per joist are enough. All nails should penetrate 1 1/2" into the joists.

You might also consider using reduced-corrosion deck screws. Although they are expensive compared to nails, they greatly reduce cupping as the deck ages.

Use a combination square and mark a true perpendicular line across each joist so that you can place all your nails in

a straight line. This takes a little more time, but your finished deck will have a much nicer appearance.

The process of nailing on the deck boards is straightforward, but there are a few things to remember. First, you need to leave a gap of 1/4" between each course of deck boards to allow water to drain off the deck. To maintain this gap, stick a flat carpenter's pencil between the courses as they are applied (Figure 16-20).

No board is perfect, and many will have bows that need to be pulled out. This is done by forcing the bow out as you nail from one end to the other. This is why you should never nail from both ends to the middle—you may trap the bow. Put in your spacer to create the gap and then force the board into place. It will usually straighten out if it is not too badly bowed. Use a smooth-headed hammer and try not to mar the wood (although the first few rains will probably draw out most of the dents). You can also use a pry bar, as shown in Figure 16-21, to force the board straight.

It is easiest to place the deck boards flush with the outside edge of one of the outer joists, let them "run wild" at the other end, and then cut this end all at once. The only other trick to applying the decking is to drill pilot holes when nailing near the end of a board, especially where two deck boards join together in the center of a joist and both ends must be nailed to the joist. If you try to nail that close to the end of the board, you will often split the wood. To prevent this splitting, drill a pilot hole that is slightly smaller than the shank of the nail, and then drive the nail into the pilot hole (Figure 16-22).

Begin to lay the deck boards from the house end of the deck. Measure out from the wall every few courses to be sure that all boards are equidistant from the wall as you progress. Make adjustments gradually and continue until you are one course away from the end of the joists. (See Step Eleven for what to do then.) Stand up and look down on the deck to be sure you are not trapping any bows in the boards and that the deck looks good in general.

Step Eleven
Cutting the Ends of the Joists and Deck Boards

Margin of Error: ¼"

Most Common Mistake

☐ Not cutting square ends.

As you apply the last deck boards, there is one final adjustment to be made. You are aiming for the outer edge of the last course of decking boards to be exactly flush with the ends of

the joists. Some builders don't bother with this detail, but it gives a nice finished look. The only way to make this work out is to cut the joists after the next-to-last course but before the last course is nailed on. This way, you can tell exactly how things are going to work out. After the next-to-the-last course is in place, measure to the ends of the joists for their final cut (Figure 16-23). The measurement is made from the outer edge of the next-to-the-last course to a point on the joists that equals the width of a deck board plus the gap between courses. For example, a 5 ½" board with a ¼" gap would equal 5 ¾". To place the band joists under the last piece of decking, deduct 1 ½".

Mark the ends of the joists at this point and draw a line across them with a combination square. When you cut the joists at this point, be sure to make good, straight cuts so the band will fit on properly. After you have cut the ends of all the joists, install your last course of deck boards. Be sure this is a good, straight course, because it will be more visible than the others. After this last course is in place you will install the band joist (the piece that goes across the ends of all the joists). This band joist is often one size wider than the joist, to act as a curb for the decking.

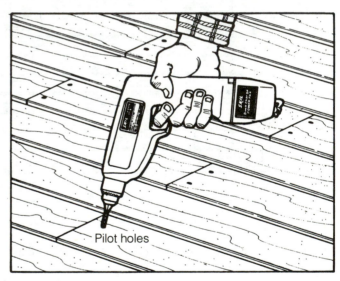

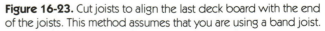
Figure 16-22. Drill pilot holes for nails near the ends of boards to prevent splitting the boards.

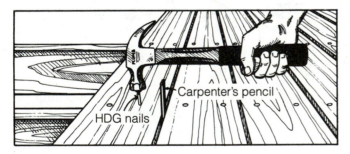
Figure 16-20. Leave a gap between deck boards for drainage.

Figure 16-21. Use a pry bar to remove bow in deck boards.

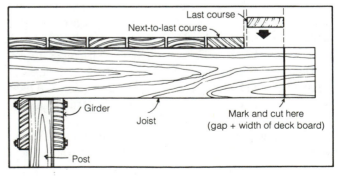
Figure 16-23. Cut joists to align the last deck board with the end of the joists. This method assumes that you are using a band joist.

Figure 16-24. Snap a chalkline to show where to cut the wild ends of the decking boards.

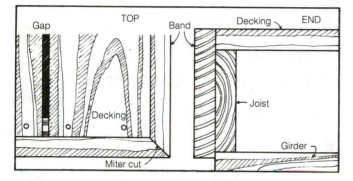

Figure 16-25. Facing the deck with band joists.

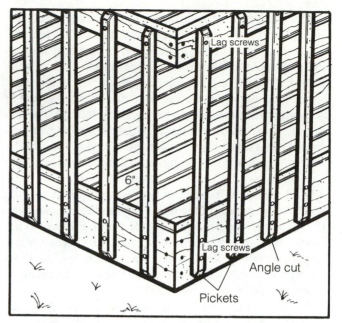

Figure 16-26. A simple, common railing design.

Now you are ready to cut the "wild ends" of the deck boards. To do this, make a mark at either end of the deck and snap a chalkline to get a perfectly straight cut. Cut off the ends of the decking boards to this line (Figure 16-24). Be sure your marks are where you want them to be, allowing for any cantilever over the joists. Set your saw to cut through the deck boards plus ¼". Stop cutting every now and then and check to be sure you are on the line and not veering into or away from the joists.

It's a good idea to paint the exposed ends of the joists and deck boards with a water-repellent material for added protection.

Step Twelve
Facing the Deck
with Band Joists

Margin of Error: ¼"

Most Common Mistake

☐ Not measuring correctly to allow for mitered ends.

After you have cut the ends of the joists and the decking boards, you are ready to apply the band joists (Figure 16-25). Sometimes the band consists only of a piece at the end of the joists where you just made your final cut. Usually, however,

the band covers all outer edges of the deck and is one size (2") wider than the joists so that it acts as a curb for the decking (refer to Figure 16-2).

The ends of the individual band pieces can be miter cut so that there is no exposed end grain. Mitering is not difficult, but it requires accurate measuring and cutting. When measuring, remember that the measurements taken off the deck refer to the inside cut of the miter, not the outside. You may want to practice on some scrap pieces to be sure you have set the correct angle on the saw. Nail the bands to the joists with HDG 10-penny nails.

Step Thirteen
Installing the Railings

Margin of Error: ¼"

Most Common Mistakes

☐ Pickets not plumb.

☐ Top railing not level.

☐ Pickets not evenly spaced.

☐ Pickets too far apart.

There are many different styles of railings for decks. Choose a style that will fit your budget, time, and energy, as well as the overall look and use of the deck. Different styles do different things. You can incorporate planters, benches, tables, and stairs into your design. A wide, flat board installed at the top of the railing is useful for holding flower pots, paper plates, drinks, and other amenities of outdoor living. A book on deck design or a ride around the neighborhood will inspire your imagination.

This section describes a simple, sturdy, widely used railing design (Figure 16-26). Most of the procedures outlined here will apply to almost any design. If you are copying a design from an existing deck, a close inspection of the deck with sketchbook in hand should enable you to understand how the railing is put together. The main thing you want to be sure of when installing a railing is its stability. There is nothing worse than building the entire deck railing, only to discover that it is weak and unstable. You don't want to be worried about a guest taking an unexpected plunge onto your lawn.

Most areas have codes that apply to deck railings. If the deck is more than a certain distance from the ground, often 18", a railing may be required. If the deck is closer to the ground, the railing may be optional. Also, the code will allow only a certain gap between the pickets, usually 6" to 8", so that a child cannot slip through. The height of the railing is regulated, too—usually 36" to 42".

The simple railing shown here is constructed of 2x2 pickets with a 2x4 top railing. Stability is provided by using two HDG lag screws to bolt the bottom of the pickets to the band joists, and by tying the railing to the house with lag screws. Remember to leave a gap between the railing and the house as you did with the ledger.

First, cut all the pickets. An angle cut on the top and bottom of each picket is an esthetically pleasing touch. After cutting the pickets, cut the 2x4 top rail. If possible, use pieces that are long enough to span the entire length of each section. If the span is too long and two pieces are needed, you must join them over a 2x4 picket. Determine where this break should occur for the most balanced appearance. Miter cut the top rail at corners so that no end grain is exposed.

After all your pieces are cut, it is best to screw or bolt the pickets to the top rail and then install the entire assembly onto the deck. Mark the top rail so that the pickets will be properly spaced. Then secure the pickets to the rail using screws or lag screws that are as long as possible without poking through the back side of the railing (about 2 ½", or 4" if you have band joists). Be sure that your marks are correct and that the pickets are attached to the proper side of the marks. A misplaced picket will show all too clearly. At the bottom of each picket, drill two holes that are one size smaller than the lag screws that will hold the pickets to the joists and band. Drill these holes so that they are as far apart as possible and yet at least 1 ½" from the edge of the band and joists.

You are now ready to install the entire assembly onto the deck. This is done by using two more lag screws at the base where the picket meets the joists and band. Use 2 ½" or longer lag screws, and be sure they are HDG or treated to minimize rust. Align the picket/railing assembly so that it is in its exact location and nail a few pickets temporarily in place to hold it there. Then use a level to locate where each picket will meet the band and joists. By using the level at each picket, you can be sure that they are all plumb and parallel to each other. It is imperative that the assembly be in its

exact location before you start plumbing the pickets. If you move the assembly, even slightly, after the pickets are attached at the bottom, the entire assembly will look askew and will need to be redone. Once you have ascertained that the assembly is in its exact location, and have plumbed your pickets, hold the picket in place while you mark the location of the holes on the band and joists. Then drill these holes on the band and joists, using a drill bit one size smaller than the shank of the lag screw.

With deck or lag screws, secure the pickets to the band joist. Do this around the entire deck until all the railings are in place. Where two railings intersect at their miter-cut railing top, drill pilot holes through one top railing into the other, and then nail them together with 16-penny HDG finishing nails, two from one direction and two from the other. Your railings are now complete.

Step Fourteen
Waterproofing the Deck

Margin of Error: Not applicable

Most Common Mistake

☐ Not sealing the deck.

If you live where freeze damage is likely, or if you want to maintain the original color of the decking, it's a good idea to treat the decking with water repellent. In temperate areas, decks are often left untreated so they can "breathe." The water repellent can be applied with a brush, roller, or spray. It goes on quite easily because it is thin. Unlike paint, it penetrates quickly. A water repellent with a mildewcide will help redwood keep its red color and not turn gray with age. (As mentioned earlier, the California Redwood Association recommends applying the sealer to all pieces before construction, including the edges, ends, and bottoms.) The sealer can serve as a base coat for other finishes. Apply another coat of the sealer to a redwood deck after it is completed, and reapply every 12 to 18 months to prevent darkening and to preserve the beautiful redwood color.

Unsealed wood is vulnerable to staining and decay, and may have to be replaced prematurely. Because of its enduring qualities, this is not as much of a problem with redwood as it is with other woods.

Color or a bleached effect can be added to redwood and other woods by using decking stains and bleaches. Use a lightly pigmented, oil-based decking stain to show the wood grain or a heavily pigmented, heavy-bodied stain if you prefer an opaque effect. Whether the wood is smooth or rough sawn, use a brush rather than a spray for application. "Shake and shingle" paints, sprays, varnishes, and lacquers are not recommended for decks.

Bleaching agents can be applied to give the decking a silvery, weathered look. If no finish is applied to redwood, it will initially darken and then weather to a driftwood gray.

17 Stairs

BUILDING STAIRS is among the most difficult and intimidating of all carpentry tasks. People expect stairs to be of certain proportions, and the codes specify many details so that these expectations will be met. Aside from understanding the code requirements and the variables that are unique to your site, some simple math is required to design a staircase.

As with electrical or plumbing work, tasks that at first seem complicated are relatively simple if you take them one step at a time, so to speak. And as with electrical work, an appropriate design with detailed drawings is an important starting point, because the design determines the materials you will need to order.

This chapter describes the design and construction of a simple, straight, exterior deck stair. Interior stairs are also discussed, but all stairs are an extension of the simple basic stair.

All stairs must be constructed for strength, and exterior stairs must use rust resistant-fasteners and be made to drain water. Handrails are required on all stairs over 18" high.

Ramps are an option that should be considered. All ramps must conform to the specifications developed for wheelchair access, as outlined at the end of this chapter.

Before You Begin

SAFETY

☐ Wear safety glasses or goggles whenever you are using power tools, especially if you wear contact lenses.

☐ Wear ear protectors when using power tools. Some tools operate at noise levels that can damage hearing.

☐ Be careful not to let loose hair and clothing get caught in tools. Roll up your sleeves and remove jewelry.

☐ Keep blades sharp. A dull blade requires excessive force and can easily slip.

☐ Always use the right tool for the job.

☐ Don't try to drill, shape, or saw anything that isn't firmly secured.

☐ Don't work with tools when you are tired. That's when most accidents occur.

☐ Read the owner's manual for all tools and understand their proper usage.

☐ Keep tools out of reach of small children.

☐ Unplug all power tools when changing settings or parts.

WHAT YOU WILL NEED

Time. The time it will take you to build a staircase depends on your familiarity with the construction methods employed; the requirements of your particular site; and the complexity of your design.

Tools

Framing square

Hammer

Handsaw

Level

Pencils

Power saw

Tape measure

Saw horses

Stair nuts

Screwdrivers

Wrenches

Dust masks

Goggles

Materials. The example illustrated in this chapter, a staircase off a redwood-covered deck, uses 2x6 redwood decking for the treads and 4x4 posts to support the handrail. The diagonal pieces that support the treads, called *stringers*, should be pressure-treated 2x12s or other structurally rated 2x12 material.

Many choices are available for the handrail and spindles; this chapter outlines some code requirements.

You can use either nails or screws; just be sure that they are galvanized or otherwise rust resistant. Joist hangers, framing clips, and other metal framing aids can all simplify the construction and make it stronger.

The amount and kind of materials required—wood, metal, and concrete for the pad—all depend on the design of the stairs.

USEFUL TERMS

Figure 17-1 shows the anatomy of a typical exterior staircase.

A **cleat** is a board attached to another board, flat side to flat side. Once used to support the treads, cleats tend to work their fasteners loose and are no longer used for this purpose. Two kinds of cleats are still used. One type is attached to

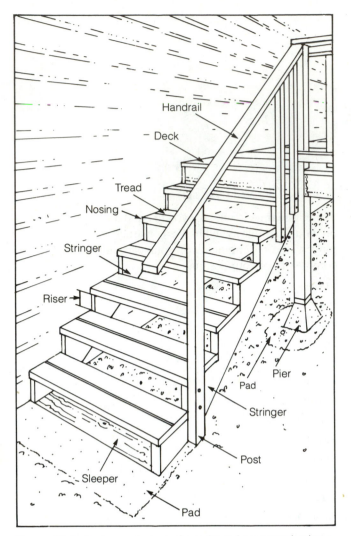

Handrail

Deck

Tread

Nosing

Stringer

Riser

Pier

Pad

Stringer

Post

Sleeper

Pad

Figure 17-1. Anatomy of a typical exterior staircase attached to a deck.

the stringer to stiffen it, and the other type is attached to the upstairs floor framing to support the top end of the stringer.

A **handrail** is a narrow rail beside the stairs to hold onto as you go up and down. If your stairs are not enclosed on one side, two handrails are necessary.

A **landing** is a flat spot in the staircase where a turn is made.

The **nosing** is the portion of a stair tread that extends beyond the face of the riser.

The **riser** is the height from step to step; or the board itself, installed vertically, that fills this space.

The **run** is the width of a tread, or the cut made on the stringer to support the tread.

A **sleeper** is much like a cleat, but it is used at the bottom of the stringer instead of the top. The sleeper is most often

partly embedded in concrete, so it must be of decay-resistant material.

A **spindle** or **baluster** is an upright support for the handrail.

Stair nuts are small clamps that are attached to the outside edge of a framing square to define the rise and run on a stringer.

Stringers are the diagonal beams that support both treads and risers. Builders call stringers by different names in different parts of the country. A carpenter who mentions a "carriage," "rough string," or "rough horse" is probably talking about a stringer.

A **tread** is the flat portion of the stair that you step on.

PERMITS AND CODES

The building codes address stairs with an eye to uniformity, so you don't have to "relearn" each stair you use. Most building codes require a minimum clear width of 36", wide enough so that two people can pass one another easily. However, the fire code requires a clear width of 44" for interior or exterior stairs used as an escape route from the building.

With this one exception, the building codes prevail in determining minimum standards. Here are some basic rules that most communities use.

1. If the total height from grade to the decking surface is 12", a stair is required.

2. The rise from stair to stair must be no less than 4" and no more than 8". This dimension may not vary more than ⅜" between any two steps in one staircase.

3. Tread depth must be between 9" and 12". Some communities allow deeper treads in some exterior applications.

4. Stairs over 40" wide require a third stringer, centered between the two outboard stringers.

5. The bottom step in an exterior location is often required to be made of cast concrete, to resist pest and fungus attack.

6. Stairways over 44" wide must have two handrails.

7. The handrail must qualify as "graspable."

8. Some communities require nonskid surfaces on exterior stairs, especially where icing is common. Some areas require supports even for short stringers if additional snow loads are expected.

In addition, fire codes address the fire resistance of exterior stairs that may be used as an escape route, particularly in high-density urban areas.

All of these requirements affect design to some extent. You need to be familiar with the code in your community to make sure that your design complies.

BUILDING AN EXTERIOR STAIRCASE

Step One
Designing the Staircase

Margin of Error: 1/8"

The staircase discussed here is a straight exterior staircase from the ground to a deck, using the same materials that were used to frame and cover the deck itself.

The first thing you need to determine is the total height the stairs will climb. Outdoors, this is often affected by the pitch of the ground; the total height from the deck to the lowest portion of the bottom step must be determined.

Figure 17-2 shows how the basic elements of the staircase are put together. Before you begin construction, you should make a similar sketch of your own project. If the deck is 44" above grade, but the soil drops about 4" where the bottom step will be, the approximate total rise is 44" + 4", or 48". The rise of each step should be about 7". Divide 48" by 7", for a rise of about 6 7/8"—close enough. This tells you that you need seven risers, each 6 7/8" high. The decking surface itself is the top tread, and therefore you will have one fewer treads than risers, or six treads. On stairs that protrude from the top surface, there are an equal number of risers and treads.

In this example, it would also be possible to divide the total rise by 6" and design a staircase with eight 6" risers and seven treads. If your local code is flexible, and you have the space, keep in mind that deeper treads and lower risers are more negotiable and easier to use, and therefore safer. If your space is limited, just remember that the smaller the riser height, the more total run length the treads will need.

In this example, the treads are 2x6 redwood boards, just like the decking. As shown in Figure 17-3, swo flat 2x6s, plus a gap of 1/4" for drainage, give a full tread width of 11 1/4" (5 1/2" + 5 1/2" + 1/4"). Code requires the tread to extend 1" beyond the face of the riser, or in this case the riser cut. Because this is a deck staircase, risers won't be used to fill in the vertical spaces. Therefore the tread width cut needs to be 11 1/4" minus 1", or 10 1/4".

Step Two
Calculating the Materials List

Margin of Error: Not applicable

Once you have determined the number of treads in your staircase, and the desired stair width, it is easy to calculate the amount of 2x6 you will need. Making a sketch like the one in Figure 17-2 will help you make up your materials list. In this example, the stairs are 48" wide, and each tread uses two 2x6's. Therefore each step requires 8' of 2x6 from stringer to stringer.

Stringers are ordered at least 2' longer than the diagonally spanned distance, so that you will have enough material to cut the piece on the ends to accommodate the top vertical face and the bottom base. Stringers are always made from structurally rated 2x12 or larger boards. It's a good idea to hand pick them for straightness. If pressure-treated material is available, it is a good choice for exterior stringers.

The handrails and spindles should reflect the overall design of your deck. The railing posts are 4x4, just like the deck rail supports. The railing height is typically 36", measured from the front of the tread.

The bottoms of the stringers are usually attached to a 2x4 decay-resistant board, called a *sleeper*, which is set flush into a reinforced concrete pad slightly above grade level. (As

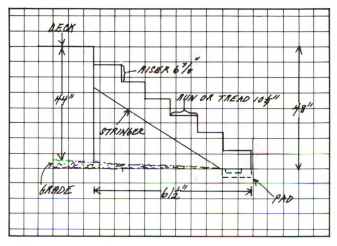

Figure 17-2. The basic elements and dimensions of an exterior staircase.

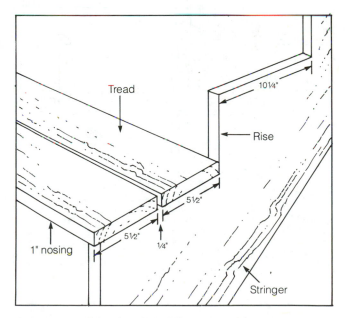

Figure 17-3. Full tread width is 11 1/4" (two 2x6 boards plus a gap of 1/4" so that water can drain off the step).

mentioned earlier, some communities require the whole of the bottom step to be cast concrete.) The pad or step should be the same width as the stair treads, or slightly wider. The sleeper should be positioned to support the heel of the stringers. Be sure to order enough steel and concrete, and the necessary form boards and stakes.

"Welded wire mesh," small steel wires welded together in a grid pattern, is often used to reinforce the pad. The mesh is cut 4" or 5" smaller than the form, in both dimensions, so that the edges are covered by a minimum of 2" of concrete. The mesh is held off the bottom of the form by small precast concrete blocks about 2" high, called "dobes" (pronounced "dough-bee," a contraction of "adobe").

Full-cast concrete bottom steps usually require two or more pieces of mesh. Larger projects usually also need some small rebar for durability.

Step Three
Building the Support Pad

Margin of Error: 1/4"

Use two long boards, cantilevered off the decking and squared to the deck edge, to mark the outside edges of the stringers (Figure 17-4). Now mark off the distance out to the bottom riser face cut. In our example, six treads, each 10 1/4" deep, means a total run of 61 1/2". Measure out 61 1/2" and make a mark. Use a plumb bob or level to drop this line to grade. This

is the front edge of the support pad. Remember that the tread will overhang the cut by 1".

Measure back from the front edge the width of one tread plus whatever is needed to support the heels of the stringers. Usually another 8" of pad width is sufficient, but this depends on the angle at which the stringer is installed. Marking the stringer itself is the easiest way to determine the actual pad width, and to keep its sizes and visual impact to a minimum.

Once you have all the dimensions of the pad, excavate or form this area as necessary to provide a concrete pad at least 4" thick. Install welded wire mesh reinforcement and pour the concrete. Then add the sleeper.

The sleeper is placed 2" or 3" in from the back edge and is usually the full length of the pad. When your form is filled within 1" of the top, place the sleeper into position and then finish filling the form with the concrete. The top of the sleeper should stick up about 1/8" to 1/4", so that the stringer does not rest directly on the concrete. You may have to pound the sleeper down or backfill beneath it to adjust its height. Besides holding the stringer slightly off the pad, all the sleeper does is provide a place to secure the stringers to the pad, so exact placement is not critical.

Step Four
Cutting the First Stringer

Margin of Error: 1/8"

Place the first stringer board, in our example a pressure-treated 2x12, flat across some sawhorses, crown facing up. Clamp a board onto your framing square, as shown in Figure 17-5, or use stair nuts, as shown in Figure 17-6, to set the rise and run. (In our example, that means a 6 7/8" rise and a 10 1/4" run.) Starting at the top, mark the rise and run of the first step on the stringer in pencil. Now move the square down so the first run and second riser marks intersect on the stringer's edge, as shown in Figure 17-7.

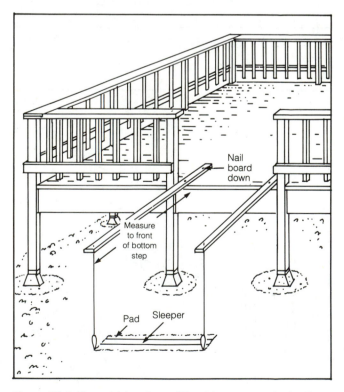

Figure 17-4. The outside edges of the stringer are marked with two long boards cantilevered off the deck.

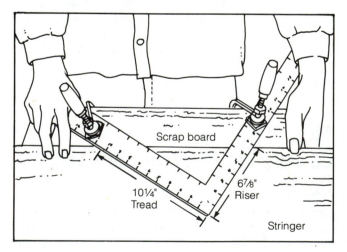

Figure 17-5. Use a square clamped onto a scrap board to mark the rise and run on the stringer.

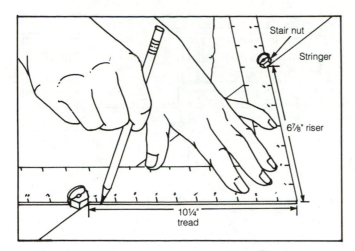

Figure 17-6. You can also use stair nuts to set the rise and run on the stringer.

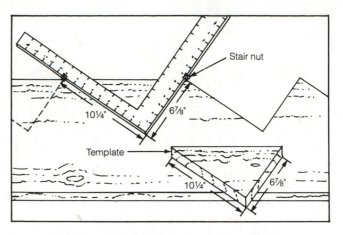

Figure 17-7. After marking the first rise and run, move the square down the stringer and mark the next rise and run.

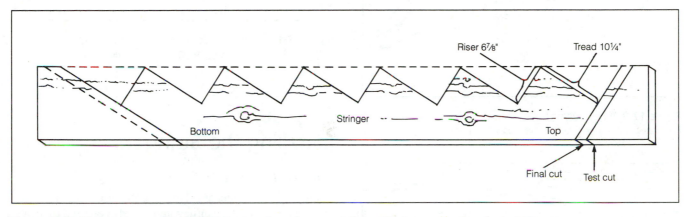

Figure 17-8. After you have marked all the steps on the stringer, mark lines at the top and bottom for test trim cuts.

Repeat this process until you have the correct number of tread cuts and a riser mark on the bottom of the stringer. Using the same tape or nut location, put the square on the other edge of the stringer and mark a continuation of the top riser cut line and an inverted tread cut at the bottom of the last riser. Once all treads and risers are marked on the stringer, make another mark 1" outside of the top riser cut line and 1" below the line at the bottom, as shown in Figure 17-8. Use a power saw to cut the stringer on the outside line.

Now place this trimmed but uncut stringer in position temporarily. The tread and riser marks should be level and plumb respectively, but displaced 1" up and 1" out. If these marks are not level and plumb, you have made a mistake that must be corrected. Double check your calculations and review your drawings for conceptual mistakes. Also check the marks themselves; a ⅛" error multiplied by seven risers makes a ⅞" error over all.

Assuming that the riser and tread marks are OK, and that the top plumb mark and bottom horizontal marks will meet their supports closely, it's time to cut the riser and tread notches and to make the final top and bottom cuts. Never overcut the notches with a power saw. Instead, you should cut to the intersecting corner of the marks and finish the cut

with a handsaw, as shown in Figure 17-9, to retain as much strength as possible in the stringer.

After you have cut the first stringer, you need to check its fit before cutting the others. To do this, mark one riser height down from the top of the decking, on the fascia or framing. Hold the top tread cut of the stringer even with this line; the bottom cut should rest securely on the pad. Mark the location of each stringer and test fit this first stringer at each spot. You may have to adjust the bottom cuts to accommodate any unevenness in the pad or stringer.

Step Five
Dropping the Stringer

Margin of Error: ⅛"

So far, we have been "pretending" that we will walk on the tread cuts themselves—but the thickness of the tread will be added to the bottom riser height, as shown in Figure 17-10, and the riser height at the top will be reduced by the same amount (in our case, about 1½").

In practice, however, instead of reducing each tread cut by this amount, the whole stringer is lowered by the thickness

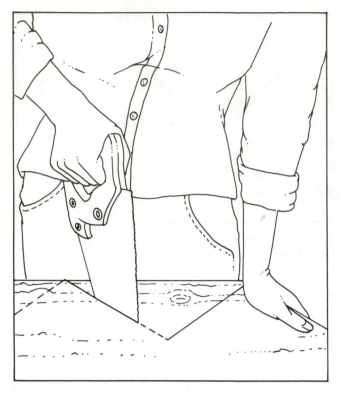

Figure 17-9. When cutting the riser and tread notches, use a handsaw rather than a power saw to finish the cut.

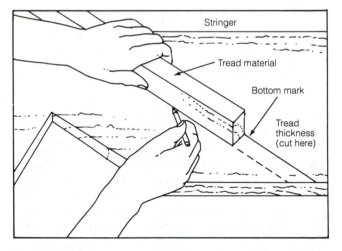

Figure 17-10. For greatest accuracy, use a scrap of the tread material to mark the bottom of the stringer.

of the tread—in our example, 1½". (This is called "dropping the stringer.") After 1½" is trimmed off the bottom of the stringer, the bottom riser height is 5⅜" (6⅞" - 1½" = 5⅜"). You may simply mark the bottom of the stringer with a tape measure, but using a scrap of the actual tread material is more reliable (see Figure 17-10). Since the tread thickness will vary with different materials, using a scrap gives the appropriate distance in each specific case.

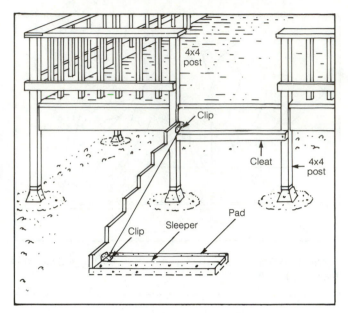

Figure 17-11. Install outside stringers first, attaching them to both the deck and the sleeper, and then install intermediate stringers.

Step Six
Installing the Stringers

Margin of Error: ⅛"

Using the first stringer as a template, cut the other two stringers. Then remove the cantilevered boards you used to locate the support pad.

The top of the stringer is usually attached to the deck with joist hangers or framing clips, and the bottom is clipped or toenailed into the sleeper in the support pad. Always install the outside stringers first, as shown in Figure 17-11, checking for level tread cuts between them, then place intermediate stringers in line with the outside ones.

Particularly where heavy snow loads are expected, long stringers need additional posts to support snow load on the stairs. If you do use additional posts, it's a good idea to use the same post to support both the stringer and the handrail, if possible. These posts are bolted into position on the stringer, leaving 6" or more of free space at the bottom to accommodate a pier block or a cast pier support. For information on installing pier blocks, see Chapter 16, Decks.

Some communities allow you to use a cleat to stiffen the stringer. Typically, a structurally rated 2x4 is bolted or screwed to the side of the stringer below the rise and run notches. The cleats are applied on the inside of the stringer, so they are not visible. Cleats look cleaner than posts, but if the staircase is long or snow is expected, local codes will probably require posts. If you do use a cleat, remember that it will be exposed to the weather. Use a decay-resistant material, caulked to reduce pest and water access to the joint between the cleat and the stringer.

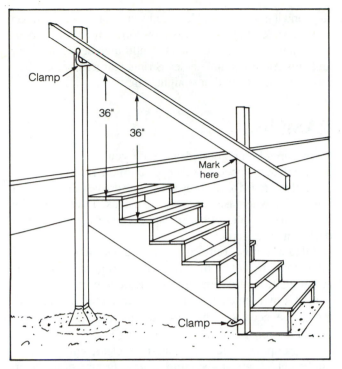

Figure 17-12. Use clamps to hold the handrail and its 4x4 support before bolting them in place.

Step Seven
Installing the Treads

Margin of Error: 1/4"

Installing treads is the easy part of building stairs. Starting at the bottom, hold the first 2x6 flush with the riser cut and nail or screw it into the stringers, using two galvanized #16 nails or treated screws per joint. Then nail on the second 2x6, again using two nails per joint. Remember the 1" nosing, and place the front nails back accordingly. Repeat this process step by step until all the treads are secured.

Step Eight
Installing Handrail Supports

Margin of Error: 1/4"

Handrail supports can be installed either before or after the treads. Clamp a redwood or pressure-treated 4x4 post to the stringers to hold it in place, as shown in Figure 17-12. Then attach it with galvanized carriage bolts, washers, and nuts.

Whatever style you choose for your handrail, remember that the top cuts must be angled to meet the railing. The bottoms are also often cut at the same angle for a neater appearance. Bolt the posts to the outside of the stringer so that you can use the full width of the stairs.

Too many 4x4 posts on your staircase look massive and can detract from the visual appeal of the lighter spindles. For this reason, our example uses one 4x4 on each outside

Figure 17-13. Plumb each spindle and mark its final location before attaching it to the stringer.

stringer, with the deck rail 4x4s supporting the tops of the handrail. To provide a place to attach the spindles and support a flat 2x4 rail on the top, another 2x4 is notched into the 4x4s vertically. Notching is not required, however, and you may want to simply cleat this support piece between the 4x4s so that the inside edge of the support is positioned plumb above the side of the stringer. In this way, flat spindles can be secured at the top and bottom without the careful notching that is common to interior stairs.

Because most deck railings are 42" high and the code requires 36" rail height measured from the front of each step, the stair rail almost always hits the deck rail 4x4 below the top of this support. When a deck rail is only 36" high, or if the top step protrudes at the deck level, the handrail will be above the top of the 4x4 in order to meet the 36" height stipulation for the stairs. In this case, you must add more 4x4 posts to support the tops of the stair rails. Temporarily clamp the rail support 2x4 in position and with a level make a mark on the support piece directly across from the bottom of the deck top rail. Mark back 1 3/4" (half the width of the 4x4), and with your level draw a plumb line here. The 4x4 will be aligned on one side to this line, so the post will support both the stair rail and a new short top rail and support piece between the stair rail and the deck rail.

Step Nine
Installing the Handrails and Spindles

Margin of Error: ¼"

Handrail height requirements vary from community to community, and the "graspable" rule means that in some areas you can't use a flat 2x6 for a handrail.

Spindle requirements for stairs also vary, as they do for the deck. The maximum allowable space between them is 6" in some areas and 8" in others. Like the stairs themselves, these pieces need to be sturdy and secure for safety reasons.

Use a level, as shown in Figure 17-13, to be sure that your spindles are plumb before nailing or bolting them to the stringer. Then drive finish nails down through the handrail into the beveled top of the spindle.

STAIRS WITH LANDINGS

Code limits the total height of stair rise without a landing to 12'; any higher and a landing is required.

While it may at first appear to be twice as complicated to build stairs with a landing as it is to build straight stairs, it isn't really. The landing should be considered as just another

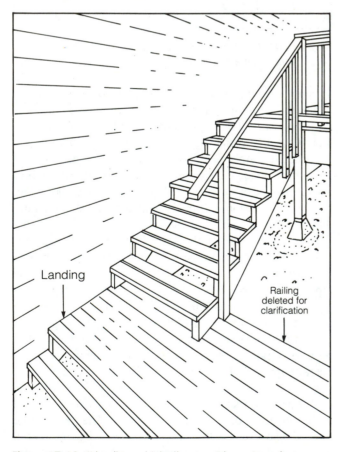

Landing

Railing deleted for clarification

Figure 17-14. A landing, which allows a stairway to make a right-angle turn, can be considered to be simply a large stair.

step, and it is calculated, designed, and framed into position as a large intermediate step, as shown in Figure 17-14. On interior stairs, your calculations should include the subfloor and finish flooring thicknesses. Stringer dimensions are then calculated just as with a straight stair.

RAMPS

Ramps are often a good idea even if you don't have an elderly or handicapped member of your household. They are easier than stairs for children to use, and create a more formal impression when used as access to a deck. They also make it easier to get sacks of soil and other heavy supplies up to a deck container garden.

All ramps must conform to standard wheelchair ramp requirements. In most communities those minimum standards are straightforward. The slope of the ramp must not exceed 1 in 12. Lower pitches are fine, but the overall ramp length must not exceed 30'. These two stipulations limit total rise, on flat terrain, to 2½' (1/12 x 30' = 2½').

The ramp width must be at least 36" clear, with the handrail height 32" above the ramp surface. Design of the ramp also requires careful consideration of such factors as landings, turns, curbs, and the possibility of icing. Like the stairs, ramps must be sturdy and braced as necessary for durability.

INTERIOR STAIRS

The basic design of interior stairs differs only slightly from the design of exterior stairs. However, because interior stairs must meet numerous code requirements and fit the available space, interior stair calculations are usually done by an architect or designer, during the planning phase.

Besides getting you from one floor to another, interior stairs must control dust, air flow, and noise, and wood-framed stairs must be protected from fire. For these reasons, risers are almost always used to fill in the vertical spaces on interior stairs.

Risers are usually installed before the treads on interior stairs, and the joints are often caulked to control dust. Riser boards are typically 1" thick, and their thickness is added to the tread cut dimensions when the stringer is marked and cut. It's often a good idea to carpet stairs to control noise, but the carpet's thickness must be considered to keep the riser heights within the ⅜" required by code once the stringer is cut.

Interior treads are made of hardwood, particle board, or plywood. These materials vary in thickness, and their thickness determines how much the stringer is dropped.

The riser boards should be secured with screws to the tread from behind, every 6" or so, to minimize the chance of squeaks developing.

The areas below the stairs are drywalled for fire protection, and little triangular "closets" often result. Full-width fireblocks are installed in these spaces from the tread-riser intersection down to the bottom of the stringer, every 4' or so, to protect the stairs and provide nailing for the drywall. In multistory buildings the stairs are often stacked in the same well to avoid these odd spaces.

Building code requirements limit the riser height to 8" inside, and often allow as little rise as 5". A minimum tread width of 11" is required for stairs that would be considered an escape route in case of fire.

Different Floor Finish Thicknesses

The final thickness of your finish floor affects the stringer design. If all your floor surfaces are the same, dropping the stringer is the same as for the deck stairs. If the surfaces are of different heights, the simplest way to accommodate these differences is to use scraps to build each level to its finish height. The total riser height is then determined off these surfaces and the stringer is designed as described earlier. Calculating these differences with your tape is not as reliable. Just be sure to include the finished surface height when you mark the top riser drop on the framing, and test fit the stringer carefully.

Headroom

It's important to provide adequate headroom for interior stairs. The code stipulates a minimum clearance of 6'8", but on a long staircase this minimum can be claustrophobic. A full 7' clearance, or even more, is advisable for most stairs. This distance is always measured from the front of a tread vertically to the ceiling.

Other Differences Between Interior and Exterior Stairs

Interior stairs are often easier to construct than exterior stairs, because they are often placed between two interior walls. In this case, all the studs in these walls can be used to support the stringers vertically, by nailing or screwing through the stringer into the studs.

However, the drywall next to these studs is vulnerable to damage. A kick could knock a hole right through the drywall. Even if you plan to install a baseboard, code generally requires blocking behind the drywall, above the tread, to prevent such damage. Blocking is also used to support

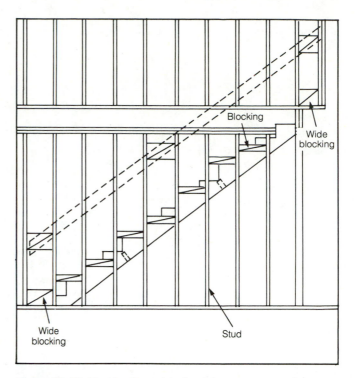

Figure 17-15. Blocking for an interior staircase prevents damage to drywall.

handrails and to provide a place to secure a curved handrail return. The blocking adjacent to the tread is also useful to secure any baseboards or trim around the treads, as shown in Figure 7-15.

Stairs will always flex to some degree, and this flexing often results in squeaks. Outside, these noises are hardly noticeable, but inside they can be annoying. To prevent squeaks, make close, careful cuts, and use both screws and adhesive to secure the treads and risers. Bugle-head drywall screws and flexible panel adhesive, available in caulking gun cartridges, are recommended.

Handrails and spindles are generally much fancier on interior stairs. Hardwood rails with 90° elbows, shaped to match the straight sections, are used to return the rail neatly to the wall or to turn a corner. Spindles may be plain or fancy, but they must be spaced as recommended by local code. If you choose to use a diagonal board above the steps themselves as a base for the spindles, the 6" to 8" maximum gap rule also applies to the little triangle below the board. Just like the stairs, the rails need to be stout and well built to pass the final inspection, as well as for your safety.

Index

A

ABS plastic pipe, 36, 38-39
Acoustic ceiling, 75
Acoustical tile ceilings. *See* Tile ceilings
Adapter fittings, 29
Adhesives, 9
    for ceramic tile, 120, 123, 127
    for drywall, 58
    for parquet floors, 109
    for plastic pipe, 38-39
    for sheet vinyl, 102-4
    for strip flooring, 112
    for wallpaper, 135
Air chambers, 29, 37-38
Air tools. *See* Pneumatic tools
Alarm systems, 172-73
Alkyd (oil-based) paint, 130, 131
Allen wrenches, 8
Alternating current, 15
Aluminum oxide sandpaper, 10
Aluminum thresholds, 156
Aluminum wire, 19
American Wire Gauge (AWG), 19
Amperes, 16
Appliances
    clothes driers, 18, 44
    codes, 18
    dishwashers, 148-49
    feeder cable path design, 18
    microwave ovens, 149
    ovens, 149
    ranges, 18, 149
    refrigerators, 18
    washing machines, 18, 44
Armored cable type BX, 19
Attachments
    drills, 4
    pneumatic tools, 12
Attics
    insulating, 48, 50-51
    ventilating, 48-50
Audits and surveys
    home security, 164
    weatherizing, 152-54
AWG (American Wire Gauge), 19
Awning windows, 159

B

Backer board, 120-21
Backsaws, 5

Backsplash, 128
Baluster, 192
Band joists, 175, 189
Bandsaws, 4
Bar clamps, 9
Baseboard, 71, 107
Basements
    caulking and sealing, 52
    drainage, 52, 53-54
    insulating, 52-54
    suspended ceiling design, 79
    suspended ceilings and basement
        windows, 84
Bathroom sinks, 40-41
Bathtubs, 42-43
Battens, 120
Battery backup systems, 28
Belt sanders, 10
Bench saw, 3-4
Beveled casing, 93-94
Bits
    drill bits, 4
    hole saw, 163, 169
    spade bit, 163, 169
Block planes, 11
Block sanders, 10
Blow guns, 12
Blown-in insulation, 46
    for attics, 51
    for new walls, 52
Bonding
    plastic pipe, 38-39
    See also Adhesives
Booking wallpaper, 129, 135
Bow, 175
Box wrenches, 8
Boxes (electrical), 20
    roughing in, 17, 22-23
    See also Fixtures (electrical); Receptacles
        (outlets)
Boxing paint, 131
Brackets, 9
Breaker boxes, 16
    grounding rods, 22
    installing, 21-22
    main breaker, 16
    subpanels, 17, 18
    See also Circuit breakers
Brushes, 129-30
Bugle head screws, 7
Building drain, 29, 36
Building sewer, 29, 36

Bulb vinyl weatherstripping, 151
Burglars. *See* Home security
Buses
    grounding bus, 22
    neutral bus bar, 17, 22
Bushing diameter, 37
BX cable, 19, 20

C

C-clamps, 9
Cabinetmaker's chisels, 6
Cabinets, 141-42
    base cabinets, 143-44
    design, 140
    installing, 141-44
    island cabinets, 144
    leveling, 141, 142
    nailing strips, 141
    permits and codes, 140
    preparation, 140-41
    wall cabinets, 141-43
Cable, 19
    clamping, 20
    connecting wires, 25-27
    installing, 23-25
    outdoor wiring, 28
    pigtailing, 25-27
    preparing studs for, 23
    pulling, 23-24
    See also Electricity; Wire
Carpenter's hammers, 6
Carpenter's pencils, 2
Carpenter's squares, 2
Carpenter's wood glue, 9
Cartridge fuses, 21
Casement windows, 159
Casing, 89
    beveled, 93-94
    See also Trim
Cast iron pipe versus plastic pipe, 38
Catspaws, 9
Caulk, 151
Caulking, 46
    basement walls, 52
    ceramic tile, 126
    weatherizing, 154-55
Caulking guns, 12, 154
Ceiling boxes, 20
Ceiling joists, 75
Ceiling tiles, 75. *See also* Tile ceilings
Ceilings, 75-87

Ceilings, *continued:*
design, 76
drywall, 59-60
permits and codes, 76
suspended ceilings, 75-84
tile ceilings, 75-76, 84-87
Cellulose insulation, 46
Cement. *See* Adhesives
Ceramic tile, 119-28
accessory installation, 125
adhesive application, 123, 127
backer board installation, 120-21
backsplash, 128
caulking and sealing, 126
counter tops, 127-28
cutting, 124
final adjustments, 124
floors, 126-27, 141
grouting, 124-25, 127, 128
laying the tile, 123, 127-28
layout, 121-23, 127
taping backer board joints, 121
trim tiles, 124
underlayment for floors, 126-27
walls, 120-26
Chalklines, 2, 79-80
Channel lock pliers, 8
Checklist of tools, 13-14
Chimneys and flues, 174
Chisels, 6, 12
Chopsaws, 3
Circuit breakers, 16, 21
ground fault circuit interrupters (GFCI), 21, 28
main breaker, 16, 21-22
See also Breaker boxes
Circuits, 16
Circular saws, 3
Clamps, 9
Claw hammers, 6
Cleanouts, 29, 36-37
Cleats, 191, 196
Closet bends, 30
Closet shelves, 73
Clothes drier venting, 44
Codes. *See* Color coding; Inspections; Permits and codes
Color coding
switch loops, 21
wire nuts, 20, 25
wires, 15, 19
Columns in suspended ceilings, 79, 84
Combination saws, 6
Combination squares, 2
Concrete
ceramic tile over, 127
vinyl flooring over, 106
Conduction, 45
Conduit, 19-20
Connectors. *See* Fasteners and connectors
Contact cements, 9
Continuity testers, 16
Continuous ridge vent, 49
Convection, 45

Coping saws, 5
Copper pipe
cutting and soldering, 30, 39-40
hard versus soft, 39
joining to galvanized pipe, 35
plastic pipe versus, 38
testing the system, 40
Corner beads, 55, 62, 63
Corners
drywall, 55, 62, 63
trim, 70-71
wallpapering, 136-37
Counter tops
ceramic tile, 119-20, 127-28
laminate, 139-40, 144-47
Coupling, 37
Coved edges for vinyl floors, 103
Crawlspace insulation, 52
Cross tees, 75
Crosscut saws, 5
Crown, 175
Cutting in, 129, 131-32

D

Deadbolts, 163, 167-68
installing, 168-70
Deadlocking latches, 163
Decking boards, 175, 177, 186-88
Decks, 175-90
band joists, 175, 189
cutting board ends, 188-89
decking installation, 186-88
design, 177-78
estimating materials, 177
footings and pier blocks, 175, 177, 183-84
foundation pier holes, 175, 177, 182-83
girders, 175, 177, 184-85
joists, 175, 177, 181-82, 185-86, 189
ledger installation, 178-81
permits and codes, 177
posts, 175, 177, 184-85
railings, 177, 189-90
stair rails and, 197
waterproofing, 190
Dedicated circuits, 18
Design and planning
ceilings, 76, 77-79
decks, 177-78
doors, 90
drywall, 56
electricity, 18
kitchens, 140
painting, 130
plumbing, 31-33
shelves, 66, 72
stairs, 193, 199
strip flooring, 111-12
vinyl floors, 100
wall paneling, 66
wallpapering, 134
Dielectric union, 35
Dishwasher installation, 148-49
Disk sanders, 10

Dismantling tools, 9-10
Door lights, 163
Door stop installation, 93
Door threshold, 151, 156-57
Doors, 89, 97
bottom seals, 157
caulking, 154-55
deadbolts and entrance locks, 163, 167-70
design, 90
door shoes, 157-58
drywall around, 58-59
head jambs, 89, 92
hinge jambs, 89, 91-92
home security, 164-67
lockset installation, 93, 168-70
painting, 133-34
paneling around, 69, 72
permits and codes, 90
pocket doors, 96-97
prehung doors, 89
reveal, 89, 93-94
sliding glass doors, 95-96
stop installation, 93
strike jambs, 89, 92-93
threshold seals, 156-57
trimming with beveled casing, 93-94
wallpapering around, 137
weatherizing audit, 153
weatherstripping, 156-58
See also Trim
Double-cylinder locks, 163
Double-hung windows, 158-59
Downspout, 151
Drain/waste/vent (DWV) system, 36-39
Drainage (basement), 52, 53-54
Driers, 18, 44
Drills, 4, 12
Drum sanders, 10, 115
Dry-backed vinyl tiles. *See* Self-adhesive vinyl tiles
Drywall, 55-63
adhesive, 58
angles, 59-60
applying the drywall, 57-58
ceilings, 59-60
corner beads, 55, 62, 63
curves and odd spaces, 60
cutting openings, 58-59
mud, 55, 61-63
paneling over, 67
permits and codes, 56
prepping the walls, 56-57
repairing, 63
stairs and, 199
tape, 55, 61-62
Drywall compound (mud), 55, 61-63
Drywall nails, 55
Drywall saws, 5, 55
Drywall screws, 7, 55
Ductwork and suspended ceilings, 83
Duplex receptacles. *See* Receptacles
DWV system (Drain/waste/vent) system, 36-39

E

Edge sanders, 10
EG (electroplated galvanized) fasteners, 176
Elbows, 37
Electric drills, 4
Electricity, 15-28
  alternative technologies, 28
  basics, 15, 19-21
  boxes, 20, 22-23
  breaker boxes, 16, 21-22
  cable, 19, 20, 23-25
  circuit breakers, 16, 21-22
  color coding, 15, 19, 20, 21
  connecting wires, 25-27
  design, 18
  dielectric union, 35
  fixture installation, 27-28
  fuses, 21
  ground fault circuit interrupters (GFCI), 21, 28
  main breaker box installation, 21-22
  outdoor wiring, 28
  permits and codes, 15, 17-18
  pigtailing, 25-27
  preparing studs for cable, 23
  receptacles (outlets), 18, 20, 25, 26-28
  rough electrical inspection, 25
  solar-powered low-voltage systems, 28
  switches, 20-21, 25, 26-27
  wire, 19, 23-27
Electroplated galvanized fasteners, 176
Emery cloth, 10
End-cutting nippers, 8
Energy conservation, 159-61
  maintenance, 153, 160-61
  thermostat, 160
  water heater, 160
Epoxy, 9
Escutcheons, 30
Exterior boxes, 20

F

Fasteners and connectors, 9
  electroplated galvanized, 176
  hot dipped galvanized, 175, 176
  nail guards, 9, 56, 57
Feathering, 129
Feeders, 16
Female-threaded fittings, 30
Fence brackets, 9
Fiberglass blankets or batts, 46
  for attic floor, 50-51
  for rafters, 50
  for walls, 51-52
Files, 11
Finish plumbing, 30, 40-44
  bathroom sinks, 40-41
  clothes driers, 44
  inspection, 33
  showers and bathtubs, 42-43
  toilets, 43
  washing machines, 44

Finishing hammers, 6
Finishing hardwood floors
  preparing for sanding, 114-15
  protective finish, 117
  repairing squeaky or cupped boards, 113-14
  sanding, 115
  staining, 116-17
Fire security, 173-74
Fish tape, 16
Fittings (plumbing), 37
Fixtures (electrical)
  illumination codes, 18
  installing, 27-28
  lighting circuit design, 18
  recessed lights, 28
  suspended ceiling design, 79, 84
  track lighting, 27-28
  wallpapering around, 138
Fixtures (plumbing), 30
  bathroom sinks, 40-41
  clothes driers, 44
  fixture system, 37
  showers and bathtubs, 42-43
  toilets, 43
  washing machines, 44
Flat bars, 10
Flat paints, 130
Flat-headed screws, 7
Flexi-vent, 46, 50
Flint sandpaper, 10
Floor register, 107
Floors
  ceramic tile, 119-20, 126-27
  hardwood floors, 107-17
  kitchen, 141
  parquet, 107-111
  subfloor, 99
  underlayment, 99
  vinyl floors, 99-106
Foam insulation, 46, 53-54
Footings, 175, 183-84
Fore planes, 11
Formaldehyde and resorcinol, 9
Foundation connectors, 9
Four-way switches. See Switches
Framing chisels, 6
Framing hammers, 6
Framing squares, 2
French drains, 52, 53-54
Full mortise locks, 168
Full-spread adhesive vinyl floors, 99, 141
  applying over concrete, 106
  coved edges, 103
  cutting the vinyl, 101-2
  design, 100
  installation, 103-4
  permits and codes, 100
  preparing the subfloor or underlayment, 100
  template, 99, 100-101
Furring, 46, 65, 75
  for insulation, 46, 53
  for tile ceilings, 75, 85-87

for wall paneling, 65, 68
  See also Shims
Fuses, 21

G

Gable vents, 49
Galvanized fasteners, 175, 176
Galvanized pipe, 35
Garnet emery sandpaper, 10
General purpose circuits, 18
Geotextiles, 54
GFCI (ground fault circuit interrupters), 21, 28
Girders for decks, 175, 177, 184-85
Glazed tile, 119. See also Ceramic tile
Glazier's points, 107
Glazing compound, 151
Gloss paints, 130
Glue. See Adhesives
Greenrock, 55. See also Drywall
Grooving planes, 11
Ground fault circuit interrupters (GFCI), 21, 28
Grounding bus, 22
Grounding rods, 22
Grounding wire, 15
Grout, 120
Grouting ceramic tile, 120, 124-25, 127, 128
Guns
  blow guns, 12
  caulking guns, 12, 154
  nail guns, 12, 65
  spray guns, 12
Gyp board. See Drywall
Gypsum. See Drywall

H

Hacksaws, 5
Half thresholds, 157
Hammering
  drywall, 58
  toenailing, 176
Hammers, 6
  pneumatic, 12
Handrails, 192, 197-198, 199
Handscrews, 9
Hardwood floors, 107-17
  finishing, 113-17
  parquet floors, 108-11
  permits and codes, 107
  strip flooring, 111-13
HDG (hot dipped galvanized) fasteners, 175, 176
Head jambs, 89, 92
Heartwood, 175
Hiding places, 171
Hinge jambs, 89, 91-92
Hole saws, 163, 169
Holes for piers, 175, 182-83
Home security, 163-74
  alarm systems, 172-73
  deadbolts and entrance locks, 163, 167-70

Home security, *continued:*
   doors, 164-67
   fire security, 173-74
   neighborhood watch programs, 173
   permits and codes, 164
   safes and hiding places, 171
   survey, 164
   windows, 170-71
Hot dipped galvanized (HDG) fasteners,
   175, 176
Hot wire, 15

I

Illumination codes, 18
Impact wrenches, 12
Inflation kits, 12
Inspections
   before applying drywall, 56
   plumbing, 33
   rough electrical inspection, 25
   See also Permits and codes
Insulation, 45-48, 50-54
   attic, 48, 50-51
   basement, 52-54
   blown-in, 46, 51, 52
   common types, 46
   fiberglass, 46, 50-52
   foam, 46, 53-54
   furring, 46, 53
   permits and codes, 47
   pipes, 161
   preparatory work, 48, 52-53
   R-values, 45, 47
   rafters, 50
   vapor barriers, 46-47, 53
   walls, 51-52
   See also Ventilation; Weatherizing
Interlocking thresholds, 156-57
Iron pipe versus plastic pipe, 38
Island cabinets, 144

J

Jack planes, 11
Jalousie windows, 151
   weatherstripping, 159
   See also Windows
Jambs, 89
   head jambs, 89, 92
   hinge jambs, 89, 91-92
   home security, 167-68
   strike jambs, 89, 92-93
   See also Trim
Jigsaws, 3
Joiner planes, 11
Joist hangers, 9
Joists, 175
   band joists, 175, 189
   ceiling joists, 75
   for decks, 175, 177, 181-82, 185-86, 189
Junction boxes, 20

K

Key-in-knob locks, 167
Keyhole saws, 5
Kitchens, 139-144
   cabinets, 141-44
   counter tops, 144-47
   design, 140
   dishwasher installation, 148-49
   electrical codes, 18
   island cabinets, 144
   oven installation, 149
   permits and codes, 140
   preparing for installation, 140-41
   range installation, 149
   sequence of installation, 141
   sinks, 147-48
Knockouts, 20

L

Lag screws, 7, 175
Laminate counter tops, 139-40, 144-47
Landings, 192, 198
Latex (water-based) paint, 130
Laundries
   driers, 44
   electrical codes, 18
   washing machines, 44
Ledger for decks, 175, 178-81
Ledging, 99
Leveling
   cabinets, 141, 142
   ceramic tile, 122
   suspended ceilings, 79-80
   tools, 2
   wallpaper, 135
Levels, 2
Lighting. *See* Fixtures (electrical)
Lighting circuit design, 18
Lineman's pliers, 8
Locking wrenches, 8
Locks and deadbolts
   installing, 93, 168-70
   types of, 163, 167-68
   for windows, 170-71
Long-nosed pliers, 8
Loose insulation. *See* Blown-in insulation
Low-voltage solar electrical systems, 28

M

Machine screws, 7
Main breaker, 16, 21-22
Maintenance
   energy conservation, 153, 160-61
   tools, 1-2
Male-threaded fittings, 30
Mallets, 6
Masonry, paneling over, 68
Masonry connectors, 9
Mast, 16-17
Mastic, 120
Metal conduit, 19

Microwave oven installation, 149
Mixing paint, 131
Moisture-resistant (MR) drywall, 55. *See
   also* Drywall
Molding. *See* Trim
Mortise, 163
Mortise chisels, 6
Mortised-in bolts, 168
Mosaic tiles, 119. *See also* Ceramic tile
MR drywall, 55. *See also* Drywall
Mud, 55, 61-63

N

Nail guns, 12, 65
Nail plates, 9
Nailguards, 9, 56, 57
Nailing strips, 141
Nails, 7
   for backer board, 121
   for decking, 187
   for drywall, 55
Nailsets, 7
National Electric Code (NEC), 15
Needle-nosed pliers, 8
Neighborhood watch programs, 173
Neutral bus bar, 17, 22
Neutral wire, 15
NM/NMB cable, 19
   clamping, 20
   sizing, 23-25
Nosing, 192

O

Oakum, 151
Oil-based (alkyd) paint, 130, 131
Open-end wrenches, 8
Orbital sanders, 10
Outdoor wiring, 28
Outlet circuits, 18
Outlet/switch boxes, 20
Outlets. *See* Receptacles
Oval-headed screws, 7
Oven installation, 149

P

Pad, 175
Pad sanders, 10
Paint, 130-31
Paint edger, 130, 132
Paint guide, 130, 133
Painting, 129-34
   cutting in, 129, 131-32
   estimating paint, 130
   large surfaces, 132
   permits and codes, 129
   preparation, 131
   rollers, 129, 132
   sequence for, 131
   trim and woodwork, 133-34
Panel boxes. *See* Breaker boxes
Paneling. *See* Wall paneling

Parquet floors, 107-111
  applying adhesives, 109
  laying the tiles, 110
  layout lines, 108-9
  permits and codes, 107
  preparing the subfloor, 108
  rolling the floor, 110-11
Paste. *See* Adhesives
Pencils, carpenter's, 2
Penetrating sealant, 107
Perimeter bond sheet vinyl floors, 99, 141
  applying over concrete, 106
  cutting the vinyl, 101-2
  design, 100
  installation, 102-3
  permits and codes, 100
  safety rules, 99
  template, 99, 100-101
Permits and codes
  ceilings, 76
  color coding, 15, 19, 20, 21, 25
  decks, 177
  doors, 90
  drywall, 56
  electricity, 15, 17-18, 47
  hardwood floors, 107
  home security, 164
  insulation, 47
  kitchens, 140
  National Electric Code (NEC), 15
  painting, 129
  plumbing, 30, 33
  ramps, 198
  stairs, 192, 198, 199
  UL (Underwriters Laboratory), 17
  Uniform Building Code, 9
  Uniform Plumbing Code (UPC),
    29, 30, 33
  vinyl floors, 100
  wall paneling, 66
  wallpapering, 129
  weatherizing, 152
  See also Color coding; Inspections
Phillips head screwdrivers, 7
Photovoltaic electrical systems, 28
Pickets for deck railings, 190
Pier blocks
  for decks, 175, 183-84
  for stairs, 196
Piers, 175, 177, 182-84
Pigtailing, 25-26
  at duplex receptacles, 26
  splitting a receptacle on a push terminal,
    26-27
  switches, 27
Pipe wrenches, 8
Pipes
  bonding, 38-39
  cast iron, 38
  conduit, 19-20
  copper, 30, 35, 38, 39-40
  cutting, 38, 39-40
  galvanized, 35
  insulating, 161

plastic, 36, 38-39
soil pipe, 30
soldering, 30, 40
vent sizing, 37
wrenches, 8
See also Plumbing
Planes, 11
Plank flooring. *See* Strip flooring
Planning. *See* Design and planning
Plaster ring, 20
Plastic pipe, 36, 38-39
Plate strips, 9
Pliers, 8
Plug, 37
Plumb bobs, 2, 175
Plumbing, 29-44
  bathroom sinks, 40-41
  bathtubs, 42-43
  clothes driers, 44
  copper pipe, 35, 38, 39-40
  drain/waste/vent (DWV) system, 36-37,
    38-39
  fittings, 37
  fixture system, 37, 40-44
  hook-up to municipal sewer, 33
  inspections, 33
  insulating pipes, 161
  kitchen sinks, 148
  permits and codes, 30, 33
  planning, 31-33
  plastic pipe, 36, 38-39
  plumbing system, 33-38
  showers, 42-43
  supply system, 34-36, 39-40
  testing, 40
  toilets, 43
  valves, 34, 35, 37
  vents, 37
  washing machines, 44
Pneumatic tools, 11-12
Pocket doors, 96-97
Polarity, 15
Pole sanders, 55, 63
Polycarbonate, 163
Polyurethane, 107, 117
Polyvinyl glue, 9
Post anchors, 9
Post caps and plates, 9
Posts, 175
  decks, 175, 177, 184-85
  suspended ceiling design, 79, 84
Power tools
  cordless, 4, 7
  drills, 4
  pneumatic tools, 11-12
  sanders, 10
  saws, 3-4
  screwdrivers, 7
Prehung doors, 89
Pressure-treated lumber, 175, 176
Primers, 130
Pry bars, 9
Pulling cable, 23-24
Pumice, 11

PVC conduit, 19-20
PVC pipe, 38-39

Q, R

Quick-connect couplers, 12
R-values, 45, 47
Rabbit planes, 11
Radial arm saws, 4
Radiation, 45
Railings for decks, 177, 189-90
Ramps, 198
Ramsets, 65, 68
Ranges, 18, 149
Rasps, 11
Ratchet wrenches, pneumatic, 12
Receptacles (outlets), 20
  electrical codes, 18
  hanging, 27-28
  installing, 25
  splitting for a switch, 26-27
  wallpapering around, 138
  wiring, 26-27
Recessed lights, 28
Recessed shelves, 73
Reciprocating saws, 3, 10
Reducer fittings, 30
Reducing coupling, 37
Redwood, 176
Refrigerator electrical codes, 18
Resorcinol and formaldehyde, 9
Reveal, 89, 93-94
Rim-mounted locks, 168
Rip saws, 5
Ripping hammers, 6
Risers
  plumbing, 30, 35
  stairs, 192, 199
Robertson screws, 7
Rod saws, 120
Rollers, painting, 129, 132
Romex (NM/NMB) cable, 19, 20, 23-25
Rottenstone, 11
Rough electrical inspection, 25
Rough opening, 89
Rough plumbing, 30, 34-40
  drain/waste/vent system, 36-37, 38-39
  inspection, 33
  supply system, 34-36, 39-40
Roughing in, 17, 22-23
Round-headed screws, 7
Routers, 4
Run, 192
Runners, 75

S

Saber saws, 3
Safes, 171
Safety glass, 163
Safety plates, 9, 56, 57
Sandblasters, 12
Sanders, 10
  pneumatic, 12

Sanders, *continued:*
   pole sanders, 55, 63
Sanding (hardwood floors), 114-15
Sandpapers, 10
   for hardwood floors, 115
Sapwood, 175
Sash brushes, 129
Sawblades, 4
Sawhorse brackets, 9
Sawing. *See* Cutting and sawing
Saws
   drywall saws, 5, 55
   hand saws, 5-6
   hole saws, 163, 169
   power saws, 3-4
   reciprocating saws, 3, 10
   rod saws, 120
   sawblades, 4
Scab, 46
Screwdrivers, 6-8
Screwdriving
Screws, 7
   drywall screws, 55
   lag screws, 175
Scribing, 65, 67, 69-70
Sealing
   basement walls, 52
   ceramic tile, 126
   waterproofing decks, 190
Security. *See* Home security
Self-adhesive vinyl tiles, 141
   applying over concrete, 106
   cutting tiles to fit, 105-6
   design, 99
   dry-backed tiles versus, 106
   laying the tiles, 105-6
   permits and codes, 99
   preparation, 104-5
Service drop, 17
Sheet metal screws, 7
Sheet paneling, 65-71. *See also* Wall
   paneling
Sheet vinyl floors. *See* Full-spread adhesive
   vinyl floors; Perimeter bond sheet vinyl
   floors
Sheetrock. *See* Drywall
Shelves
   closet shelves, 73
   design, 66, 72
   recessed shelves, 73
   suspended shelves, 72-73
Shims, 46, 65, 89. *See also* Furring
Shoes, door, 157-58
Showers, 42-43
Side jamb, 89
Silicate compound, 46
Silicon carbide sandpaper, 10
Single pole, single throw switches. *See*
   Switches
Sinks
   bathroom, 40-41
   kitchen, 147-48
Sizing
   vent pipes, 37

wires and cables, 19, 23-25
Sizing for wallpaper, 129, 134
Sledge hammers, 6
Sleeper, 192, 193-194
Sliding glass doors, 95-96
Sliding windows
   weatherstripping, 159
   See also Windows
Slip joint pliers, 8
Smoke detectors, 174
Socket chisels, 6
Socket wrenches, 8
Soffit, 151
Soffit ventilation plugs, 48-49
Soil pipe, 30
Solar-powered low-voltage electrical
   systems, 28
Soldering copper pipe, 30, 40
Spacers, 120
Spade bit, 163, 169
Spindles, 192, 198, 199
Spray guns, 12
Spring clamps, 9
Spring latches, 163
Spring metal weatherstripping, 158
Square-headed screws, 7
Squares, 2
Staining hardwood floors, 116-17
Stair nuts, 192, 194
Stairs, 191-199
   cleats, 191, 196
   deck rails, 197
   design, 193, 198
   exterior staircase, 193-98
   handrail supports, 197
   handrails, 192, 197-98, 199
   headroom, 199
   interior stairs, 198-199
   landings, 192, 198
   permits and codes, 192, 198, 199
   ramps, 198
   risers, 192, 199
   sleepers, 193-94
   spindles, 192, 198, 199
   squeak prevention, 199
   stringers, 192, 194-96, 199
   support pad, 194
   treads, 192, 197
Staplers, pneumatic, 12
Steel wool, 10
Stop molding, 89
Storm glazing, 155
Strap wrenches, 8
Strike jambs, 89, 92-93
Stringers, 192, 194-96, 199
Strip flooring
   applying the adhesive, 112
   laying the planks, 112-13
   permits and codes, 107
   planning, 111-12
   preparing the subfloor, 108, 111
Stud shoes, 9
Subfloor, 99, 107
   for parquet flooring, 108

for vinyl flooring, 100, 104-5
Subpanels, 17, 18. *See also* Breaker boxes;
   Circuit breakers
Supplies. *See* Materials
Supply system (plumbing), 34-36
   installing, 39-40
   testing, 40
Support pad for stairs, 194
Surface finish, 107
Surveys and audits
   home security, 164
   weatherizing, 152-54
Suspended ceilings, 75-84
   border tiles, 77-78
   care of, 84
   chalklines, 79-80
   design, 76
   fitting around openings and supports,
     83-84
   grid installation, 82
   grid layout, 77, 78-79
   level lines for, 79-80
   lighting fixtures and, 79, 84
   panel installation, 82-83
   permits and codes, 76
   reference strings, 80-82
   runners, 75, 80, 81-82
   wall molding installation, 80
   wire fastener and hanger wire
     installation, 80
   See also Tile ceilings
Suspended shelves, 72-73
Sweating (soldering), 30, 40
Switches, 20-21
   installing, 25
   for receptacles, 26-27
   switch loops or legs, 20-21
   wiring, 27

T

T fitting, 37
Table saws, 3-4
Tack hammers, 6
Tang chisels, 6
Tape (drywall), 55, 61-62
Tape measures, 2
Taping knife, 55
Tegular panels, 75
Tempered glass, 163
Template for vinyl floors, 99, 100-101
Thermal thresholds, 156
Thermostat, energy conservation, 160
Thinset, 120
Three-way switches. *See* Switches
Thresholds, 151, 156-57
Tile adhesive, 120
Tile ceilings, 75-76, 84-87
   design, 76
   furring strips, 75, 85-87
   layout, 85
   metal furring strip installation, 85-86
   most common mistakes, 76
   permits and codes, 76